# The evolution of international business

This book surveys how international business has developed over the past two hundred years. It conveys the complexities and dynamism of this area of business, as well as providing an overview of the evolution of international business from its nineteenth century origins until the present day.

Because multinational investment is a cumulative process, the structure of contemporary international business can only be satisfactorily explained in many respects by examining its history. The approach taken by Jones is thematic, and the discussion does not require prior knowledge of economic history or the theory of the multinational enterprise. The book is internationally comparative throughout. It examines services and natural resources alongside manufacturing and demonstrates the long-term role of multinationals as transferors of technologies and cultures across borders.

By making specialist literature on the subject accessible to a wider audience this will be an essential text both for students of international business seeking an evolutionary perspective on their subject and historians looking for an introduction to multinationals.

**Geoffrey Jones** is Professor of Business History in the Economics Department, University of Reading.

# The evolution of international business

## An introduction

Geoffrey Jones

London and New York

First published 1996
by Routledge
11 New Fetter Lane, London EC4P 4EE

Simultaneously published in the USA and Canada
by Routledge
29 West 35th Street, New York NY 10001

© 1996 Geoffrey Jones

Typeset in Times 10/12 by Florencetype Ltd, Stoodleigh, Devon
Printed and bound in Great Britain by Redwood Books, Trowbridge, Wilts

*British Library Cataloguing in Publication Data*
A catalogue record for this book is available from
the British Library

*Library of Congress Cataloguing in Publication Data*
Jones, Geoffrey
    The evolution of international business / by Geoffrey Jones.
        p.  cm.
    Includes bibliographical references and index.
    ISBN 0–415–10775–X (hb : alk. paper). – ISBN 0–415–09371–6
(pb : alk. paper)
    1. International business enterprises – History.  2. International
trade – History.  3. Cartels – History.  4. Competition,
International – History.  I. Title.
HD2755.5.J67   1996
338.8′8′09–dc20

ISBN 0–415–10775–X
ISBN 0–415–09371–6 (pbk)

# Contents

# Figures

# Tables

# Preface

This book is an attempt to draw together a highly diverse, multi-disciplinary, international, rapidly expanding and challenging literature on the evolution of international business. It draws upon my own research in this subject over the last fifteen years, but the debt owed to the work of numerous other researchers is fundamental. The bibliographical references serve as my acknowledgements to these many colleagues worldwide. I would like to acknowledge my especial debt, both personal and academic, to Mark Casson, Alfred D. Chandler Jnr, John H. Dunning and Mira Wilkins. I have learned a great deal about multinationals over the years from discussions with T.A.B. Corley, Jean-François Hennart, Peter Hertner, Tetsuya Kuwahara, Akira Kudo, Harm G. Schröter, Keetie E. Sluyterman and Ken'ichi Yasumuro. Their influence on this book is self-evident. The ideas expressed in this book have been substantially refined and improved as a result of stimulating discussions during seminars held in Geneva, London, Oslo and Urbana-Champaign in 1994 and 1995. Helga Nordvik and Tom Roehl made especially insightful comments.

At various times the sheer complexity of this subject produced crises of self-doubt about the wisdom of attempting to write such a book. The support of Mira Wilkins, who read every draft chapter, was critical in preventing me from abandoning the project. Mark Casson, David Merrett and Mary B. Rose also read all or parts of the book, and provided numerous insightful – as well as supportive – comments. I remain responsible for the judgements and opinions expressed here.

The Division on Transnational Corporations and Investment of the United Nations Conference on Trade and Development was an indispensable source of information about the recent activities of multinationals. Its annual *World Investment Report* and related publications are an outstanding source of data and analysis. I owe special thanks to Karl P. Sauvant for his assistance. Lilach Nachum was a valued supplier of recent FDI data.

I also need to thank three other patient and supportive people. Fabienne Debrunner spent much time assisting me with the German and French literature. Rosemary Nixon of Routledge commented helpfully on a very imperfect first draft, and stayed calm as deadlines came and went. And Lynn Cornell played an indispensable role in typing the manuscript and getting the book ready for publication.

Geoffrey Jones
Reading, March 1995

# Introduction

This book provides an overview of the development of international business from its nineteenth century origins until the present day. There is a very large literature written by economists, political scientists, policy-makers and others about multinationals. Most of the analysis and the conclusions have been based on the experience of the last four decades. As this book shows, international business is a process which has gone on for a much longer time period.

An evolutionary perspective on international business offers important advantages. Because multinational investment is a cumulative process, the structure of contemporary international business can only be satisfactorily explained in many respects by examining its history. A striking number of today's largest multinationals established their leading positions in world industries many decades ago, and retained them despite the challenges posed by technological, social, political and other changes. More fundamentally, an evolutionary perspective demonstrates the dynamic nature of international business. The structures, strategies and impact of multinationals have changed considerably over time, and will continue to change in the future. It is this dynamic element of international business which is one of its most important characteristics.

This approach to international business was pioneered by Mira Wilkins, who in a two volume study of the history of US multinationals (Wilkins 1970, 1974a), discussed the evolutionary and cumulative nature of international business, revealing how its form and organisation changed over time. Subsequently, many aspects of the history of international business have been researched, even though many gaps remain to be filled. This book seeks to make this specialist literature accessible to a wider audience. It assumes little prior knowledge of either economics or political and economic history. As a result, it is hoped that it can be used both by students of international business seeking an evolutionary perspective on their subject, and historians wanting an introduction to multinationals. The approach is internationally comparative throughout.

The approach taken is thematic. Chapter 1 introduces the key concepts used in research on multinationals. The discussion is non-technical and does not require prior knowledge of the theory of the multinational enterprise. Chapter 2 presents an overview of the development of international business over time. It provides estimates on the size and direction of multinational investment over time, and discusses the reasons why such quantification is full of uncertainties. These two chapters provide the theoretical and chronological framework for the book. Chapters 3, 4 and 5 examine in more detail the growth of international business in natural resources, manufacturing and services. Chapter 6 is concerned with the relationship between multinationals and their home countries. Chapter 7 turns to the impact of multinationals on the host countries for their operations. Chapter 8 discusses the policies pursued by host governments. A short conclusion in Chapter 9 summarises the main themes of the book. Three appendices provide a listing of the largest multinationals in 1992, a definition of key terms and a brief chronology intended for those with little historical knowledge.

The development of international business worldwide over two hundred years is a diffuse subject. This book attempts to convey some of the complexities, but nonetheless it is by definition an exercise in simplification. It makes no attempt to provide a comprehensive history of all multi-nationals, and it is selective in the issues surveyed and the topics covered. The bibliography at the end of the book provides a means of pursuing topics which can only be treated briefly here.

# Chapter 1

# Multinationals: theories and concepts

## ISSUES

Multinational enterprises, or MNEs, have attracted an enormous literature, but the reason for their significance in the world economy is often misunderstood. The largest MNEs are very large indeed. Their business interests stretch over much of the world. But the real significance of MNEs rests on neither their size nor their span, impressive as it appears, but on their function. MNEs control a package of resources which they move across national borders, and continue to control over those borders. Often this transfer is conceived solely in financial terms, but in practice the role of MNEs in transferring capital between countries is one of their less important functions. The critical resources which MNEs transfer across borders are found in the areas of technology and organisation, entrepreneurship and culture. MNEs are important because they have the capacity to move technologies and ideas around the world. This gives them the potential to serve as engines of growth.

The existence of such firms raises a number of issues. A first set of issues is related to *why* MNEs exist. The existence of MNEs might seem obvious, in the sense that firms in the capitalist system exist to make profits, and investing in foreign countries could be seen as a logical way of making more money than staying in one country. Yet not all firms in the world are multinational. In addition, although some industries are dominated by MNEs, others are not. And while some countries are the home countries of many MNEs and/or attract many foreign MNEs, other countries neither possess nor attract many MNEs. The study of MNEs involves explaining these differences between firms, industries and nations, and the choices they make – or are made for them – regarding MNEs.

A second set of issues is concerned to explain *how* MNEs exist. The control of packages of resources in different countries is a complex undertaking. Of course, firms operating in a single economy very often need to monitor and control operations in more than one location, and have to acquire skills in the co-ordination of diverse activities. The managerial challenge of running a nationwide business in geographically large countries like Brazil, Russia and the United States is self-evident. Yet the managerial problems appear even more daunting when firms cross borders. In different countries, the problems of co-ordination over distance are joined by those of co-ordination between different business, legal and political systems, which are often conducted in different languages by people with different cultural values and preferences than at home. What kind of organisation do firms need to control their operations in foreign countries?

A third set of issues concerns the *impact* of MNEs. What are the consequences of the transfer of skills and ideas around the world? Does it bring benefits, or are there costs? What are the consequences for a country of having some of its companies controlled by companies owned abroad? Do the consequences vary by firm, industry and nation? Can the consequences be predicted?

These three central issues are constant in international business, but they have been resolved in different ways in different circumstances. This book surveys how the resolution of these issues has changed over time.

## DEFINITIONS

An MNE is usually defined as a firm that controls operations or income-generating assets in more than one country. Attempts have sometimes been made to define MNEs in a more restrictive fashion. It has been suggested that multinationality requires operations in a minimum number of countries, usually five or six, or that a firm which is active across borders should be a certain size before it can be called an MNE. In practice, attempts to restrict the definition of 'MNE' encounter such difficulties that most researchers prefer the broad definition offered above. This is the approach taken here.

Although MNEs can be very large, firms that operate across borders can be of any size, and many are small by any definition. Their organisational forms differ enormously. MNEs can be engaged in manufacturing, services or the exploitation of natural resources. A broad distinction can be made between firms engaged in *market-oriented* investments and those engaged in *supply-oriented* investments. In the former, firms locate a facility in a particular overseas market to serve that market directly. In the latter, firms locate in a particular country to gain access to sources of supply of (for example) raw materials. MNEs can be *horizontally integrated* – a firm which performs the same kind of value-added activities in each geographic market. They can also be *vertically integrated*, where the enterprise produces outputs in some of its plants that serve as inputs to others of its plants. Firms can engage in *backward vertical integration* to obtain raw materials and other inputs for production facilities, or in *forward vertical integration* into distribution facilities for their products in foreign countries. MNEs can also be *diversified* across products as well as countries.

The simplest way that a firm can engage in business outside its national borders is by exporting. The term MNE is not used for a firm whose sole international involvement is the exporting of goods or services from its home base. The essence of the multinational concept is that the firm controls income-generating assets in at least two countries. The acquisition of such assets involves a foreign investment, which may be one of two types. *Portfolio* investment involves the acquisition of foreign securities by individuals or institutions without any control over the management of the foreign entity. *Foreign direct investment* (FDI) involves management control. Control is the critical factor. MNEs engage in FDI because they both own and control assets in foreign countries.

The basic idea that MNEs engage in FDI which enables them to own and control assets in foreign countries is straightforward. FDI is conventionally used as a proxy to measure the extent and direction of MNE activity. This convention is used in this book. Yet in practice FDI figures have serious drawbacks and do not fully capture the essence of the multinational enterprise. Control can be exercised in numerous ways. International FDI statistics are bedevilled by the problems of defining 'control'. The easiest aggregate measure of 'control' is the share of the equity of a company, but there remains no international consensus on the minimum equity stake deemed necessary for 'control' to exist. Currently, in the United States an investment is regarded as direct if at least 10 per cent of the equity is owned. In the United Kingdom the percentage is 20 per cent and in Germany 25 per cent. Most countries have changed their definitions over time. Prior to 1980, Japanese data was based on 25 per cent minimum stock ownership. The current figure is 10 per cent (Julius 1990: 14–20, 109–12).

These problems are in fact only the beginning of the technical difficulties involved in using FDI data. Measures of flows of FDI between countries have numerous drawbacks, one being that they do not include direct investment financed from sources that do not pass through the country of the original investor, including capital markets in the host countries. Stock data is usually based on the historical value of an investment and not updated at market prices. Given that countries have varied widely in the timing of their direct investments, this introduces major distortions into international comparisons of FDI stocks (Cantwell and Bellak 1994). An evolutionary study of international business faces the additional and major problem that only fragmentary and partial estimates of the size of FDI exist before the 1960s.

The most straightforward example of FDI occurs when an enterprise establishes a wholly-owned subsidiary in a foreign country. Such a subsidiary can be established either by taking over an existing local firm or by a *greenfield* investment involving the establishment of a completely new operation. However, there are in reality a range of intermediate and alternative contractual modes available between operating abroad through wholly-owned foreign subsidiaries and exporting. These modes involve both equity and non-equity arrangements.

MNEs often operate abroad using a *joint venture*, when two or more companies own a foreign firm. Companies also engage in cross-border activity using non-equity arrangements which can achieve control with no – or very little – actual investment. These international business strategies are not captured in a financial measure such as FDI. There are a number of such strategies available to firms. *Licensing* involves a contract between independent firms to transfer technologies, rights or resources. *Franchising* is a specialist type of licensing under which a foreign company grants an individual or company the right to do business in a certain way over a certain period of time in a specified place. *International cartels* involve agreements between independent firms to maintain prices or limit output. *International collaborative agreements* and *strategic alliances* are arrangements between firms to share facilities or co-operate in new product development. *Long-term contracts* between firms are also an important component of international business.

The existence of intermediate modes between exporting and wholly-owned FDI re-inforces the critical point that the real significance of MNEs is not as an institutional vehicle for foreign investment. The issues raised by MNEs are not those concerned with capital flows between nations. The focus is rather on the package of resources possessed by MNEs. While each package can be regarded as specific to each firm, it also draws on the characteristics of the *home economy* where they are based. Equally, while the transfer of these assets by each firm will be a unique experience, it can be expected to have an impact on the *host economy* more generally. It will raise issues of sovereignty, and the possibility of countries gaining access to technologies and management systems which they currently lack. In considering such impact issues, the quantity of FDI flows is not an ideal proxy for the significance of international business. It is necessary instead to look at more qualitative attributes of MNE activity: the sectoral and industrial distribution, the technological content, and the nature of the linkages to the local economy.

## THEORIES OF THE MULTINATIONAL ENTERPRISE

The term 'multinational enterprise' is a comparatively recent one. In 1958 the French economist Maurice Byé coined the expression 'multi-territorial firm' (Dunning 1993: 68–9). In 1960 David E. Lilienthal, one-time head of the Tennessee Valley Authority in the United States, delivered a paper on the problems of US corporations with overseas operations, which he defined as 'multinational corporations' (Fieldhouse 1986: 10–11). However the concept of multinationals pre-dated the name itself. During the interwar years, a number of mainly American academics published FDI estimates and analyses of the determinants and impact of enterprises engaged in FDI. These studies contain explicit discussions of the managerial and technological as well as financial aspects of this phenomenon (Southard 1931, Remer 1933, Lewis 1938). There was also a wider public discussion in interwar Europe about the consequences and dangers of foreign firms controlling domestic industries (Wilkins 1974a: 154–5).

In contrast, the significance of MNEs was only belatedly realised by economic theorists (Dunning, Cantwell and Corley 1986). A major difficulty was that the assumptions of mainstream neoclassical economic theory had the consequence of making all the issues raised by MNEs appear unimportant. The Heckscher-Ohlin theory, which sought to explain how a country's comparative advantage determined its trade, assumed atomistic competition, which meant that the issue of ownership did not matter, and that all technology was public, so that proprietary technology was also not an issue. As a result, the phenomenon of foreign firms moving technology and other assets between countries and controlling them across borders could not be identified as a matter requiring analysis.

Until the 1960s mainstream economic theorists treated MNEs simply as arbitrageurs of capital, moving equity from countries where returns were low to those where it was higher. A major conceptual breakthrough came in a Ph.D thesis at the Massachusetts Institute of Technology completed by Stephen Hymer in 1960. This thesis, which was entitled *The International Operation of National Firms*, asserted that FDI involved the transfer of a whole package of resources and not simply finance. This insight – and a number of others in the Hymer thesis – was the basis for much subsequent theoretical development (Dunning 1993: 68–95).

**Ownership and locational factors**

Beginning with the Hymer thesis, an underlying assumption of many theories of the MNE was that a firm required some form of 'advantage' in order to operate and compete in an unfamiliar foreign environment. In foreign markets, local firms were assumed to possess superior knowledge about the markets, resources, legal and political system, language and culture, and all the many other things which separate one country from another. In so far as this is true, foreign firms would have no incentive to locate in that market or ability to survive in it without an advantage.

This reasoning led to the view that a foreign firm required *ownership* (or competitive) advantages over its local rivals. There are many possible sources of advantage to foreign firms. In the post-Second World War period, access to superior technology, information, knowledge and know-how has been extremely important. The most tangible component of the technological advantage of an MNE is seen in access to new products and processes. This access can be derived from heavy spending on *research and development* (R & D). It might be protected by patents or other means which prevent competitors copying or acquiring the technology. When technologies are standardised, the ability to differentiate products can be a significant source of advantage for an MNE. As a result, *branding* and *product differentiation* strategies are often an important source of advantage for firms in foreign markets.

A second ownership advantage lies in superior management and organisation techniques. These can arise from superior organisational structures compared to local rivals or from superior management skills, such as better marketing skills or accounting methods. Advantages might also be derived from better trained or educated managers. Managerial and technological advantages are closely related and interdependent. The concept of technology should not be confined to the narrow sense of the mechanics of the production process or the physical characteristics of the products made, but encompasses all aspects of the organisation of production. The ability of a firm to innovate and generate new technology is a critical ownership advantage, which eventually results in a stream of new ownership advantages.

A third source of ownership advantage can be found in access to finance. MNEs might have access to cheaper capital than local competitors. This might arise from privileged access to capital markets which may not be so accessible to firms from certain countries, or from the large size of an MNE which enables it to borrow cheaply. In some countries where close relationships exist between banks and industrial companies, the latter might have privileged access to funding. Financial or accounting techniques might also provide ownership advantages in this area. Conversely, capital constraints can force divestments or otherwise have a major impact on the choice of contractual arrangements for international business operations (Casson 1987: 45–8).

Further ownership advantages can be derived from the size of a firm. MNEs which are also very large firms possess an important source of market power because of economies of scale. The main advantages are derived from the centralisation of R & D, marketing, finance and other management functions which will not be available to smaller local competitors. According to the theory proposed by Knickerbocker (1973), MNE strategies can be understood in terms of the rivalry of oligopolistic firms which follow one another into new foreign markets as a defensive strategy.

Firms derive ownership advantages from privileged access to raw materials. This may arise from control over production of the material, or over processing, or over the final markets for raw materials. The availability of a mineral or other raw material in the home economy can generate ownership advantages for firms of that nationality, because they develop product-specific capabilities and knowledge which can be utilised elsewhere.

Firms can possess any number of these – or other – ownership advantages when they operate in a foreign market. The type of ownership advantage which may stimulate a foreign investment will differ considerably between products and industries. Within manufacturing, superior technology and innovative capacity are especially important in the case of production goods. Product differentiation will often be more important for consumer goods. Ownership advantages can be generated internally within the firm, or acquired in some way – by licensing a technology from a foreign competitor or buying an entire foreign firm.

MNEs can also be said to derive ownership advantages from being multinational. These advantages of common governance derive from the ability to co-ordinate separate value-added activities across national boundaries. Multinationality can enhance operational flexibility by offering wider opportunities for global sources of input. It can provide more favoured access to international markets. It can provide the ability to diversify or reduce risks. Ownership advantages derived from the possession of intangible assets and those derived from the common governance of geographically dispersed assets are conceptually different. This distinction is examined further below.

It can be assumed that the greater the ownership advantages of business enterprises, the more incentive they have to exploit them in foreign markets. However the existence of ownership advantages alone does not provide an explanation for international business. A firm could exploit these advantages through exporting from its home country rather than engaging in FDI. It could also employ one of the intermediate modes considered earlier. To explain the choice of FDI over the alternative of exporting, a number of *locational* factors have to be considered.

Ownership advantages can explain why firms should wish, and are able, to operate in foreign countries. Locational factors within the host economy can be used to explain where they locate, and why a company should undertake FDI in a foreign country rather than exploit its ownership advantage by exporting. There are a considerable number of possible locational factors whose relative importance differs between different industries.

Among the most important locational factors are *tariff* and *non-tariff* barriers to trade. In so far as exporting and local production represent two alternative ways of servicing a foreign market, measures that make exporting difficult will encourage local production, although a firm also has the option of withdrawing completely from supplying a foreign country. There are numerous examples of manufacturing firms which would have preferred to export to a particular market, but which had to engage in FDI because trade protectionism or non-tariff barriers such as import quotas rendered this strategy ineffective. Host countries may impose trade barriers for reasons completely unassociated with FDI, or they might be designed with the specific intention of inducing foreign firms, which had previously exported, to set up local manufacturing facilities.

Host government policies impact the locational decisions of MNEs in a variety of other ways. Governments can seek to attract foreign companies by offering subsidies, or else discourage them by restricting or prohibiting foreign participation in local industries. Government policies have a considerable influence on the *investment climate* of a country. Government spending on physical infrastructure and educational facilities can make a country an attractive location for foreign investors. At the other extreme, a government that is unable to provide a legal framework which offers security to foreign investors will contribute to the existence of a high-risk environment to which only risky or speculative investments will probably be attracted.

The nature of the host country market is often an important locational factor. The size and income level of a market, its growth and stage of development are important considerations. Firms can often have a better appreciation of the idiosyncrasies of a particular market if they manufacture in it rather than export to it. On the other hand, the adaption of products to cater for differences in tastes may only be economic if the host country market is sufficiently large. Sometimes a particular host country may be an attractive location less for itself, than because of its membership of a wider free trade area or regional economic bloc. Another important locational factor can be differences in labour costs. In products in which labour costs form a significant proportion of total production costs, there might be incentive to transfer production to lower wage economies.

The spatial distribution of resource endowments is a critical locational factor for MNEs engaged in the exploitation of natural resources. In the case of non-renewable resources such as mining and petroleum, there is a fundamental difference from manufacturing or service industries because the location of mines or oil wells is determined by geology. The distribution of minerals and petroleum around the world is fortuitous and asymmetric with respect to final markets. Business enterprises which seek to exploit a particular mineral can sometimes choose between host economies, but the choice can only be between countries which possess the resource. In some services, the spatial distribution of created resource endowments can be a critical locational determinant. In international banking, banks are drawn to the agglomerations of human skills and informational infrastructures found in international financial centres.

## Internalisation and the boundaries of firms

Transactions cost theory provides a different perspective on the reasons for the growth of MNEs. The fundamental insight is derived from a pioneering article by Coase (1937) which sought to explain the boundaries of firms. Coase's focus was on the multi-plant domestic firm rather than the international operations of firms. He argued that firms and markets represent alternative methods of organising production. This theory suggested that the market is costly and inefficient for undertaking certain types of transactions. The *transactions costs* of the market include the cost of discovering relevant prices and in arranging contracts for each market transaction. The existence of such costs means that whenever transactions can be organised and carried out at a lower cost within the firm than through the market, they will be *internalised* and undertaken by the firm itself. Firms will internalise transactions until the marginal cost of doing so exceeds the marginal revenue.

This theory attracted little attention from economists until the 1970s, when it was extended and refined by Oliver Williamson (1975, 1981, 1985). Williamson suggested that transactions costs could be examined systematically in relation to three factors. These are *bounded rationality*, *opportunism* and *asset-specificity*. Bounded rationality refers to the impossibility of anyone knowing all possible information, which means that people invariably make less than fully rational decisions. Opportunism refers to the tendency of some people to cheat or misrepresent. Asset specificity reflects the extent to which types of transaction, in order to be carried out, necessitate investments in material and intangible assets (such as knowledge) which are dedicated to particular uses, and how much their value will be diminished if used in alternative ways. If it is difficult to measure the value of goods and services, and if the opportunities for bargaining and dishonesty are therefore high, there is an incentive to replace the market by hierarchy. The combination of bounded rationality, opportunism and asset specificity produces the strongest incentive to internalise a transaction rather than to use contracts in the market. A party which has invested in equipment (for example) specifically designed to carry out a transaction and which has a lower value in other areas will fear that its trading partner will opportunistically renegotiate the terms of trade. This provides an incentive to internalise the transaction within the same firm.

Internalisation is concerned with imperfections in the markets for *intermediate products*. Intermediate products embrace all the different types of good or service that are transferred between one activity and another within the production process. As applied to MNEs by McManus (1972), Buckley and Casson (1976), Hennart (1982) and others, this theory proposes that firms expand across borders because the transaction costs incurred in international *intermediate product* markets can be reduced by internalising these markets within the firm.

The MNE is conceptualised in a different fashion in this theory than in the earlier discussion on ownership and location factors. Instead of being a firm which owns or controls production facilities in more than one country, the MNE is perceived as an institution which co-ordinates the use of intermediate products produced in one country with subsequent value-added activities in another country. The primary analytical concern is not to understand the advantages held by MNEs over local rivals, but the ways in which cross-border transactions are organised within the same firms, rather than through arm's length trade between independent firms.

Internalisation theory can be used to explain patterns of both vertical and horizontal integration across borders (Casson 1987). The internalisation of tangible intermediate product flows between upstream and downstream production explains vertical integration between mining and manufacture, agriculture and food-processing, component production and final assembly. Vertical backward integration – for example, by steel firms into iron ore or rubber manufacturers into natural rubber plantations – can be seen as arising from *small number conditions*, when the number of parties to the exchange is small, which can often arise from the presence of physical asset specificity, and from *information asymmetry*, which can cause problems of quality control because of opportunistic behaviour (Hennart 1991a: 89–92). The internalisation of flows of intangibles such as knowledge and reputation can explain patterns of cross-border horizontal integration.

This body of theory is of considerable value for understanding international business, and it will be used throughout this book. But there are a number of caveats about the application of the theory to the history of international business. There are continuing differences of emphasis between leading internalisation theorists, and a number of criticisms have also been made of the theory as a whole. These include that it is a theory of market failure rather than of firm success, and that it is so preoccupied with the costs of organising transactions in markets that it does not consider the organising – or management – costs incurred by firms (Demsetz 1988). It has also been objected that the theory neglects the complexity of actual business by focusing on the extremes of markets and hierarchies, while in reality there are elements of markets within hierarchies and vice versa (Perrow 1986). The significance of networks of firms rather than pure markets and hierarchies is discussed below. Although transactions costs theorists are addressing such criticisms (Hennart 1993), the limitations of the existing theory need to be borne in mind.

## The eclectic paradigm

John H. Dunning's *eclectic paradigm* provides an organising framework in which different theoretical approaches are incorporated, and which attempts to explain all forms of international production (Dunning 1993: 76–86). The eclectic paradigm maintains that firms will engage in international production if they possess ownership advantages in a particular foreign market; if the enterprise perceives it to be in its best interest to add value to these ownership advantages rather than sell them to foreign firms – internalisation advantages; and if locational advantages make it more profitable to exploit its assets in a particular foreign location rather than at home.

The eclectic paradigm has evolved considerably over time. In its latest formulations, it incorporates numerous different factors as well as conflicting theoretical approaches. It is for this reason that Dunning now describes it as a paradigm rather than as a theory. The disadvantage of the paradigm is that it has very little predictive power, but it is also very realistic in reflecting the diversity and complexity of international business. Dunning incorporates a large number of non-economic variables into the paradigm, and this interdisciplinary approach undoubtedly provides important perspectives on many aspects of international business. Political, legal and cultural influences can have a decisive impact on ownership, location and internalisation factors.

The necessity for ownership advantages in the eclectic paradigm has attracted particular criticism from internalisation theorists. Casson suggests that a combination of internalisation and location advantages is itself sufficient to explain multinational activities, arguing that too much weight has been placed on the assumption that MNEs incur additional costs when they do business abroad. These costs, he suggests, should be seen as 'simply one component of the overall cost of integrating activities in different countries, and it is only the overall cost that is crucial to the theory'. The eclectic paradigm uses both the types of ownership advantage identified earlier in this section: i.e. both those derived from the possession of intangible assets and those derived from internalisation itself. But for Casson the first type is not a necessary condition – though they may be useful for explaining the success or failure of a company – while the description of the second type of advantage as an 'ownership' one is tautological (Casson 1987: 32–6).

These theoretical debates over the necessity or otherwise of ownership advantages are complicated by the fact that different questions are often being asked. Internalisation theorists are concerned to explain why MNEs in general displace international trade in intermediate products. The theory is concerned with explaining the boundaries of the firm. The concept of ownership advantages is used to explain the growth of a particular firm or group of firms *vis-à-vis* other firms. The generation of ownership advantages can be regarded as a key element of competitive success and survival (Cantwell 1991: 44–51).

In some ways, theories can be seen as evolving alongside international business. In the 1960s, when the first theories were formulated, the most powerful image of an MNE was of a large US corporation with advanced technological and managerial systems. It appeared a very superior form of business organisation compared to its competitors in Europe or Japan. Moreover, foreign markets appeared very 'foreign' to American academics of that period. By the 1990s the information revolution and the globalisation of the world economy had combined to make foreign countries look less dangerous and distant places. Large US corporations no longer seemed to possess enormous ownership advantages, while no single organisational form had replaced them as a paragon of international business. Theorists were, as a result, less inclined to look for some enormous 'ownership advantage', and attention turned to exploring more subtle advantages held by firms in foreign markets.

There remains no universally agreed theory of international business. Disagreements persist about the relative importance of ownership, location and internalisation factors. There are other theories which approach the subject from different perspectives, such as the product cycle theory which is discussed later in the book. There is now a widespread recognition that in so far as economic theories address single issues, international business can only be understood by combining a number of theories. The problem is how to integrate these different theories in a consistent way.

## ENTREPRENEURS, FIRMS, HIERARCHIES AND NETWORKS

There are a number of further concepts relating to the role and function of entrepreneurs and firms which are important for understanding the development of international business.

### Entrepreneurship

Entrepreneurs have been conceived in a restricted fashion in neo-classical economic theory. The basic problem is that the theory provides 'a static analysis of a fundamentally dynamic problem' (Casson 1985: 175). A state of equilibrium is assumed in which transactors' plans are fully reconciled by the prices prevailing in equity and management markets. The emphasis on the final state rather than the process of getting there diverts attention from the distinctive contribution of the entrepreneur, for it is self-evident that equilibrium is constantly disrupted by unforeseen changes in the environment. These unforeseen changes are frequently the result of innovation by an entrepreneur, which proceeds to disturb the environment of other entrepreneurs.

A number of economists have attempted to model entrepreneurship in a more dynamic fashion than in mainstream economic theory. Knight (1921) suggested that entrepreneurship was associated with uncertainty bearing. Uncertainty was distinguished in this model from risks to which some possible outcome can be ascribed and insured against. Kirzner (1973, 1979) suggested that entrepreneurs are persons who are alert to hitherto unexploited possibilities for exchange. In contrast to Knight, entrepreneurship is distinguished from ownership, and entrepreneurial rewards are derived solely from the possession of the knowledge that opportunities exist which no-one has spotted before. For Kirzner entrepreneurship is associated with disequilibrium, and concerns the process by which the economy moves towards equilibrium.

In the model of Schumpeter (1943), the entrepreneur is an extraordinary person who brings about extraordinary events. The entrepreneurial figure is an innovator who disturbs and disrupts markets, technologies and organisational methods. Entrepreneurs constantly destabilise the world by innovation – rather than, as in Kirzner's model, take the best advantage of the existing situation. Schumpeter argued that the growth of large corporations was in the process of rendering the entrepreneur obsolescent, because innovation would become routine. Kirzner, on the other hand, regards large corporations not as alternatives to entrepreneurship, but as magnets attracting entrepreneurial talent, and as institutions which permit a more effective use of entrepreneurial alertness.

For Casson, an entrepreneur 'specialises in taking judgmental decisions about the co-ordination of scarce resources' (Casson 1982: 66). A key feature of the model is the importance of judgement and not the ownership of resources *per se*. Unlike Schumpeter and Kirzner, the entrepreneur in this model is not the force behind change so much as a person who makes difficult judgements in a changing world. An entrepreneur synthesises information through diverse sources and exploits it. Casson uses this model to explain the growth process of a typical horizontal foreign direct investor. An entrepreneur gains information on an overseas market through varying channels, such as travel or news from relatives who might have migrated. On the basis of this information, he/she may decide to export and set up a distribution subsidiary. A sales subsidiary gives the exporting firm access to further information, which might provide the basis for a decision to set up a factory. This will provide detailed information on factor costs which can be compared with other information from other factories, and enable over time the rationalisation of international production (Casson 1985: 186–8).

Entrepreneurship is extremely important in international business. Whether they are conceived as extraordinary innovators or as 'alert' individuals or as taking judgemental decisions, a great deal of what happens in international business can be termed 'entrepreneurial'. Entrepreneurial ability can be a critical ownership advantage and an important part of the explanation of why and how firms expand across borders. The amount and quality of entrepreneurship differs between countries, for complex social, economic and ideological reasons (Casson 1982).

## Firms and innovation

In neo-classical economics firms transform inputs of factors of production into outputs of goods and services. The central assumption is that firms face known choices assuming prevailing technologies and given resources, and that they have no difficulty taking the right decisions to achieve profit maximisation. In such a theory, firms are 'black boxes' and what goes on inside them is of little importance. Managers have no important role in this view. Also of little importance are differences between firms. Firms facing different markets will behave and perform differently, but if the market conditions changed so would the behaviour of firms. Though firms differ, the differences have no great significance. Transactions cost theory also treats firms and managers as passive reactors rather than dynamic entities. The theory is one of exchange which seeks to predict the existence of a firm or MNE, but it does not address the internal sources of growth within firms.

Recent theories on innovation, technology and business treat firms and their organisation in a different fashion. In the evolutionary theories of technological innovation associated with Nelson and Winter, Dosi and others, firms do not dip freely into some general stock or pool of 'prevailing' technological knowledge. Instead, firms produce things in ways that are differentiated technically from the production methods of other firms, and they make innovations largely on the basis of in-house technology. The search process of industrial firms to improve and diversify their technology involves them building on their existing technological base and on their existing markets (Nelson and Winter 1982; Dosi 1988).

These theories stress the role of the dynamic capability of individual firms. These capabilities have three components. The first is the strategy of the firm, or how it defines and rationalises its objectives and how it intends to pursue them. The second is the structure of the firm, or how it is organised and governed. Thirdly, strategy and structure mould organisational capabilities. Nelson and Winter propose that firms which work well can be understood in terms of a hierarchy of organisational routines. At any time the practised routines that are built into an organisation define the range of things the organisation can do. In industries where technological innovation is important, a firm needs a set of core capabilities in R & D, and the extent of these will limit the extent of innovation a firm can undertake. *Corporate competence* is found in the tacit capability of a firm that results from a process of continued and collective learning. It is embodied in the firm's localised skills and organisational routines. This aspect of technology – unlike brand names or patents which can be copied or purchased – is strictly specific to a firm (Nelson 1991).

The evolutionary theories of technological innovation help to explain why a number of enterprises have remained prominent MNEs over long time periods. They deepen the discussion of ownership advantage by showing how firms develop the competence which enables them to become and remain competitive in innovation. This literature also emphasises the fact that firms differ and that these differences matter. Finally, the theories suggest that the critical area of difference will be found in the organisation of the firm. 'It is organisational differences, especially differences in abilities to generate and gain from innovation, rather than differences in command over particular technologies, that are the source of durable, not easily imitable, differences between firms' (Nelson 1991: 72).

## Hierarchies and networks

Alfred D. Chandler's research on the emergence of the modern industrial enterprise provides a series of key concepts to understand the competitive advantages of firms and the reasons why they can be a more efficient means of co-ordinating transactions than markets (Chandler 1962, 1977, 1990). Chandler has been concerned to explain the development of large corporations administered by a hierarchy of salaried professional managers. Until the last decades of the nineteenth century, production and distribution of goods all over the world was carried on by small enterprises whose managers were also the owners. Business enterprises in the nineteenth century normally operated a single unit of production or of distribution. The flow of goods between these enterprises was co-ordinated by the 'invisible hand' of the market.

In explaining the shift from these personally managed enterprises to the modern corporation, Chandler identifies two crucial variables. These are changes in technology and in markets. The coming of modern transportation and communication in the nineteenth century – especially railroads, telegraphs, steamships and cables – made possible mass production and mass marketing for the first time. The first corporations with managerial hierarchies appeared in the United States in the 1850s and 1860s to co-ordinate the movement of trains and the flow of goods on the new railroad networks and messages over the new telegraph system. Transportation improvements coincided with the development of new technologies in certain industries which permitted much greater reduction in cost per unit of output as volume increased. The first industries to secure these economies of scale included oil refining, metallurgy and food processing, where continuous flow techniques were applied. Mass production in turn required assured mass markets, with the result that manufacturing enterprises in these industries typically built their own extensive marketing organisations. In those industries that integrated mass production and mass distribution, managerial hierarchies emerged to provide a 'visible hand' to co-ordinate the flows of goods within the enterprise.

The large managerial enterprise which emerged in the capital-intensive manufacturing industries of the late nineteenth and early twentieth centuries achieved economies of scale from their size and integration and of scope from diversifying into new products and, eventually, countries. According to Chandler, the success of firms in moving in this direction depended on their *organisational capability*, which in turn rested on their willingness to make three interrelated investments in production facilities, marketing, and management. The successful firms were those that recruited and organised the managers needed to supervise the functional activities pertaining to the production and distribution of products, and to co-ordinate and monitor the flow of goods.

Chandler demonstrates the frequency with which the *first movers* in making the three-pronged investments remained leaders in their industry over the long run, and have proved capable of innovating and moving into new lines of business. These first movers had very considerable advantages from their investments, and in many cases their industry quickly became and remained oligopolistic. Latecomer firms – or *challengers* – thereby encountered considerable barriers to entry.

In the first half of the twentieth century the modern industrial enterprise continued to grow through horizontal and vertical integration, and expansion in new products and countries. This growth brought into being a new basic organisational form or structure to replace the existing, centralised and functionally departmentalised U-Form. This was the *multi-divisional structure* (or M-Form). M-Form firms had a corporate headquarters and a number of product or geographical operating divisions. The headquarter executives carried out two related functions. The first was entrepreneurial and involved the determination of long-term strategies for the entire firm and the allocation of resources within the firm to allow these strategies to be pursued. The second function was administrative and consisted of monitoring the performance of the operating divisions.

The Chandlerian model has major implications for understanding the development of international business. The modern industrial enterprise is conceived as playing a central role in creating the most technologically advanced fast-growing manufacturing industry of each generation. The visible hand of managerial co-ordination is treated as the key to industrial innovation, and a major force behind the growth of MNEs. 'Although not all ... integrated industrial enterprises became multinationals', Chandler writes, 'nearly all industrial multinationals evolved from such enterprises' (Chandler 1986: 409).

Chandler also provides an explanation for country-specific differences in international competitiveness. It was the United States that took the lead in the creation of large corporations, and US firms remained larger and more numerous than those of other countries. The United States had many more and many larger managerial hierarchies than those of other nations. In some other countries, such as the United Kingdom, industrial firms remained smaller, at least until the interwar years, and continued to be dominated by their founding families. The persistence of British *personal capitalism* – which Chandler contrasts with the *competitive managerial capitalism* of the United States as well as the *co-operative managerial capitalism* seen in Germany – caused a lag in that country's competitive abilities in the capital-intensive industries of chemicals, machinery and electric equipment. 'It was in just these industries that the Americans and the Germans successfully invaded the markets of the world and of Britain itself' (Chandler 1980: 427).

There are strong parallels between the internalisation explanation of the existence of firms and Chandler's historical account of the replacement of the invisible hand of the market by the visible hand of managers, even though the approaches are conceptually distinct (Lazonick 1991). However a considerable complication for both approaches is that firms and markets are not the only ways of organising production. Co-operative agreements between firms can provide an alternative both to the firm as a co-ordinated system, and to the market, through their ability to compensate for market failures (Mariti and Smiley 1983).

The Japanese business system provides the most widespread example of this phenomenon. Modern Japanese capitalism evolved a structure which combined characteristics of both the market and hierarchy. Before the Second World War a number of family-owned holding companies called *zaibatsu* had controlled groups of trading companies, banks and other enterprises, between which there were substantial trading and other links. *Zaibatsu* were broken up after the Second World War, but networks of independent firms which co-ordinated their activities in some fashion and for various reasons persisted. The two most important types of inter-firm network or enterprise group were *keiretsu*, or vertical groupings of successively smaller companies dominated by major firms at the top of an industry, and *kigyo shudan*, horizontal groupings of companies from a range of sectors. These groups were sometimes linked by cross-share-holdings, but their most conspicuous feature was stable and preferential transactional relationships (Fruin 1992).

Japan was not alone in possessing *network* forms of organisation. In northern Italy, there are highly successful networks of small independent firms manufacturing wide ranges of consumer goods and engineering components. Networks of inter-firm co-operation developed around Silicon Valley and Route 128 in the United States. Networks are – in certain conditions – more flexible than firms, and yet can achieve higher levels of co-ordination than markets (Powell 1990).

A great deal of international business activity has always been organised through collaborative or network arrangements rather than through hierarchies. While MNEs are frequently seen as large firms engaging in FDI through wholly-owned subsidiaries in foreign countries, the reality is that MNEs consist of enterprises of all sizes which can operate in foreign countries using a wide range of equity and non-equity strategies. MNEs have employed complex organisational forms in response to the complex challenges of operating in foreign environments. From the nineteenth century to the present, firms have collaborated with, as much as competed against, other firms when they crossed borders. These joint ventures, contracts, licensing agreements and alliances blur the boundaries of firms. Wilkins refers to firms having 'ragged edges' (Wilkins 1986a: 90–1).

## THE ORGANISATION OF MNEs

The organisation of international business has always posed formidable organisational challenges. The control and co-ordination of value-added activities in different countries requires formidable managerial skills. While transactions cost theory indicates that technology and other rent-seeking assets can often be transferred more efficiently and cheaper within a firm than between independent firms, there are also considerable costs in terms of commitment of managerial (and other) resources if an FDI strategy is employed.

At the simplest level, firms that operate across borders face the problem of how best to ensure that managers of foreign subsidiaries respond effectively to the directives of the parent company. In economic theory this is a *principal/agent* problem. The principal is the parent company and the subsidiary is the agent which agrees to act on the parent's behalf. Bounded rationality, opportunism and moral hazard mean that transactions between agent and principal involve problems of policing and enforcement. The firm can be regarded as a highly developed mechanism of contract enforcement, or – in Oliver Williamson's terminology – a *governance structure* (Williamson 1985). The problems of enforcing contracts and monitoring behaviour – or governance costs – are particularly acute in firms operating across borders. The organisational design of MNEs can be regarded as an attempt to minimise the cost of contracting and of monitoring these contracts.

There are a considerable number of organisational choices open to an MNE. These include the relationship between its domestic and international operations, and whether managerial responsibility should be subdivided according to functions such as finance, marketing, product lines or geographical areas. Enterprises operating across borders frequently experience conflicting pressures between centralisation at the head office and greater autonomy for subsidiaries. The resolution of such pressures depends on a considerable number of variables, including industry-specific factors such as the nature of the external markets which the firm faces; region-specific factors, including the geographical and social distance between the centre and subsidiaries; nation-specific factors, such as the political and fiscal relations between the countries spanned by the firm; and factors specific to the firm itself, including the availability of skills and cost of management in each location (Buckley 1988).

While the use of Chandlerian-style managerial hierarchies provides one model for the appropriate organisational structure, Ouchi (1980) and others have argued that types of corporate culture or *clans* can be more effective than bureaucracies in certain circumstances. Bureaucratic hierarchies resolve the problems of monitoring their employees by means of rules and other policing methods. The 'clan' – whose members are heavily socialised and share common goals and understandings – can offer a superior organisational form in situations in which there are considerable problems of measurement and far too much uncertainty exists for prices or rule systems to be able to function well. The clan form has less need for formalised and sophisticated flows of information, because common ideas, beliefs and values instead function as information carriers and provide sufficient guidance for management action (Alvesson and Lindkvist 1993). Although the Ouchi concept of clan can be criticised, the basic idea is especially helpful among other ways in understanding how firms were able to control distant operations before modern communications and transport developed.

The organisational history of international business is one of constant change as managers have sought the most effective means to control foreign operations. In the search for the optimal structure at any one time, a firm's past structures and management culture exercise a considerable influence – and often constraint – on what can be done. The importance of this *administrative heritage* serves as a further justification for an evolutionary approach to international business (Bartlet and Ghoshal 1989).

## SUMMARY

MNEs control income-generating assets in more than one country. They transfer a package of resources across national borders using a range of equity and non-equity strategies, which include wholly-owned subsidiaries, joint ventures, licensing agreements, alliances and long-term contracts. The existence of MNEs can be explained by a mixture of ownership, locational and internalisation factors, but international business is so complex that it can be understood only by combining a number of theories, and by considering political, legal and cultural factors alongside economic ones.

The development of MNEs reflected in part differences between countries in their entrepreneurial capabilities, while MNEs performed entrepreneurial functions in the countries in which they operated. As firms, they possessed unique capabilities which provided the basis for sustained innovation. The growth of large managerial enterprises in the United States and elsewhere over the last one hundred years provided a major source of sustained innovation and stimulated the growth of MNEs, but alternative institutional arrangements were also capable of innovation. When firms sought to operate in foreign countries, the use of markets, hierarchies or network relationships were all possible alternatives. The boundaries of firms are frequently blurred in international business. The organisation of international business presents a constant challenge to managers. MNEs are in a continuous process of searching for the most effective structures, though their ability to find solutions is often constrained by their past history.

# Chapter 2

# The evolution of international business

## THE ENVIRONMENT OF INTERNATIONAL BUSINESS

Although the history of modern international business goes back to at least the early nineteenth century, its growth and evolution has been discontinuous. Periods of rapid growth have alternated with ones of stagnation or even decline. In different periods, different choices were made between alternative modes of operating abroad, and alternative forms of organisation. The relative importance of particular industries has varied markedly over time. During the nineteenth century the exploitation of natural resources and related service activities provided the most dynamic component of international business. Cross-border manufacturing was progressively more important as the twentieth century progressed, but services became the most dynamic sector of international business from the 1970s.

This chapter provides an overview of the main long-term trends in the development of international business. It relates these trends to changes in the environment in which firms have found themselves. Five exogenous factors which influenced the growth and structure of international business over time are identified. Needless to say, every single corporate decision to invest abroad was influenced by its own idiosyncratic mix of factors.

First, trends in international business were related to overall macro-economic conditions. Periods of fast economic growth have generally stimulated the growth of MNEs, while depressed or static market conditions have discouraged them, or else encouraged alternatives to FDI. Countries experiencing rapid economic growth have generally been more attractive hosts to MNEs than ones in dire economic circumstances. MNEs have typically originated from higher income economies rather than lower income ones, although the national differences in propensity to engage in FDI show that no automatic correlation existed between rising incomes and international business activity. While corporate decisions can be heavily influenced by movements in interest rates and exchange rates, these kind of macro-economic variables are not considered as major influences on long-term patterns in international business.

A second influence on the growth of international business has been the degree of receptivity to foreign enterprises. This issue has both international and national dimensions. In the case of the former, the existence and enforcement of international property rules has had a major influence. At a national level, international business has been stimulated when countries permitted or encouraged foreign-owned companies to operate, and discouraged when discriminatory regulation was applied against them. Receptivity has varied greatly over time and between countries. Government regulations have often played an important part in corporate decisions to operate in a foreign country through wholly-owned subsidiaries, joint ventures, licensing or other means. The degree of political risk can be related to receptivity. Wars and political instability have had long-term impacts on international business activity.

A third influence on international business has been the degree of capital liberalisation. MNEs have flourished in periods when capital has been permitted to move freely across borders. Exchange controls have discouraged FDI, distorted the form and direction it took, or encouraged the use of alternative strategies.

A fourth influence on the growth of international business has been trade protectionism. This has been extremely significant where a choice existed between exporting and FDI, because trade barriers stimulate market-oriented FDI by discouraging exports.

A fifth influence on the growth of international business has been transport and communications technology. This has been a particularly important factor in explaining how MNEs have been able to control operations across borders. Improvements in communications and transport which have facilitated managerial control over foreign operations have stimulated FDI by reducing the risks of overseas investment. Falling transport costs have opened up new markets, made the exploitation of natural resources feasible, and enabled firms to choose where to allocate value-added activities.

It was the interaction of these five factors which shaped developments in international business. The co-existence of capital liberalisation and trade protectionism usually stimulated manufacturing FDI, but when high tariff levels co-existed with exchange controls or high levels of political risk, they provided less of a stimulus for firms to manufacture abroad. These factors need to be seen as working together – and with other factors also – rather than as isolated entities. Moreover, the relationship between firms engaged in international business and their environment has also been a two-way one. While exogenous factors played critical roles in corporate strategies and investment decisions, MNEs also shaped the world in which they operated, by transferring skills and technologies between countries. The relationship between international business and the world economy has been a dynamic one.

The following discussion identifies five chronological periods in the history of international business, but this should not be interpreted in too rigid a fashion. The selection of periods is arbitrary, and has more logic for some industries and countries than for others. Many themes and trends overlap different periods.

## ORIGINS BEFORE 1880

### Overview

The emergence of international business on a significant scale occurred in the middle decades of the nineteenth century, but the phenomenon of FDI had a longer history. Individuals, merchants and bankers had exchanged goods and services across borders for many centuries. They had sometimes sent representatives to live in foreign countries. Family members were often used: the poor state of transport and communications ruled out close monitoring of representatives abroad and dictated instead the use of people who could be 'trusted' not to act opportunistically. Entrepreneurs sometimes invested in mines or factories in foreign countries. These were direct investments, but they were almost never sustained for more than a short period. Typically the foreign entrepreneur would settle in the host economy and the element of control from abroad would be lost. However, there were exceptional cases of international business which were sustained over long periods. Between the sixteenth and eighteenth centuries, large European chartered trading companies – such as the English and Dutch East India Companies – co-ordinated substantial business activities across national borders (Blussé and Gaastra 1981).

During the early nineteenth century direct investments began to be made in a growing range of activities and countries, and they began to take on a more permanent character. British companies began to exploit the goldfields of Brazil in the 1820s, and by mid-century there were a significant number of direct investments in minerals in various European countries. British banks began opening branches in Britain's Australian, Canadian and West Indies colonies in the 1830s. Cross-border investments in manufacturing occurred also in the 1830s, when Swiss cotton companies erected plants in southern Germany in that decade (Schröter 1993b: 51). From the 1850s FDI in manufacturing began to grow. An early example was an investment in Russia by the German electricals firm Siemens. Singer's sewing machine factory in Glasgow, Scotland, opened in 1867, is considered the first sustained multinational investment by a US manufacturing company (Wilkins 1970: 37).

There are no estimates of the overall size of FDI before 1880. It seems that the largest number of cases of direct investment were found in financial services, transport and energy utilities, and natural resources, while multinational manufacturing was confined to a limited number of companies. It would be most surprising if both the total amount of FDI and the number of enterprises engaged in it were not small relative to overall economic activity. Total foreign capital flows (both portfolio and FDI) between 1815 and the 1870s were modest. The real significance of these decades is that the direct investments which were made sometimes proved far more durable than in the past. Although older patterns continued – within a short period managerial control from Switzerland was lost over the south German cotton factories – in other cases the investments of these years were sustained for long periods stretching into the twentieth century. Examples included the foreign factories established by Siemens and Singer, and the British mining companies in Brazilian gold and British colonial banks.

The ability of firms to sustain direct investments in foreign countries gave a new significance to international business. In some cases, and over time, firms established value-added activities in several countries, creating the possibility of flows of services and goods not only between a home economy and a host economy, but between different host economies in a firm's business empire. The existence of sustained direct investments also deepened the impact of multinationals on host economies. While merchants and entrepreneurs had made one-off transfers of technology to foreign countries in the past, sustained investments meant that there was a continuous flow of resources into (as well as out of) a host economy within the multinational enterprise.

## The business environment

Macro-economic conditions and, especially, the importance of the British economy in the first half of the nineteenth century, exercised a fundamental influence on this early stage of international business. Britain's position as the birth place of the Industrial Revolution in the late eighteenth century gave that country a unique importance in the world economic system. Britain held, for a time, supremacy in the textiles, coal, iron and steel, engineering and shipbuilding industries which were at the centre of the first phase of modern industrialisation. In 1850 the United Kingdom accounted for 43 per cent of total world exports of manufactured goods. Twenty years later, well after the steady diffusion of industrialisation to other parts of Western Europe and the United States, Britain still accounted for one-third of total world industrial production (Chandler 1990: 4).

Britain's position as the first industrial nation explains its pre-eminence in international business. Many of the earliest cases of direct investment were British. The British position as a centre of technological innovation was reflected in the advanced mining technology employed by the British gold mining companies in Brazil. The demand of the British economy for agricultural products and raw materials was a factor in the extensive investment in the banking services which financed trade flows.

Conversely, the overall insignificance of Japanese outward FDI in this early period – and until much later – is readily explicable by that country's stage of economic development. For over two hundred years until 1853, Japan had been a closed economy with virtually no foreign trade. Although the Japanese economy in the Edo Period had seen some remarkable advances in agricultural productivity and human capital formation, it had been untouched by the Industrial Revolution, and possessed no modern industry. A process of modernisation began with the Meiji Restoration in 1868, but until the 1930s Japan's modern industrial sector was largely limited to consumer goods, especially cotton and silk textiles.

The emergence of international business was facilitated by high world-wide receptivity to foreign enterprises. The end of the prolonged period of warfare in 1815 following the defeat of Napoleon was followed by a century of relative world peace, despite the importance of a number of major regional conflicts such as the Crimean War, the American Civil War and the Franco-Prussian War. This period saw the spread of inter-national property law which greatly reduced some of the risks of international business. Seventeenth century European governments had started the process of reducing the risks of trade by signing bilateral commercial treaties that protected alien property, but it was only in the nineteenth century that these treaty standards hardened into international law, the core principle of which was that the property of foreigners could not be taken without prompt, full compensation. Uncompensated seizure was considered robbery, and the use of unilateral force was considered a legal and legitimate response.

The principles of this law were strongly supported by European governments, and enforced on much of the rest of the world by Britain and, later, the United States. Western concepts of property rights were imposed through treaties, the securing of extraterritorial rights (especially at Far Eastern ports) and by the spread of colonial rule over large areas of Asia and Africa. The upshot was the creation of a favourable legal environment for the growth of international business. Until 1914, there were no large-scale sequestrations of foreign property (Lipson 1985: 37–64).

Imperialism made a growing part of the world safe for foreign investors, but the inherited monopolistic policies of earlier centuries took time to pass away. The East India Company, the private British company which had accumulated growing political power over large parts of India from the eighteenth century, held a monopoly over British trade with India and elsewhere in Asia and blocked its British competitors. It was the abolition of this monopoly over trade with India in 1813, and China in 1834, which opened the way for the spread of British mercantile, financial and other companies in Asia.

Capital liberalisation and trade protectionism were less important influences on the emergence of international business. There were no legal controls on capital movements, but portfolio investment – by far the largest element of capital flows – was a high risk business. Many Latin American borrowers defaulted in the late 1820s, while a financial panic in 1837 in the United States followed by the default of two state governments resulted in a virtual collapse of foreign investment in the United States in the 1840s (Wilkins 1989: 66–76). Trade protectionism was a factor behind certain early manufacturing FDI: the Swiss investments in the German cotton industry followed the formation of the German customs union in 1834, which threatened Swiss exports (Schröter 1993b: 51). Yet the growth of sustained manufacturing FDI in the 1850s and 1860s coincided with a widespread adoption of free trade policies in much of the developed world.

Advances in transport and communications technology were more significant for the timing of the emergence of international business. The application of steam to land and sea transport was fundamental. In 1800 land transport was based on dirt roads and water transportation. Both were slow and dependent on the weather. The international spread of railroads from the 1830s brought a new speed and reliability. The earliest railroads were built in Britain and the eastern United States, but their subsequent spread was rapid. Sea travel was also transformed. In the first half of the century improvements in sailing-ship technology helped to produce a sharp fall in ocean freight rates. From the mid-century the use of steamships expanded, which continued the process of cheapening and speeding up transport across the sea. The cutting of ship canals speeded up sea transport. The opening of the Suez Canal in 1869 was critical in providing a shorter route between Europe and Asia. There were also significant improvements in communications. The telegraph was the most important nineteenth century innovation. In 1852 London and Paris were joined by electric telegraph. The first successful trans-Atlantic cable connection was in 1866. In 1870 Bombay and London were linked by cable. The cable reached Australia in 1872.

By 1880 transport and communication advances had opened new markets and made the exploitation of natural resources in distant lands more feasible. More significantly, they had lessened the risk of FDI by making the managerial task of controlling businesses over long distances easier. These developments did not 'cause' the emergence of MNEs. Indeed many of the improvements in the world's transport and information infrastructure were the result of multinational investment. Yet these developments in turn prompted further multinational growth, by making it easier to sustain direct investments. Before the nineteenth century the best means of sustaining direct investments was if a government awarded a monopoly or special privileges. It was on this basis that the European chartered trading companies were able to build and preserve complex international organisations. Improvements in transport and communications enabled firms to sustain operations across borders more easily without government privileges. The coincidental absence of major wars, the spread of international property law, and the growth of imperialism made foreign business opportunities appear less risky than in the past.

## GROWTH 1880–1930

### Overview

Between 1880 and 1930 the size and significance of international business in the world economy expanded greatly. There was a rapid increase in cross-border trade and investment flows, and most of the world was drawn into the international economy. International business was at the centre of these developments. Multinational trading companies evolved on a large scale; multinational banking expanded; and there was substantial international business in transport and communications. Large corporations emerged in petroleum exploitation and distribution worldwide. There was also FDI in agriculture and raw materials, including tea, sugar and rubber plantations in the developing world, and livestock production in the United States and Latin America. By the time of the outbreak of the First World War in 1914 multinational manufacturing was undertaken in a wide range of products, including chemicals, pharmaceuticals, electricals, machinery, motor cars, tyres, branded food products and cigarettes.

Although the qualitative evidence leaves no doubt about the dynamic growth of international business, the quantification of its dimensions remains difficult. It is universally agreed that there was an enormous amount of foreign investment from the 1870s to 1914, but there remains considerable uncertainty about the dimensions and composition of pre-1914 cross-border capital flows. The total world stock of foreign investment by 1914 is usually estimated at between $40 and $45 billion, but no great faith can be placed on such figures. Even the size of the capital exports from the world's largest creditor nation – the United Kingdom – is disputed. Until recently it was generally agreed that British capital holdings abroad stood at around £1,000–£1,200 million in 1875, and had risen to £4,000 million (or $19,440 million) in 1914, but there is a debate about whether these figures should be reduced by as much as a quarter (Platt 1980, 1986; Feinstein 1990).

It is difficult to estimate the stock of FDI from the existing data on total foreign investment because of the uncertainty about the breakdown between its direct and portfolio components. It was long believed that almost 90 per cent of capital flows in this period were portfolio in character, but since the 1970s there has been a progressive re-evaluation of this assessment. Dunning's estimates of world FDI stock for bench-mark years, which provide the basis for many of the statistics used in this chapter, was a landmark stage in this revisionist process (Dunning 1983, 1988a, 1992). These estimates suggest that by 1914 around one-third of total world foreign investment, or some $14,582 million, took the form of FDI. This sum was tiny compared to later levels of FDI, but its relative importance can be seen if compared to the overall size of economies at that time, even though such comparisons are extremely crude. If the higher estimates of FDI size are accepted, FDI represented around 9 per cent of world output in 1913. This proportion declined subsequently, and even in the early 1990s FDI only represented around 8.5 per cent of world output (United Nations 1994: 130). These figures need, however, to be placed in the context of the warnings given in Chapter 1 that FDI is only a partial indicator of the significance of international business.

Figure 2.1 analyses world FDI in 1914 by home economy. It is based on Dunning's original estimates, which have been modified to reflect new research on German, Dutch and British FDI. These revisions raise the estimated world outward stock to $18,204 million, but the raw data is so poor that no great faith should be put in this number. Even the figures for the United States, which has the best data, are full of problems, while little research has been undertaken on the FDI of major investors such as France.

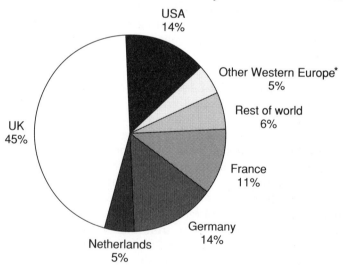

* Principally Belgium, Sweden and Switzerland

*Figure 2.1* Percentage share of FDI stock in 1914 by home economy
*Source*: Dunning 1992 (adjusted)[1]

The most striking feature of Figure 2.1 is the concentration of ownership of world FDI. The United Kingdom alone accounted for almost one-half of the total stock. If the United States and the Netherlands are added, these three countries accounted for two-thirds of the stock. If the analysis is made on a regional basis, Western Europe accounted for four-fifths of world FDI. This concentration of multinational ownership has been one of the most persistent features of international business.

The distribution of world FDI among host regions by 1914 is given in Figure 2.2. These estimates are even cruder than those for home economies, and can at best only be regarded as providing orders of magnitude.

The estimates show that although FDI originated from a small number of countries, it was widely dispersed around the world. Latin America and Asia were especially important as recipients of FDI inflows in the nineteenth century. Within these regions, particular countries were the magnets for direct investors. It is likely that the major Latin American hosts were Brazil, Argentina and Mexico, while in Asia both India and China received considerable amounts of FDI. However, the largest individual host economies were not in the developing world, but were the prosperous economies of the United States and Canada. Chapter 7 gives a more detailed breakdown by individual host economies.

Figure 2.3 estimates the sectoral distribution of world FDI in 1914.

The enormous relative importance of natural resources in international business at this time stands out. Given that a considerable amount of the service sector investments was concerned with financing, insuring,

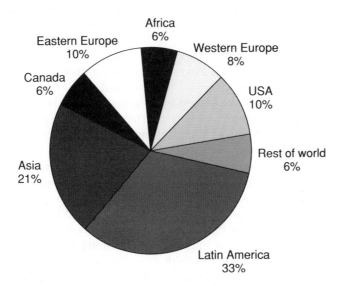

*Figure 2.2* Percentage share of FDI stock in 1914 by host economy
*Source*: Dunning 1992

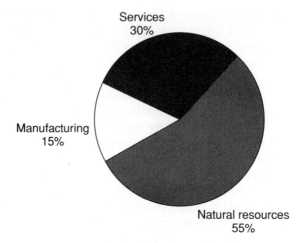

*Figure 2.3* Estimated distribution of accumulated world FDI by sector in 1914
*Source*: Dunning 1992

transporting and otherwise making possible international trade in raw materials and foodstuffs, it can be estimated that at least three-quarters of world FDI was concerned with the exploitation of natural resources. This sectoral distribution largely determined the geographical distribution. Manufacturing investment was overwhelmingly located in Western Europe and North America, while much of the FDI in natural resources and services was in the developing world, although the United States, Canada and Eastern Europe also received considerable sums.

From the perspective of the business enterprise, the separation of manufacturing, service and natural resource sectors is misleading. The firms which crossed national borders had no hesitation about crossing borders between different economic sectors. The process of vertical integration took manufacturing companies into distribution; petroleum companies into shipping, distribution and manufacturing; and trading companies into the exploitation of natural resources and manufacturing.

Many of the firms which made these direct investments, especially in manufacturing, grew and were organised in ways which were to become familiar in the twentieth century. They can be termed 'classic' MNEs: these were firms which had begun by undertaking value-added activities in their home market, and then established wholly or majority-owned subsidiaries abroad. Among the pioneer multinational manufacturers, Singer and Siemens were major examples of such firms. They had developed managerial and technological competences at home before venturing abroad. These competences gave such firms the ability to sustain their investments, although numerous failed or short-lived investments were made also by

*Table 2.1* Numbers and types of business enterprise engaged in international business in 1914

| Home economy | 'Classic' MNEs | | |
| | No. of enterprises | No. of production subsidiaries | Sector |
| --- | --- | --- | --- |
| USA (1) | 39 | 116 | Manufacturing |
| UK (2) | 200 | n.a. | Manufacturing |
| Switzerland (3) | 160 | 265 | Manufacturing |
| Germany (4) | 51 | 153 | Chemicals |

| Home economy | 'Free-standing' companies | | |
| | No. of enterprises | | Sector |
| --- | --- | --- | --- |
| UK (5) | 2,643 | — | All but especially primary and service |
| UK (6) | 'Several thousand' | — | All but especially primary and service |
| UK (7) | 957 | — | Metal mining |
| Netherlands (8) | 184 | — | Especially tropical agriculture, also banking, mining, transport |

*Sources*: (1) Vaupel and Curhan 1969[2]; (2) Nicholas 1989; (3) Schröter 1990b; (4) Schröter 1990a; (5) Houston & Dunning 1976; (6) Wilkins 1988a; (7) Harvey and Press 1990a; (8) Sluyterman 1994

'classic' MNEs. This was the type of firm which was predominant in international business after the Second World War, when the theory of the MNE was developed. Before 1914, almost all US and many European MNEs in manufacturing were classic MNEs, though they differed in size from very small to very large. Table 2.1 gives some estimates of the numbers of classic MNEs in the world economy by 1914.

The classic MNE formed only a part of the world of international business. The 'ragged edges' of firms were evident in the late nineteenth century. European firms often expanded abroad in collaboration with other firms, although there was a great variety of such collaborative arrangements. French and Belgian enterprises often invested abroad through complex holding companies. Financial intermediaries controlled substantial direct investments in both utilities and manufacturing. These strategies reflected the 'mixed banking' tradition prevalent in these countries, where banks often held equity stakes in a range of industrial companies. The use of such strategies in international business makes it hard to quantify the scale of FDI involved, for many activities fall into a grey world between direct and portfolio investment.

Much British and Dutch international business before 1914 was undertaken by firms floated on the capital markets to undertake business activities exclusively or mainly abroad. Their boards of directors met in Europe, and were usually supported by very small head offices, but they undertook no other economic activity in their home economy. Typically they specialised in a single commodity, product or service, usually in a single country. They were predominantly located in the natural resource and service sectors, but were also found in some manufacturing and processing operations. These were entrepreneurial enterprises, formed in the context of the booming world economy and of expanding imperial frontiers.

By the time the theory of the MNE began to be developed this type of firm was rare. Because these British and Dutch firms undertook no prior production in their home economies before investing abroad, early researchers on the history of MNEs did not consider them as engaging in FDI (Stopford 1974). This view was reinforced because before the Second World War the term 'direct' was used in many countries simply to describe foreign investment that did not pass through the capital markets (Wilkins 1977: 13). However the application of modern definitions of FDI – with their emphasis on management control – led to the reinterpretation of these firms as being engaged in FDI, since their head offices in one country controlled operations in another country (Houston and Dunning 1976; Svedberg 1978). The upward revision of FDI estimates for this period rests largely on this re-evaluation. Wilkins later coined the term *free-standing company* to describe these firms: she considered them to be 'the most typical mode of British direct investment before 1914' (Wilkins 1986a, 1988a). Table 2.1 gives estimates of the large numbers of this type of firm active by 1914.

The British and Dutch free-standing companies were widely spread over the developing world, with a distinct colonial orientation. This was particularly noticeable in the case of the Dutch. No less than 140 of the 184 Dutch free-standing companies operated in the Dutch East Indies (Sluyterman 1994). In contrast, there were large numbers of British free-standing companies active outside the British colonies, especially in the United States.

There are many unresolved issues concerning free-standing companies which have implications for how they should be treated in FDI estimates. Undoubtedly the key element of FDI – management control – was evident in many cases, but the thousands of free-standing firms are not a homogenous group. While in some instances managerial control was exercised from a head office in the home country, in other cases the firms appear more as vehicles for portfolio investment, with managerial decision-making located in the host economies. Some firms were engaged in a form of property development. Once the short-lived need for their specialised project management skills dried up, management control shifted to locals, and the investment ceased to be 'direct' (Casson 1994a). There were numerous transient free-standing companies, but also instances of longer-lived firms, and in some cases underlying continuities were disguised by a change of legal structure for one reason or another.

These free-standing companies were part of wider business networks. In the British case, Wilkins identified 'clusters' linking nominally separate firms around original promotors, financial intermediaries, solicitors, accountants, mining engineers, merchant banks, trading companies and influential individuals. Common to all clusters was the provision of services – a reflection of the tiny head offices of the British free-standing companies. On the whole, these 'clusters' seemed fragile affairs. 'While the resulting governance structure sometimes approximated to a multinational enterprise', Wilkins judged, 'in most cases the connections within the clusters were too partial and too weak to be so designated' (Wilkins 1988a: 265).

Chapman identified a somewhat similar phenomenon amongst British business interests in the developing world before 1914. He identified some thirty British-based *investment groups* active in Asia, Latin America, Russia and South Africa before 1914. These were 'an entrepreneurial or family concern whose name and reputation was used to float a variety of subsidiary trading, manufacturing, mining or financial enterprises, invariably overseas and often widely dispersed' (Chapman 1992: 233; Chapman 1985, 1987). The groups, which were primarily merchants in origin, included the large British trading companies active in Asia and Latin America, as well as the more mining-centred groups operating in South Africa. Although usually concentrated on specific geographical regions, these investment groups were diversified across the service, natural resource and consumer manufacturing sectors. Typically they consisted of networks of enterprises joined by a number of factors, including (often) minority equity shareholdings, interlocking directorships, and trading relationships. Managerial competences were distributed throughout the network. This diffusion of 'control' within these business networks makes them very difficult to quantify in terms of FDI.

The significance of such clusters and networks of firms is difficult to interpret. Their rationale and managerial competences are discussed further in later chapters. There are interesting parallels with the complex cross-border relationships which developed in international business in the 1980s and 1990s. This might suggest that in periods of fast and deep globalisation, flexible networks of firms have advantages over firms with clearly defined boundaries.

Although the outbreak of the First World War is a major turning point in world political history, it did not bring a halt to the dynamic growth of international business, even though it caused massive short-term disruption to international firms. The wartime events did, however, prompt important long-term significant shifts in both outward and inward FDI flows. The United States emerged as the most dynamic direct investor in the world economy, though its stock remained well below European levels. United States FDI almost doubled in the 1920s. This growth more than compensated for the wartime-induced collapse of German FDI, almost all of which was sequestrated. The sequestration of foreign capital in Russia following the Communist Revolution in 1917, which resulted in the loss of a large amount of French and Belgian FDI, also appears to have dampened new investment flows from those countries in the 1920s. While Russia was eliminated as a host economy, there seems to have been an especially rapid growth of FDI into Canada.

The numbers of MNEs of the 'classic' type expanded further in the 1920s, and their operations became more complex, involving more countries and more products. Hundreds of US manufacturing companies established foreign operations. New US industries became involved in multinational expansion on a substantial scale for the first time, notably automobiles and food and consumer chemicals (Wilkins 1974a: 60–91). The estimated numbers of British-owned manufacturing MNEs expanded from 200 before 1914 to almost 450 by 1939 (Nicholas 1989).

In contrast, many of the European free-standing firms active in the United States seem to have disappeared or passed into local ownership during and after the First World War. In Latin America, a swathe of British free-standing firms were acquired by US companies. Yet in some sectors – such as banking and utilities – and some regions – such as Southeast Asia and Africa – the free-standing type structure survived (Hennart 1994a). Networks of loosely co-ordinated firms evolved tighter organisational structures over time (Greenhill 1995). Some free-standing firms in mining and petroleum evolved into large diversified extractive MNEs. Even a new generation of free-standing firms appeared on the New York stock market. United States investors floated companies that owned sugar plantations and mines in Latin America, while a number of foreign entrepreneurs set up US-based free-standing firms (Wilkins 1993a; Hennart 1994b).

**The business environment**

The spread of international business after 1880 took place in a world economy which was growing rapidly. International trade grew at much higher rates than world output, sometimes growing more than 60 per cent per decade, as the industrialised economies of Western Europe and North America exchanged manufactured goods for the raw materials and food-stuffs produced in the Third World and Southern Hemisphere economies.

The unprecedented movements of people across national boundaries in the late nineteenth century, as Europeans flooded into the United States and other settler economies, Russians moved out to the empty lands of Siberia, and Chinese migrated to south-east Asia and California, had important influences on international business. Emigration spread consumption patterns. Business often followed the emigration patterns of its nationals across borders. The flows of trade and people, as well as capital, created a truly worldwide economy for the first time in human history.

The growth of the new capital-intensive industries such as chemicals, machinery and packaged food products in the late nineteenth century was very important in the development of international business. These industries were ferocious consumers of raw materials. The growth of chemical and electrical production caused a large increase in the demand for minerals such as copper, aluminium and zinc. The motor vehicle industry needed tin for solder and for the alloys used in bearings. In the late nineteenth century petroleum began to be used as an alternative to coal to drive trains and steamships, while it was the only fuel that could be used in motor cars. The new industries of this era, therefore, stimulated an extensive worldwide search for new sources of supply of raw materials.

The enormous organisational significance of the new industries has already been indicated when Chandler's work on the emergence of the modern industrial enterprise was discussed in Chapter 1 (pp. 17–19). The growth of large corporations and the creation of managerial hierarchies forms an important element of the explanation of how firms were able to control the range and scale of cross-border activities. The first movers in these industries became and often stayed among the largest MNEs of the twentieth century. Yet a great deal of multinational activity was not undertaken by large firms with managerial hierarchies, but by small firms owned by families, or by firms joined in networks.

There were important shifts in global economic power which influenced the development of international business. The large British share of world FDI reflected the continuing overall importance of the United Kingdom in the world economy. Even in 1913 the British economy still had a 28 per cent share of total world exports of manufacturers. The world's largest capital exporter, Britain was the home of an enormous agglomeration of financial services and institutions in the City of London, which became the world's premier international financial centre. Britain was the lynchpin of the Gold Standard, to which most of Europe, the United States and much of the rest of the world subscribed from the 1870s. Sterling, the British currency, was regarded as being as good as gold, and as a result came to be used to finance not only British trade but also that of most of the rest of the world as well. Nevertheless the growth of US and other European FDI during the late nineteenth century testified to the spread of industrialisation and economic development. The United States replaced the United Kingdom as the world's largest economy by the beginning of the twentieth century. However, there was to be a considerable time lag before the overall size of the US economy translated into giving it the world's largest stock of FDI.

The First World War disrupted almost every aspect of the world economy as it had developed over the previous half century. The postwar economy featured a new instability. There was a severe recession soon after the end of the First World War, which was followed by the Great Depression at the end of the 1920s. Yet there were sufficient continuities with the pre-War economy to continue to provide a favourable climate for FDI. Although some countries, such as Britain and Japan, experienced considerable difficulties of economic adjustment, there was rapid industrialisation in the United States, Australia, Canada, Brazil, India and elsewhere. While in the developed economies industrialisation involved the further spread of industries such as automobiles and chemicals, and the increasing use of mass production methods, in developing countries it took the form of the expansion of textiles and other consumer products. In both types of industry there were opportunities for MNEs. World trade also recovered in the 1920s: by the end of that decade the ratio of world trade to world product had probably returned to its 1913 level (Kenwood and Lougheed 1992).

The great expansion of international business in the late nineteenth century occurred in a world economy where receptivity to foreign enterprise remained high. This was related in part to the limited role played by governments in economies as a whole. In some countries, particular industries – such as banking – were regarded as so sensitive or strategic that foreign ownership was restricted, but overall restrictions on the foreign ownership of assets remained remarkably few right down to the First World War. With some exceptions, business enterprises were free to seek out the most profitable opportunities worldwide. It was a borderless world.

An important aspect of the high receptivity to international business was European imperialism. The late nineteenth century was the age of imperialism. The already extensive British Empire grew further and on the eve of the First World War the United Kingdom, whose population was 45 million, presided over a worldwide empire of 400 million inhabitants. The population of the United States at that time was less than 100 million. The British Empire spanned large parts of Asia, Africa and elsewhere, and included the countries settled by British emigrants, such as Australia and Canada. France, Belgium and Germany also occupied substantial parts of Africa. France had large Asian possessions, including the modern states of Vietnam, Laos and Cambodia. In south-east Asia, the Dutch East Indies (Indonesia) was a colonial possession of the Netherlands, while at the end of the nineteenth century the United States occupied the Philippine Islands following a war with Spain, the former colonial ruler.

Western imperialism facilitated international business activity in many ways. Colonial governments established similar legal and administrative structures to those in the home country, thereby greatly reducing the risks of FDI. Colonial administrators often favoured firms of their own nationality, granting them contracts and concessions, and supporting them against foreign firms and sometimes even indigenous firms. These factors encouraged the large amounts of FDI in natural resources and related service sector activities in colonial territories. Imperialism also spread consumption patterns worldwide. This was most evident in countries settled by European emigrants, but the African and Asian colonies also experienced many metropolitan influences.

It has been suggested that investments in colonies should be excluded from the concept of FDI (Schröter 1993c: 94), but there are considerable difficulties with this view. On the one hand, British colonies such as Canada and Australia evolved into independent states over time, and there would be great difficulties in ascertaining when these countries became sufficiently 'foreign' for the British-owned firms active in them to be considered as engaged in FDI. On the other hand, metropolitan enterprises investing in colonial territories faced sufficiently different administrative, legal and business conditions for their activities to be regarded as FDI, even if the political risks they faced were lower than those in fully sovereign nations.

This issue has to be placed in the context of the desire of firms to reduce the managerial costs of controlling businesses outside their own country. One of the most effective strategies of early multinationals was to invest in countries which were geographically and/or culturally close to their own. The two most important host economies for US FDI before 1914 were Mexico and Canada (Wilkins 1970: 113–72). The same geographically 'nearby' phenomenon was found in the investment patterns of Swiss, Swedish, Dutch, German and other continental European direct investors, even though they also invested further afield, in the United States and elsewhere. German businesses 'spilled over' their border into neighbouring Austria, Switzerland and France (Wilkins 1988b; Schröter 1993a; Schröter 1993c). These investments in neighbouring countries were often more accurately described as 'multi-regional' than 'multinational'. Like the colonial investments of the British, Dutch and others, investors in neighbouring countries faced fewer problems than those that chose radically different host economies.

The borderless world suffered its first setbacks as a consequence of the First World War and its aftermath. During the 1920s there was an increase in the growth of restrictions on foreign companies in various countries, although these remained limited compared to later decades. Far more serious was the Soviet sequestration of foreign property after the Russian Revolution. This was the first significant attack on the international property law regime which had been so widely accepted in the nineteenth century. The Soviets acknowledged a legal obligation to compensate foreign property owners, but only if Western countries paid for the damage their armies had caused after they intervened in the civil war which followed the Communist Revolution. Throughout the 1920s the League of Nations (the predecessor to the United Nations) held conferences designed to clarify the obligations of host states to foreign capital, but the European states were unable to secure their aims in the face of resistance from Latin American and other 'peripheral' countries (Lipson 1985: 65–76).

International business expanded in the late nineteenth century when restrictions on the movement of capital across borders were effectively non-existent. The widespread adoption of the Gold Standard further facilitated foreign investment and, taken together with the boundless opportunities of the period, helped to produce the unprecedented scale of cross-border capital flows. The existence of European free-standing companies was closely related to this situation. They flourished in the world's largest capital exporting economy, the United Kingdom, although their comparative absence in other large European capital exporting countries – such as France – implies that explanations of their existence must go beyond capital availability.

The international mobility of capital began to falter in the 1920s. The international monetary system was severely disrupted by wartime inflation and the suspension of the Gold Standard. Though many countries returned to the Gold Standard in the mid-1920s, world financial and economic conditions had changed greatly compared to pre-1914. Capital flows often assumed a speculative and short-term form. The war transformed Germany from a major creditor country to a debtor, whereas the United States emerged as the world's largest creditor. New York came of age as a major international financial centre. United States foreign investment rose from $7 billion to $17 billion between 1919 and 1929, but – exceptionally for the United States – portfolio lending grew faster than FDI (Lewis 1938: 450, 605). In contrast, the British international lending position was weakened by the wartime liquidation of foreign assets, and by poor export performance subsequently. These trends help to explain both the appearance of US-based free-standing companies, and the disappearance of British free-standing companies operating in the United States.

Trade protectionism was a major influence on the rapid growth of manufacturing FDI after 1880, as the worldwide trend towards free trade went into reverse. The American Civil War (1861–5) led to a substantial rise in US tariffs to raise revenue. The wartime tariffs were retained after 1865, increased in the 1880s, and then raised by the McKinley Act of 1890 to an average level on protected commodities of 50 per cent. A brief lowering of the US tariffs in 1894 was followed three years later by an increase to 57 per cent. In Europe there was a return to protectionism after 1880, stimulated by a severe recession in the previous decade and encouraged by the growth of European nationalism and the emergence of new European nation states, such as Germany and Italy. By 1914 the only remaining European countries pursuing free trade policies were the United Kingdom, Netherlands and Denmark. After the First World War protectionism spread. By the early 1920s US tariffs had been raised to their highest ever levels by the Fordney-McCumber tariff. Australia, India and some Latin American countries were among those that turned to tariffs, import quotas and other trade barriers to help infant industries and foster their manufacturing sectors by import substitution.

The improvements to transport and communications from the late nineteenth century had more of an incremental than a revolutionary character. The growth of railroad systems continued to open up new markets and provide opportunities for the exploitation of natural resources, while sea journey times and costs continued to fall through developments such as the opening of the Panama Canal in 1915. The impact on international business in natural resources was particularly important. These improvements in transportation aided the growth of production from mining areas like those in Bolivia, central Africa and Malaysia, by reducing the cost of shipping the ores and metals to the major markets in Europe and North America (Schmitz 1979: 25). The development of the telephone and the automobile, and the rapid spread of the aeroplane in the interwar years, opened new sectors for international business activity, and provided further tools to facilitate managerial control over distant operations.

## ALTERNATIVES TO MULTINATIONAL ENTERPRISE

### Overview

During the 1930s and 1940s the growth of world FDI slowed considerably. In a range of industries, firm strategies shifted from seeking to own and control assets in foreign countries to seeking collaborative agreements with competitors to control markets. This was the heyday of international cartels.

The continuing paucity of data makes it difficult to test hypotheses about changes in the overall size of FDI in the 1930s. A picture of overall stagnation emerges for the only economy for which FDI estimates exist, the United States, although the data is far from robust. Moreover, while the stock of outward US FDI fell, inward FDI into the United States

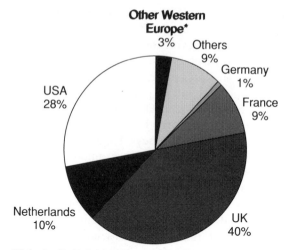

*Principally Belgium, Sweden and Switzerland

*Figure 2.4* Percentage share of FDI stock in 1938 by home economy
*Source*: Dunning 1992 (adjusted)[3]

between 1935 and 1940 may have risen from $1.6 billion to $2.9 billion (Lipsey 1988: 485–7). However these figures also need to be treated with caution, as the 1940 number was not only derived by a different measurement criterion than that used for the earlier one, but was far more comprehensive in its coverage. It is certainly unlikely that inward FDI into the United States rose as rapidly as inward portfolio investment, the flow of which was greatly boosted by flight capital from Europe (Wilkins forthcoming).

By 1938 Dunning estimated total world stock of FDI had reached $26,350 million. An analysis by home economy is given in Figure 2.4.

The United Kingdom still emerged as the world's largest holder of FDI stock, but the ranking of other home economies had changed considerably compared to 1914. There had been a collapse in the size of German FDI, while the relative importance of the United States had grown. Britain's continued pre-eminence in terms of stock reflected its historical involvements, and it is likely that in terms of new activities, the United States overshadowed Britain in FDI during the interwar years. Netherlands was the world's third largest holder of FDI stock. Neutrality in the First World War meant that Dutch FDI survived intact, while the colonial empire continued to provide opportunities for resource-based investments during the interwar years. Together, the United Kingdom, the United States and the Netherlands accounted for over three-quarters of world FDI.

Figure 2.5 provides an estimate of world FDI stock by host country or region in 1938.

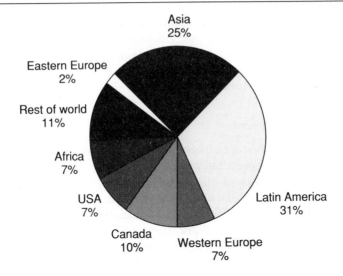

*Figure 2.5* Percentage share of FDI stock in 1938 by host economy
*Source*: Dunning 1992[4]

These estimates continue to highlight the importance of the developing world as the principal recipient of FDI, although once more Canada and the United States are identified as the two single largest host economies.

It is probable that the 1930s saw marked differences in the sectoral propensity to invest abroad. There were both new entrants to multinational manufacturing and divestments. Within manufacturing, new FDI was far more frequent in some products than in others. There was considerable new FDI in the world petroleum industry. In the service sector, trading companies found profitable opportunities, but multinational banking stagnated.

The Second World War and the immediate aftermath saw – not surprisingly – little new international business activity. Both sides in the conflict sequestrated the assets of the other. The entire stock of German and Japanese FDI was lost. The spread of Communism to Eastern Europe in the late 1940s, and to China in 1949, resulted in further falls in the stock of FDI. The United States was the only country to have significantly increased its actual FDI during the war and subsequently. By 1950 that country's stock of FDI was considerably higher than ten years previously.

There was a widespread use of alternatives to FDI in international business. Numerous international cartel agreements were formed between manufacturing firms. In some industries – and collusion was much more widespread in some industries than in others – cartels became the pre-eminent form of international business activity, and their overall significance in the control of world manufacturing activity was considerable.

The spectacular spread of international collusion in manufacturing was matched by its importance in many primary commodities. The Second World War and its aftermath saw the dismantling of most of these agreements, except in certain commodities and services, where in some cases their influence was sustained.

## The business environment

The depressed economic conditions and high unemployment following the onset of the Great Depression in 1929 reduced the numbers of attractive investment opportunities in the world economy. US real GNP fell by almost a third between 1929 and 1933. In some cases companies experienced such difficulties in their home markets that they had to withdraw from their international operations. These economic conditions provided more incentives for firms to engage in international cartels, which offered the opportunity to influence prices, output or market share without the risks of FDI. While much of the industrialised world in the 1930s experienced high levels of unemployment, declining primary commodity prices caused sharp falls in real incomes for the producer countries in Latin America, Asia, Africa and Australia. The deteriorating fortunes of the commodity economies was a major incentive behind the cartelisation of many primary products.

Nonetheless, manufacturing MNEs had new opportunities in countries which industrialised as a result of import substitution behind high tariff barriers. In some developed countries falling world food and raw material prices in the 1930s caused cheaper imports and higher real incomes, at least for the proportion of the working population which remained in employment. This created growing markets for new consumer products like vacuum cleaners and refrigerators, which MNEs could exploit.

The continued evolution of managerial capitalism was important. Interwar merger waves resulted in the growth of large firms in economies which had previously featured more fragmented industrial structures. While in 1912 there were only three industrial firms in the world with a capitalisation of more than $300 million, by 1937 there were forty-three (Schmitz 1993: 31). The growth of concentration facilitated – though did not necessarily cause – international collusion. Collusive behaviour on an international scale was made much easier by the existence of oligopolistic and cartelised domestic markets. It was far easier to organise industries when there were only a handful of major corporations than in a situation of hundreds or thousands of competing firms.

Receptivity to international business declined in the 1930s. There were a number of major conflicts between host governments and MNEs active in natural resource exploitation in the developing world. The oil industry became a particular area of dispute. The Mexican nationalisation of foreign oil companies without compensation in 1938 was a landmark event which asserted national sovereignty over natural resources, and represented a further assault on international property rules. While the political conditions for FDI deteriorated, participation in international cartels was often backed by governments, especially in Europe. Subsequently, it was a resurgence of antitrust policies in the United States in the 1940s which was a particularly important factor behind the decline of international cartels (Wilkins 1974a: 291–300).

The international mobility of capital fell sharply in the 1930s. The onset of the Great Depression was followed by the collapse of the international financial system. The repatriation of the large amounts of American portfolio lending from Europe provoked a major financial crisis in central Europe and Germany in 1931. The Gold Standard was fatally undermined when Britain was forced to abandon it in September of that year, followed by the United States two years later. In its place a number of regional currency blocs developed, each supported by extensive exchange controls. A US dollar area included Latin America; a sterling bloc included most of the British Empire and some northern European countries; a German bloc extended over parts of central Europe; a yen bloc included parts of Asia; and a residual 'gold bloc' included France and some other Western European countries. In this environment, cross border capital flows fell sharply, and were often confined within currency blocs (Kenwood and Lougheed 1992; Cain and Hopkins 1993: 76–105).

The consequences for international business were considerable. Exchange controls were a major disincentive to engage in new FDI as dividends and profits could not be repatriated, though they could give rise to 'enforced investment' as funds that could not be repatriated were ploughed back into business. This helps to explain the almost 50 per cent increase in the level of US FDI in Germany between 1929 and 1940 (Wilkins 1974a: 185–9).

The decline in capital mobility rendered the continued increase of protectionism in the 1930s a less potent force in prompting market-oriented FDI. The Smoot-Hawley Act of June 1930 substantially increased the US tariff level, and other countries also raised their tariffs. By the end of the 1930s almost half of the world's trade was restricted by tariffs. Tariffs continued to encourage foreign firms to establish local manufacturing, but they also strengthened the bargaining positions of national firms in international cartel negotiations (Wurm 1993).

The 1930s saw further improvements in international transport and communications. Air travel became faster, safer and more regular. Transatlantic and trans-Pacific services were inaugurated. As a result it continued to become physically easier to supervise foreign subsidies, but this did not provide a great incentive to FDI given the mounting political, regulatory and legal obstacles faced by foreign investors.

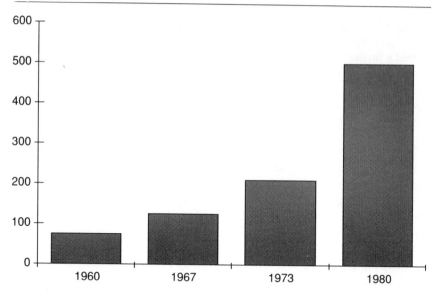

*Figure 2.6* World stock of outward FDI 1960, 1967, 1973 and 1980 (US$bn)
*Source*: Dunning 1992: 17, 117

## RESURGENCE 1950–1980

### Overview

There was a recovery in the growth rate of world FDI from the 1950s. The international cartel system was dismantled, and large US-owned corporations became the symbol of international business in the postwar world. These were the years when the term 'multinational' was invented, when economic theorists turned their attention to explaining their existence, when many governments began to collect statistics on FDI for the first time, and when the role of MNEs in the world economy became the subject of controversy. Figure 2.6 shows the growth in the world outward stock of FDI between 1960 and 1980.

The rapid growth rate of FDI in this period is evident,[5] though even by 1980 it is unlikely that FDI had regained the relative importance it had held in the world economy before 1914. The world FDI stock amounted to 4.8 per cent of world output in 1980 – still far below the estimated level of 1914 (United Nations 1994: 130).

A striking feature of postwar international business was the role of the United States as the leading home economy. United States MNEs expanded abroad on a colossal scale, with US FDI growing faster than the US economy as a whole. Between 1945 and the mid-1960s the United States may have accounted for 85 per cent of all new FDI flows, though within a decade the proportion had fallen to 40 per cent of total outflows.

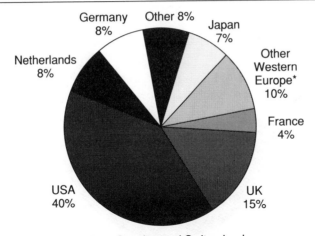

*Principally Belgium, Sweden and Switzerland

*Figure 2.7* Percentage share of FDI stock in 1980 by home economy
*Sources*: Dunning 1992: 17; United Nations 1993: 248

The result was a radical change to the home country distribution of the stock of FDI. In 1960 and 1970 the United States accounted for almost one-half of the total world stock of outward FDI. Figure 2.7 shows the situation in 1980, by which time the US share had begun its relative decline.

The relative importance of the United States as the world's leading home economy rivalled and at times exceeded that of Britain before the Second World War. The US share in FDI outflows in the 1950s and 1960s was far above the US share in the world's income or output even at its peak level in 1950 (Lipsey 1993: 144). However, the British remained prolific foreign investors, replacing the large amounts of FDI lost during the war and through sequestration. Together, the United States, the United Kingdom and the Netherlands accounted for two-thirds of world FDI in 1980, but twenty years previously their share had stood at three-quarters. Nevertheless, there were pointers towards a more pluralistic situation. In the twenty years after the end of the Second World War both German and Japanese FDI had been remarkably low, despite the rapid recovery of their economies from wartime devastation. Their companies preferred to export rather than establish extensive foreign operations. However, during the 1970s both economies re-emerged as significant outward investors, although the relative importance of FDI remained rather low compared to the overall size of these two economies.

Figure 2.8 shows the radical re-distribution of FDI stock among host economies which had occurred by 1980.

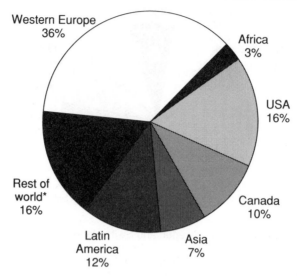

*Principally Australia, New Zealand, South Africa, and Southern Europe

*Figure 2.8* Percentage share of FDI stock in 1980 by host economy
*Sources*: Dunning 1992: 20; Stopford and Dunning 1983: 12

By 1980 almost two-thirds of world FDI was located in Western Europe, the United States and Canada. Britain, the largest single host economy in Europe, had more inward investment than the whole of Africa and Asia combined. Within this overall picture, there were some important trends. In 1967 Canada, as in 1929, had been the world's single largest host economy, accounting for 18 per cent of all world inward investment. But by 1980 Canada was only the third largest host, after the United States and the United Kingdom. In contrast, the United States had begun to grow rapidly as host economy. The FDI inflow to the United States was less than 10 per cent of the total inflow to developed countries in the early 1960s; it reached a quarter in 1973–4; and over a third in 1975–80 (Lipsey 1993: 116). At the opposite spectrum was Japan, which even in 1980 accounted for less than 1 per cent of world inward FDI stock.

The relative shift of world FDI to the developed world was related to a new emphasis in international business on market-oriented investment, particularly manufacturing, rather than supply-oriented activities. There was a sharp relative decline in FDI in natural resources which had been so important before the Second World War. In agriculture and mining, and later in petroleum, foreign firms lost the ownership of production facilities in many developing economies, though often they remained very powerful in the transportation, processing and marketing of commodities.

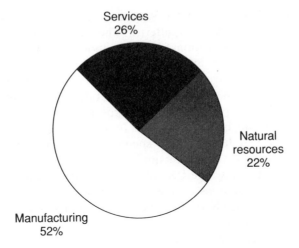

*Figure 2.9* Distribution of accumulated world FDI by sector, c. 1978
*Source*: Stopford and Dunning 1983: 18

The result, as shown in Figure 2.9, was a radical redistribution among sectors of world FDI.

Manufacturing FDI was now larger than the natural resource and service sectors combined, but there were also significant changes within each sector. In the service sector, transport and utility investments were no longer important, while new investments had been made in professional business services, fast food, restaurants, hotels and other services. Above all, from the 1960s multinational banks, trading companies and international commodity dealers began rapid international expansion.

It is likely that the overall number of MNEs in the world economy grew considerably. One estimate suggests that by the end of the 1960s some 1,240 US firms had production or marketing affiliates in more than one country: seventy-five of this number had affiliates in more than twenty countries (Houston and Dunning 1976: 22). This was the era of the classic MNE in manufacturing. The 'typical' US MNE had gone abroad on the basis of a well-developed domestic business, and possessed a 'clean' organisational structure consisting of wholly-owned subsidiaries.

**The business environment**

The macro-economic environment provided the essential context for the resurgence of international business activity. Between 1950 and 1973 the annual real GNP growth of the OECD countries averaged around 5 per cent. This growth was smooth, with none of the major recessions seen in the interwar years. The results included the creation over time of large prosperous markets, especially in Western Europe and later in Japan, and the spread of consumption patterns. The environment was a highly favourable one for international business, though from the early 1970s it gave way to low growth, inflationary and unstable conditions.

The world economy was dominated by the United States until the 1960s. The Second World War left the United States in a uniquely powerful position. While Europe and Asia had experienced extensive destruction and loss of life, no battles had been fought on the soil of the United States. Europe and Japan had to spend the immediate postwar decade undergoing extensive reconstruction, heavily dependent on official aid from the United States. The US dollar became the world's major reserve currency. US corporations assumed leading positions in many manufacturing industries, usually facing little initial competition from European or Japanese competitors.

Nevertheless the fast economic growth rates experienced by Western Europe and Japan in the 1950s and 1960s eventually reduced the scale of US hegemony. These economies were effectively 'catching up' the technological and productivity lead of the United States: as they did this, their income levels rose rapidly and their economies underwent structural transformation. The emergence of a US deficit on its balance of trade in the 1960s, and the devaluation of the US dollar and the end of its convertibility into gold in 1971, can be taken as the symbolic signs of the ending of an era.

Receptivity towards foreign business fell further after 1950. MNEs were entirely excluded from the communist states of Russia, China and elsewhere. In the twenty years after 1945 the European colonial empires were dismantled. In some cases, decolonisation was followed by an aggressive reaction against the FDI of the former colonial power, and sometimes all foreign investment, though in other cases independence had less radical consequences. Almost invariably, the end of colonialism brought new political, economic and legal uncertainties for Western companies in the developing world.

The relatively small number of expropriations without compensation until the late 1960s – when a period of large-scale expropriation began – reflected the power and determination of the United States to protect foreign investments. Given the American domination of the world economy outside the Communist bloc, the threat of economic sanctions – and the American capacity for military intervention – were major deterrents. However the Americans and Europeans were unable to get international bodies such as the United Nations to guarantee the property rights of international investors. In the postwar decades a series of United Nations resolutions affirmed the right of member states to nationalise natural resources. The Charter of Economic Rights and Duties of States, passed by the General Assembly in December 1974, provided a wide-ranging endorsement of national efforts to control foreign companies, by expropriation, contract abrogation and other tactics. The decline in the ability of the United States to enforce its will in the 1970s enabled the governments of the developing world to follow their own rules regarding foreign property (Lipson 1985: 85–139).

Even in the developed world receptivity towards international business fell. In a number of Western European countries many public utilities, industries and companies were taken into state ownership. This did not involve the nationalisation of foreign companies – which were rarely active in the sectors taken into public ownership – but it confined their potential area of operation. Japan was an extreme case of this trend. Its governments systematically discouraged inward FDI, and managed to restrict it to a low level. The growth in the importance of Western Europe as a host region, and the continued importance of Canada and the United States, reflected the fact that these were the few remaining regions where MNEs could operate with comparative freedom and safety.

The postwar years did not see a reversion to the liberal capital movements regime which had existed before 1929. In the late 1940s and early 1950s only the US dollar was available as a major convertible currency. Elsewhere exchange controls regulated capital movements. They were often the instruments used by governments to screen or monitor FDI flows. The worldwide controls over capital movements were related to balance of payments concerns and the system of fixed exchange rates established at Bretton Woods. It was not until 1958 that most European countries adopted non-resident convertibility, which permitted foreigners to move funds for current account purposes freely from one country to another. This was the key development in the establishment of a liberal and open international economy. It had an immediate impact on FDI flows, with an increase of US FDI into Europe (Wilkins 1974a: 342). This open economy did not extend to large parts of the world, because most developing countries continued to exercise tight controls over capital movements, while even most developed countries retained some exchange controls. It was only after the collapse of the Bretton Woods system of fixed exchange rates in the early 1970s that controls over capital movements began to be dismantled.

There was a partial decline in world trade barriers in this period. Under the auspices of the General Agreement on Tariffs and Trade (GATT) signed in 1947, tariffs were reduced. This process peaked in the 1960s, when the Kennedy Administration in the United States made major efforts to secure radical reductions in tariff rates. During the mid-1960s there was a comprehensive reduction of barriers to trade in manufactured goods. While the growth of trade barriers had initially stimulated multinational manufacturing, their subsequent decline also stimulated FDI by increasing the trading opportunities of foreign subsidiaries. By the end of the 1960s, however, the US-inspired drive for trade liberalisation showed a distinct loss of momentum, as US balance of payments deficits began to cause concern about the scale of foreign imports. The following decade saw the re-emergence of new kinds of protectionism in the world economy.

The formation of regional trading blocs was both part of the process of reducing trade barriers, and a limitation on it. The European Economic Community (later known as the EC, and, from 1993, the European Union) was formed in 1957, and initially consisted of six Western European countries. It developed common tariffs against external imports. An extreme case was the Common Agricultural Policy, adopted in 1966, which severely restricted US agricultural exports to Europe. However, within Europe, free trade was established between the member countries, although many non-tariff barriers persisted. The creation of such a large 'Common Market' attracted US MNEs to Western Europe.

The development of international business in the 1950s and 1960s was facilitated by radical advances in transport and technology. In 1958 the first commercial jet made an Atlantic crossing. This was followed by a phenomenal increase in air traffic. The development of telex was a considerable advance over telephones in facilitating international communications and co-ordinating multinational business (Wilkins 1974a: 328). In 1965 the first satellite for commercial telecommunications was launched. During the 1970s the use of the facsimile machine took off. The movement of goods across the world was considerably facilitated by the development of larger ocean-going ships or super-freighters, and the growth of containerisation.

## GLOBAL BUSINESS

### Overview

In the 1980s the average annual growth rate for FDI outflows reached 14 per cent. This decade was probably the fastest period of growth for FDI since the late nineteenth century. The growth of FDI was faster than that of both world exports and world output. Figure 2.10 illustrates the absolute scale of this growth.

The considerable shift in the distribution of world FDI between home countries is shown in Figure 2.11.

During the 1980s the United States no longer dominated new flows of FDI. Between 1986 and 1990 it accounted for around 13 per cent of world FDI outflows, compared to Britain's 17 per cent and Japan's 19 per cent (Dunning 1992: 18). Western Europe returned to its traditional position as the largest source of FDI, with the United Kingdom remaining the most prolific European outward investor (United Nations 1994). German, French and other Western European FDI also expanded, and it was the

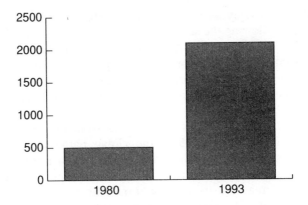

*Figure 2.10* World stock of outward FDI 1980 and 1993 (US$bn)
*Source*: United Nations 1995

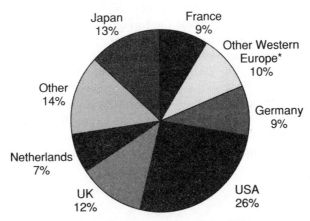

*Switzerland, Sweden and Italy. Remaining European
Countries are included in the 'other' category along with
Canada, Australia, etc.

*Figure 2.11* Percentage share of FDI stock in 1993 by home economy
*Source*: United Nations 1995

re-emergence of these continental European economies as large-scale
outward investors which caused the rise in Western Europe's overall share
of world FDI. By 1993, the once-dominant trio of the United States, the
United Kingdom and the Netherlands still accounted for around 45 per
cent of world FDI stock, while in terms of outflows the United States
recovered its leading position in the early 1990s.

Japanese FDI rose from only around 3 per cent of world outward stock
in 1971 to reach 13 per cent in 1993. Japanese FDI moved up sharply in
the early 1970s; fell back following the oil shock of the mid-1970s;

increased very sharply again in the early 1980s; and then increased even more sharply following the sharp appreciation of the yen in 1985 (Strange 1993: 64–71). During the 1980s the outflow of Japanese FDI was much faster than that of any other major economy: the growth rate was 22 per cent between 1980 and 1985 and 35 per cent between 1986 and 1990. By 1993 Japan held the world's second largest stock of FDI after the United States.

Virtually all FDI continued to originate from the developed market economies. Up to the late 1970s the global pattern of FDI could be characterised as bi-polar, dominated by North America (the United States and Canada) and Western Europe, but the subsequent rapid growth of Japanese FDI created a tri-polar pattern. The Triad of North America, the EU and Japan accounted for around four-fifths of total outward stocks and flows in the early 1990s. This percentage was substantially higher than that in the area of trade, where the Triad accounted for around one-half of the total world trade (United Nations 1991). The most significant exception from this pattern was the foreign expansion of MNEs from the Asian newly industrializing countries (NICs), but in quantitative terms these countries still accounted for only a small proportion of world FDI.

Figure 2.12 shows the distribution of world FDI by host economies in 1993.

By this date the concentration of world FDI stock in North America and Western Europe was striking. Although the United States had always been one of the world's most important host economies, its share of total inward world FDI was unprecedented. This reflected the transformation of the

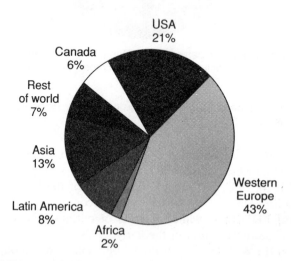

*Figure 2.12* Percentage share of FDI stock in 1993 by host economy
*Source*: United Nations 1995

United States from – in the 1970s – a country whose outward FDI greatly exceeded its inward FDI – to one in which the inward investment exceeded outward investment. Even more striking than the role of the United States as a major host was Japan's continued insignificance in this capacity.

The place of the developing countries as hosts was more complicated. Their share of the total stock declined further between 1980 and 1993, but the share of developing countries in total flows of FDI began to rise around 1990 and reached almost 40 per cent by 1993. The distribution of this inward investment was highly skewed. Latin America, the Caribbean and most African countries attracted relatively little investment, but East and South Asia and China became increasingly important as hosts (Dunning 1993: 289). Between 1980 and 1990 ten countries accounted for almost 70 per cent of total FDI flows to the developing world. These were, in order of importance as hosts: Singapore, Mexico, Brazil, China, Hong Kong, Malaysia, Egypt, Argentina, Thailand and Taiwan (United Nations 1993). The concentration of FDI flows became even greater subsequently, as the flows of investment to China accelerated to reach more than a third of the total FDI in all developing countries in the mid-1990s.

Figure 2.13 provides an estimate of world FDI by economic sector in 1992.

While services represented around a quarter of the total world stock at the beginning of the 1970s, by the early 1990s they accounted for over a half. Although there are a large and diverse group of service sector activities, 85 per cent of service FDI was in trade-related activities and banking and finance. The same percentage of the stock was located in developed

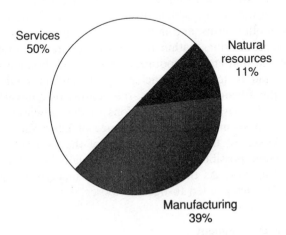

*Figure 2.13* Distribution of accumulated world FDI by sector in 1992
*Source*: United Nations 1993: 62

countries, where advantage was taken of the growing demand for consumer services resulting from rising real incomes, the growing technological, information and knowledge component of many activities, and the new opportunities offered by deregulation and liberalisation.

By the mid-1990s the scale of MNEs was considerable. There were estimated to be over 37,530 MNEs active controlling over 200,000 foreign affiliates located worldwide, although a considerable proportion of total activities was in the hands of a 100 or so really large MNEs. If the level of world FDI is related to the world output, the globalisation of international business was approaching that obtained before the First World War. However international business was not merely regaining its former importance in absolute size. MNEs had a much greater flexibility to locate different parts of their value-added activities in different parts of the world. Production of goods and services became internationalised at a deeper level than in the past. A striking manifestation of these trends was a rapid growth of intra-firm trade in manufacturing, especially in high technology industries such as automobiles and machinery which had experienced the greatest rationalisation on a world scale. In the early 1970s intra-firm trade was estimated to account for around 20 per cent of world trade. By the early 1990s, that share was around one-third. Intra-firm exports and imports accounted for one-third and over 40 per cent respectively of all US trade (United Nations 1994: 143).

As the integration of international production by MNEs proceeded, organisational forms evolved. The 'clean' organisation of the classic MNE gave way to more complex worlds of networks and alliances. This trend was observable in manufacturing, natural resources and service industries. The idea of an MNE as a tightly defined managerial hierarchy gave way to a looser structure, in which firms had many – often fluctuating – alliances with other firms, and in which they no longer sought to produce all value-added activities within their own corporate borders. It was no longer apparent that large corporations with 'clean' boundaries were able to innovate and to learn at sufficient speed, and in some of the most technologically advanced industries, the centres of innovation appeared to have moved from inside corporations to the networks linking them. In retrospect, it seems that the dominance of international business by the classic MNEs of the middle decades of the twentieth century may only have been possible because of the relatively subdued levels of international activity. As the pace of internationalisation quickened, the boundaries of firms needed to become looser.

## The business environment

An important feature of the macro-economic environment was a redistribution of economic power in the world economy. From the 1970s the overwhelming influence of the United States on the world economy gave way to a situation whereby economic power was distributed between North America, Western Europe and Japan, which together accounted for three-quarters of world manufacturing production.

The decline in the pre-eminence of the United States in FDI flows mirrored its relatively less important role in the world economy. In the early 1960s the United States accounted for 40 per cent of world manufacturing output. Thirty years later it was responsible for less than a quarter. Through the 1970s and most of the 1980s American growth rates lagged behind those of its major competitors. In contrast, the Japanese economy grew rapidly for two decades from the late 1950s. This 'high growth' era ended in the early 1970s, but subsequently Japan's economy displayed a dynamism and resiliance to external shocks which enabled it to grow much faster than its Western competitors. Japan's share of world manufacturing production increased from 5 per cent in the early 1960s to around 20 per cent at the beginning of the 1990s.

There were other shifts in world economic power. The most important was the rapid economic growth experienced by several East and South-east Asian economies. The lead was taken by the 'four tigers' of Hong Kong, Singapore, South Korea, and Taiwan, which from the 1960s achieved high rates of economic growth and structural transformation. Between 1966 and 1990 Singapore grew by an average 8.5 per cent per annum, or three times as fast as the United States. The 'four tigers' were followed by a second wave of Asian economies including Malaysia, Thailand, Indonesia and parts of China, whose growth rates accelerated in the 1980s and 1990s.

From the 1970s many of the restrictions on international business which had accumulated over the previous fifty years were swept away. The borderless world began to be restored. Policy in many developing countries shifted towards export-led growth and more active participation in the international division of labour. The attraction of inward FDI was increasingly seen as a valuable means to develop new technologies, products and skills. China's adoption of market-oriented policies in the 1980s, and the demise of Communism in Russia and Eastern Europe at the end of that decade, opened up huge parts of the globe once more to international business. Deregulation and privatisation opened many new opportunities for international business in both developing and developed countries, including service activities such as air transport, tourism and telecommunications which had long been closed to foreign companies. In the new policy environment, MNEs faced few risks of expropriation. Nevertheless, the international property rules of the nineteenth century were not restored. In China, in the former Communist states of Eastern Europe, and elsewhere, MNEs faced numerous uncertainties regarding their legal rights and the enforcement of contracts. In this respect, the

MNEs investing in these regions faced a far more uncertain world than had their nineteenth century predecessors.

The restrictions on capital flows which had accumulated since the 1920s were dismantled. The key development was the emergence of the Eurodollar markets from the 1960s. The rapid growth of the unregulated global money and capital markets resulted in the widespread internationalisation of financial markets. National controls over cross-border capital flows were largely swept away during the 1980s as financial deregulation occurred in all major economies. The new environment provided great opportunities for MNEs in financial services, and restored the kind of capital mobility which had existed in the nineteenth century.

In contrast, there was a new wave of trade protectionism in the world economy which stimulated market-oriented FDI, just as it had in previous decades. While GATT contributed to a declining general level of tariffs, non-tariff barriers such as voluntary export restraints (VERs) proliferated. By the early 1990s non-tariff barriers affected more than a quarter of all industrialised country exports, and they were even more widely used by developing countries (Dicken 1992: 151–5). The new protectionism was related in part to the further growth of regional trading blocs. The European Union (as it is now called) was enlarged in 1973, 1981, 1986 and 1995. The Single European Act of 1985 set a target to complete a Single Market in 1992, and considerable progress was made in the intervening period in the creation of a single unified market. In 1994 the United States, Canada and Mexico formed Nafta (the North American Free Trade Area). A year later the Mercosur customs union was launched by Brazil, Paraguay, Uruguay and Argentina.

The real costs and risks of managing at a distance were sharply reduced by changes in communications and transport technologies. Developments in information technology revolutionised communications. The use of 'geo-stationary' satellites, which orbited the earth at heights of between 12,000 and 25,000 miles, expanded spectacularly to provide simultaneous cheap voice, data and video links worldwide. The likely growth of 'low earth orbit' satellites in the 1990s promised the provision of voice and data telecommunications to anyone anywhere in the world. Optical fibre cables provided an alternative means of transmitting very large volumes of information at very high speeds.

Information and its use emerged as a driving force in international business. Manufacturing systems were transformed by the use of information technology (IT) to control production processes. Advances in IT included the development – and then the linking – of CAD (computer-aided design) and CAM (computer-aided manufacturing) systems – and the rapid and changing use of computers in business, including a change from mainframes to personal computers, and then work stations. Rapid and immediate access to information developed as an important source of competitive advantage. It was particularly important in the international growth of service firms.

The major advances in communications were often achieved through a convergence of once discrete technologies. Multimedia technology combined communications with computer graphics and video, hi-fi sound, computer data and – especially – interaction between the system and the user. The need to combine quite different technologies was an important influence behind the formation of cross-border alliances, as the boundaries of even the largest MNEs could no longer contain all the technological knowledge and organising skills needed for competitive success.

## SUMMARY

This chapter has surveyed the chronological development of international business from the early nineteenth century. It has shown that this development has been a complex process which has not been continuous. Between 1880 and the 1920s international business reached a significance in the world economy which it was not to approach again until the 1980s. Trends in international business over time have been shown to have been influenced by the macro-economic environment, the degree of receptivity to foreign enterprises, the level of protectionism, the existence of capital controls, and transport and communication technology. These factors have interacted with one another, and have themselves been shaped in varying degrees by international business.

Over time the nature of international business has changed greatly. In the nineteenth century international business was heavily concentrated on the exploitation of natural resources. Subsequently manufacturing and, more latterly services, became the leading sectors. Most multinational investment has always originated from a small number of advanced countries, but it has been more widely distributed. Until the Second World War the developing world attracted the largest proportion of world FDI, but subsequently it became concentrated largely in the developed market economies of Western Europe and North America. There have been significant shifts in organisation also. Large classic MNEs with clean organisational boundaries were pre-eminent in the middle of the twentieth century, but in earlier and later periods networks and alliances of firms have been common features of international business.

## NOTES

1 Dunning's estimates for home countries in 1914 is the basis of Figure 2.1 (Dunning 1992: 117). However, the UK figure has been raised from $6,500 to $8,172 million on the basis of Corley (1994). The German figure has been raised from $1,500 to $2,600 million using V. Schröter (1984). The French figures has been raised from $1,750 to $2,000 billion as the former figure is too low for

Europe's largest capital exporter. Dunning estimated $1,250 million for Belgium, Italy, Netherlands, Sweden and Switzerland. Gales and Sluyterman (1993) give $925 million for the Netherlands alone. This figure has been taken, and another $925 million allocated to the four remaining countries, given that Belgium, Sweden and Switzerland are all known to have made substantial direct investments. Dunning's estimates of $2,652 million for the United States, $680 million for Canada and $780 million for 'other developed countries' of Russia, Japan, Australia, New Zealand and South Africa have been used. This has raised the total world stock of FDI to $18,204 million, which has been used in the calculation of percentages.

2 The low number of US MNEs is misleading. The figure is from the Multinational Enterprise Study Project conducted at the Harvard Business School in the 1960s. This pioneering study identified a sample of 187 large US MNEs with manufacturing subsidiaries in at least six countries in the *mid-1960s*, and then traced their historical growth backwards. This procedure missed many smaller firms, as well as those which no longer existed in the mid-1960s.

3 Figure 2.4 is based on Dunning's 1938 estimate (Dunning 1992: 117). A Dutch figure of $2,700 million has been used from Gales and Sluyterman (1993: 65). This has been subtracted from the Dunning figure of $3,500 million in 1938 for Belgium, Italy, Sweden, Switzerland and the Netherlands, and the residual $800 million allocated to the other countries. This is likely to be an underestimate. Although Belgian FDI appears to have stagnated in the interwar years (Devos 1993: 204), Swedish and Swiss FDI seem to have grown.

4 Figure 2.5 is taken from Dunning's 1938 estimate (Dunning 1992: 118). However Dunning's figure for inward FDI into the United States of $1.8 billion is too low given the more widely accepted figure of $2.9 billion for 1940.

5 Distortions arise because the data are expressed in current US dollars. The 1970s in particular were a decade of high inflation as well as shifting exchange relationships (Stopford and Dunning 1983: 7–11).

# Chapter 3

# Multinationals and natural resources

## INTERNATIONAL BUSINESS AND NATURAL RESOURCES

The leading place occupied by the exploitation of natural resources in the development of international business has been stressed in Chapter 2. Before the 1950s more than a half of total world FDI was located in this sector, while a much higher percentage of the inward FDI stock of developing countries was in primary activities. However, the significance of this sector was much greater than its quantitative importance. It has generated some of the world's largest MNEs, whose leadership of their respective industries has proved long-lasting. While the growth of intra-firm trade in manufacturing since the 1970s has been striking, extensive intra-firm trade in international resource products dates back to the nineteenth century. Finally, the impact of resource MNEs on many host economies, and on the way in which the world's natural resources have been exploited, has been fundamental.

The development of international business in natural resources, as a result, provides crucial evidence on the three central issues of why MNEs exist, how they exist, and their impact. Unfortunately, the examination of these issues is complicated because of the heterogenous nature of this sector. An essential distinction is between renewable resources (agriculture and forestry) and non-renewable resources (mining and petroleum). These sub-sectors have different characteristics. FDI in non-renewable resources differs fundamentally from that in manufacturing or service industries because the location of mines or oil wells is determined by geology. The distribution of hard minerals and petroleum around the world is fortuitous and asymmetric with respect to final markets. There are significant scale economies in the exploitation of minerals. Minerals can also only be used once in their original form. This makes questions of ownership and optimal exploitation of the resource of great strategic importance. These characteristics tend to create a different industry structure than in renewable resource industries, where there are often multiple sources for many agricultural commodities, and where products can often be developed by small investors with relative ease (McKern 1993: 1–11).

Within the wider renewable/non-renewable categories, there are industry-specific variations which have exercised a considerable influence on how international business activity has developed. Mining industries generally share a number of common features: these include the importance of geology, the capital-intensity and high-risk nature of their business, and the fact that most metals are homogenous products sold in world markets. But there are also important differences between minerals. Minerals differ widely in their availability. Bauxite, the raw material from which aluminium is normally derived, is not widely distributed, at least in terms of sufficient richness for commercial use. In contrast, tin and zinc are far more widely found around the world.

## ORIGINS AND GROWTH

International business activity in resource exploitation began early, and expanded rapidly from around 1880. Table 3.1 shows some of the enterprises engaged in multinational investment before 1914.

Table 3.1 International business in natural resources before 1914: illustrative cases

| Company | Nationality | Principal business | First FDI | Countries/ operations c. 1914 |
|---|---|---|---|---|
| St John d'el Rey Mining | UK | Gold mining | 1830 | Gold mining and related utilities in Brazil |
| Rio Tinto | UK | Metals | 1873 | Pyrites, sulphur, copper in Spain |
| Metallgesellschaft | German | Metal trading | 1887 | Smelting, refining, mining and distribution of metals in USA, Mexico and Europe |
| Jersey Standard | US | Petroleum | 1879 | Oilfields, refineries and distribution in Canada, Latin America and Europe |
| Shell Group | Dutch/UK | Petroleum | 1890 | Oilfields, refineries and distribution in USA, Venezuela, Dutch East Indies, Russia and Europe |
| United Fruit | US | Tropical fruit | 1887 | Plantations and utilities in Caribbean and Central America; shipping; distribution in UK and Europe |

## Mining

The tradition of foreign investment and foreign entrepreneurial activity in mining began well before the nineteenth century (Wilkins 1977: 578). In the early nineteenth century, mining was one of the first activities to attract free-standing firms. In the 1820s and 1830s six British-owned companies were formed to exploit Brazilian goldfields. The pioneer venture was formed in 1824, but the most substantial, and sustained, British FDI in Brazilian gold mining was the St John d'el Rey Mining Company, which was organised in 1830. By 1913 this free-standing company operated the deepest mine in the world employing over 2,500 workers, including 150 European expatriates. It also held large real estate holdings around the gold mine, built hydroelectric plants, and owned and operated a private electric railroad (Eakin 1989).

From the middle of the nineteenth century there was growing European mining FDI which took the form both of horizontal integration – with mining firms undertaking FDI in mining abroad – and backwards vertical integration – with metallurgical companies seeking mineral deposits. During the 1850s the Belgian mining companies Vieille Montagne and La Providence began to invest in iron ore and coal mines in France, Germany and elsewhere as mineral deposits became scarcer in Belgium. In the late nineteenth century the Cockerill business enterprise, a large Belgian industrial group originally founded by a British family, invested in Russian minerals, as did a number of other French and Belgian companies (McKay 1970).

A massive growth in FDI in mining took place from the 1870s. The United Kingdom became the centre of the international mining industry in this era, retaining this role until it passed to New York after the First World War. The number of British companies engaged in FDI in non-ferrous metal mining rose from 39 in 1875 to 957 in 1913. In 1875 one-third of this British FDI was invested in Europe, mainly Spain, and one-third in North America, mainly the United States, with copper as the single most important mineral. This pattern changed considerably following the discovery of the South African goldfields. In 1913 over a fifth of the British firms active in FDI in mining, and two-fifths of the capital invested, was in the southern African gold industry (Harvey and Press 1990a: 106–7).

The hundreds of British mining companies were usually small affairs, but there were occasional exceptions, such as the Rio Tinto Company. Rio Tinto was founded in 1873 to buy mines from the Spanish government for the then large sum of $18 million (£3.68 million). Within a decade Rio Tinto had constructed a mining and metallurgical complex in southern Spain, and secured a leading position in the world markets for sulphur and copper. Subsequently the emergence of new producing regions, especially the United States, eclipsed Rio Tinto's Spanish production, but it dominated the world pyrites industry before 1914. The company also diversified beyond Spain. At the end of the 1920s it became involved in the development of the Northern Rhodesian (now Zambian) copper belt (Harvey 1981).

A trio of German metal trading companies before 1914 also became large-scale corporate players in world metals. The firms were Aron Hirsch and Sohn; Beer, Sondheimer & Co.; and Metallgesellschaft, the largest of the three. Metallgesellschaft was a trading firm, founded in 1881, which diversified into the mining, processing and distribution of copper, lead and zinc with extensive investments in the United States and Mexico as well as Europe, where it had a large London-based trading operation. Its United States subsidiary, the American Metal Company, formed in 1887, invested in coal mining, but its main focus was smelting and refining. Metallgesellschaft also had mining and processing companies in other European countries, and in 1912 built the largest refinery in Europe in Belgium to process ore from the Belgian Congo. The German metal traders succeeded separately and jointly in vertically integrating on an international scale the mining, smelting, refining, sale and manufacturing of all the most important non-ferrous metals. In certain metals, such as lead, zinc, copper and nickel, their control was such as to amount to a preponderant influence upon international prices (Wilkins 1989: 267–71; Chandler 1990: 487–8).

In the late nineteenth century US-based companies undertook substantial FDI in mining and smelting, mostly in the neighbouring countries of Canada, Mexico and Central America (Wilkins 1970). After the First World War, US mining companies expanded their stakes abroad. Substantial investments were made in mining and smelting in Latin America and Canada, and smaller ones in Europe, the Far East and Africa. The greatest US investments in Latin America were made in nitrates and copper in Chile, copper, lead and zinc in Peru, and tin in Bolivia; but US firms were active in almost the full range of minerals including asbestos, chrome, coal, diamonds, gold, nickel, platinum, silver tungsten and vanadium. The major US enterprises involved included American Smelting and Refining (ASARCO), Kennecott, American Metal (whose ownership passed from German to US hands as a result of the First World War), Anaconda, and Alcoa, the giant US aluminium company (Wilkins 1974a: 102–13; Navin 1978: 117–32).

## Petroleum

It was in petroleum that some of the largest MNEs were to develop. The United States was the home of the modern oil industry, for it was there that the first oil well in the world was drilled, in Pennsylvania, in 1859. The United States was the world's largest oil producing country through to the First World War, though in the late nineteenth century Russian oil production also became substantial. Smaller oilfields were developed in Canada, Romania, Indonesia, Mexico, Iran and elsewhere.

The dominant business enterprise in the late nineteenth century oil industry was the Standard Oil Company, whose power rested on control over much of the pipelines and refinery capacity of the United States. Standard became a large oil exporter. In some years of the late nineteenth century as much as three quarters of its sales came from the export trade. Its first FDI came in 1879, when a refinery was built in Austria-Hungary; but this was abandoned within seven years. In the 1880s refineries were built in Mexico and Cuba to refine imported American oil, and other refineries followed when foreign tariffs on refined oil were high. The company's main focus was foreign distribution and marketing. By 1907 Standard Oil controlled fifty-five foreign companies capitalised at around $37 million.

In 1911 the United States Supreme Court decided that Standard Oil was a monopoly which infringed the antitrust laws, and it was dissolved into 34 separate companies, nine of which had foreign facilities. Standard Oil of New Jersey (later known variously as Jersey Standard, Esso and Exxon) obtained the largest foreign assets, including the oilfields and refineries in Romania and Canada; refineries in Germany and Cuba; and marketing operations in Canada, most of Latin America and Western Europe. Two of the independent firms formed out of the 1911 dissolution were Standard Oil of New York (later Mobil), which took over Standard's Far Eastern distribution companies, and Standard Oil of California, which both developed into two of the world's largest oil companies. The beginning of the twentieth century also saw new American entrants into multinational oil, especially the Texas Company (later Texaco) which began to establish overseas sales offices from 1905. By 1913 it was selling oil through its own outlets in Europe, Latin America, Asia and elsewhere (Wilkins 1970: 84–6).

The leading European oil companies which appeared in the late nineteenth century displayed a different pattern of development from the American companies. The oilfields of Eastern Europe, and especially Russia, played an important part in the growth of European oil companies. The Russian oil industry was transformed by the introduction of modern technology by members of the Swedish Nobel family, who had settled in Russia in the 1870s. Their company – which produced around one-tenth of total Russian oil in the late nineteenth century – was not a 'Swedish multinational', for although members of the Swedish family managed it, they did so from headquarters in Russia with no control from a Swedish parent company. Its equity was held in various Western European countries, as well as in Russia, with German banks as the single most important institutional shareholders. The firm might be better categorised as a Russian-based oil multinational, for it established foreign distribution companies, the largest of which was in Germany (Fursenko 1991).

A number of European banks made large-scale investments in petroleum. During the 1880s the Paris branch of the Rothschilds acquired Russian oil producing interests. The Rothschilds had diversified into the oil business in the previous decade, importing American oil into France, and building a refinery there. After plans to acquire a quarter of the equity of the Nobel company fell through, they decided to buy their own Russian oil company in 1886. Their venture became the largest exporter of Russian kerosene, and they also created a network of distribution companies in Western Europe. The Deutsche Bank also entered the oil industry. In 1903 it gained control of a leading Romanian oil producer which was placed under the control of a holding company in which the bank had a 50 per cent shareholding and overall management control. A vertically integrated oil business was created which included distribution companies in a number of European countries (Pohl 1989).

From the late nineteenth century the European oil industries sought to cartelise the world oil market, and to involve Standard Oil in these plans (Jones 1981: 53–4). While negotiations with Standard Oil were never successful, in 1906 the Deutsche Bank, Nobels and Rothschilds did establish the jointly owned Europäische Petroleum Union (EPU), which had its own distribution companies and an oil tanker company. EPU alternated between competition with Standard Oil on the European markets, and further attempts to reach co-operative agreements with it.

The Shell Group, destined to be one of the world's largest oil companies, originated in separate British and Dutch oil companies. The 'Shell' Transport and Trading Company's origins lay in the activities of a London merchant who began his career in the 1830s selling boxes made from shells brought from the East. The business expanded the number of commodities sold, and the Samuel family established a large shipping and trading business in the Far East. During the 1880s the firm began selling the Russian oil of the Rothschilds to the Far East, breaking the monopoly previously held by Standard Oil. A major competitive assault on Standard Oil was possible after 1892, when permission was given for the firm's oil tankers to pass through the Suez Canal, which greatly reduced the cost of Russian oil in Asia. Subsequently fears that Russian supplies might be reduced led to a search for oilfields nearer the Far Eastern markets, and in 1898 a major oilfield was discovered in the Dutch colony of Borneo, a year after the 'Shell' Transport and Trading Company was founded.

The Royal Dutch Petroleum Company was established in the Netherlands in 1890 on the basis of a concession to drill for oil in the Dutch East Indies. Henri Deterding, who became chief executive in 1901, sought to build an oil company to rival Standard Oil. In 1907 he obliged Shell, weakened by organisational problems and failed business strategies, to enter a merger agreement, with the Dutch holding 60 per cent and the British 40 per cent of the shareholding. Over the next decade the Shell Group purchased the Rothschilds' oil assets in Russia and major production assets in Venezuela. In the United States, marketing and oil exploration activities began in 1912, followed a year later by the acquisition of a Californian oil producing company (Jones 1981).

British Petroleum (BP) began as one of the dozens of British free-standing companies formed in 1901 to search for oil in various parts of the world. Its origins went back to a British syndicate formed to exploit a concession granted by the Iranian government to search for oil in Iran. In 1908 oil was discovered, and the Anglo-Persian Oil Company was formed in the following year. In 1914 the British government – anxious to secure reliable supplies of cheap fuel oil for the Royal Navy and concerned about British dependence on oil from foreign countries supplied by foreign firms – took a majority shareholding in the company (Jones 1981, Ferrier 1982).

The First World War caused a major discontinuity in the ownership structure of the world oil industry. The sequestration of German foreign assets and the nationalisation of Russian oil eliminated the Nobels and the Deutsche Bank from the industry (Pohl 1989: 89–90). The war also both demonstrated the strategic and commercial importance of oil, and raised fears about the exhaustion of existing oil supplies. The result was a worldwide search for oil in the face of a perceived oil shortage. The main centre of attention was Venezuela, whose production increased rapidly and by 1928 was ranked second only to the United States. There was also great activity in the Middle East, where extensive oil reserves were widely suspected beyond Iran. However, it was not until 1927 that oil was discovered in Iraq, and it was a further seven years before a pipeline was completed which enabled the export of Iraqi oil. The first major discoveries in Saudi Arabia and Kuwait came only in 1938.

United States, British and Anglo-Dutch companies were pre-eminent in the worldwide search for oil, with each of the major oil companies possessing their distinct corporate profiles. Before the First World War US oil companies had primarily made market-oriented investments abroad, but in the 1920s they also made extensive supply-oriented invest-ments. Jersey Standard was the largest US oil company active abroad, though it was not always the most successful one. In Venezuela, Gulf Oil and Standard Oil of Indiana were the leading US oil producers in the 1920s, and it was not until 1928 that Jersey Standard found oil (Wilkins 1974a: 113–22). Shell, like Jersey Standard, had worldwide marketing activities and diversified production interests. Shell was the largest producer in Venezuela in the 1920s, while by the end of the 1920s it was selling gasoline throughout the United States through its 65 per cent owned affiliate, Shell Union. A complete contrast was the Anglo-Persian Oil Company, which held a much smaller share of world oil markets, and whose competitive position rested on the control of the prolific Iranian oil reserves (Bamberg 1994).

## Renewable resources

Over the course of the twentieth century FDI in non-renewable resources came to far exceed that in renewable resources, but in the nineteenth century there was extensive international business in agriculture and related activities. In commodities such as sugar, tea, bananas and rubber, foreign-owned plantations in Asia, Latin America and elsewhere became very important, though in the cases of other agricultural raw materials, such as cotton and tobacco, production remained in the hands of local commercial or peasant farming. In such commodities, foreign companies usually became prominent at the marketing and processing stage. There was also substantial direct investment in cattle ranches, especially in the Americas. A variety of corporate forms were used by these direct investors, even in the same product. There were numerous free-standing companies, manufacturing companies which had integrated backwards, and other firms which began as producers and integrated forwards into distribution.

In the late nineteenth century cattle-raising attracted considerable FDI. Many British free-standing companies invested in cattle ranges in the United States, acquiring major properties in Texas, Wyoming, Colorado and New Mexico, though by 1914 most of these ranches were back in American hands (Wilkins 1989: 299–307). The British also established large land companies in Latin America, especially in Argentina from the 1880s, intended to raise livestock. While some of these investments were free-standing, others were part of large integrated enterprises. One example was the Liebig's Extract of Meat Company, which originated in 1863 when a Belgian engineer established a factory at Fray Bentos in the river Uruguay to produce a beef extract by means of a new German technology. A British incorporated company was formed in 1865, and by 1913 the firm owned vast estates in Argentina and Uruguay on which cattle were raised for processing (Stopford 1974: 177–8). The large US meat packing companies, Armour and Swift, established packing plants in these countries also, and came to dominate their beef exports, but unlike Liebig they chose not to integrate into ranching (Wilkins 1970: 189–90).

A worldwide surge in demand for and prices of rubber from the early 1900s led to the remarkable growth of plantation rubber, which over-turned the previous dominance of world markets by wild or natural rubber collected by labour intensive methods. European-owned plantation companies were established throughout the colonial possessions in Southeast Asia, which by the First World War accounted for two-thirds of total world output of rubber. These were free-standing firms, although

– as will be discussed later – they became embedded in wider business networks. US companies invested in rubber in Mexico and elsewhere in Latin America. By 1912 Americans controlled 68 per cent of Mexico's rubber business (Schell 1990: 237–8; Wilkins 1970: 121–2, 187–8).

Rubber and tyre manufacturing companies also undertook backward vertical integration in this period. This strategy was stimulated by high prices before the First World War, and subsequent supply constraints as various restrictive cartel agreements came into force in the interwar years. Before the First World War Dunlop had acquired rubber estates in Malaya, while US Rubber leased land in Sumatra, in the Dutch East Indies. There were further US plantation investments during the war and in the 1920s. Firestone leased a small Liberian plantation in 1925, while Goodyear acquired a large plantation in Sumatra as well as one in the Philippines. By the mid-1920s US Rubber supplied 20 per cent of its own rubber, and the plantations subsidiary was for a time more profitable than its parent company. The tyre companies retained these investments over a long period, even though they purchased the bulk of their natural rubber on world markets. A less successful strategy was that of Ford, which in 1927 began to establish plantations in Brazil. This proved a loss making venture, through a combination of indigenous pests and other difficulties, but despite a substantial net loss, Ford's plantations continued until 1945 (Wilkins 1974a: 99–101; French 1991: 121–5).

There were other instances of backward vertical integration by manufacturers. In the 1900s, Lever Brothers – Unilever's British predecessor – began to establish palm oil and copra plantations, which were initially designed to guarantee supplies for the soap manufacturing business in the face of a predicted secular shortage of vegetable oils. A concession was secured covering huge areas of the Belgian Congo. A Belgian-registered company, Huileries du Congo Belge (HCB), was founded to work the concession. The strategy was not to set up plantations of oil palms, but to collect, mill and export the fruit of natural palms (Fieldhouse 1978: Chapters 8 and 9).

The tropical fruit sector was unusual in the emergence of vertically integrated MNEs which came to exercise a predominant influence on the world banana trade, and some other fruits also. The United Fruit Company's origins went back to the Boston Fruit Company, which had begun by purchasing bananas in Jamaica for shipment and sale in Boston. In the late 1880s Boston Fruit purchased Jamaican banana plantations. By the time the United Fruit Company was formed in 1899 the business owned or leased over 320,000 acres of land in the Caribbean, including Jamaica, Cuba, Costa Rica, Columbia and Nicaragua. This land was primarily used for growing bananas, but United Fruit also had orange groves, coconut trees, rubber trees, sugar production, cacao and cattle land (Wilkins 1970: 157–9).

The introduction of mass production cultivation techniques enabled United Fruit to expand the proportion of bananas it grew itself rather than buying on the open market. The fruit was shipped in company-owned vessels. In 1904 United Fruit took a large holding in the leading firm in the European banana trade, Elders and Fyffes, and in 1913 it acquired full control (Davies 1990). In the Caribbean, United Fruit built drainage and water systems in central America to facilitate its agricultural investments. It also established and operated railroads to facilitate the transport of its products, engaged in other infrastructure investments and established company towns in former jungle areas. During the 1920s United Fruit's business interests continued to expand, and it diversified into other products, such as coffee, sisal, cacao, sugar and African oil palm (Wilkins 1970: 159–60; Wilkins 1974a: 96–8; Read 1986a).

## DETERMINANTS

### Entrepreneurship and risk

The fundamental reasons behind the rapid growth of international business in natural resources lay in the industrialisation of Europe and the United States, which provided a large market growth for minerals and foodstuffs, and so prompted a global search for sources of supply. Until the early nineteenth century the world's demand for non-ferrous metals, for example, had been met by long-established mining regions in Europe – Cornwall, Spain, Sweden and Saxony – as well as Latin America. But as demand soared, and newer metals such as aluminium and nickel were required, these traditional sources of supply were inadequate. New discoveries were made in remoter parts of the globe, and their exploitation was often undertaken using direct investment strategies of one kind or another. The exploitation of natural resources in distant regions was facilitated by improved communications and falling transport costs.

FDI in natural resources arose from entrepreneurial perception of these profitable opportunities. The initial exploitation of overseas natural resources in the nineteenth century was typically in the hands of large numbers of small firms or individual prospectors. Mining was – and remains – a high-risk industry not only because of the exploration process, but also due to uncertainties regarding cost and completion time if a mine is constructed, and the subsequent performance of a mine or oilfield. In all commodities price fluctuations provide a further dimension of risk. Entrepreneurs seeking to exploit resources on the world's frontiers encountered a formidable combination of logistical problems arising from inadequate or non-existent infrastructure and, often, political instability or the lack of a modern legal structure.

Entrepreneurial risk-taking was at the forefront of business strategies in this environment. There was, as a result, a high level of firm creation and destruction. Fraud and financial malpractice were common. In the nineteenth century mining and petroleum industries, the division between speculative, fraudulent and entrepreneurial activities was particularly thin. In Britain some 8,400 companies are known to have been formed between 1880 and 1913 for mining and mine exploration abroad, the great majority of which generated little or no serious activity (Harvey and Press 1990a). The individuals behind these companies can be conceived as Kirzner-style entrepreneurs taking advantage of the opportunities of the period, but by transferring technologies and organisational methods across the world they were also Schumpeterian innovators, as much destabilisers of the environment as taking advantage of it.

Entrepreneurial activities sometimes took the form of diversification from one activity to another perceived as offering profitable opportunities. An important example was the virtual foundation of the modern Mexican oil industry by the British entrepreneur Weetman Pearson. Pearson became involved in Mexico through the activities of his firm of contracting engineers which undertook infrastructure projects in various countries, including the United States and Mexico. Petroleum deposits were discovered in Mexico when the firm's staff were looking for rock for harbour construction, while a missed train connection which left Pearson spending a night at the Texan town of Laredo, which was in the grip of an oil boom, led him to perceive the possibilities that could arise from discovering oil in Mexico.

From 1902 Pearson was able to use close contacts with the Mexican government to secure large oil concessions. Ahead of finding oil, he invested in downstream facilities by building a refinery and buying oil tankers to transport oil, and signed contracts to supply oil products to distributors in Europe. This was a risky strategy before a large supply of oil had been found and by 1908 the firm was reduced to buying Texan oil on the open market for refining and re-export to Europe. But, in 1910, after the drillers had moved to explore a new region, a hugely prolific oilfield was discovered. By 1914 Mexico had become the third largest oil producing country in the world, and Pearson owned 60 per cent of the output. The prior investment in downstream capacity then enabled Pearson to build a large integrated oil business which was sold to Shell in 1919 (Spender 1930; Jones 1981).

The Pearson case was a rare example of success in an industry where most investments failed. Pearson was exceptionally well-placed because of pre-existing information about the business and political environment, and the ability to divert resources from other activities. Even then long-term persistence and flexibility, including a willingness to abandon original exploration sites, were needed. And the whole enterprise would still have failed if oil had not in fact been present.

## Internalisation factors

Transactions cost theory provides important perspectives on the systematic factors behind the development of international business in natural resources. The theory helps to explain the large numbers of European free-standing firms active in resources before the First World War. Hennart suggests that this corporate form was favoured when capital could be more efficiently transferred through equity links than through international capital markets. High transactions costs arose in capital transfers in the nineteenth century because of the risks that debtors might not repay their obligations. Information asymmetries and opportunistic behaviour made the effective monitoring and screening of borrowers very costly. A strategy of taking collateral as security for a loan was possible, but not effective for investments in mining and agriculture in which capital sunk into unsuccessful projects could not yield saleable assets.

The free-standing firms in resources can be regarded as providing an institutional alternative to capital markets with high transaction costs. They were created in capital-rich countries to bring additional funds to firms located in capital-poor countries which could not obtain local financing. Rubber plantation companies – and their tin equivalents – in early twentieth century Malaya, owned either by European expatriates or local Chinese, were unable to find sufficient local sources of capital and needed the resources of the London capital market. However their reputations and the nature of their collateral were insufficient to attract London investors. The solution was to reorganise the ventures as free-standing firms, through which British lenders could monitor the use of their funds and exercise some managerial control over the venture. In support of this argument, Hennart points to the evidence that European free-standing firms survived longer in countries with underdeveloped capital markets, such as Malaysia and Nigeria, where they were still to be found in the 1960s; by contrast, in the United States, where an efficient stock market developed, they had all but disappeared by the 1920s (Hennart 1991a).

Transactions cost theory can explain patterns of vertical integration in minerals and agricultural products. The presence of physical asset specificity often led to vertical integration rather than the use of markets. This can be seen in the differing patterns of growth of the Bolivian and Southeast Asian tin industries. The former was characterised by greater vertical integration than the latter. The different types of tin found in the two regions help to explain these differences. The tin found in Southeast Asia, including Malaya, was alluvial. It was low grade but easy to mine as it was found close to the surface. The ores could be easily concentrated, and the concentrates were homogeneous and contained few impurities, and were easy to smelt. Mining firms and smelters felt no pressure to integrate but used the market to exchange products. Bolivia's lode deposits, on the other hand, were found underground. The ores were more complex and contained impurities. Smelting lode concentrates was difficult, and had to be tailored to the particular characteristics of an ore. The smelters in this sector were characterised by physical asset specificity. The costs of switching partners were high, while there could be fears that the more flexible party would opportunistically renegotiate the terms of trade. The result was an incentive for vertical integration between mining and smelting in the lode sector of the tin industry (Hennart 1986b; 1987).

Problems of quality control arising from situations of information asymmetry encouraged vertical integration in tropical fruit products such as bananas. Bananas are highly perishable. Moreover, as a tropical fruit, feasible production locations are at a distance from the major consumer markets. Vertical integration was pursued to ensure adequate supplies, and as an important means of quality control. Consistent quality was better assured by vertical integration because it reduced the incentive to cheat at each stage. Improvements in quality control enabled the MNEs to introduce consumer brands, whose bananas sold at a premium price compared to the unbranded bananas which could be supplied on an irregular basis through an arm's length export trade. Banana production itself offered few economies of integration, and in fact numerous small producers co-existed with the major companies. It was in the co-ordination of production and marketing that the economies of integration and internalisation were found (Hennart 1987; 1991a).

## Ownership factors

European and US companies were by no means always 'first movers' in the exploitation of minerals or commodities in Asia, Africa and Latin America, yet by the middle of the twentieth century foreign-owned firms were dominant in virtually every extractive enterprise in the developing world producing for export, and they held significant shares in a range of agricultural products also. This raises the question of the nature of the ownership and competitive advantages which these Western firms possessed. This issue is not specifically addressed by the transactions cost model, for although the theory predicts that an inefficient market will be internalised, it does not predict by whom (Hennart 1991a: 107–8).

The advantages of foreign-owned firms rested in part on information and better market access. The markets for minerals and commodities were overwhelmingly in the advanced economies. European and US firms had much better knowledge of conditions in the final market, and greater ease of establishing and maintaining relations with customers in the consuming countries. Their reputations could serve as guarantees of quality to consumers. This provides an important dynamic explanation for backward integration into raw materials (Buckley and Casson 1985: 189–90).

The existence of natural resources at home provided firms from the home country with access to skills and technologies which could be exploited abroad. This was obvious in the case of the United States, which in 1900 was the world's largest producer of copper, lead and petroleum, and second largest producer of bauxite, gold and zinc. The importance of French companies such as Péchiney in aluminium reflected France's position as the world's leading producer of bauxite until the Second World War. Even the prominence of British firms can be partly explained by this mechanism. By 1900 the United Kingdom was no longer an important producer of any mineral except coal, but that country had the legacy of being, until around 1850, the world's largest producer of tin, copper and lead. The use of skilled miners and technology from the old mining region of Cornwall was a prominent feature of British mining ventures in many regions in the late nineteenth century and afterwards.

The importance of countries as major consumers of particular commodities yielded advantages to their firms. The extensive British activity in sugar and tea plantations reflected that country's very high level of sugar and tea consumption (Chalmin 1990: 14). In the twentieth century the United States was the largest market for virtually every commodity. Firms based in that market had a considerable competitive advantage.

There were some obvious advantages in technology. Advances in mining and other technologies enabled Western firms to discover and exploit new sources of minerals, sometimes replacing indigenous producers in the process. Foreign-owned firms had better access to advanced technology, and were better able to recruit professionals trained in Europe or the United States. The importance of technological advantages can be seen in the case of Malayan tin. Local Chinese entrepreneurs had developed the Malayan tin industry during the nineteenth century. The large surface deposits of alluvial tin were easily mined using labour-intensive working methods, and Western mining companies had no obvious advantage. The situation changed as the more easily accessible and rich ore deposits were exhausted. During the 1900s British companies introduced a new technology – bucket-dredging – which had been first developed in New Zealand in the 1880s. Dredges could operate in swampy areas where drainage was impossible and work low-grade deposits profitably through economies of scale. Few Chinese miners adopted dredging, which was more capital-intensive than previous methods. FDI in Malayan tin surged, and by the end of the 1920s tin production by Western-owned firms in Malaya exceeded that of Chinese enterprises (van Helten and Jones 1989).

Patented technology provided the basis for the early growth of aluminium MNEs. Alcoa and its European competitors held the patents to new technology invented in the 1880s which sharply reduced the cost of reducing alumina (refined bauxite) into aluminium (Smith 1988). On the basis of its patent, Alcoa was able to monopolise the American market and control virtually all the bauxite deposits within the United States.

Access to capital markets and other sources of finance provided ownership advantages. The London Stock Exchange was not only the world's leading source of mining finance but also offered a vibrant entrepreneurial environment. The importance of London as an international financial and trade centre enabled it to function as the centre of a 'global information network'. British merchants, shippers and other businesses throughout the world sent back to London details of investment opportunities, offers of mining concessions, and information about local contacts (Harvey and Press 1990a: 115–16). A large number of company promoters, financiers, speculators and other intermediaries resided in London and specialised in the provision of venture capital for speculative mining and other ventures (Turrell and van Helten 1986).

The capital-intensive nature of mining operations helps to explain the involvement of banks and investment houses in the mining groups which emerged in the late nineteenth century. From the late 1880s the London and Paris branches of the Rothschilds held a large interest, amounting to around one-third of the ordinary capital in 1905, in the Rio Tinto Company. For a time in the late 1890s the Rothschilds also controlled the Anaconda Copper Company in the United States, then the largest copper producing company in the world (Wilkins 1989: 266–8). The Mellon banking family loaned Alcoa much of its start-up capital, and controlled a substantial minority stake in the firm for many years. The long-term nature of this financier-mining house relationship was not unusual. The links between the Rothschilds and Rio Tinto, and the Guggenheims and Kennecott and ASARCO, lasted through much of the twentieth century (Bosson and Varon 1977).

Ownership advantages in management were evident. In petroleum and aluminium, US companies grew as large enterprises within the United States before venturing abroad. These firms exploited abroad organisational capabilities developed at home, and they fit comfortably in the 'classic' MNE model. The managerial advantages held by European firms were often different. They sometimes made effective use of non-equity strategies to achieve their goals. Metallgesellschaft's powerful international position rested on a group of companies joined by interlocking shareholdings and market sharing agreements. The basis of its control over many metals was the ability to enter into long-term contracts either for the purchase of untreated concentrates or for the treated metal output. It was able to offer such contracts because it offered subsidised freight rates from mines to the European smelters; because it either owned or controlled large smelting works in Europe and the United States; and because its links with German banks helped to provide the funds needed to buy in bulk and invest heavily in smelting and other processes (Richardson 1987: 14–18).

The managerial advantages held by the European free-standing companies were different again. The organisational structures of these thousands of entrepreneurial ventures looked fragile, but this may be misleading because many of them were linked to wider business networks. In Malaya, the British 'agency houses' or trading companies took the lead in the creation of the new rubber plantation industry at the turn of the century. These enterprises either created their own plantations or purchased ones established by expatriates or local Chinese, and then used their reputations to float free-standing companies on the London Stock Exchange. The British agency houses usually retained part of the equity of the new rubber companies, and usually retained the day-to-day management of the companies as 'managing agents'. As a result, the hundreds of British rubber plantation companies established to operate in Malaya were in practice linked to a small number of trading companies. There was a similar situation in the neighbouring Dutch East Indies (Sluyterman 1994), and close parallels in other commodities and regions.

The organisational capabilities of these wider business groups were considerably more substantial than the apparent structure of numerous independent free-standing firms would imply. A comparison between West Africa and Malaya is instructive. The formation of a group of British free-standing firms to engage in both wild and plantation rubber investments in West Africa between 1905 and 1914 ended in almost total failure, often involving fraud. A crucial difference with Malaya was that the British trading companies declined to become involved in the rubber industry (Munro 1981: 275–6). Genuinely free-standing firms were high risk and vulnerable to fraudsters, but firms embedded in wider business networks could be effective. Even US FDI in mining in this period sometimes took the form of entrepreneurial firms linked with wider networks. There were many small, speculative and/or free-standing US mining ventures in Mexico. The Guggenheims operated in Mexico more as an investment group than as a classic US MNE. They used a variety of loosely linked companies in that country, as well as their main corporate vehicle, ASARCO (Harvey and Press 1990a: 166).

First mover advantages were strong in many commodities. There were several reasons for this, but one of the most fundamental was the role played by concessions. In the late nineteenth century and the first half of the twentieth century mining, petroleum and plantation investments in developing countries often operated on the basis of concessions from the host governments. The lack of bargaining skills and technical know-how on the government side, and the control over technology, capital and markets on the company side, made most of these concessions appear remarkably favourable to the foreign companies.

Most of the oil, mineral and plantation concession agreements of this period awarded the concessionaire virtually unrestricted rights in exploiting one or more natural resources. The concessionaire was typically granted extensive rights over a key large land area, often for fifty or more years. The financial obligations imposed on investors were rather limited, and often royalty payments were based on volume of output, rather than on value. It was not until the 1950s that the concept of taxation of concession income began to gain wide acceptance (Smith and Wells 1975: 31–7).

The concession system effectively placed much of the world's best plantation land and mineral resources in the hands of the first mover companies which had secured them before 1914. Subsequently, it was difficult for new entrants to make great progress, because of the economic conditions and falling price of commodities in the interwar years. Greater opportunities emerged in the 1950s, when host governments began to negotiate and/or cancel concessions, but by this time the first movers were frequently large vertically integrated corporations providing further large barriers to entry.

## Political influences

Political factors generated both firm-specific and nation-specific ownership advantages and were an important influence on the development of international business and natural resources. While the internalisation model assumes that firms are free to choose the most efficient form to operate in a foreign market, in natural resources in particular, political influences have often dictated the mode employed. European colonialism in Asia and Africa not only reduced the risks of investments, but also provided the environment for wide-ranging concessions, privileges and even overt discrimination against local producers. A large proportion of British, French, Dutch and Belgian FDI in primary activities was located in their respective colonies, and was in this sense far more 'colonial' in character than their investments in manufacturing. However US companies were also involved in resources on a global basis, and it is evident that possession of a large colonial empire was not the only influence prompting this kind of investment.

Governments provided competitive advantages for their firms in certain products believed to have a strategic value. The growth of European-owned petroleum companies was encouraged by European governments. The most important example was the British government's investment in the Anglo-Persian Oil Company in 1914. It is extremely unlikely that this enterprise would have survived as an independent entity without this government shareholding, given the scale of investment required to develop international distribution facilities to sell its crude oil. After 1914 the British government provided the funds necessary for Anglo-Persian's growth, a market for its products, and assistance in growing as an integrated oil company by selling to it the sequestrated British Petroleum

Company, the Deutsche Bank-controlled petroleum marketing and distribution company in Britain (Jones 1981; Ferrier 1982). Although Anglo-Persian retained virtual management independence from the British government, the government's support at a critical time provides the main explanation of how a wholly British-owned company became one of the world's seven oil majors. During the 1920s several other European governments also created their own companies, notably France's Compagnie Française des Pétroles (CFP) in 1924 (Melby 1981: 64–73; Nowell 1994).

Political considerations were increasingly influential in the development of resource industries in the interwar years. The pursuit of oil concessions involved extensive political and diplomatic considerations. The securing of concessions invariably involved negotiating with host governments, as in most countries the rights to the subsoil resources of liquid hydrocarbons was vested in the state. In the Middle East, most of whose states were under British or French 'protection' after the war, there were prolonged diplomatic rivalries as the US State Department supported the efforts of US oil companies to gain access. Subsequently, as fears of shortage turned into a problem of surplus oil by the end of the 1920s, the Middle East was divided into monopoly concessions operated by international consortia. Under the terms of the Red Line Agreement of 1928, control of the Iraqi oilfields was in the hands of the Iraq Petroleum Company, jointly owned by Shell, Anglo-Persian, CFP and a consortium of five US companies, including Jersey Standard (Wilkins 1974a: 122, 207; Venn 1986). Diplomatic rivalries – especially between the United States and Britain – frequently impacted on corporate strategies in other industries in the interwar years. British corporate strategies in copper were in part determined by considerations of blocking US firms (Alford and Harvey 1980).

Political events – in the form of Germany's defeat in the First World War – also exercised a major impact on FDI in resources. While the low German level of FDI in mining and petroleum has often been regarded as a long-term historical feature (Schröter 1993a: 38), this overlooks the extensive international investments of the metal trading companies and the Deutsche Bank in oil before the war. These business strategies were disrupted on a long-term basis. A significant German presence in the international oil industry never re-appeared, while the Metallgesellchaft did not resume substantial FDI in mining production until the 1970s.

## INTERNATIONAL COLLUSION

During the interwar years, and especially the 1930s, extensive international cartel agreements were formed in many primary commodities. These agreements were driven by the sharp falls in commodity prices in these years. However there were considerable differences in the effectiveness and longevity of these cartels. While in some products collusive arrangements proved difficult to sustain even over the short term, at the other extreme a small number of commodities remained controlled by international cartels down to the 1990s.

In the petroleum industry, the pressures towards cartelisation which had been present since the late nineteenth century became much stronger towards the end of the 1920s, and US companies became involved. As in many other commodities, expanding production in the early 1920s resulted in a growing problem of over-supply within a few years. In 1928 the world's three largest oil companies – Jersey Standard, Shell and Anglo-Persian – responded with the 'As Is' or 'Achnacarry' Agreement, named after the Scottish castle where their chief executives met.

This wide-ranging agreement was designed to bring surplus productive capacity into balance with demand by controlling competition. Each company was to accept its existing market share and not seek to increase it. They were to make their existing distribution facilities available to other producers at below the cost which a producer would incur by creating new facilities. New facilities were only to be built to meet increases in consumption. Each market was to be supplied from the nearest producing area with the object of securing the maximum economies in transportation and preventing different production areas competing for the same business. Each member of the cartel was allocated a quota for each product in each market, and would direct oil shipments on the geographically most favourable basis. Prices were to be based on those at the US Gulf of Mexico. It was intended that this agreement should apply to all countries, except the domestic market of the United States, where it faced objections under the antitrust laws. However, arrangements were also made to control US exports through the formation of associations consisting of US oil companies which accounted for almost one-half of US oil exports.

Although they became infamous symbols of the power of the 'seven sisters', in reality the oil cartels had a limited overall effect, and were unsuccessful in stabilising prices. Attempts to control US production – whose overcapacity was made worse by the discovery of the huge East Texas field in 1930 – failed, partly because of US antitrust laws. The failure to cartelise the US domestic market left the oil majors trying to organise co-operation in individual markets. Even this proved difficult. The inability to control US oil exports, as well as exports from Soviet Russia and Romania, undermined the 'As Is' Agreement, which had to be renegotiated. In a recent study, the majors emerge less as the 'masters of the environment in which they operated', and more as large but vulnerable business enterprises attempting to respond to their 'unstable and uncertain environment' (Bamberg 1994: 107–17, 517).

The experience of the oil industry was repeated in many mining industries. Wide-ranging cartel agreements were put in place, but most attempts to reduce price competition and stabilise prices were unsuccessful (Schmitz 1995). But there were contrasting experiences. The attempts to cartelise the world copper industry in the 1930s were particularly unsuccessful, largely because of the rapid growth of production from the copper belt in Africa and Canada (Navin 1978: 132–8). The cartelisation of the tin industry, which took place in response to a dramatic price fall at the end of the 1920s, was far more successful. A Tin Producers Association was formed in 1929 which established voluntary output controls, and a year later the governments of British Malaya, the Dutch East Indies, Nigeria and Bolivia signed a Tin Agreement, which established compulsory production quotas. This producers' cartel was successful in sustaining prices and became the basis of one of the world's longest running commodity agreements, which endured until 1985. A major reason for the success of international collusion in tin, as opposed to copper, lay in the willingness of the governments of the major tin producing countries to support it using their statutory powers (Hennart 1986b: 232–4; van Helten and Jones 1989: 169–70).

The world aluminium industry also became highly cartelised. Alcoa, the dominant US producer, stayed out of formal membership of the international cartels for antitrust reasons, and instead it engaged in implicit collusion with the cartels, supported by equity investments in various European producers, as well as in bauxite and water-power properties in Europe. In 1931 world cartelisation of the industry reached a new stage when the 'Aluminium Alliance' was formed, designed to stabilise markets in the wake of the Great Depression. Alcoa participated in this Alliance through its nominally independent Canadian subsidiary – Alcan – to which it had transferred virtually all its foreign properties three years previously (Stocking and Watkins 1946: 216–73).

The longevity and performance of producer cartels was heavily influenced by the structure of the market for their commodity. The fewer the number of producers and the higher the barriers to entry, the more likely it was that a cartel strategy was feasible. The greater the number of significant outside or fringe producers, the more likely that a cartel would break down. Also important in facilitating cartels was non-substitutability with other products and non-differentiation, which meant that producers could not engage in non-price competition while still maintaining high prices. The support, or otherwise, of governments was crucially important also. In the interwar years, there was substantial governmental support for commodity cartels. After the Second World War US antitrust policies made it extremely difficult to operate a cartel in a commodity in which the United States or its firms were significantly involved.

Spar suggested also that a crucial determinant of whether co-operative behaviour among producers succeeds or not lies with the internal characteristics of the producer firms. This is because the ability to make credible commitments and believable threats – both essential to the survival of cartels – is dependent on possessing a certain type of organisation, which Spar describes as autonomous and even authoritarian. It is resistant to outside pressures and lacks conflicting power groups within itself (Spar 1994).

The long-running international cartels in gold and diamonds lend support to this thesis. In both commodities there was sustained collusion and a very prominent position for the Anglo-American Corporation, which had developed into the world's largest mining company by the 1990s, with a current value (in 1993) of almost $12 billion (Ericsson and Tegen 1993). This enterprise originated as a gold mining company in South Africa, the world's largest gold producer since the late nineteenth century. In 1929 Anglo-American became a leading force in the world diamond industry through its acquisition of around one-third of De Beers, the dominant world producer (Innes 1984: 102–8). Between 1945 and 1960 Anglo-American, following the development of the Orange Free State gold-fields, became South Africa's largest gold mining group, diversified into other minerals and countries, and acquired extensive manufacturing investments in South Africa, where the largest part of its assets was located (Innes 1984; Kaplan 1983).

Anglo-American has been controlled from its inception in 1917 until the present day by the Oppenheimer family, which in the 1990s still owned around 8 per cent of the total equity, but exercised control through a complex web of cross-shareholdings in partially-owned companies. This business group was exactly the kind of autonomous and authoritarian organisation which Spar believed to be most effective in cartels. The Oppenheimer companies were highly centralised; effectively immune from takeover; and virtually free from government interference, given their enormous importance in the South African economy.

Anglo-American pursued a long-term strategy of 'orderly marketing' in the gold industry. It was able, through its leading position in the South African gold industry and that industry's importance in world gold production outside the Soviet Union, to exert a considerable influence over gold prices. This control was facilitated by long-term collusion with the Soviet gold industry, which like Anglo-American had an authoritarian and secretive structure able to sustain collaborative agreements over the long term. Although no formal cartel agreement was made, for decades the Soviets and South Africans met to regulate the supply of gold so as to keep prices high and curb speculation (Spar 1994: 137–77).

In diamonds, more formal collusion has existed over a long period up to the present day. The international diamond cartel was organised by De

Beers' London-based Central Selling Organisation (CSO), established in 1934, which controlled at least 80 per cent of world trade in rough (uncut) diamonds. De Beers' influence was initially based on South Africa's position as the only source of diamonds in the world, but over time South African production lost relative importance and by 1990 only accounted for 9 per cent of total world gemstone production. De Beers responded to this situation by developing collaborative links and long-term contracts with the new diamond producers. The cartel was (and is) based on De Beers' role as both the sole purchaser and price setter and the CSO's position as the sole distributor. By extremely close regulation of the number and types of diamonds permitted to enter the market, the cartel controls both the supply and price of diamonds. After the discovery of a large supply of diamonds in Siberia in the 1950s, the Soviets entered the diamond cartel. De Beers purchased most of the Soviet production of gems, and then marketed the stones through the CSO. The diamond cartel was an almost uniquely successful commodity cartel which kept the supply of diamonds limited and their price high for decades, though the collapse of the Soviet Union and consequently a growing threat of unofficial Russian sales reaching the market posed new challenges to the cartel's survival (Spar 1994: 29–87).

## THE GROWTH OF LARGE INTEGRATED FIRMS

### Mining

By the middle decades of the twentieth century the world mining industry had become noteworthy for its high degree of concentration of ownership and control in the hands of a relatively small number of MNEs. A fundamental influence on this process was that from the nineteenth century mining became highly capital-intensive, and required longer gestation periods following an initial investment before a product could be produced and sold (Mikesell and Whitney 1987). In the copper industry, the exploitation of copper minerals worldwide involved the mining of low-grade ores from increasingly large individual deposits. These two characteristics were linked because the lower grade ores were generally found in the larger scale ore bodies. The result was that mining companies had to finance larger-scale and more capital-intensive ventures, which yielded returns over longer time periods. The exploitation of larger and lower-grade ore deposits required capital-intensive techniques. In addition, as new regions were explored for copper, mines were established in remoter and underdeveloped areas, forcing copper companies to invest in infrastructure and forcing up the costs of labour and materials. The upshot was strong pressure towards a larger scale of operations and the growth of large companies (Schmitz 1986).

The rise of large firms was accompanied by extensive horizontal and vertical integration across borders. Horizontal integration occurred as firms sought to utilize their skills and expertise developed in one country in others, and to diversify sources of supply. This was the traditional strategy for the growth of mining firms. Vertical integration also occurred as firms sought to control all or some of the stages of production from mining or drilling, through processing and refining, to distribution and manufacture of final products. But there were considerable variations between both different minerals and different firms in the same industry. The extent of vertical integration and the way it was achieved varied considerably. Some mining firms began their corporate careers as ore-producers, before integrating forwards into smelting, refining or semi-fabrication. Others started as smelters or refiners, before integrating backwards into mining. A third variant was provided by metal trading firms, which became involved in other stages of the industry.

These differences can be shown by examining the role of MNEs in aluminium, copper, tin and iron ores. Table 3.2 identifies the major MNEs in each mineral and provides a (very crude) estimate of their share of total world production in the 1950s.

*Table 3.2*  Large MNEs in selected minerals in the 1950s

| Mineral | Combined share of world production (%) |
|---------|----------------------------------------|
| *Aluminium*: Alcoa, Reynold Metals, Kaiser Aluminium, Alcan, Péchiney, Alusuisse | 90 |
| *Copper*: Kennecott, Anaconda, Phelps Dodge, Roan-AMC, Anglo-American, Union Minière, International Nickel | 65 |
| *Tin*: London Tin Corporation, Patiño, Billiton | 45[1] |
| *Iron Ore*: Bethlehem Steel, Republic Steel, US Steel | 10? |

*Sources:* Vernon (1983: 44) for aluminium; United Nations (1980: 30) for copper; Hennart (1986b: 250) for tin; author's estimates for iron ore
*Note 1:* Before 1952

For most of the twentieth century the world aluminium industry was controlled by a small number of large vertically integrated MNEs. In the interwar years they had collaborated closely in the extensive international cartel agreements, but these arrangements were subsequently disrupted by regulatory intervention. In 1945 Alcoa was the subject of a historic Federal antitrust decision when it was ruled that although Alcoa had not intended to create a monopoly, the fact remained that it had a monopoly on the American domestic market which was in violation of antitrust law, and it would be in the nation's best interest to break it up. In the wake of this decision, US government-financed wartime aluminium plants which had been run by Alcoa were sold off to two new rivals: Reynolds Metals and Kaiser Aluminium and Chemical. In 1950 the US courts also ordered the separation of Alcoa and Alcan, its Canadian affiliate, on the grounds that the same nine shareholders controlled 44.65 per cent of Alcan's stock and 46.43 per cent of Alcoa's stock (Smith 1988). During the 1950s and 1960s these four North American firms co-existed with France's Péchiney and Alusuisse of Switzerland, and together they formed a 'big six' in the world aluminium industry.

These six MNEs were internationally vertically integrated across all three stages in the production of aluminium. They controlled almost all the world's bauxite reserves, which were largely concentrated in a number of developing countries, especially in the Caribbean and later in Africa. Once mined, the bauxite was transferred internally between the affiliates of the six MNEs for refining into alumina. Little refining was undertaken in the bauxite-producing countries, although Alcan, whose longer shipping routes made cutting transport costs important, built alumina plants in Jamaica and Guyana during the 1950s. A number of other alumina refineries were built in the Caribbean region in the 1960s, as host governments pressured companies for local processing. At the next stage a smelting process converted alumina into aluminium. This electrical process was highly energy intensive, so smelting facilities were located near low-cost sources of energy. Until 1970 the only aluminium smelter built in the Caribbean was a small one in Surinam owned by Alcoa (Rodrik 1982: 193–4).

In 1956 the six major MNEs produced most of the world's alumina and accounted for 85 per cent of the smelting capacity of the world outside the Communist countries. The strength of these companies was mainly derived from control of this processing stage. More than three-quarters of world trade in bauxite and alumina occurred internally between MNE affiliates, and no open competitive markets for these materials developed (Cobbe 1979: 26–7; Vernon 1983: 44).

The rationale for such extensive vertical integration in aluminium lay in its extremely capital-intensive nature and the existence of high economies of scale associated with the refining process. There were substantial advantages to operating smelters at as near full capacity as possible, which necessitated a continuous supply of raw material. The need for security of supply of bauxite also explained why each MNE used bauxite from a number of sources (Cobbe 1979: 27–9). A particular feature of the industry was the high asset specificity in bauxite refining, arising from the cost savings that could be obtained when refineries were built to process a single type of bauxite. As bauxites are heterogeneous, each refinery needed to obtain its bauxite from a limited number of mines, and switching costs were high. There was an obvious incentive for vertical integration by refiners to avoid opportunistic behaviour by suppliers of ores (Hennart 1987: 90–1).

Large vertically integrated MNEs were also for a time a prominent feature of the world copper industry. Based in the world's leading producer and consumer of copper, large US companies secured world leadership in the industry. In copper, unlike aluminium, control of rich ore deposits was a decisive competitive advantage. In 1911 the three largest US copper groups controlled between them 48 per cent of world copper refining output (Schmitz 1986). The largest US copper companies all became involved to some degree in FDI – even though the North American copper market can be regarded as segmented off from the rest of the world – but the degree of internationalisation and integration differed considerably. Kennecott originated as a copper mining company. It integrated into semi-fabrication in 1929, but until 1958 the company's ores were smelted and refined by ASARCO, an outcome of the Guggenheim participation in both companies. ASARCO originated as a lead smelter, and became involved in the smelting of copper in 1899. It entered the copper mining business in 1922 with an investment in Peru, and subsequently it purchased mining interests in Canada, Mexico and Australia, but it did not mine copper in the United States until 1954. ASARCO diversified abroad much more than either Kennecott or Phelps Dodge, but was less integrated into fabrication. Phelps Dodge started as a copper trader and began copper mining in the 1880s. Unlike Kennecott, it integrated into fabricated copper at a relatively early stage, and by the early 1930s was refining most of its smelter output. Phelps Dodge became the first fully integrated US copper company (Navin 1978: 228–73; Read 1986b: 300–4).

Barriers to entry to the copper industry were lower than in aluminium. Copper smelters and refiners were less capital-intensive. The ongoing discovery of large sources of copper not only undermined the interwar cartels, but provided the basis for challengers to the American leadership. A vast mineral zone was discovered in the Belgian Congo before 1914. By 1929 the Union Minière du Haut Katanga, which exploited these deposits, emerged as one of the world's leading suppliers of copper. The development of the Zambian copper deposits in the interwar years provided further opportunities for new entrants. Nevertheless the degree of concentration in the industry became considerable for a time. In the 1950s the seven largest copper mining companies accounted for 60–70 per cent of total copper output of the market economies.

The importance of large integrated MNEs in the world tin industry peaked in the interwar years. During the 1920s and 1930s a process of consolidation occurred in the industry. In Malaya, which dominated world production, many of the British free-standing companies active in tin production came under the control of the London Tin Corporation (LTC), which was formed in 1925. By 1937 the LTC controlled, through its subsidiary Anglo-Oriental, about one-third of Malaya's tin output. This company also controlled tin companies in Thailand, Burma and Nigeria. Although the alluvial nature of Southeast Asian tin provided no strong incentive for integration forwards into smelting, LTC became part owner of one of the two large smelters which smelted the whole of Malaya's output of tin concentrates.

In contrast, a vertically integrated MNE developed from the Bolivian tin industry. The Bolivian entrepreneur Patiño displaced the foreign companies which had initially developed the Bolivian industry and by 1910 had become the largest Bolivian producer of tin concentrates. This output was at first sold to smelters in Britain and Germany. In 1916 Patiño secured control of the British smelter, in partnership with the US-owned National Lead Company, a major consumer of tin. This was a rare case of a tin user acquiring interests in mining or smelting. The high physical asset specificity of the smelters required to deal with Bolivia's lode ores provided an incentive for this strategy. In 1929 Patiño also obtained control of one of the two Malayan smelters (Thoburn 1981: 64–5; Hennart 1986b: 230–2). During the 1920s the main corporate vehicle for this Bolivian company, the Patiño Mines and Enterprises Consolidated, was registered in the United States, apparently to assist the raising of capital (Klein 1965; Wilkins 1993b).

By the 1930s three groups – LTC, Patiño and the Dutch government and private company (Billiton) interests which controlled the Dutch East Indies tin industry – accounted for almost half of the world's mining and tin smelting (outside the Soviet Union) (Hennart 1986b: 250). This concentration facilitated the cartelisation of the industry, and Patiño and LTC were behind the first producers' cartel. But during the early 1950s – much earlier than in most other minerals – host governments began to take control of the production of tin. In 1952 Bolivia became the first country to take over its tin industry. This left the Patiño group still important in the marketing and smelting of tin, but broke the vertical integration with mining. From 1953 the Indonesian government began excluding Dutch companies from mining, a process which was completed by the end of the decade.

A distinguishing feature of the world iron ore industry was the modest level of FDI. The large US and European steel corporations established in the nineteenth century grew up close to their own domestic sources of iron ore and coking coal. They integrated backwards within their own economies and became integrated from mining through fabrication, but plentiful domestic supplies and high transport costs did not provide incentives to invest abroad. The iron and steel industry became characterised by powerful domestic firms which were vertically integrated within their own borders, which were protected by high tariffs and – in the interwar years – extensive international cartels. Both international trade and investment in iron ore were low. In 1950, measuring by the iron content of ore, less than 20 per cent of the world output of iron ore was exported, and over half of those exports were in intra-European trade (Cobbe 1979: 34).

From 1950 the large US steel companies began to invest on a substantial scale in mining ore overseas. The principal reasons for the change of strategy were the feared exhaustion of domestic iron ore supplies; improvements in bulk shipping capacity which reduced the cost of long ocean hauls; and the discovery of new iron ore bodies. By 1964 US-controlled companies held 74 per cent of Canada's iron ore producing capacity. The US steel companies also exploited iron ore in South America and Africa. Bethlehem Steel developed mines in Chile, Venezuela and Liberia; Republic Steel mined ore in Liberia, where by the 1960s iron ore exports were more important than rubber exports; and US Steel invested in Venezuela (Wilkins 1974a: 305–6; McKern 1976: 49–50).

Nevertheless, the role of MNEs in iron ore remained less than in bauxite, copper or even tin. Barriers for entry into production of iron ore were relatively low. The growth of the Japanese steel industry in particular provided vast opportunities for new independent producers. The iron ore industry developed as one where international vertical integration from iron ore to steel remained low, but where two-fifths of trade took place under long-term arm's length contracts between major producers and consumers (principally Brazil and West Germany, Australia and Japan), while another two-fifths was sold on more short-term contracts (Brown and McKern 1987: 56).

## Petroleum

By the middle decades of the twentieth century the world oil industry – outside North America and the Communist bloc – was dominated by a handful of large vertically integrated MNEs. In 1950 the seven major oil companies or 'seven sisters' – five American (Jersey Standard, Gulf Oil, Texaco, Standard Oil of California and Mobil) together with BP and Shell – accounted for 85 per cent of gross crude oil production and 72 per cent of refinery throughput in the world excluding North America and the Communist countries (Penrose 1968: 78). In a ranking of the world's largest industrial firms (measured by turnover) in 1956, all of the seven sisters were among the world's top twenty-five enterprises. Jersey Standard and the Shell Group were in second and third place respectively. No mining company could match them in size. Anaconda, at that time the world's largest mining company, was ranked the world's fifty-fifth largest industrial firm by this measure (Schmitz 1995).

The large petroleum companies were all vertically integrated internationally, operating at all stages of the industry beginning with the exploration and production of crude oil and ending with the distribution of the finished product to the final consumer. In the early 1950s they probably controlled 90 per cent of the oil moving in international trade. They were also extensively diversified into petrochemicals, fertilisers and other industries which used petroleum derivatives as raw materials. Vertical integration in the industry arose – or was said to arise – from the benefits to companies from assured outlets for crude oil; the more efficient operation of refineries as a result of assured and managed flows of crude oil; and the greater ability to adjust to short-run changes in the demand for different products in different areas (Penrose 1968: 46–50).

Vernon has suggested that the strategies of the large international oil companies rested on their search for stability and their 'special sense of unease' at the prospect of unregulated oil markets (Vernon 1983: 20). The investments required to develop an oilfield or build a refinery were extremely large. Once these sums had been committed, operation of the facility entailed high fixed costs. As a result, small variations in price or in output had a relatively powerful effect on profits. Short-term elasticities of both supply and demand have been low, which meant that they were both very slow to respond to price changes. Both the interwar cartels and the extensive vertical integration can be seen as responses to these conditions.

### Renewable resources

In plantation agriculture, large vertically and horizontally integrated MNEs exercised a major role in the trade of certain commodities. Table 3.3 gives examples of large MNEs which were active in agriculture in the 1950s and 1960s.

A high proportion of world trade in bananas was controlled by US MNEs. Between 1929 (when it absorbed a rival) and the late 1960s United Fruit and another US MNE, Standard Fruit, exercised a duopolistic control over the world banana export trade. Both firms were vertically and horizontally integrated MNEs which controlled the flow of bananas from the point of production through to the point of final sale. They also held geographically dispersed locations of production linked either by purchase contracts or by plantation ownership. During the 1930s United Fruit both deepened its investments in Central America, and expanded elsewhere – such as the French West Indies and Africa (Wilkins 1974a: 194–7). The size of the firm dwarfed that of several host economies. In 1955 United Fruit, by itself, contributed in tax payments 15 per cent of the total government revenues in Costa Rica and 12 per cent in Panama (Wilkins 1974a; 406–7).

*Table 3.3* Large integrated MNEs in agricultural commodities in the 1950s
and 1960s

| Company | Nationality | Activities |
|---|---|---|
| *Tropical fruit/bananas* | | |
| United Brands | US | Central American and other plantations; shipping; worldwide |
| Castle & Cooke | US | distribution |
| Del Monte | US | |
| *Palm oil/other commodities* | | |
| Unilever | UK/Dutch | Plantations in Africa, Asia, Pacific; transportation; manufacture |
| *Tea* | | |
| Brooke Bond Liebig | UK | Tea plantations in Asia and Africa; blending, packing and distribution in UK and elsewhere; cattle ranges in Africa and Latin America; manufacturing and processing in Latin America and Europe |
| *Sugar* | | |
| Tate & Lyle | UK | Sugar plantations in West Indies and Africa; shipping; refineries in UK and Canada; commodity trading |

There were modifications to the corporate structure of the banana
industry over time. Following antitrust proceedings, United Fruit was
enjoined not to acquire further banana companies, and in 1967 it had to
spin off part of its business to form a new company. Two years later
it was involved in a long takeover attempt by another company. The
resultant enterprise, renamed United Brands, experienced a series of
mishaps in the 1970s, including a hurricane which destroyed 70 per cent
of its Honduran plantations, and a Federal court conviction for bribery
of a Honduran government minister. The second member of the banana
duopoly, Standard Fruit, was acquired in 1968 by Castle & Cooke, a
Hawaiian shipping and food processing company. Finally, a third major
competitor emerged, when the Del Monte Corporation, a large US multinational fruit and vegetable processor, diversified into bananas. These
three companies continued to account for almost two-thirds of the world
banana trade through the 1980s. Their position rested on barriers to entry.
The major companies had the advantage of access to the best plantation
sites. Much of their land was obtained through concessions in return for
the provision of infrastructure improvements. Control of refrigerated
transport and contacts with retailers provided further barriers to entry
(Read 1986a: 320–1).

Beyond tropical fruits, Unilever inherited the extensive agricultural investments of its British predecessor, Lever Brothers, and over time added to them, becoming the world's largest agribusiness. The HCB subsidiary in the Belgian Congo made large losses in the early 1930s when world commodity prices collapsed. The initial strategy of collecting and transporting natural oil palm products from trees dispersed over vast areas proved too high-cost compared to the palm oil produced by plantations elsewhere. Subsequently a new strategy of intensive plantation production – not only of palm products but also of other tropical products – was implemented. By 1959 HCB had a planted area of 140,000 acres producing 54,000 tons of palm oil, as well as smaller quantities of cocoa, coffee and tea, and was probably the world's largest single plantation enterprise. Unilever also had smaller plantation investments in seven other countries. This made Unilever responsible for around 12 per cent of total world exports of palm oil in 1960 (Fieldhouse 1978: 494, 553). It has remained the world's largest single producer of palm oil.

Lever Brothers had initially engaged in vertical integration for defensive reasons, but by the 1920s the agricultural investments increasingly resembled a form of horizontal rather than vertical integration. They charged 'market prices' to the manufacturing part of the business, and were seen as autonomous business units whose function was to make a profit. Their rationale became that they already existed. The initial investment had been so large, and was so unlikely to be recovered by selling them, that Unilever considered it might as well retain the plantations and attempt to make a profit from them (Fieldhouse 1978: 450).

The growth of larger enterprises was a prominent theme of the tea industry. In the nineteenth century numerous British tea plantation companies had flourished in South Asia, but over time these came under the control of the large British managing agencies or trading companies. By 1900 one of these enterprises alone controlled numerous tea companies in India and Ceylon employing 70,000 workers (Bagchi 1972: 162). Through to the 1970s British companies controlled large shares of the total tea production in South Asia.

A number of British companies were vertically integrated from tea production to marketing. Brooke Bond developed as a tea grower, blender and packer which held at least one-third of the British tea market by the 1950s. The firm established a purchasing office in India in 1900 in order to gain more control over the source of supply rather than relying on the vagaries of the London market. After the First World War it purchased its first tea estates in India and Ceylon, and in the mid-1920s it introduced tea growing to East Africa. In both India and East Africa the firm also built blending and packing factories, and marketed its tea products. In 1968 the firm merged with another integrated British food concern, Liebig's Extract of Meat Company, which owned 2.7 million acres of cattle ranges in Argentina, Paraguay and Southern Africa together with extensive foreign manufacturing operations for meat packing in South America and for other products (such as meat cubes and canned convenience foods) in Western Europe (Wainwright nd).

Large integrated MNEs also developed in sugar cane. The sugar industry consisted of two complementary agricultural crops: cane from tropical areas and beet from temperate ones. The beet sugar industry and refineries were in the hands of strong national oligopolies usually supported by protectionist policies. Historically these firms undertook little FDI. Sugar cane was produced by estates which sold their raw sugar on the world sugar commodity markets in New York, London and Paris. There was substantial FDI in sugar plantations, some of which took the form of vertically integrated businesses. US sugar refiners invested in Cuban sugar factories. US-owned companies controlled as much as 70 per cent of Cuba's sugar output in 1934, falling to 37 per cent in 1958 (Wilkins 1974a: 406). A prominent British sugar plantation company was Booker McConnell, a trading company which had bought plantations in British Guyana in the 1830s. By the early 1950s it accounted for 70 per cent of Guyana's sugar output. The firm also owned a shipping company which transported most of Guyana's sugar to Britain (Chalmin 1990: 691–2).

The striking element in the growth of Tate & Lyle as a fully integrated sugar MNE was its timing. The firm was more a 'last-comer' than a first mover in its decision to invest in plantations. It purchased its first sugar estates in Jamaica and Trinidad only in 1937. The company, which was Britain's leading sugar refiner, had tried to invest in the emergent British beet sugar industry, but had been forced out by the creation of a quasi-state monopoly. The initial investments in the West Indies were motivated by the desire to employ resources released from the unsuccessful beet sugar venture. Over the next three decades Tate and Lyle acquired large estates and factories in Jamaica, Trinidad (where it accounted for 80 per cent of the local production), Belize, Zambia and Zimbabwe. During the 1950s it acquired large shipping interests, which included ships specially built for the transport of sugar. It also acquired the largest sugar refining company in Canada, the other major export market of West Indian sugar apart from Britain. Tate and Lyle also owned road transport to deliver refined sugar, and engineering services to build sugar factories and refineries. In 1965 Tate and Lyle diversified into commodity trading when it acquired United Molasses, the world's largest trader in molasses (Chalmin 1990).

## NEW ENTRANTS AND THE
## DECLINE OF INTEGRATION

Since the 1950s the development of international business in natural resources has represented a considerable contrast with manufacturing. As a relative proportion of world FDI, the significance of the natural resource sector has progressively and sharply declined. While manufacturing MNEs began to integrate their production internationally, in most resources there have been strong trends towards less concentration, the fragmentation of vertical integration, and the decline of intra-firm trade flows. Yet there are also parallels between manufacturing and natural resources. In both sectors, hierarchical firms with strong boundaries have given way to more complex and fluctuating patterns of control and power.

## The ownership of resources

A major reason for the decline of vertical integration was the policies of the governments of many developing countries to increase national ownership and control over natural resources. This trend led to a considerable number of expropriations of foreign assets, especially from the late 1960s. The extension of national control over resources was often accompanied by the formation of 'producer associations' – or cartels of national producers – designed to enhance the bargaining power of host countries against the vertically integrated companies. In 1973–4 OPEC emerged as the role model for such producer cartels following its unilateral huge increases in the price of oil – though it became apparent over time that this cartel was probably even less successful than the 'seven sisters' in regulating prices over the long term.

In agriculture, there was widespread nationalisation of foreign-owned plantations. In sugar cane, foreign ownership of production was virtually eliminated in many countries by nationalisation or enforced localisation during the 1970s. Tate & Lyle no longer had any sugar production facilities by the end of the decade, though Lonrho – a diversified British trading company – retained plantations in Malawi, Mauritius and other parts of Africa (Chalmin 1990: 503–30). In the tea industry, foreign plantations in Sri Lanka were nationalised in 1972, while in India the British-owned companies were required to localise their equity ownership (though not their management) in the 1970s. By the 1980s foreign-owned plantations had become unusual, although they had a continuing importance – sometimes in a partly-owned form – in products such as bananas and palm oil (Graham and Floering 1984: 49–59).

There were similar developments in minerals and petroleum. In tin, the Bolivian and Indonesian nationalisations of the 1950s were followed by the extension of state ownership, or at least state participation, in production in many other countries. A landmark event was the takeover in 1976 of the London Tin Corporation – the largest tin mining MNE – by the Malaysian government to form the Malaysia Mining Corporation (MMC). In copper, there were widespread nationalisations during the 1960s and 1970s by the established producing countries of Chile, Peru,

Zambia and Zaire (Shafer 1983). By the early 1980s about one-half of the mineral production capacity located in developing countries was state-owned (Radetzki 1989: 48). Between 1971 – when Algeria and Libya nationalised their oil industries – and 1976 virtually every major oil producing developing country nationalised their oil industry. As a result the long-established pattern of equity ownership of oil-producing concessions by the oil MNEs was virtually eliminated (Kobrin 1985: 13–17).

These developments meant that the natural resource MNEs became increasingly dependent on arm's length transactions for their raw material needs. As their international vertical integration was broken up, they became more vulnerable to the vagaries of the market. Figure 3.1 shows the scale of the loss of control over production by the oil majors.

This pattern was repeated throughout the primary sector, though the timing and extent of change varied. While in 1960 the leading seven copper corporations still controlled between 60 and 70 per cent of copper production, two decades later the seven largest private companies controlled less than 23 per cent of copper production (United Nations 1980: 30). In the 1980s the copper industry was integrated, but mainly within national boundaries, where state-owned enterprises accounted for over 40 per cent of copper mining capacity and substantial percentages of smelting and refining capacity. In iron ore also, the internationally vertically integrated structure was curtailed by widespread nationalisations and the consequent

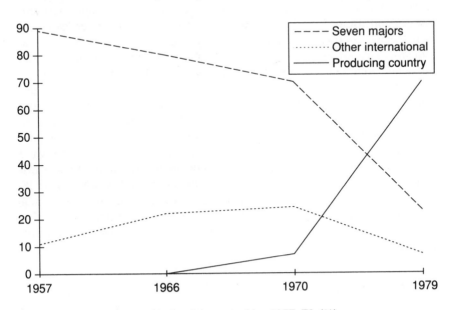

*Figure 3.1* Crude oil production by ownership, 1957–79 (%)
*Source*: Vernon 1983: 27
*Note*: Excludes crude oil produced in the United States and communist countries

formation of state-owned enterprises, which by the late 1970s accounted for almost 40 per cent of internationally traded ore (Vernon and Levy 1982: 172–3).

The loss of ownership did not always imply a decline in the control which MNEs exercised over the production of commodities. While the ownership of plantations declined, MNEs continued to exert considerable influence over developing country agriculture through various forms of contract. In the banana industry, the US MNEs developed the 'Associate Producers' system under which they sold or leased some of their plantations to local independent producers. The Associate Producers remained dependent on the companies through the latter's control over production inputs and technical assistance, and through the long-term contracts in which the MNEs set the purchase price of a given grade of banana. The MNEs also retained control over transport and distribution in the main markets – so that third party companies could not purchase the surplus fruit and the local producers could not dispose of unsold supplies. This kind of contract farming enabled MNEs to avoid conflicts over land ownership and labour issues, and lessened the risk of expropriation because fewer assets were located within the host country (United Nations 1987: 11; Glover 1986).

In many cases MNEs responded to the new circumstances by increasing the importance of transportation, international marketing and distribution, and by increased use of marketing strategies involving product differentiation, and use of brand names in order to maintain customer loyalty to firm-specific products, as well as to strengthen barriers to entry in the industry. This kind of strategy was particularly prominent in the food and beverage commodities. The large US banana MNEs pursued product differentiation strategies in the 1960s and 1970s. When US antitrust rulings obliged the banana companies to limit their control over marketing and distribution intermediaries in the United States, United Fruit followed by construction and renovation of ripening rooms, staff training, and the maintenance of warehouses and retail distribution. The US-owned companies also geographically diversified through expansion into Western Europe and Japan. At the end of the 1970s the three US MNEs held 90 per cent of the US market. In Japan, the US companies increased their market share from 33 per cent to 84 per cent in the first half of the 1970s – displacing in the process the independent Ecuadorian banana producer, Noboa (United Nations 1987: 17–18).

## New entrants

The emergence of new competitors to the established MNEs changed the corporate structure of world resource industries as much as host government policies. Some of the leading new competitors were in fact state-owned companies which had acquired the production assets of the MNEs. By the early 1980s state-owned entities controlled about one-half of the mineral production capacity in the developing countries (Radetzki 1989: 48). In most cases state mineral enterprises did not undertake FDI and did not attempt to integrate forwards, although there were a small number of exceptions, especially in copper. Both Codelco of Chile and ZCCM of Zambia made investments in European downstream processing of copper. Codelco became the world's largest copper producer on the basis of copper mines formerly owned by the US MNEs in Chile. These state-owned mining companies were often perceived as relatively unsuccessful. ZCCM became a byword for the management problems and resulting inefficiency of the new state-owned firms (Radetzki 1989: 49–50). But other state-owned mining companies developed as sound business enterprises, well capable of competing with the Western MNEs.

The MNEs often developed contractual and equity relationships with the state-owned mining enterprises. While the state companies could sell products such as copper for which there existed a competitive world market, in the case of products like bauxite in which no open market existed, they often formed joint ventures with foreign companies. The joint venture form became increasingly common in the aluminium industry, and often worked to the advantage of the MNEs, which were frequently able to negotiate favourable supply and management arrangements (Rodrik 1982: 207). These provided foreign minerals companies with assured sources of raw material, and the state company with an assured market.

In the petroleum industry, a few state-owned companies became vertically integrated MNEs. The Kuwait Petroleum Company (KPC) pursued one of the most ambitious strategies. During the 1960s the Kuwaiti government obliged the company which controlled its oil production – a joint venture between BP and Gulf Oil – to relinquish part of its concession to a state company, which also established a refinery in Kuwait. During the early 1970s foreign ownership of Kuwait's oilfields was completely eliminated, and in 1980 the Kuwait Petroleum Company was established to manage the various government oil activities. During the 1980s KPC expanded into exploitation and distribution abroad, buying (in 1983) Gulf Oil's refining and marketing networks in various European countries.

State-owned entities were far from the only new entrants into natural resources in the primary sector. In the oil industry, the rise of 'other' international oil companies is clear from Figure 3.1 These included European state-owned oil companies such as CFP – which was virtually the eighth member of the seven sisters – and AGIP of Italy, which was part of Italy's state energy-holding corporation, Ente Nazionale Idrocarburi (ENI). During the 1950s AGIP developed an innovative strategy for negotiating oil concessions with producer states by offering them a 'partnership' in the exploitation of their natural resources. The same strategy was applied when the Italian company sought concessions to build refineries and distribute its refined products in developing countries. AGIP also formed distribution companies in many European countries and Africa. Using imported Soviet oil, AGIP could offer the lowest gasoline prices in Europe. Among the other oil independents which competed for concessions and markets were the US independents such as Getty Oil, Occidental, Amerada, Ohio and Continental. These US and other independents seriously weakened the influence of the oil majors on world prices and increased the bargaining power of the producer governments.

While the oil majors were under competitive challenge in their own industry, they sought to diversify by entering metal mining. An early example of this phenomenon was Shell's acquisition in 1970 of Billiton, a company which had diversified from tin mining in the Dutch East Indies into bauxite, and subsequently into other minerals (Thoburn 1981: 67). In the copper industry, in 1977 Anaconda was purchased by Atlantic Richfield Company – the pioneer oil explorer in Alaska. In 1981 BP acquired Kennecott through its US affiliate Standard Oil of Ohio. Among the US oil companies, Exxon made substantial investments in Chilean copper, while Standard Oil of Indiana (Amoco) undertook FDI in copper, gold and other minerals. This diversification into minerals proved less than successful in many cases, and was reversed subsequently, sometimes after heavy losses. In 1989 BP sold most of its mining and minerals business, including Kennecott, to its fellow British MNE, RTZ. Five years later Shell sold its Billiton metals and mining assets to Gencor, a South African mining group.

The large mining MNEs also diversified into other products to reduce risks and to achieve more balanced earnings (Mikesell and Whitney 1987: 37–9). This led to some minerals attracting substantial FDI for the first time, such as black coal (McKern 1976: 67–70). The mining MNEs became holders of broad portfolios of investments in a substantial range of minerals. The growth of RTZ into one of the world's largest mining MNEs demonstrated this trend. In the late 1940s the Rio Tinto Company possessed only its old Spanish mines – finally sold in 1954 after many difficulties with the Fascist government in Spain – and a share of the Zambian copper belt, acquired in the interwar years. But subsequent product and geographical diversification led to the firm's transformation. Its acquisition of Kennecott – which doubled its size – extended and deepened the range of mines in which it held a substantial share of the world production. In the early 1990s RTZ was the world's leading producer of titanium, among the three largest producers of bauxite, copper, iron ore and lead, and among the ten largest for – among other things – tin, silver, lithium and molybdenum (Ericsson and Tegen 1993).

During the 1970s and subsequently, affiliates of mining MNEs themselves became large international firms. RTZ's partly-owned Australian affiliate Conzinc Rio Tinto of Australia (CRA) developed into one of the large Australian mining companies, with diversified activities in Australia and beyond, including subsequent FDI in copper mining in Papua New Guinea. Another example in the aluminium industry was Alcoa of Australia, formed in 1961 as a joint venture between Alcoa and a group of Australian mining companies, which became the world's largest aluminium producer over the following three decades.

In aluminium, the large integrated MNEs retained their market share much later than in many other products. After 1971 there was considerable nationalisation in the industry, which included the major bauxite exporting countries of Guyana and Jamaica, but the aluminium MNEs exploited new ore deposits in places such as Australia (Rodrik 1982: 199–205). In 1982 six major MNEs still controlled 46 per cent of world bauxite production, and 50 per cent and 45 per cent respectively of the refining and smelting of alumina and aluminium (Brown and McKern 1987: 92). But subsequently the vertically integrated MNEs progressively lost control over the industry. State-owned companies in Venezuela and the Arabian Gulf built large smelters, whose location was increasingly decided by the availability of the cheapest sources of energy. Japanese companies invested in smelting capacity in foreign countries or supplied technology to foreign smelters in return for long-term contracts to supply the Japanese market. Markets developed for bauxite and alumina. Nevertheless the level of intra-firm trade remained high, and by the beginning of the 1990s about two-thirds of alumina was still traded among affiliates (Wells 1993: 337–52).

In agriculture, MNEs also diversified into new products in response to changed circumstances and the breaking of old lines of vertical integration. In the sugar industry, Tate & Lyle evolved first towards becoming a commodity trader, and then, after a catastrophic collapse in world sugar prices in 1978, diversified into other sweeteners, especially corn syrup. The firm focused on the sugar and sweeteners market in Europe and the United States, where it made a series of large acquisitions, culminating in 1988 with the purchase of Staley, one of the four US firms producing high-fructose syrup (Chalmin 1986, 1990).

As in minerals, MNEs specialising in a single or a few products were often absorbed into wider conglomerates. In 1984 Brooke Bond Liebig, by then Europe's leading tea company, was acquired by Unilever. This purchase complemented Unilever's Lipton brand of tea in the United States, and made Unilever the world's largest tea business (Chalmin 1990: 707–8). Del Monte, the tropical fruits MNE, was first acquired by the US tobacco company R. J. Reynolds in 1979, and then in the early 1990s sold off in several parts, with its branded food and beverages business coming into the orbit of the Anglo-American Corporation.

## SUMMARY

During the nineteenth century international business played a key role in the global search for raw materials and foodstuffs for the markets of the industrialised world. Numerous entrepreneurial firms were formed to engage in this search. Western-owned firms brought a large proportion of the world's resources under their ownership or control. These firms possessed ownership advantages in technology, management, finance and information, and were often able to construct large barriers to entry by virtue of the concession system. MNEs employed a variety of strategies including vertical integration, networks, and long-term contracting to secure and retain control of natural resources in the face of unpredictable changes in markets, technologies and political conditions.

In many commodities there were strong internalisation arguments for integration and, together with the capital-intensive nature of mining, this led to the emergence of large oligopolistic firms in many industries. A high proportion of the world trade in commodities such as petroleum, aluminium and bananas was intra-firm inside the large integrated MNEs. In the interwar years – and sometimes later – these firms also co-operated in extensive international cartels designed to stabilise markets, though this aim was rarely achieved over the long term.

This business structure began to change from the 1950s, and the pace of change accelerated from the 1970s. The advantages of long-established MNEs were eroded by host government intervention, the increased bargaining strength of hosts, and the diffusion of technology and management skills. Vertical integration down to the production level was weakened or eliminated in most commodities. MNEs responded by moving into higher value-added transportation, processing and marketing activities and by horizontal diversification strategies. The boundaries of firms became more flexible as control was exercised by contracts rather than equity, and as joint ventures proliferated. MNEs in many commodities faced new sources of instability and risk as even some of the most organised of markets, such as diamonds, encountered problems in controlling new entrants. Nonetheless, the resource MNEs remained among the most powerful forces within international business in the 1990s.

# Chapter 4

# Multinational manufacturing

## INTERNATIONAL BUSINESS AND MANUFACTURING

Multinational strategies have figured prominently in nearly all of the world's most dynamic manufacturing industries since the late nineteenth century. The firms that pioneered the capital-intensive technologies of the Second Industrial Revolution of the late nineteenth century – chemicals, electricals and machinery – rapidly expanded into international markets. The automobile producers followed in their path, as did their post-Second World War successors in petrochemicals, pharmaceuticals, computers and semiconductors. These industries transformed living standards and lifestyles in each generation through the development of countless new products. International business was at the heart of the process whereby such innovation in manufacturing was spread across borders.

The scale and significance of multinational manufacturing raises the key issues in international business. How and why did MNEs become so important in the world's leading industries? While resource MNEs had to invest abroad because of the realities of geology or climate, why did manufacturing companies choose not to export their products but rather to build factories in foreign countries? How were complex technologies and products transferred between countries by firms? And how did managers control such transfers?

Manufacturing, like natural resources, is heterogeneous. International business strategies and organisational patterns have been conditioned by industry-specific conditions. The approach taken here is to offer broad generalisations about developments in multinational manufacturing over time, but to illustrate the diversity in the historical experience by focusing on specific industries at particular stages in their development.

## ORIGINS AND GROWTH

### Overview

Multinational manufacturing grew from the 1830s, planted stronger roots in the 1850s and 1860s, and by 1914 was an important element of the world economy. Many early investments were short-lived, but the mid-century saw direct investments in manufacturing which were more durable. In 1855 Siemens and Halske, the German firm which pioneered the development of telegraph and cable equipment, built a factory at St Petersburg following orders from the Russian government for the construction and maintenance of a telegraph network. This was managed by a brother of the firm's founder. In 1863 another brother established a factory for the production of sea cables in Britain (Hertner 1986). Both these foreign businesses lasted until the First World War. Also in 1855 Saint-Quirin, a French glass company which was a predecessor to Saint Gobain, built a factory in Mannheim, Germany, which also became a long-lasting venture (Daviet 1989). In 1865 J & J Clark, a Scottish cotton thread producer, opened a factory in Newark, New Jersey, and two years later Singer opened its sewing machine factory in Glasgow, Scotland. By 1914 numerous other multinational manufacturing investments had been made by firms which differed greatly in terms of size, longevity, organisation, nationality and industry.

In terms of size, a number of large-scale MNEs developed over the course of the late nineteenth century. Singer provides a striking example. Singer's growth was based on the invention at the beginning of the 1850s of the world's first commercially successful sewing machine. By 1867 Singer had become the largest manufacturer of sewing machines in the world. Singer's first foreign factory at Glasgow proved a great success. It began by assembling parts imported from the United States. Over time it manufactured the heavy stands of the machines, and assembled them with imported machine heads. Finally, it began to manufacture entire machines and supply them to other markets. In 1885 Singer opened a new factory near Glasgow. This was the largest sewing machine factory in the world. The firm opened other factories in Canada, Austria and Germany, and in 1901 a Russian factory was opened outside Moscow, which by 1914 employed over 3,000 workers.

The growth of Singer's manufacturing outside the United States was intimately connected with the firm's dynamic and successful investment in overseas marketing. Building on its practice in the United States, Singer used its own sales offices to market sewing machines, selling its products through hire purchase. By 1890 Singer's sewing machines were sold virtually worldwide and almost entirely by its own employees, and the firm controlled around 80 per cent of the world market. As its markets in North American and Western Europe became saturated, Singer employed its sales strategies to great effect in new markets, especially Russia. Singer's sales in Russia rose from 70,000 machines in 1895 to almost 700,000 machines in 1914. Singer's Russian company had an elaborate network of offices and around 4,000 depots, stores and shops, and employed over 27,000 people. Thousands of Singer agents – who received a weekly salary plus commission – were responsible for selling machines, collecting instalment payments, and even doing minor service on machines (Davies 1976; Carstensen 1984).

Singer was unusual, and co-existed with many far smaller investments. Multinational manufacturing was far from the preserve of big business. Many MNE investments, especially by European firms, were on a modest scale, and sometimes undertaken by very 'small' companies. Numerous examples of such small investments can be cited before 1914. In the 1900s the French manufacturing subsidiary of the Swiss chemicals company Ciba had a mere twelve workers (Schröter 1991, 1993c). The Norwegian firm of Mustad & Son, which built a factory in Britain in 1911 to manufacture horseshoe nails, had a workforce of less than fifty (Bostock and Jones 1994).

The multinational investments of this era varied as greatly in their longevity as in their size. Many of the largest US and European MNEs of the 1990s (or their predecessor companies) had made considerable direct investments before 1914. The list includes Nestlé, Unilever, General Electric and Siemens. They were first movers in their industries, and were able to establish market positions which proved hard to challenge. These positions were preserved by sustained corporate competences which were renewed generation after generation. However such enterprises, although of great importance, were atypical. Numerous failed investments and divestments co-existed with more successful ones. Multinational manufacturing was a high risk strategy in which a high failure rate was to be anticipated.

The organisational forms used to engage in multinational manufacturing varied greatly also. Singer developed a considerable managerial hierarchy which was capable of co-ordinating and controlling production, distribution and sales on a worldwide basis. This worked well with that firm's highly standardised products, but other US MNEs faced by more complex product markets used looser organisational forms (Carstensen 1984). Modern managerial firms were not the only ones to engage in FDI. A considerable number of the pre-1914 MNEs from European economies were family owned and managed. Examples included many Swiss MNEs (such as Geigy in chemicals and Maggi and Wander in food production), as well as Swedish, Dutch and Belgian firms (Schröter 1993b). Free-standing firms appeared in some sectors. This mode was employed in the British investment in US beer-making in the late nineteenth century, which for a time resulted in British-owned breweries being ranked among the largest business enterprises in the United States (Wilkins 1989: 324–30).

The nationality of these pioneer manufacturing MNEs was as mixed as their other characteristics. There were considerable and very significant US firms active abroad by 1914, but in sheer numbers Western European-owned companies were pre-eminent. German and British companies appeared the most numerous and included some of the larger multi-national groups, but many French, Swiss, Swedish, Belgian and Dutch firms were active abroad by 1914. There were rarer examples from other countries such as Italy, where the electrical firm Pirelli made direct investments in Spain, Britain and Argentina between 1902 and 1913 (Wilkins 1986c, 1988b; Schröter 1993c; Montenegro 1993). Even the first Japanese FDI in manufacturing occurred in these years. This largely took the form of small investments in textile spinning and weaving in China in the 1900s, but also included the opening of a soy sauce factory in Denver, Colorado in the 1890s by Kikkoman (Wilkins 1986b, 1989).

There were examples of multinational manufacturing in numerous products by 1914. FDI strategies were prominent in the high technology industries of this era – chemicals and machinery – but were also found in numerous consumer goods. British companies manufactured dog food and toffee in the United States, and marmalade in Germany. A German firm manufactured malt coffee – a cheap coffee-substitute made from barley – in Austria, Sweden, Russia and Spain. United States, British and German MNEs made gramophone machines and records all over Europe, as well as in India, Brazil and Argentina (Wilkins 1989: 352–9; Hertner 1986; Jones 1985).

A common element of an otherwise diverse picture was that MNEs were engaged in moving the latest and the newest technological accomplishments, products and processes around the industrialising nations of the world (Wilkins 1974a). For the most part, MNEs were active in the products which developed during the Second Industrial Revolution rather than the First. This can be seen in the case of the United Kingdom, where there was a considerable contrast between the industrial structure of its manufactured exports and that of its manufacturing FDI. By the end of the nineteenth century textiles still accounted for around two-fifths of total British exports, with iron and steel and machinery accounting for a further one-quarter. These were the products in which the United Kingdom held a comparative advantage in the world economy. The British firms in these industries undertook almost no FDI, in contrast to their counterparts in branded consumer products, cotton thread, tyres and artificial silk. Multinational enterprise flourished in industries in which technology, brands and product differentiation were important features.

## Chemicals, machinery and consumer goods

The late nineteenth century saw remarkable developments in the chemical industry, associated with the application of scientific research to industrial processes. Thousands of new products were invented. It was an industry in which European, especially German, companies were immensely strong. The German chemical companies grew as large managerial enterprises which made long-term investment in research and production. In some sectors the German superiority was crushing. In artificial dyestuffs the total value of the production of the eight German firms (including their foreign subsidiaries) amounted to three-quarters of total world production in the 1900s. German firms were vigorous exporters of their new products, but they also invested abroad on a substantial scale (Schröter 1990a).

The leading German dyestuffs firms, BASF, Bayer and Hoechst, established their first foreign subsidiaries in Russia and France in the 1870s and 1880s, followed later by the United States and Britain. Bayer, the largest firm, had taken a minority interest in a US manufacturing company in 1871, and although this particular investment was later disposed of, Bayer became a substantial manufacturer in the United States. In 1914 Bayer owned three of the seven dyestuff plants in the United States, and it also manufactured there the new pharmaceutical products which it had developed, notably aspirin. The German companies supported their manufacturing operations in the United States with extensive nationwide sales organisations (Wilkins 1989: 389–95). In Russia, five German manufacturers established six dyestuffs factories which accounted for around 80 per cent of the German dyes sold on the Russian market in 1913 (Plumpe 1990: 59).

Bayer and Hoechst had large pharmaceutical operations, but there were also specialised German pharmaceutical firms which went abroad before 1914. E. Merck, to give one example, began manufacturing pharmaceuticals (including morphine, codeine and cocaine) in the United States in 1899, and started production in France in 1912 (Hertner 1986). Further FDI was undertaken by the leading German electrochemical firms, such as Degussa, the largest German producer of cyanides by the electrolytic process. By 1914 this firm's US subsidiary had four manufacturing plants in operation producing a variety of cyanides, bleaching agents, sodium and chloroform (Wilkins 1989: Chapter 11; Chandler 1990: 474–86).

While the importance of German firms in chemicals was striking, other European firms were active in particular sectors. Swiss dyestuffs firms invested in neighbouring countries, and sometimes further afield. The first Swiss chemical FDI occurred in 1882 when a dyestuffs firm built a small factory near Lyon, France to supply the textiles industry. Ten years later this factory was sold to another Swiss firm, Geigy, which had already begun manufacturing in Russia in 1888. By 1914 Geigy, Ciba and Sandoz had small-scale manufacturing in the United States, Britain, France and Germany, while the Swiss pharmaceuticals manufacturer Hoffmann La Roche had opened a factory in Britain in 1909 (Schröter 1991: 230–66). The Belgian chemical firm Solvay & Cie also developed a large multi-national business to exploit its invention of a continuous process to make caustic soda, which was used in the manufacture of glass, textiles and other chemicals (Bolle 1968). In contrast, the US manufacturers of industrial chemicals and pharmaceuticals, such as Du Pont, Dow Chemical and Monsanto only rarely ventured beyond their home market before the Second World War (Chandler 1990: 175–87).

The machinery industries of the late nineteenth century resembled chemicals in the proliferation of new products. Unlike chemicals, machinery was an industry in which US-based companies became prominent international investors. They pioneered the mass production of machinery by fabricating and assembling interchangeable parts, and as a result US firms became world leaders in many products (Chandler 1990: Chapter 6). A considerable proportion of US manufacturing FDI in Europe originated from this sector. Otis Elevator became the first world-wide producer of lifts, with factories in Britain, Germany, France and Canada by 1914. National Cash Register became the world's firstmover in cash registers, and had factories in Germany and Canada by 1914. Among the European enterprises active in standardised light-machinery products was Germany's Accumulatoren-Fabrik AG, which from the 1890s built a network of storage battery factories across Europe from Britain to Russia, and an international marketing network which extended from Buenos Aires to Cairo and Tokyo (Chandler 1990: 403–8).

In electrical engineering two German firms – Siemens and Allgemeine Elektricitäts-Gesellschaft (AEG) and two US firms – General Electric (GE) and Westinghouse – formed a global oligopoly which dominated the world electrical industry until the 1940s. By 1914 Siemens had ten foreign factories spread over five countries (von Weiher and Goetzeler 1977: 58–60). AEG, which was founded in 1883, acquired factories in Russia and Austria-Hungary and established joint venture production subsidiaries with GE in Italy and Siemens in Russia (Chandler 1990: 464–74). From the formation of GE in 1892 the firm expanded abroad, building a network of overseas subsidiaries in which it had equity stakes, though not always controlling ones, mostly operated by its Thomson-Houston subsidiary. A contrasting strategy was that of Westinghouse, who constructed a number of large overseas factories, beginning with a giant plant in Manchester, England in 1899. By 1914 other large factories were owned in Germany, France, Russia and Canada. Size was no guarantor of profitability, and during the First World War the firm divested from European manu-facturing (Wilkins 1970: 93–6).

Swedish electrical engineering companies also became internationally important in a number of specialist products. ASEA, which pioneered methods of electrical transmission in the 1890s, acquired a British manufacturing company in 1898. L. M. Ericsson developed a large overseas business – exporting 95 per cent of its production at the turn of the century – and then built factories in the United States, Russia, Britain and elsewhere in Europe, manufacturing telephone exchanges and sets for local markets (Olsson 1993: 103–4).

In consumer goods industries also, MNEs transferred the latest products and processes between countries. Nestlé originated as one of a cluster of Swiss firms producing condensed milk, baby food and chocolates. The Anglo-Swiss Condensed Milk Company, which despite its name was a purely Swiss company, established a British factory to produce condensed milk in 1872, and an American plant ten years later. This enterprise also expanded elsewhere, although in 1902 it divested from the United States by selling its business to the US company Borden. Three years later Anglo-Swiss merged with another Swiss firm Nestlé, which had itself established foreign condensed milk factories by the turn of the century. By 1914 the combined business manufactured condensed milk and baby food products in Britain, the United States, Australia, Norway, Germany and Spain. Nestlé also had a large shareholding in a Swiss chocolate company which manufactured chocolate in the United States and elsewhere (Wilkins 1989: 331–5).

The Dutch and British predecessors of Unilever were large-scale multinational investors prior to 1914. Van den Bergh and Jurgens, the leading Dutch margarine companies, established factories in Germany and Belgium; by 1914 each Dutch firm had seven margarine factories in Germany. In Britain, the Dutch companies invested in distribution, forming relationships with retailing groups which led, by 1914, to the acquisition of full control over several chains of retail shops (Wilson 1954, II: 122–38). The British predecessor to Unilever was Lever Brothers, the soap manufacturer, which between 1890 and 1914 erected or purchased factories in numerous countries, in several of which it controlled multiplant operations. In Canada, the British firm had eight factories in six cities by 1914, while in France Lever had three factories in two cities (Wilson 1954, I: 98–110, 188–210).

### Significance by 1914

Multinational manufacturing was widespread by 1914. Amidst the galaxy of small or failed investments, some manufacturing companies had established extensive multi-country and multi-plant manufacturing. Table 4.1 lists some of these multinational giants.

*Table 4.1* Some large multinational manufacturing enterprises, c. 1914

| Company | Nationality | Product | No. of foreign factories in 1914 | Location of foreign factories |
|---|---|---|---|---|
| Singer | US | Sewing machines | 5 | UK, Canada, Germany, Russia |
| J & P Coats | UK | Cotton thread | 20 | US, Canada, Russia, Austria-Hungary, Spain, Belgium, Italy, Switzerland, Portugal, Brazil, Japan |
| Nestlé | Swiss | Condensed milk/ baby food | 14 | US, UK, Germany, Netherlands, Norway, Spain Australia |
| Lever Brothers | UK | Soap | 33 | US, Canada, Germany, Switzerland, Belgium, France, Japan, Australia, South Africa |
| St Gobain | French | Glass | 8 | Germany, Belgium, Netherlands, Italy, Spain, Austria-Hungary |
| Bayer | German | Chemicals | 7 | US, UK, France, Russia, Belgium |
| American Radiator | US | Radiators | 6 | Canada, UK, France, Germany, Italy, Austria-Hungary |
| Siemens | German | Electricals | 10 | UK, France, Spain, Austria-Hungary, Russia |
| L. M. Ericsson | Swedish | Telephone equipment | 8 | US, UK, France, Austria-Hungary, Russia |
| Accumulatoren-Fabrik | German | Batteries | 8 | UK, Austria-Hungary, Spain, Russia, Poland, Romania, Sweden |

The manufacturing subsidiaries of these companies were often large business enterprises, employing a thousand or more workers, and even larger numbers when the firms also undertook FDI in marketing and distribution. For some firms multinational manufacturing had already become an important part of their business. Saint Gobain's German factories accounted for almost two-fifths of the French firm's total glass production in 1913 (Daviet 1989: 130). By the same date Singer's sales in Russia alone accounted for over 30 per cent of its total worldwide sales (Carstensen 1984: 55). In 1914 almost one-fifth of Siemens's total workforce of 80,000 were employed outside Germany (von Weiher and Goetzeler 1977: 60).

In terms of market share, foreign-owned manufacturing affiliates had secured prominent positions in their host economies. In the United States, the production of a number of products was either wholly dominated by, or substantially in the hands of, foreign MNEs, including cotton thread, rayon, magnetos, cream separators, alkali and dyestuffs (Wilkins 1989: 621). There were similar examples elsewhere. In Germany, foreign-owned companies were pre-eminent in products as diverse as elevators and margarine. In Britain, they were the major forces in strategic parts of the dyestuffs and electrical engineering industries. In Japan, foreign affiliates controlled the rubber industry and a number of other advanced technology products.

**The interwar followers**

The First World War produced distinct winners and losers among the established manufacturing MNEs. The winners included the firms owned by the European countries which had managed to stay neutral, notably Sweden, Switzerland and the Netherlands. Their subsidiaries were free to operate in the countries on both sides. In some cases the war presented considerable opportunities. The growth of the Swedish company SKF to become the world's largest ball-bearing manufacturer was greatly facilitated by its ability to undertake war production on both sides. Wartime profits enabled the Swedish company to buy up the entire German ball-bearing industry in the 1920s (Lundström 1992: 156–7).

German companies were the most prominent losers, and in many cases the dynamic international strategies of the pre-1914 era gave way to risk-averse alternatives in the interwar years. A striking case was the chocolate manufacturer Gebrüder Stollwerck, which had built the second largest chocolate factory in the United States – in Stamford, Connecticut – as well as smaller factories in Britain and Austria, and also diversified into the multinational manufacture of vending machines. Having lost its foreign factories, in the interwar years Gebrüder Stollwerck confined its FDI to Eastern Europe (Chandler 1990: 399–400, 515). In chemicals, the loss of intangible assets such as brand names and patents was perhaps even worse than that of physical assets. Bayer only recovered the right to use its own brand name in the North American market in 1994, and then at a cost of $1 billion.

In the interwar years German manufacturing companies, reluctant to re-enter multinational production, often preferred to participate in international cartels and other arrangements which did not involve the investment of large sums of capital abroad, though German MNE activity was greater than the overall FDI estimates might suggest. The number of German-owned foreign production subsidiaries in chemicals fell from 153 in 1913 to a mere 24 in 1920, but the numbers had grown to 128 in 1930, and 144 by 1938 (Schröter 1990a; Schröter forthcoming). The large German enterprises often re-built extensive international distribution networks after the War, even if their foreign production remained modest. IG Farben – a giant chemicals company formed in the mid 1920s by the merger of eight firms including Bayer, BASF and Hoechst – had 726 subsidiaries or partly-owned affiliates in foreign countries by the end of the 1930s. Two-thirds of these were sales agencies, and most of the remainder were engaged in the finishing and packaging of pharmaceuticals and dyes (V. Schröter 1984: 388).

Manufacturing grew in complexity in the interwar years. Companies went to more foreign countries, and built more plants, and manufactured more products in individual foreign countries. An extreme case was the Swedish Match Company, which during the 1920s expanded rapidly from its Swedish base led by the entrepreneurial figure of Ivar Kreuger. At its greatest extent Swedish Match controlled 144 producing units in thirty-three different countries. By 1930 companies owned at least 50 per cent by Swedish Match accounted for more than 40 per cent of the total world match production. These subsidiaries were linked through a diverse range of equity and contractual arrangements. In certain countries (such as Germany and much of Eastern Europe), Swedish Match operated state match monopolies, sometimes secured by the company providing loans to the respective governments. Even after Kreuger's suicide in 1932, which led to a complete reconstruction of Swedish Match, the group remained a widespread multinational manufacturer, with seventy manufacturing companies in thirty-one countries (Hildebrand 1985).

Complexity of a different sort was illustrated by British American Tobacco (BAT). The origins of BAT lay with the American Tobacco Company, which had exploited the commercial possibilities of the invention of continuous-process cigarette machinery to become the biggest cigarette enterprise in the United States by the turn of the century. During the 1890s American Tobacco made manufacturing investments in Australia, Canada, Germany and Japan. The acquisition of a leading British producer in 1901 led to a violent reaction from British competitors, thirteen of which combined to form the Imperial Tobacco Company. In 1902 a compromise was reached between the Americans and the British. The US market was reserved for the American Tobacco and the UK market for Imperial Tobacco, while they created a new company, BAT, to control tobacco production and marketing in the rest of the world. It developed a global cigarette business. New factories were established in Belgium, Denmark,

India, Egypt, Palestine and Brazil, and a series of factories were established in China (Cox 1989).

Although British-based, BAT was initially US-controlled and managed, but this American influence was diluted after American Tobacco was ordered to be dissolved under US antitrust law in 1911, and by the early 1920s BAT had become British-controlled. BAT's multinational manufacturing expanded rapidly. By 1914 it was manufacturing in China between one-half and two-thirds of the 12 billion cigarettes it sold in that market. In the 1920s it had around 25,000 Chinese working in its factories. The firm was fully integrated from control over the growing of tobacco through all stages of production and forward to distribution and marketing in China. During the 1920s BAT not only took shares in Chinese distribution companies, but also made large numbers of films – designed to promote cigarettes – and purchased a network of cinemas to show them in. The number of cigarettes sold by BAT in China reached 80 billion in 1928 (Cochran 1980). By the 1930s the firm's factories spread from Australia to Africa to Latin America (Cox 1989).

The interwar years also saw the creation of Unilever. This firm was formed in 1930 through a merger of Britain's Lever Brothers and the Margarine Union of the Netherlands, which included the firms of Van den Berghs and Jurgens. The combined business had a worldwide distribution of assets which included not only soap and margarine factories, and the huge plantation interests discussed in Chapter 3, but also trading companies, ships, retail shops and much more. This extensive multinational was distinguished by its joint British and Dutch ownership and control. The business was controlled by two holding companies – Unilever Limited registered in London and Unilever NV registered in the Netherlands – with identical boards of directors. The structure was such that the British and Dutch shareholders would receive dividends of equal value. The new concern had two head offices, in London and Rotterdam. The latter supervised Unilever's extensive business in continental Europe, while London supervised the British and overseas activities. Beneath the boards a complex administrative system was developed to control the business (Wilson 1954, II: 309–72). Unilever thus became one of a handful of companies – like its Anglo-Dutch twin Shell – whose ownership and management was shared between two different countries.

## Automobiles and food in the interwar years

The interwar years saw divergences in the international business strategies pursued in different manufacturing industries. In industries characterised by high levels of oligopoly, such as chemicals and electricals, international collusion became extensive (see pp. 123–7). In other industries, such as automobiles and branded and packaged foodstuffs, multinational strategies were preferred.

The growth of the multinational automobile industry began before the First World War. The world automobile industry developed first in France in the late 1890s (Laux 1992: 7–8), and it was European companies which initially undertook FDI. French car companies such as Renault established distribution operations in the United States and elsewhere, and in a limited number of countries small assembly plants were established, particularly in Italy, but also in Spain, Britain and the United States. The German Daimler Company, which began manufacturing in Austria in 1902, had a claim to be the world's 'first multinational motor company', but Italy's Fiat probably had the most extensive foreign manufacturing business before 1914, with factories in Austria, the United States and Russia. These European companies were making small numbers of expensive cars for the wealthy (Fridenson 1986).

In the 1900s Henry Ford revolutionised the industry by the development of a standardised product – the Model T – manufactured on a moving assembly line. Ford was able to achieve large economies of scale from production in large volume, interchangeable parts and flow production. As a result, costs were dramatically less than for cars produced – as in Europe – in small batches by skilled craftsmen. But Ford's moving assembly line at Detroit was only completed in 1914, and the US dominance of the world industry was far from overwhelming. Before 1914 Ford only had two foreign factories, in Canada and Britain, plus a small assembly unit in France (Wilkins 1970: 96–7).

The 1920s saw extensive multinational growth by Ford and General Motors. The American industry (or parts of it) underwent further transformation as Alfred P. Sloan undertook large-scale organisational innovation at General Motors which led to the adoption of an M-form structure. This organisational innovation led to General Motors replacing Ford – still personally managed by Henry Ford – as the US market leader by the end of the 1920s. In this period the United States made the automobile industry its own, and by the end of that decade US firms made 85 per cent of the world's automobiles. Ford erected assembly plants in Europe, Latin America and Japan, and in 1928 began building a new British factory at Dagenham, near London, which became the largest car factory in the world outside the United States. General Motors expanded abroad through acquisition. In 1929 it acquired Opel, one of the ten largest industrial companies in Germany and the manufacturer of Germany's best-selling car (Wilkins 1974a: 72–5).

European automobile manufacturers undertook FDI, but on a smaller scale than the Americans. French companies were the most prominent. Citroën – Europe's largest automobile firm – opened factories in Germany, Britain, Belgium, Italy and elsewhere during the 1920s, while

Peugeot began assembly in Italy and Germany. After Citroën divested from many foreign investments following its rescue from financial collapse and takeover by Michelin in 1935, Renault emerged as the leading French car multinational, with factories in Belgium, Britain and elsewhere (Fridenson 1986: 160–1). Among smaller niche European producers was Switzerland's Sauer, which manufactured trucks in the interwar years in Germany, France and Austria (Laux 1992: 132).

The automobile industry carried in its wake numerous component and supplier firms. Automobiles provided a huge demand for rubber tyres. European firms initially took the lead in multinational tyre manufacture. Both France's Michelin and Britain's Dunlop undertook considerable direct investment before 1914 (Wilkins 1989: 423–4; Jones 1984b). By contrast, the four large US rubber and tyre manufacturers initially limited their foreign manufacturing to Canada. In the interwar years, the US tyre firms followed the car makers abroad. The world tyre industry became dominated by large US and European companies which opened foreign factories both in aggressive competition with one another and in response to tariffs. Between 1927 and 1938 Goodyear opened tyre factories in Australia, Britain, Argentina, the Dutch East Indies, Brazil and Sweden. US Rubber, Firestone and Goodrich had similar strategies (French 1987, 1991). Among the European manufacturers, Dunlop, Michelin and Pirelli continued to make large-scale multinational investments. Michelin opened new factories in Britain, Italy, Germany, Spain, Czechoslovakia, Belgium and the Netherlands, though it closed its pre-war American factory. Pirelli's new tyre factories included ventures in Spain, Britain, France, Brazil and Argentina.

The US car makers were followed abroad not only by tyre companies, but by a host of other US supplier firms which manufactured wheels, batteries, roller bearings, spark plugs, window glass and other products. Most of their factories were concentrated in Europe in the interwar years, and were often located physically near the factories of their main customers, the automobile manufacturers ( Wilkins 1974a: 75–6; Wilkins and Hill 1964: 192, 204).

United States food manufacturers pursued dynamic international business strategies in the interwar years. They established considerable numbers of plants to serve each of the different national markets of Europe and elsewhere. Corn Products Refining established market-oriented operations on six continents during the interwar years (Wilkins 1974a: 63). On a smaller scale, firms such as Quaker Oats, Kellogg, Heinz, Carnation, Pet Milk, Kraft and Wrigley set up foreign production facilities, often in other English-speaking countries with similar market conditions. The international operations of Coca-Cola expanded greatly, especially after 1930 when the firm established the Coca-Cola Export Corporation subsidiary to sell and promote its soft drinks in all countries except the United States, Canada and Cuba. By the end of the 1930s Coke could be purchased in seventy countries. As inside the United States, Coca-Cola's international growth involved a franchise system. The firm established its own syrup factories abroad to supply local independent bottlers which were given exclusive licences for their territories (Mason 1992a: 162–3; Giebelhouse 1994).

European companies were important international investors in other food products. By 1938 Nestlé operated 105 foreign plants (Heer 1966). The British chocolate companies Cadbury and Rowntree, which had relied on exporting before 1914, opened factories in Australia, Canada, New Zealand, South Africa and Ireland in the interwar years (Jones 1986a: 96–118). On a smaller scale, the British manufacturers of jams, mustards and condiments established or acquired production facilities in Europe, United States and elsewhere (Chandler 1990: 371–3).

## Equity and non-equity strategies

As manufacturing firms expanded into foreign markets in the nineteenth century and the interwar years, they employed the full spectrum of possible strategies between a wholly-owned production subsidiary and exporting. There were both firm and industry-specific differences in the propensity to use one mode more than another. In the case of a company such as Swedish Match, virtually every possible strategy was employed in pursuit of control of the world match market in the 1920s.

Manufacturing MNEs made extensive use of joint ventures. Partnerships with local interests were often used in industries which involved contracts with public authorities or else where there was reason to believe that a local identity would yield competitive advantage. They were often used by the British and French multinational armaments companies before the First World War (Davenport-Hines 1986; Beaud 1986). Risk-sharing was often an important motive. In the interwar years financial pressures encouraged some manufacturing MNEs to sell part of the equity of foreign affiliates to local investors. Sometimes there was an explicit recognition that a firm's managerial resources were insufficient for it 'to go it alone' abroad. Joint ventures were sometimes used to resolve tensions between two competitor companies (Jones 1986b: 121–3).

Joint ventures often reflected the 'negotiated environment' prevalent in business activity outside the United States before and after 1914 (Wilkins 1970: 76). In Europe and elsewhere, no antitrust tradition existed, and firms frequently employed co-operative strategies. During the 1900s the German dyestuffs firms were divided into two Interessengemeinschaften – BASF, Bayer and Agfa formed one, and Hoechst, Cassella and Kalle the other – and their FDI often took the form of joint ventures between allied firms (Hertner 1986: 123–4). It was not until the 1950s that US-style antitrust laws began to be adopted in other countries, and even then their scope was usually much narrower than in the United States.

Firms responded to changing political and economic conditions in foreign markets by shifting between strategies. The case of IG Farben in interwar Japan illustrates this process. During the 1920s IG Farben preferred to export its chemical products to the Japanese market. The German firm undertook FDI in distribution facilities in order to assist this strategy. It refused to license its technology to Japanese firms for fear of losing control over it. However in the 1930s growing Japanese tariffs rendered the export strategy very difficult, as did the continued expansion of the indigenous Japanese chemical industry. Japanese government restrictions made it impossible for IG Farben to contemplate investment in manufacturing in Japan. IG responded by offering Japanese firms licences for dyestuffs and nitrogenous fertiliser technology. Part of the reason IG Farben felt able to shift its strategy was that the firm considered that its position had been strengthened by the growing strength of the worldwide cartel in dyestuffs and other products, in which IG Farben played a central role. As a result, IG Farben was able to negotiate price and market agreements with the Japanese companies, either on its own or as a member of the international cartel (Kudo 1994).

Licensing strategies were employed by some firms in preference to FDI because of real or perceived weaknesses in managerial experience or financial resources. This was the case of the Dutch firm Océ-van der Grinten, which exploited its technology for manufacturing copying paper in the interwar period through a network of international licences. The limited shelf life of copying paper as well as tariffs and patent law provided incentives to engage in FDI, but the Dutch firm's small financial resources and limited marketing experience pushed it towards a licensing strategy. By the end of the 1930s the company, which had a policy of granting exclusive rights to one firm in every country, had entered contracts with firms in most European countries, the United States, Latin America and Japan (Sluyterman 1992).

The main problem with licensing agreements is that they may increase the transaction costs with the misuse or dissipation of property rights whenever they cannot be fully protected through a contract or where the litigation procedure is costly or ineffective. Singer encountered precisely this problem at the very beginning of its international expansion. After the invention of the sewing machine in the 1850s, Singer first attempted to exploit the invention outside the United States by licensing. A licensing agreement was made with a French company in 1855 under which Singer sold its French patent to an independent French merchant in return for cash and the payment of a royalty. Singer rapidly encountered the problem of opportunistic behaviour. The French firm declined to pay Singer all its fees, handled competitive sewing machines and declined to disclose information on sales. This experience led Singer never again to sell a patent to an independent business. Instead the firm became completely committed to controlling both its own marketing and production abroad. When the French firm's patent from Singer expired in the 1870s, Singer went into direct competition with it using its own marketing company (Wilkins 1970: 38–44). Singer's experience was repeated many times in subsequent decades. The problems of opportunism provided a constant incentive to firms to internalise transactions within their own hierarchy.

## Organisation and performance

Manufacturing MNE's faced complex challenges when they sought to establish and exercise sustained control over production facilities in foreign countries. As noted in Chapter 2, such problems often encouraged firms to make their initial investments in countries which were physically or culturally close. Most US firms before the Second World War built foreign factories either in Canada or Europe, where there was a strong bias towards English-speaking Britain. United States FDI was sometimes quite literally 'nearby': Ford's first Canadian factory was just across the Detroit River from its US operations (Wilkins 1970). In Switzerland, firms from French-speaking cantons had a strong preference for making their first FDI in France, while those from German-speaking cantons had a strong preference for Germany. Many Swiss investments were within walking distance from the Swiss border. Basel-based chemical and pharmaceutical companies Geigy and Hoffman-la-Roche built factories in Grenzach, which was effectively a suburb of the Swiss city, but located just over the German border (Schröter 1990b: 401–2). 'Nearby' investments provided managers with useful experience, and were often followed by ventures further afield.

The first multinational manufacturing investments – or at least those of 'classic' MNEs – were made to serve foreign markets which, for a variety of reasons, could be better serviced by local production than by exports or other alternatives. A 'typical' investment might have begun as a distribution company, developed as an assembly operation importing components from the parent, and then become a local producer. The free-standing company had a different organisational development, in so far as it was from the beginning focused on supplying products to its host economy.

Although the focus of such manufacturing subsidiaries was the local market in which they were established, it was by no means unusual in the early years of manufacturing operations for exporting activity to assume a prominent role. By 1879 – twelve years after the factory opened – foreign sales of Singer's Glasgow-assembled sewing machines outnumbered domestic sales (Carstensen 1984: 24). There were early examples of manufacturing FDI which were entirely of the 'export platform' variety. The Swedish match producer Jönköping and Vulcan built a factory in Britain in 1910 in order to supply the Australian market, as Australia levied only 50 per cent of the standard import duty on matches of British origin. All the production of Jönköping and Vulcan's London factory was sold in Australia before 1915 (Lindgren 1979: 46, 168–9).

The organisational structure of multinational manufacturing at this stage was relatively simple. Describing the initial growth of US MNEs, Wilkins used the term *monocentric* (Wilkins 1974a: 416). Foreign subsidiaries 'began as spokes on a wheel, with the parent company at the hub'. At the initial stage, the connections between the parent and the subsidiary were rather close, or at least as close as the prevailing transport and communication situation permitted. The parent would be closely involved with the establishment of the foreign business. The products manufactured and sold by foreign subsidiaries would normally be identical to those produced by the parent. There would be close links in terms of finance, technology and staffing. However controls would often be ad hoc or exercised by personal visits from headquarters to subsidiaries, and few MNEs before the First World War had systematic standardised reporting procedures. Although managerial hierarchies were evolving rapidly, especially in the United States and Germany, most companies underwent a process of trial and error as they sought to find the appropriate management structures for international business.

In the interwar years the ties between MNE parents and their subsidiaries often loosened. Wilkins refers to a *polycentric* relationship between them. Parents often exercised little control over their affiliates, while the affiliate became responsible for most of the value-added chain in its output. Foreign units 'developed their own separate histories and their own satellite activities', sometimes undertaking their own R & D and even making their own (third country) investments (Wilkins 1974a: 417–8).

The increased autonomy of affiliates was stimulated by several factors. The spread of trade barriers discouraged the import of components from parents, while encouraging a move to manufacturing a full range of products and a focus on national markets. Exchange controls and other limits on the movement of resources and the general growth of economic and political nationalism had the same effects. A study of the multinational growth of IBM, Ford and General Motors pointed to the impact on these US firms of the competitive response by European producers, who were able to learn American production techniques and apply them. IBM, Ford and General Motors responded by the development of new products for major overseas markets which were distinct from those produced for the domestic American markets. By the end of the 1930s their foreign subsidiaries were 'transformed into producers operating under the same structure of costs and constraints as other local producers'. The decentralisation of production was accompanied by the decentralisation of administration as operating control was transferred to subsidiaries (Dassbach 1989: 483–7).

United States MNEs sometimes decentralised their administrations on a regional basis in this period. In 1928 Ford decentralised its foreign operations by placing its British affiliate in control of its overall European business. United States corporations sometimes used Canadian holding companies to manage part or all of their non-US operations. Some US MNEs formed separate international divisions to control their foreign business, in part in recognition of the managerial problems caused by operating abroad. In 1919 General Electric formed the wholly-owned International General Electric for this purpose. It took over a large and complex foreign business which included wholly-owned manufacturing subsidiaries – the preferred form in developing economies – joint ventures, and small equity stakes in some European firms (Wilkins 1974a: 138–51).

As a generalisation, it can be said that in the interwar years foreign manufacturing affiliates were weakly integrated at the production level (United Nations 1994: 122). This fitted with the prevailing economic trends of the period of stagnant trade flows and industrialisation through import substitution. Nevertheless, the model of entirely stand-alone foreign affiliates needs partial qualification. Many of the foreign – mainly US – manufacturing affiliates in Britain were engaged in some exporting activity, and were not simply supplying the domestic market. The United Kingdom was used as a production base by US MNEs to supply markets in the sterling currency area (Bostock and Jones 1994: 116–7). In exceptional cases, the degree of intra-firm transactions reached significant proportions. In the interwar years, Ford's British factory at Dagenham manufactured many of the components of Ford cars produced in Germany before the Nazi regime came to power in 1933, while British-made Ford tractors were sold to many countries including the United States (Wilkins and Hill 1964: 247, 304).

Internationalisation of technological activity reached a high level in the interwar years, though there were substantial differences between countries and industries. US and Swedish MNEs located substantial R & D operations abroad in the interwar period. US-owned electrical equipment firms in the 1930s had a higher degree of internationalisation of technological activity than they were to have at any time since. GE and RCA were especially important in this respect. The internationalisation of research in both US and Swedish MNEs fell after the Second World War, before reviving from the late 1960s. While US-owned electrical firms were highly internationalised, in Germany, France and Britain it was the large chemical firms which internationalised their R & D from the 1930s (Cantwell 1995).

The risks of multinational manufacturing were high, and even substantial first mover advantages could be overturned by inadequate strategies, sub-optimal organisation, or exogenous circumstances. Ford, which dominated the British market by the end of the First World War, saw its market share decimated by British-owned competitors in the 1920s, as managerial failings afflicted the American company. Its huge Dagenham plant was poorly located, and too large for the market at that time (Church 1994). The firm's performance in Germany was even worse, again because of chronic over-capacity in a depressed market (Wilkins and Hill 1964). Ford's problems were severe, but leading European manufacturing MNEs are also known to have made long-term losses in various markets in the interwar years (Jones 1986d).

There was nothing automatic about the growth of multinational manufacturing, and numerous failed investments co-existed with successful ones. Although the number of MNEs in world manufacturing grew over time, this was composed of a changing population of firms, even though there were some long-term players. The 1930s seems to have seen an especially high 'turnover' of MNEs. Du Pont and Monsanto were among the US MNEs which either withdrew from European manufacturing altogether, or sold part of the equity of European subsidiaries to local investors. Yet there were also new US entrants to multinational manufacturing in the 1930s, and US firms opened new plants in Latin America, Asia and Australia (Wilkins 1974a: 184–91).

## DETERMINANTS

### Ownership factors

The manufacturing companies which undertook multinational investment from the nineteenth century possessed (in greatly varying degrees) the range of ownership advantages identified in theory. As in natural resources, entrepreneurship often stands out as an important advantage, and its significance is particularly easy to discern before the growth of large corporate bureaucracies masked the influence of individuals on business decisions. In the United States the late nineteenth century was the classic era of the 'robber barons' – the businessmen who built giant corporations, and became immensely rich in the process. Many of these US industrial leaders had global ambitions and their personal influence on the international strategies pursued by their firms is evident. A noteworthy example was James B. Duke, the founder of the American Tobacco Company, and subsequently the chief executive of BAT during its period of dramatic expansion as a multinational cigarette manufacturer before 1914. BAT's extensive FDI in China originated with Duke's entrepreneurial vision of the huge potential market opportunities of that country (Cochran 1980: 10–11). The late nineteenth century contains numerous other instances of the weighty influence of founder entrepreneurs on multinational strategies.

The creation of large corporations with professional managerial hierarchies gave US and German firms ownership advantages in the new capital-intensive, technically advanced and fast-growing industries of the late nineteenth century. At the heart of these capabilities was the ability to innovate. The importance of technological innovation was a critical factor in the multinational growth of the capital-intensive industries. The international competitiveness of the German chemical firms rested on the success of their corporate research laboratories in developing new products, and more fundamentally on the willingness of these firms to make sufficient investments in organisation and production to sustain and exploit these innovations. In the late nineteenth century firms such as Bayer developed the corporate competences in innovation which they were to retain through the twentieth century. The successful exploitation of high-volume production and packaging technologies lay behind the success of the US producers for branded and packaged consumer products. Product development and innovation was facilitated by investment in research and development. At GE a pioneer research laboratory was created in 1901, which was soon doing innovative research in lighting, vacuum tubes, X-rays and other products. Through the interwar years the laboratories of GE were responsible for a remarkable number of innovations in electricals, communications and even chemicals (Chandler 1990: 218–19).

Yet it also evident that, especially but not only in consumer industries, it was quite possible to undertake and succeed in multinational manufacturing with an organisational structure far removed from the Chandlerian ideal. The British case is the most intriguing. While the British attachment to personal capitalism until the Second World War is evident, the consequences of this attachment are debatable. Wilkins has identified organisational weakness as the principal reason why most of the thousands of British free-standing companies active in the United States in the late nineteenth century proved either unsuccessful, or short-lived, or else were transformed into American enterprises by removing 'what was an essentially superfluous British corporate structure' (Wilkins 1989: 162). The management structures of some of the most active British multinational manufacturing investors of this period (such as Dunlop and Vickers) have been shown to have been haphazard, and this – together with inappropriate business strategies – contributed towards sub-optimal performances (Jones 1986a). Nonetheless, British-owned enterprises did control extensive foreign manufacturing assets with managerial structures and systems very different from the American ones. This was part of a wider European experience. Family ownership and control, and firms with 'ragged edges', were not overwhelming handicaps in building and sustaining an international competitive advantage, at least in some industries.

While the importance of a technological advantage in multinational manufacturing is evident, firms could secure such an advantage in several ways. Firms such as Bayer and GE generated their own innovations internally, but others gained a technological advantage by buying it. Early Swedish MNEs often utilised technology obtained in Germany (Wilkins 1988b). As Chandler has stressed in his account of the growth of US big business, it was rarely the inventors of new products which built the successful enterprises of the late nineteenth century: it was the entrepreneurs who matched inventions with investment (Chandler 1990: 227–8).

Technological advantages, even if in the form of patented technology, were hard to sustain over the long term. A case study of US machinery MNEs in Germany before 1914 showed that German firms, in some products at least, found more difficulty in matching the Americans in marketing skills than in technology and production process. Singer's German competitor Pfaff was able to adopt American manufacturing methods, and developed a product able to compete with the Singer machine (Blaich 1984: 36–9). It would appear that even in a high technology sector like the German electrical industry, marketing techniques and after-sales service were sources of ownership advantage which were at least as important as technology defined in a narrow sense, and probably more so (Hertner 1986).

In branded and packaged consumer products ownership advantages were often derived from skills in marketing, such as branding, advertising and product differentiation. The use of brand names proliferated from the late nineteenth century (Wilkins 1994b). While the British excelled in trademarked consumer products, German firms sometimes used trademarks in different strategies. In the United States, Bayer advertised its trademarked aspirin to doctors and to the trade rather than to the final consumer. Stollwerck sold most of its trademarked product as a cooking chocolate to other producers in the United States (Wilkins 1988b: 21).

Firm size itself was of limited importance as an ownership advantage in manufacturing FDI before 1945. Many large US and European manufacturing companies made their first direct investments before the First World War. But even in the US case, 'small' manufacturing firms also made direct investments, and US firms were by no means always larger than those of their local competitors in host countries. United States FDI in the German machinery sector before 1914 included several investments from small companies, as well as instances when investing US firms were smaller in size than their German competitors (Blaich 1984: 80–3). Many European firms at early stages of their corporate careers made both distribution and manufacturing investments overseas. Swedish enterprises faced such a small home market that they went abroad almost immediately they were founded. In some cases by the time Swedish firms were created, foreign firms dominated the limited Swedish market (Olsson 1993; Lundström 1986a).

Ownership advantages in finance were particularly clear in the case of the European free-standing firms. As in the case of natural resources, British companies could benefit from the relative cheapness of capital and the ease of raising funds on the well-developed London capital market (Wilkins 1988b: 11). Firms secured access to capital by other means than through capital markets. In Continental European countries where – unlike Britain – the ties between banks and industry were close, banks facilitated multinational manufacturing. In Sweden, Germany and Switzerland the role of banks in financing the international expansion of companies was an important, if passive, factor (Jones and Schröter 1993a: 19). In Sweden – which like the United States was a net capital importer before 1914 – banks served as both advisers and financiers to Swedish companies going abroad (Lundström 1986b: 205–14).

In the interwar years lack of access to capital has been frequently cited as a major constraint on the ability of German firms to engage in FDI (Schröter 1993a: 30). In fact the situation was more complex. In the 1920s the small size of the German capital market and high interest rates made it difficult for German firms to raise capital, but the larger enterprises were able to raise considerable sums by issuing long-term debentures on foreign capital markets. Foreign subsidiaries were used to finance foreign investments, especially after the introduction of German exchange controls. In the second half of the 1920s IG Farben set up foreign holding companies to finance its foreign activities. In 1928 it established IG Chemie in Switzerland. IG Farben transferred its foreign investments to this Swiss company, including its important US interests which were placed under the control of the American IG Chemical Corporation (AIG). IG Chemie and AIG were used to raise considerable sums from foreign capital markets (V. Schröter 1984: 394–408).

It is not always easy to separate access to capital from other sources of ownership advantage. Swedish Match's spectacular growth in the 1920s, based in part on its willingness to make sovereign loans, might suggest it had privileged access to capital in its home country. In fact Kreuger financed his operations mainly from borrowing from the United States. This strategy was made possible by a close relationship with various leading American financiers, who regarded the seemingly respectable match company as a safe intermediary to lend funds to Europe, and Kreuger's ability to construct convincing fraudulent balance sheets (Hildebrand 1985: 172–81). Swedish Match's real advantage lay in Kreuger's entrepreneurial abilities.

While it can be maintained that manufacturing MNEs before the Second World War possessed ownership advantages that they exploited in foreign markets, the significance of these advantages needs to be put in perspective. The concept works best when applied to major corporate innovators such as GE and Bayer. Moreover, these firms were able over time to derive further ownership advantages from the common governance of their geographically dispersed assets. But the scale of the ownership advantage possessed by hundreds of other manufacturing MNEs was unlikely to have been of such magnitude. The scale of their innovations was far smaller, while a limited number of foreign affiliates yielded fewer advantages of common governance. Moreover, the existence of failed and unsuccessful multinational investments suggests that often companies misjudged their competitive strengths and organisational abilities or they dissipated their initial ownership advantages.

## Locational factors

Before the Second World War the most important locational factors which encouraged firms to exploit their ownership advantages abroad through FDI rather than exporting were structural market failures, especially the spread of tariffs from the late nineteenth century. While manufacturers of cheap and undifferentiated products could shift their exports to developing countries and colonial markets if protectionism damaged markets in the United States or Europe, the makers of high-technology products, or branded consumer goods, needed markets with high per capita incomes and industrial sectors. If their exports were rendered uncompetitive, the choice was to jump tariff barriers and engage in local manufacture, or else lose the market.

Tariffs were a major factor in the spread of US manufacturing companies abroad. Wilkins notes that Canadian protectionism was the 'most crucial' factor behind US FDI in that country before 1914 (Wilkins 1970: 142). Tariffs were equally important in stimulating inward FDI into the United States in this period (Wilkins 1989: 179). Country-specific studies of British (Jones 1986a), German (Hertner 1986), Dutch (Gales and Sluyterman 1993), Swedish (Olsson 1993) and other MNEs stress the rise of protectionism as a stimulus to multinational investment. There are plentiful corporate-level case studies which show that the level of tariff protection can explain not only when and where firms undertook foreign manufacture, but also what stages of production were involved (Plumpe 1990: 58–9).

Nevertheless, there were many individual corporate foreign investment decisions which were not influenced by tariffs. Free-standing enterprises did not have a domestic business engaged in exporting prior to foreign production, so there was no question of jumping tariff barriers (Wilkins 1989: 179). Tariffs do not explain the importance of the United Kingdom as a host economy before the 1920s. Free trade Britain was the most popular destination for US manufacturing FDI after Canada, attracting a disproportionate share of the American investment in Europe (Jones 1988).

Non-tariff barriers to trade also stimulated manufacturing FDI. While outright government restrictions on foreign MNEs were few before the 1920s, the growth of nationalism, especially in Europe, sometimes led governments to favour local producers, or else led foreign companies to undertake local manufacture in order to appear as national enterprises (Wilkins 1970: 101–2). Nationalistic pressures grew in the interwar years. GE had a strategy to take shares in local electrical companies in recognition of the growth of national feelings and hostility to foreign products (Wilkins 1974a: 68). Some governments put foreign companies under direct pressure to manufacture locally. In many countries, MNEs felt some pressure to give their subsidiaries a more 'local' appearance by selling part of the equity to local investors or appointing nationals to local boards.

In certain countries, and in certain industries, patent legislation in host countries influenced the choice between exporting and FDI. In Canada patent legislation in 1872 stipulated that patents were null and void if not worked within two years of issuance, while imports also nullified patents. This stimulated US electrical FDI in Canada (Wilkins 1970: 142). British patent law was modified in 1907 to prescribe that a foreign patent, after its transfer to Britain, had to be exploited there or else be reworked. Immediately the German dyestuffs firms BASF and Hoechst established plants in Britain, but few patents were subsequently worked as it became clear that the British legislation would not be rigorously enforced (Plumpe 1990: 60).

As manufacturing FDI seldom occurred in very labour-intensive industries, labour costs were rarely an influence except in the limited number of instances when Western firms established production facilities in developing countries. BAT's investments in Chinese cigarette production provides one example. This MNE took advantage of Chinese cheap labour by using labour-intensive rather than capital-intensive production techniques, employing thousands of unskilled labourers in China to perform tasks that were already mechanised in the United States (Cochran 1980: 24–5).

The overall size and per capita income of markets was a more important locational factor than labour costs. The emphasis on structural market failure can be wrongly interpreted as suggesting that most FDI was defensive. In fact, multinational investments were often aggressive. American protectionism certainly encouraged FDI in that country, but so did the enormous opportunities of the fastest-growing and largest market in the world (Wilkins 1989: 166). The United Kingdom had the highest per capita income in Europe before 1914, as well as a high population density. In such attractive markets, FDI offered greater business opportunities than exporting, even when exporting strategies were feasible. Firms discovered that producing in a market gave them greater sensitivity to local tastes, and a better ability to respond quickly to market needs, an important competitive advantage in consumer products. Transportation costs also often meant that it was cheaper to produce locally – near the consumer – than to export.

Local production offered one of the most effective responses to competitors based in major markets. If a US company attacked a European market, a European competitor might retaliate in the United States (Wilkins 1989: 178–9). Companies had to respond if the actions of competitors threatened a valued market. In the interwar years the increasing domination of certain industries by large companies gave a strong element of oligopolistic rivalry to corporate strategies. While in some industries the oligopolists co-operated in cartels, in others they competed by erecting factories in different host economies.

**Internalisation factors**

The growth of multinational manufacturing can be seen as a response to transactional market failure. This explains why multinational investment was especially prominent in the industries of the Second Industrial Revolution rather than the First. The difficulty of writing contracts for complex technologies or brand names encouraged firms to transfer the new manufacturing technologies and products using direct investment rather than through market-based transactions. Singer's initial use of licensing – discussed earlier – provides a good example of the problems of protecting proprietary assets in non-equity strategies.

Transactions cost theory can explain the changing modes used by MNEs to operate in foreign markets. Using a sample of 119 British manufacturing firms which made a direct investment between 1870 and 1939, Nicholas showed that 94 per cent of firms for whom information is available exported their product before undertaking FDI. Virtually every company had agency agreements with foreign companies before investing abroad. These agency agreements often involved high transaction costs in terms of enforcement by the principals, as many agents sought large discounts or were inefficient in various ways. Such problems led firms to replace agents with selling companies. 'Selling and distributing organisations and branch production replaced exports through costs', Nicholas concluded, 'because the costs of transacting using the market were greater than internal firm costs involved in selling and production' (Nicholas 1982: 629; 1983).

**THE INTERWAR CARTELS**

There was a growth of international cartels in manufacturing from the 1900s, and during the 1930s a considerable proportion of world manufacturing was controlled by these agreements. A number of characteristics of the period encouraged this trend. These include the depressed market conditions, growing political risk, exchange controls and the support of governments. Interwar European governments supported the spread of cartel agreements as a solution to the economic problems of the period. The German government had a long tradition of supporting cartels. German criticism of cartels grew during the Great Depression, but the Nazi government after 1933 was an enthusiastic supporter of such arrangements. British policy was generally permissive of cartels, but during the 1930s British governments positively encouraged the participation of British companies in cartels in some, if not all, industries (Wurm 1993).

There were strong industry-specific influences on cartelisation. They proliferated in industries where there were a relatively small number of producers, especially those producing semi-finished products and capital goods. The larger the number of firms in an industry, and the greater the variety of products, the greater were the problems faced by organisers of cross-border collusive agreements. International cartels flourished in chemicals, parts of the engineering industries, and iron and steel. They were rare in most finished consumer goods, where there was a considerable variety of products, and in industries like textiles with large numbers of producers. They were also rare in such fast-growing and dynamic industries as automobiles.

The 'classic' interwar cartel was concerned with price and output, but within that generalisation an enormous variety of arrangements existed. A common type of price agreement permitted each national group of producers to decide the price to be charged in their home market, prices which were followed by exporters to that market. The international cartels in aluminium, matches and electric lamps were of this type. A second type of cartel – common in steel products – involved the fixing of export prices for a market or several markets. Cartels designed to restrict the quantity or value of sales were frequent. These often featured sales or export quotas, expressed as a percentage of total sales or exports. It was common for home markets to be reserved entirely, or in part, to the nationals of that market. In some cases foreign firms were allowed to supply particular markets to the extent of a certain proportion of home consumption – and these supplies could either come from imports from the parent or from its own production subsidiaries in that market. However some cartels, for example in wire products, specifically prohibited FDI in particular markets.

Many international cartels divided up sales territories. A classic formulation would be for the British participant to be allotted the British Empire market, and the American firm the North American market, leaving the German participant with continental Europe. The wide-ranging agreements in the interwar chemical industry between ICI, Du Pont and IG Farben took this form (Reader 1975).

International cartels of this era differed extensively in their durability. Terms of agreement varied from three to five years, but were also found for one year only. Many broke down during the term of the agreement, and renewals often involved changes in the original terms. Although some collusive arrangements proved extremely durable – Du Pont's far-reaching arrangements with ICI were in place from the late 1920s until the late 1940s – interwar cartels as a whole are best regarded as being in a continual state of flux.

Given that a central preoccupation of cartels is to prevent cheating and opportunistic behaviour by members, it was not surprising that the majority of cartel agreements provided for sanctions. Fines were imposed for companies exceeding quotas, and compensation was paid for under-selling or under-production. Sometimes compensation payments were available to manufacturers which refrained from extending capacity. In the shipbuilding and railway rolling stock cartels, there were agreements for joint consultation on tenders, and compensation was paid by firms that received orders to firms which refrained from tendering.

International cartels differed widely in their membership. Some cartels consisted of individual firms from different countries. The arrangements between ICI, IG Farben and Du Pont were of this type. There was a second type where domestic cartels in different countries formed a cartel. This was the structure of the International Steel Export Cartel which was in existence between 1933 and 1939: at its peak this consisted of the export cartels of France, Germany, Belgium, Luxembourg, Britain, Czechoslovakia, Poland and the United States (Barbezat 1991). The rayon and potassium cartels were among those of which both domestic cartels and individual firms were members (Hara and Kudo 1992: 4).

In some industries, such as chemicals and engineering, patent agreements were an important feature of the international cartel system. This was the basis of the relationship between Du Pont and ICI which provided for the sharing of know-how and R & D results. Another example concerned arrangements between Jersey Standard and IG Farben concerning hydrogenation technology. In its original form in 1929, the American and German firms agreed to pool their patents. Standard was allocated the use in the oil industry outside Germany, while IG Farben was given the entire world in non-petrochemical developments (Smith 1992: 151–2).

The international cartels developed complex organisational forms. The administration of cartels was sometimes handled by representatives from the member corporations, who implemented the decisions made at regular meetings of members' representatives. This system was more effective for straightforward matters such as setting minimum price levels, than for when more complex arrangements were being administered. In such cases, separate companies were sometimes formed, independent from the member companies, to deal with the administration. There were also cases when joint sales organisations were established, which collated orders and distributed them among member corporations (Hara and Kudo 1992: 4–5). The more highly organised cartels placed their headquarters in small European states such as Switzerland, Belgium, Luxembourg or Liechtenstein, both to avoid scrutiny from governments and to take advantage of more liberal company laws.

The formal participation of US companies in international cartels was made difficult by US antitrust laws. As a result, such participation was often disguised. This was seen in the world electric lamp cartel, which controlled about three-quarters of world output of electric lamps between the mid-1920s and the Second World War. The Convention for the Development and Progress of the International Incandescent Electric Lamp Industry was signed in 1924. A Swiss corporation – Phoebus S.A. – was established to administer production quotas, prices, exchange of technical information, and sharing of patent rights. Within Phoebus, the General Assembly of members set policy; an administrative board issued rules to implement that policy; and a board of arbitration adjudicated disputes. There was also a testing laboratory to ensure consistent quality among members' products. A marketing division promoted the use of electric lighting, especially the lamps of cartel members. Companies' production was restricted to the share of the lamp market that they held in 1922–3. The overall aim of the cartel was to assure each company of as much of its home market as it wished plus a fixed share in other, common, markets.

GE took the initiative to establish the cartel, and had a decisive influence on its policies, but was never one of the member companies, which came to include the major European lamp manufacturers and, later, Tokyo Electric of Japan. GE wished to avoid any US antitrust scrutiny, and preferred to match the cartel's policies informally. The American firm was able to effectively enforce its wishes, in part because of its enormous importance in the world industry, arising from its strong patent position, and the fact that its home market accounted for almost half of total world sales in the 1930s. GE also held equity in the major corporate members. In 1929 its holdings included 29 per cent in Osram of Germany, 17 per cent in Philips of the Netherlands, 25 per cent in AEG of Germany, 44 per cent in Compagnie des Lampes of France, 46 per cent in Britain's AEI and 40 per cent in Tokyo Electric. GE also joined in joint ventures with cartel members. It manufactured lamps in China with Osram and Philips, and in Mexico with Osram (Reich 1992: 218–24).

Although much of the literature on collaborative agreements between firms points to their unstable nature, some of the interwar cartels were both durable and effective in achieving their specific goals (Barbezat 1991). The electric lamp cartel was able to control a high proportion of world lamp sales outside the United States in the 1930s, though its success in keeping prices arbitrarily high meant that some new entrants were attracted into the industry (Reich 1992: 224). The international dyestuffs cartel is estimated to have accounted for around 70 per cent of world sales in 1938, and to have been successful in maintaining prices. The use of a 'large part' of the earnings of the dyestuffs cartel to finance R & D also suggests that the effects of cartels on welfare may not have been as negative as might be anticipated (Schröter 1990c: 143).

The Second World War massively disrupted the international cartels in manufacturing. It severed the long-standing relationships which had existed between German firms and their US and British counterparts. The importance of German firms in the cartel system linked it in the public mind to the Nazi war machine. This was one factor behind a resurgence of aggressive US antitrust policies against cartels after the war had ended. There were a series of major antitrust actions in the United States against US companies active in international cartels. Even non-US companies faced the risk of being taken before US courts if they had any agreement with a US corporation, even if it did not affect the United States itself. However, in practice, international cartel agreements in industries such as chemicals were weakening even without this regulatory onslaught, as the new economic conditions of the postwar world made a resumption of direct investment strategies more attractive.

International cartels shaped the evolution of some of the world's most important capital-intensive industries over a considerable period of time. They showed that whatever the organisational and technological achievements of single firms, co-operative agreements between them could offer viable alternative methods of organising international production, at least in certain circumstances.

## RENEWAL AND GROWTH

### Overview

From the 1950s the growth of manufacturing FDI resumed. United States MNEs were pre-eminent. They invested abroad in a range of products, though machinery, chemicals, transportation equipment, food products and primary and fabricated metals were especially important (Wilkins 1974a). The British and Dutch – the leading European outward investors in manufacturing in the postwar decades – had their own distinctive specialisations. British manufacturing FDI was heavily biased towards the materials and consumer goods industries, especially food, drink and tobacco, although from the 1960s British FDI in chemicals and electrical engineering grew. The preferred Dutch sectors were chemicals and electrical engineering, as well as food products (Gales and Sluyterman

1993: 81). The manufacturing firms of other European countries, such as France and Germany, undertook comparatively little multinational investment in the two decades after the end of the war, preferring to use export strategies to take advantage of the fast world trade growth and the opportunties offered by European economic integration (Neebe 1991).

Multinational factories were mostly located in developed market economies. US manufacturers built most of their factories in Canada and Western Europe. The economic recovery of Western Europe, its growing attractiveness as a market, and the emergence of a regional market with the formation of the European Economic Community in 1957 made Western Europe an attractive location for US manufacturers. Nevertheless the 1950s and 1960s also saw quite substantial US and European FDI in Latin American manufacturing, while British MNEs had a strong preference in this period for the developed economies of the Commonwealth, especially Canada, Australia and South Africa.

The consequences of the continued growth of industrial concentration in most developed economies were seen in the relative importance of large corporations in multinational manufacturing. This trend was striking in the case of the United States, which as late as the 1970s was the home of more than half the companies worldwide with 20,000 employees or more (Chandler 1994: 26). In 1957 less than 6 per cent of the 2,800 US enterprises with foreign operations controlled over 80 per cent of total US overseas assets and sales. Forty-five US enterprises, or less than two per cent of the total, controlled more than a half of assets and sales (Dassbach 1989: 1). There was a similar pattern in Europe as merger waves led to the creation of larger firms, and there was a spread of American management practices, including – especially in Britain – the widespread adoption of the M-form (Channon 1973: 80). The result was that although numerous British and Dutch manufacturing firms invested abroad, a small number of large MNEs, such as Unilever, Shell, BAT, Philips and AKU, accounted for most of the FDI by the 1970s.

US companies were the world's technological innovators in a range of products, including chemicals (especially petrochemicals), electricals and computers, and retained their strong world market positions in products such as automobiles, electricals, office equipment and sewing machines (Wilkins 1974a: 402–5). They were the leaders in capital or technology-intensive production methods. Through the 1960s the United States was the world centre of innovation and entrepreneurship: in 1967 the United States accounted for almost 70 per cent of the R & D undertaken in the OECD (Dunning 1988a: 93–4). United States industrial productivity was the highest in the world. In almost every host economy the productivity performance of US manufacturing affiliates was superior to that of indigenous competitors (Houston and Dunning 1976: 27).

The spread of US manufacturing MNEs abroad reflected their strong ownership advantages, which US antitrust regulations discouraged them from exploiting by international collusive agreements (Wilkins 1974a: 300). US entrepreneurs benefited from the fact that their home economy was the world's largest and richest market, and that the US dollar was the world's major reserve currency. Indeed, a worldwide 'shortage' of US dollars, which lasted until the mid-1950s, encouraged US manufacturing MNEs to establish factories in Europe to supply customers in countries that lacked dollars to buy American products (Wilkins 1974a: 310).

The timing and location of investments was often influenced by competitive rivalries between the major US corporations (Knickerbocker 1973, Graham 1978). In the automobile industry, the scale of FDI reached unprecedented levels in the 1950s and 1960s as rising world incomes created an ever-expanding market for automobiles, while the proliferation of import barriers and local content requirements discouraged importing. Competitive struggles between the major US firms in the American domestic market were reproduced abroad. Chrysler, the third biggest US producer after Ford and General Motors, had almost no FDI before 1945, but thereafter perceived the need to match its two US competitors in the world market if it was to sustain its position in its domestic market. Given its late entry into multinational manufacturing, Chrysler's strategy was one of acquisition of foreign firms. By 1973 it had purchased full control over French, Spanish and British manufacturing companies and secured control of around 7.5 per cent of total Western European vehicle production. However a major financial crisis at the end of the 1970s resulted in the sale of most of these foreign operations (Maxcy 1981).

Although the three decades after the end of the Second World War can be regarded as the high point of the influence of large, integrated corporations in multinational manufacturing, joint ventures and other equity and non-equity strategies continued to be used alongside the creation of wholly-owned subsidiaries. Multiple reasons led firms to use joint ventures. Equity sharing continued to occur when foreign projects were risky or very large. Joint ventures were frequently used when an investing firm had little knowledge of a particular economy and where speed of entry was essential. After 1945 host governments were often critical in affecting the ownership structure of multinational affiliates, and there was strong pressure from many developing country governments for MNEs to take local partners (Gomes-Casseres 1990). In Japan – for reasons to be discussed in Chapter 8 – almost all US and other foreign MNEs were obliged by the government to either license their technology or invest in Japan with local firms as partners.

There were strong industry and nation-specific influences on the proclivity of MNEs to use joint ventures. MNEs which possessed important intangible assets in product and/or process technologies were often reluctant to engage in joint ventures because of the dangers of the loss of such assets to their partners (Stopford and Wells 1972). US MNEs in particular tended throughout the postwar period to have a lower propensity to engage in joint ventures than those of other nationalities (Caves 1982: 89–90). The American evidence that the use of joint ventures was inversely correlated with R & D intensity was contradicted by research on the extensive use of joint ventures by Japanese MNEs investing in US manufacturing in the 1980s which found no correlation with R & D intensity. However there were some similarities between Japanese and American corporate strategies. The use of joint ventures was most common when the Japanese firms entered the United States for the first time and when they needed local resources to exploit fully their ownership advantage (Hennart 1991b).

The photocopier industry saw a particularly striking use of joint ventures in international business. In 1956 the Haloid Co. (which became the Xerox Corporation in 1960) formed a joint venture with Britain's Rank Organisation. The (then) small US corporation needed a partner to penetrate foreign markets with its new product, while the British company – an entertainment and leisure group – wanted to diversify out of the declining cinema industry in Britain. Rank Xerox, a 51/49 per cent joint venture between the Americans and the British, proved a highly effective vehicle to penetrate many eastern hemisphere markets for office copiers. In 1960 Xerox formed a 50/50 joint venture with Fuji Photo Film – Fuji Xerox – which was used to penetrate Asian markets.

A striking feature of these particular arrangements was their long-term durability. There was also a considerable difference in their outcome. In 1969 Xerox secured voting control over Rank Xerox, and thereafter was in effective management control over the affiliate, though it was only in 1995 that Xerox raised its share of the equity in Rank Xerox from 51 per cent to 71 per cent. Fuji Xerox evolved as a dynamic and innovative manufacturing company in its own right (Fuji Xerox 1994). By the 1980s the joint venture was considerably more successful than its American parent. As a result, there were considerable tensions arising both from the geographical restrictions as to where Fuji Xerox could market its products, and from duplication in product development.

The US manufacturing MNEs of the postwar decades were extremely important vehicles for the transfer of new products, processes and organising methods to Europe and elsewhere. They transferred the principles of mass production, American management techniques, and the M-form, and to varying degrees these US innovations were adopted by domestic businesses.

## Chemicals and electronics

In the interwar years the chemicals companies had preferred cartels to FDI, but from the 1950s there was a radical change in international business strategies. This change co-existed with a sharp expansion of world markets for chemical products: ever since 1945 the growth of demand for chemical products has consistently exceeded overall rates of growth in the developed world. US firms became prolific foreign investors. By 1970 FDI by US chemical companies (excluding the large investments made by oil companies in petrochemicals) reached $13 billion, or one-third of their domestic plant investment. No other US industry approached either the total sum or the ratio (Chapman 1991: 91, 224).

The new strategy of US chemical companies was evident in the case of Du Pont, whose FDI – and even exports – had been marginal to its overall business before the mid-1950s. The catalyst was the ending of collaborative links with ICI in 1952 – which had to be finally severed because of antitrust rulings – followed a few years later by ICI's decision to acquire a dye plant in the United States. Du Pont retaliated and in 1958 opened a new factory in Britain, designed to supply the European market. Between 1959 and 1972 Du Pont's total FDI increased from $300 million to more than $1.6 billion, by which date its foreign sales reached one-fifth of the firm's total sales volume (Taylor and Sudnik 1984: 187–94). Du Pont's foreign expansion was part of a wider trend by US chemical companies to invest abroad. While Du Pont and Monsanto concentrated on plastics and synthetic fibres – or downstream operations – Union Carbide and Dow were particularly prominent in petrochemicals. US FDI in chemicals increased six times in the 1960s (Wilkins 1974a: 376).

International competition to American firms after the trauma of the Second World War revived faster in chemicals than in almost any other capital-intensive industry (Chandler 1994: 34–5). As a result, European companies returned quite early to multinational strategies. British and Dutch MNEs such as ICI, Shell and AKU (AKZO in 1969) were initially prominent, but they were not alone. The German chemical industry, which was radically changed after the end of the Second World War by the break-up of IG Farben and the re-emergence of BASF, Bayer and Hoechst as independent companies, returned to foreign production. The German firms initially re-invested in Latin America, often repurchasing plant they had lost in the war, and then invested elsewhere in Western Europe and North America. By 1965 German chemical companies had 150 foreign production plants: the largest numbers were in France (eighteen), the United States (fourteen) and Switzerland and Brazil (ten each) (Schröter, forthcoming). The leading three Swiss chemical companies – Ciba, Geigy and Sandoz – abandoned their cartel in 1950, partly because of US antitrust pressure on their American subsidiaries, and reverted to extensive FDI. Within a decade the Swiss companies held $250 million of US assets and were the largest foreign-owned chemical manufacturers in the United States. The merger in 1970 of Ciba and Geigy created a $1.4 billion company with widespread manufacturing operations in Europe, North America and Brazil (Taylor and Sudnik 1984: 195).

The fastest growing part of the chemicals industry was petrochemicals, an industry which developed in the interwar years out of the technological convergence of the oil and chemical industries. Initially it was an almost exclusively American industry: in 1950 98 per cent of world production of ethylene, a key petrochemical product, was located in the United States. Subsequently, the petrochemicals industry grew exponentially with surging demand from the automobile, textile and construction industries, the growing use of synthetic materials, and falling costs of petroleum raw materials. World ethylene capacity grew twenty-six times between 1950 and 1970. While in 1950 98 per cent of this capacity was in the United States, by 1970 the share of the United States was 48 per cent, Europe 33 per cent and Japan 14 per cent. More than one-third of world ethylene capacity outside the United States and Japan was foreign-owned in 1970.

It was the oil companies, with their long experience of multinational operations, which were initially the most active direct investors. Exxon and Shell – whose US subsidiary had undertaken pioneering research in the industry – made large-scale FDI in European petrochemical manufacture in the 1950s. They were subsequently joined by the US chemical companies, led by Dow and later Union Carbide. The final entrants to the international industry were the major European chemical companies, which began to switch from coal to petroleum as the basic raw material for organic chemical manufacture in the 1950s. Some firms developed a petrochemicals capacity independently, while others co-operated with oil companies which were able to supply feedstocks from their refineries. These included BASF and Bayer which made partnerships with Shell and BP (Chapman 1991: 202–25).

United States MNEs were pre-eminent in the international growth of the new and fast-growing electronics industries. The first companies to appreciate the opportunities for the commercial applications of computers were a group of business machinery firms, including IBM, National Cash Register (NCR), Burroughs and Remington Rand whose origins dated back to the nineteenth century. These companies had benefited from the huge wartime demand for typewriters, adding and calculating machines and punched card tabulators – the contemporary tools of data management and processing. The US government became the largest customer in the world for such equipment, and its funding and encouragement of specific types of research – held to be essential for national security – led directly to the development of electronic digital computers, and miniaturised electronics (Cortada 1993: 221). Later the sheer size of US industry – as well as its readiness to accept the new technology – created a formidable non-military domestic market.

The US business machine companies took advantage of their unique nation-specific ownership advantage in the form of their domestic market. Remington Rand developed the first computer designed for business use, the Univac. IBM's subsequent recognition of the importance of electronics for the data processing industry resulted in the firm undertaking massive investment in research and production. By 1958 IBM had secured a predominant position in the United States market, accounting for over 80 per cent of the nearly 6,000 computers installed in that year (Dassbach 1989: 312–13). In the face of a proliferating number of incompatible computers, IBM's strategy focused on the creation of a single family of compatible computers which would enable it to reach as wide a commercial market as possible by utilising the cost advantages of the economies of scale. The result was the launch of System 360 in 1964, a broad line of compatible mainframe computers with peripherals for a wide range of uses. This proved an immense marketing success, and became the benchmark against which all other machines were measured. By the time IBM introduced its 370 range in 1970, IBM was the largest computer and electronic computer manufacturer, and one of the largest manufacturing enterprises in the world.

IBM and several other of the business machine firms had often engaged in FDI well before the Second World War (Wilkins 1974a: 77). After the war IBM's foreign factories were modernised, and in 1950 all its foreign assets were transferred to a new wholly-owned subsidiary, IBM World Trade Corporation. By 1960 World Trade operated in eighty-six countries and had a non-US workforce of around 33,000. In the 360 era IBM's non-US operations became increasingly important. In 1961 World Trade generated around 30 per cent of IBM's total profits and revenues. Nine years later it generated over 50 per cent of corporate profits and 40 per cent of revenues (Dassbach 1989: 349–55).

The modern semiconductor industry – which became one of the world's fastest growing industries from the late 1950s – also originated in the United States. The critical innovation was the fabrication of the first successful transitor at Bell Laboratories – owned by American Telephone and Telegraph – in 1948. These first transistors used germanium as their base material, but in 1954 Texas Instruments (TI) introduced the silicon transistor which had superior characteristics, and within a decade production of silicon transistors had overtaken that of germanium ones. At the end of the 1950s researchers at TI and Fairchild Semiconductors independently discovered the means of combining transistor and other discrete electrical components into a single, or integrated, circuit (IC). This opened up the modern era of integrated circuits. As in computers,

US semiconductor firms derived strong competitive advantages from their home market. In 1960 the United States accounted for over three-quarters of world consumption of semiconductors, a reflection of the importance of military and aerospace demand in the initial growth of the industry (Langlois 1988: 29–33). It was only in 1986 that Japan replaced the United States as the world's largest market for semiconductors.

US firms moved quickly to exploit their technological innovations abroad. In Europe they jumped tariff barriers and built fabrication facilities. TI was responsible for the first FDI by a US semiconductor firm when it established a manufacturing plant in Britain in 1957. The company hoped to qualify as a local producer by this strategy and thus received production contracts from the British government, Europe's largest defence spender. A factory in France followed three years later, designed to provide devices for IBM's French computer subsidiary, a reflection of the latter industry's emergence as the main user of semiconductors. By 1974 thirty-two US semiconductor producers had established in Europe nineteen wholly-owned subsidiaries and three joint ventures engaged in full manufacturing, together with twenty-four subsidiaries engaged in assembly (Langlois 1988: 68–9). In Asia, the US semiconductor firms invested in assembly and test facilities to take advantage of low labour costs (see pp. 141–2).

## Organisation

After the Second World War multinational manufacturing continued to be organised on a polycentric basis. The US manufacturing firms which expanded abroad after the Second World War would typically begin by founding autonomous foreign subsidaries, but once a number of these were in place, an international division would be formed, headed by a senior executive (Stopford and Wells 1972). The control system used in these international divisions varied widely between corporations, and depended in particular on the number of foreign subsidiaries and the nature of the transactions among the subsidiaries. While in some companies each subsidiary served a single national market and had little contact with other companies, in other cases a few large foreign manufacturing subsidiaries acted as supply points for marketing subsidiaries in other countries. Generally, the level of intra-firm manufacturing imports and exports was low in the postwar period (Wilkins 1974a: 435). As the numbers and spread of subsidiaries grew, some firms responded by appointing regional general managers, each responsible for the performance of one group of the foreign subsidiaries, and each reporting to divisional headquarters. Despite their importance in host economies, the sheer size of their domestic market meant that many US MNEs viewed their foreign operations as rather peripheral.

The organisation of multinational operations was heavily influenced by the nationality of the parent company. The spread of the M-form in postwar Britain was reflected in the use of the international division structure by many British manufacturing MNEs, but this took place in the context of a tradition whereby overseas subsidaries were allowed considerable autonomy, and this practice continued in many cases (Channon 1973: 78–85). In general, most European companies into the 1970s allowed their national companies considerable autonomy. There was little attempt at production co-ordination between national companies even at a company such as Nestlé, which accumulated a growing number of products in the postwar years ranging from its traditional dairy interests to instant coffee, soups and frozen foods (Channon 1973: 171–2; Heer 1966).

In so far as generalisation is possible given the considerable organisational diversity, US firms made greater use than Europeans of bureaucratic procedures to try to control their foreign manufacturing affiliates. European firms had a far greater reliance on a decentralised, parent-affiliate structure, and on informal, personalised control. This was termed the 'mother-daughter' form of organisation, which remained the pre-eminent form used in continental European MNEs until at least the 1970s. The most important bond was the personal relationship between presidents of parent companies and presidents of foreign ventures. European firms had little standardisation of reporting periods and document formats, while US firms usually had a high degree of standardisation. In contrast to US firms, written rules and procedures were much less important in European firms. The mother-daughter firms employed a higher proportion of home-country expatriates as presidents of foreign manufacturing subsidiaries than did firms with alternative structures. These expatriates were often heavily socialised into the parent's corporate culture. This made written rules and reports less important, because headquarters managers could usually predict how their foreign presidents would act (Franko 1976, 1978; Egelhoff 1984).

There are important caveats to these generalisations about organisation. Organisational structures differed between industries. There remained marked differences between the firms of different European countries, reflecting the diverse managerial traditions in that region. In both Europe and the United States there continued to be very considerable firm-specific differences in the organisation of MNEs. These reflected the distinct corporate cultures and unique competences possessed by each enterprise. And even the largest MNEs in the postwar period continued to reflect not only the values and practices of their home economies, but also the influence of the home cities or regions in which the company had originated and was based. Thus the organisation of Du Pont reflected its origins in Wilmington, Delaware; that of Fiat its origins in Turin, Italy, and that of Philips its origins in Eindhoven, Netherlands (Humes 1993: 111).

During the 1960s new strategies for the organisation of multinational manufacturing began to appear, involving both geographical and functional integration. The considerable autonomy given to national subsidiaries, even in US MNEs, gave rise to extensive duplication of products, R & D and other functions. The formation of the European Economic Community, worldwide lowering of barriers of trade, cost reduction in transportation, and a convergence of consumer demand in some sectors, pointed the way to solutions to these problems involving the integration of formerly isolated subsidiaries. United States MNEs began to abandon their international division structures in recognition of the fact that the presence of an international division as a separate, autonomous international unit could act as a constraint against the co-ordination of production on a worldwide scale (Stopford and Wells 1972: 21–7).

A few large US MNEs were prominent in the emergence of new strategies. During the 1950s IBM's foreign subsidiaries were hardly co-ordinated at all. They were primarily concerned with tabulating machines rather than computers, and they developed and produced different types of machines for their markets, as well as manufacturing American models. IBM's System 360 computers, which were designed to be manufactured and sold worldwide, required a far greater degree of international co-ordination. The domestic company took overall responsibility for development engineering and manufacturing. Responsibility for the development of specific processors or peripherals in the 360 line was assigned to different laboratories in Europe and the United States. The integration of product development and manufacturing planning on a world scale enabled IBM to offer its most current technologies to customers in all markets, and to make major cost savings from the elimination of overlapping products. By the end of the 1960s the firm had two regional production networks, in North America and Europe (Dassbach 1989).

During the mid-1960s Ford began to integrate its manufacturing on a regional basis. Following the removal of tariffs on assembled vehicles between producers located in the United States and Canada in 1965, Ford began to integrate its operations in the two countries. Canadian demand for many models was met by assembled vehicles imported from the United States and local production ceased, while Ford relocated and concentrated certain manufacturing operations in Canada. By 1974 the Canadian company was transformed into a unit of the US company. Subsequently Ford integrated its European operations. Its major European subsidiaries – Ford-UK and Fordwerke – had operated virtually independently, and produced unrelated passenger car models. The British subsidiary was not even wholly-owned between 1928 and 1961. By 1961 Ford US had reacquired ownership of all its European interests, and in 1967 Ford of

Europe was formed as a wholly-owned subsidiary of the US parent (Dassbach 1989: 377–9).

The creation of Ford of Europe was followed by the integration of the previously autonomous national affiliates. It had become the locus of strategic decision-making and financial planning. Product development was integrated through design and development of the first Europe-wide model – the Capri – in 1969. Falling trade barriers within Europe permitted growing cross-border movements in components and final products. Ford of Europe developed as a regionally integrated manufacturing operation. Its models were specific to Western Europe, and it possessed considerable autonomy from its parents (United Nations 1993: 147; McKinlay and Starkey 1994).

United States MNEs were the main beneficiaries of the first stage of regional integration in Europe. They were ahead of most of their European competitors in perceiving Europe as a unified market. A striking example was Unilever, whose European national subsidiaries produced and sold their own range of products well into the 1970s. Even in detergents – which lend themselves to extensive international standardisation – Unilever's European subsidiaries sold a wide range of different brands in packages of different sizes, and manufactured by a patchwork of plants, each designed to make a wide range of products for one national market. Although attempts at product rationalisation began in the 1970s, it was only under the competitive pressure of Procter & Gamble – which created an integrated European business – that Unilever moved substantively in this direction.

## GLOBAL INTEGRATION AND NETWORKS

### The changing structure of international competition

The period after 1980 combined continuities with the past with growing changes in the strategies and organisation of international production. Manufacturing FDI continued to grow rapidly, especially in the second half of the 1980s, when the annual growth rate reached almost 20 per cent, and it still accounted for almost 40 per cent of the outward FDI of developed countries. Multinational investment remained particularly prominent in certain industries, such as chemicals, electrical and mechanical machinery, automobiles and food, drink and tobacco (United Nations 1993: 72). However the era of US hegemony in multinational manufacturing gave way to one of competitive rivalries between US, European and Japanese firms.

The rapid growth of Japanese manufacturing MNEs reflected the strong ownership advantages they held in certain industries as a result of organisational innovations which challenged the American management and production methods which had been so important for much of the century. The new production system, which evolved at Toyota over a very long period extending from the 1930s until the 1960s, has been described variously as a form of 'flexible specialisation', 'post-Fordist', or 'lean production'. It can be differentiated from earlier systems of craft and mass production. The craft producer used highly skilled workers to make a small number of items. Mass production manufactured standardised products in very high volumes using unskilled or semi-skilled workers tending expensive single-purpose machines. In contrast, lean producers employed teams of multi-skilled workers trained to operate several different machines to manufacture products in enormous variety at a lower cost than mass production (Womack, Jones and Roos 1990: 13).

A central feature of this production system was the use of 'just-in-time' (JIT) systems which were based on the philosophy that work was only done when needed and in the necessary quantity and the necessary time. This resulted in a low level of inventories compared to a mass production factory. While mass production plants were as much warehouses as factories, JIT factories functioned with less than a third of the floor space. Japanese manufacturers also adapted ideas of quality control originally introduced into Japan by the US Army after the Second World War. Shop floor workers were empowered to stop assembly lines if problems emerged, and there would be a team effort to solve them. This system virtually eliminated major defects in manufacturing and design.

JIT necessitated changed relationships between manufacturers and their suppliers. In a mass production system, automobile manufacturers had distant and short-term relationships with their suppliers: large stocks had to be held just in case supplies were disrupted. In contrast, the lean producers had close relationships with a functionally tiered system of suppliers. Design and production of components was carried out in close consultation. The system developed by Toyota, and later adopted by other Japanese manufacturers, was one of tiered suppliers. The first-tier suppliers related directly to the customers, second-tier suppliers to first-tier suppliers and so on. The use of JIT methods encouraged geographical proximity, and suppliers were often located nearby their customers. Relationships with suppliers was critical because around 70 per cent of the entire value of a finished car was contracted out to suppliers, a much higher figure than in the mass production system. These tiers of firms in supplier *keiretsu* were not unitary firms organised in hierarchies, but in formal networks of relationships with flexible boundaries. They replaced arm's-length markets with intercompany co-operation, and the development of long-term relationships between independent enterprises (Gerlach 1992; Fruin 1992). The resulting system appeared to secure the advantages of both large organisations – economies of scale and scope – and those of small firms, including flexibility and entrepreneurship.

This new production system changed the economics of automobile production. Its consequences were seen in the shifting geographical location of the world industry. In 1960 the United States accounted for over 50 per cent of world production: thirty years later it accounted for less than 20 per cent. Japan's share of world automobile output rose from 1 to 25 per cent over the same period, although a subsequent revival in American production restored the United States to the position of the largest car manufacturing country in 1994.

The emergence of Japan as a major automobile producer was achieved without multinational manufacturing. Japanese car exports began increasing in the 1960s, and achieved considerable import penetration in the United States and parts of Europe in the 1970s. They were greatly assisted, especially in the United States, by an increased demand for small cars which the US manufacturers were too slow to meet. The Japanese companies initially exploited these market opportunities through exporting, together with a number of assembly operations, mainly in developing countries. Before 1982 there was not a single Japanese automobile production plant outside Japan. However, beginning in that year, when Honda opened a production facility, there was a rapid opening of Japanese transplants in the United States. Beginning in 1986 the leading Japanese automobile producers also constructed large-scale production facilities in Western Europe (Kenney and Florida 1993; Strange 1993: 172–85).

The multinational growth of the Japanese automobile industry was part of a wider process whereby Japanese companies shifted production overseas. The electronics companies led the process of internationalisation in the 1970s, automobile production followed in the 1980s, and semiconductor manufacture from the end of that decade (Yoffie 1993). In the 1990s many textile producers shifted production offshore. By 1994 nearly one-third of cars and machines made by Japanese-owned companies came from outside Japan, and 16 per cent of total Japanese-owned manufactured output was made abroad. The equivalent US figure remained much higher (around 27 per cent) but nonetheless the internationalisation of Japanese manufacturing over a short period was striking.

Lean production gave Japanese firms considerable competitive advantages in industries involving multi-assembly operations. In these industries, productivity and cost were determined by the efficiency with which parts were supplied and the flow of goods was co-ordinated. The *keiretsu* system of long-term mutual transactions between independent firms proved more efficient in this regard than integrated US corporations. In other manufacturing industries, such as chemicals or food, Japanese firms were not able to generate large ownership advantages. During the 1990s it also became evident that lean production had drawbacks as well as advantages. There were costs to the environment caused by the queues of trucks waiting outside lean factories to deliver components just-in-time, while the Kobe earthquake in 1995 showed that the entire production system was extremely vulnerable if an unforeseen event disrupted the flow of goods.

In many industries, such as chemicals, pharmaceuticals, computers, office machinery and electrical equipment, US MNEs remained powerful international competitors. A period of excessive diversification in the 1960s and 1970s, sometimes associated with financial engineering and excessive short-term time horizons, led to the demise of famous US MNEs such as Singer, and the rapid decline of US ownership in certain other industries, such as rubber. But a re-focusing on core activities and – as in the case of automobiles – a determined attempt to adopt Japanese production methods, enabled US firms to renew their competitive advantages (Chandler 1994). Meanwhile the largest European MNEs – such as Nestlé, Unilever, Bayer, Michelin, Electrolux and Glaxo – were global leaders in their respective industries.

These – and other MNEs – possessed considerable organisational capabilities, which were often the result of decades of cumulative experience, but the concept of an ownership advantage is less compelling than in previous periods as an explanation of multinational growth. The rapid diffusion of technologies and production systems made ownership advantages harder to sustain. A great deal of multinational activity took the form of strategic asset seeking. Enterprises bought or sold assets across borders to spread risks, open up new markets, or sometimes to make financial gains.

MNE strategies continued to deliver a range of outcomes from very successful to highly unsuccessful. The gap between the profitability of foreign-owned manufacturing firms in the United States and US manufacturers widened in the late 1970s and again in the 1980s. Although there was some evidence that poor recorded returns may have been caused by corporate strategies to minimise their fiscal obligations, the rapid rate at which foreign firms divested from their US subsidiaries suggested that many investments performed genuinely poorly. The predominant mode of entry into the United States was by acquisition, and in aggregate foreign companies paid high prices for poor quality companies. In the 1980s foreign MNEs purchased US manufacturers that were only a quarter as profitable as a broad US norm (Laster and McCauley 1994). The British remained the largest direct investors in the United States, but a substantial number of their acquisitions went awry (McCauley and Eldridge 1990). Japanese MNEs were not immune from major difficulties either. Sony and Matsushita were able to dominate world consumer electronics, but their acquisition of US entertainment companies such as Columbia Pictures, CBS Records and MCA proved slow to deliver expected gains. Matsushita's sale (to Canadian-owned Seagram) of 80 per cent of the equity of MCA only five years after the initial acquisition in 1990 was indicative of the problems encountered by the Japanese companies in attempting to manage Hollywood film studios.

### Locational factors and the growth of integrated production

Locational factors assumed a new importance in the growth of multinational manufacturing. There is no doubt that the growth of the 'new protectionism' from the 1970s stimulated the growth of multinational manufacturing, especially from Japan. As the US deficit mounted, American administrations became involved in growing trade disputes with Japan and Europe, alleging that their 'unfair' trading practices were hindering American exports. The United States pursued 'orderly marketing agreements' with Japan in sectors such as textiles, automobiles and electronics. Growing trade friction between the United States and Japan led to the passage by the US Congress in 1988 of the Omnibus Trade and Competitiveness Act, which provided – under the so-called 'Super 301' provisions – for unilateral retaliatory measures against trade partners found guilty of 'unfair trade practices'. Though this law expired in 1990, the United States persisted with unilateral trade restrictions, and Europe followed the American path (Strange 1993: 84–99).

There was a close correlation between the proliferation of voluntary export restraints (VERs) and orderly marketing agreements in the United States in the late 1970s and the sudden upsurge of Japanese FDI in the electronics and automobile industries (Encarnation 1992: 117–46). However, it should be stressed that as European exports were not subject to VERs, they provide at best a partial explanation for the growth of inward investment into the United States. The growth of European import restraints subsequently worked also to promote Japanese FDI into European manufacturing during the 1980s. The Single European Market project after 1985 greatly stimulated the growth of Japanese FDI by combining the promise of a very large and prosperous regional market with the threat that Japanese manufacturing exporters might have their access to it limited (Strange 1993: 106).

There was a new emphasis on production costs in decisions on the location of multinational manufacturing. A key development was the growth of outsourcing, which involved the transfer of part of a manufacturing (or other) operation to a host economy which was linked to work done elsewhere, mainly in the home country. The use of offshore assembly plants by firms in the semiconductors industry in the 1960s was a landmark event. Fairchild was the first US firm to establish offshore assembly – in Hong Kong in 1963 and South Korea in 1964. The other US semiconductor firms were forced by competitive pressures to follow the Fairchild example. The period was one of intensifying competition within the

United States as new firms entered the industry. By 1974 twenty-six US semiconductor firms had established fifty-six offshore assembly facilities, especially in Mexico, Singapore and Malaysia. In that year almost four-fifths of American production was assembled abroad (Langlois 1988: 51–6; Yoffie 1993).

The nature of the semiconductor industry made it ideal for outsourcing. Transport costs to foreign markets were low because of the high value per weight of semiconductors, while workers in Asia and Latin America could be trained quickly to undertake the tedious assembly work required. Initially the pioneering US firms established wholly-owned affiliates and most corporate functions remained with the parent. Wafers manufactured in the United States were air-freighted to Asia, assembled into circuits, and then air-freighted back to the parent firm for testing and distribution. Subsequently, local firms developed manufacturing skills and acted as subcontractors, and – especially when Japanese semiconductor MNEs expanded into Asia from the 1970s – more sophisticated parts of the production process, such as R & D and wafer fabrication, began to take place in Asia (United Nations 1993).

While protectionism encouraged Japanese manufacturers to build factories in the United States and Europe, it was cost considerations which led to their investments elsewhere. By the 1970s Japanese economic growth had resulted in rising real incomes, and hence rising labour costs. The Japanese yen was on a rising trend from 1972, when the postwar rate of Y360 to the dollar – which increasingly represented a gross undervaluation of the Japanese currency – was abandoned. These cost pressures resulted in Japanese electronics and textile producers – like their US and European counterparts – shifting assembly and lower value-added processes to offshore plants in the developing world, especially in Southeast Asia.

During the 1980s and 1990s cost-driven strategies became of increasing importance. As Asian newly industrial countries (NICs) such as Taiwan and South Korea experienced growing labour costs, they shifted their lower value-added activities to less developed neighbouring regions such as Malaysia, Thailand and, later, Vietnam and parts of China to take advantage of lower labour costs.

Outsourcing became an increasingly important practice in most industries, as MNEs focused on core activities and purchased intermediate goods and services from other firms. But over time the strategy became guided by a less exclusive emphasis on production costs, and a greater concern for matters such as quality and reliability. Closer and longer-term relationships developed between firms and their principal suppliers, with the latter taking greater responsibility for quality and design. As national markets became less protected, firms were freer to search worldwide for the lowest cost sources of supply. There was evidence of the boundaries of MNEs being redrawn to concentrate on sales and distribution, with production being subcontracted (Casson 1995).

MNEs had a growing ability to shift production or supply to wherever it was most profitable. While many companies integrated their production systems on a regional basis, in a number of cases this process was extended and deepened. In such 'global' MNEs, any affilate anywhere could perform functions for the firm as a whole. These firms located functions – not just production, but also R & D, finance and procurement – wherever they could be done best to fulfil a firm's overall strategy. This corporate structure resulted in substantial flows of technology, skills and goods within the firm, not only between parent firms and their affiliates, but between affiliates. The result was the rapid growth of intra-firm trade in both intangible and tangible assets. This increase in intra-firm trade was led by such industries as automobiles and electronics.

By the 1990s most US MNEs had abandoned their corporate-wide international divisions and had globalised their product divisions, though considerable firm-specific differences remained. European MNEs also moved further away from their 'mother-daughter' structures towards global product divisions and the employment of a wide range of American management methods. Bayer was among the large European MNEs to reorganise on global product lines, though other MNEs – such as Unilever and Nestlé – continued to use a more decentralised structure with relatively autonomous operating companies. There was evidence of a convergence between US, European and Japanese organisational structures as all MNEs sought to achieve the most efficient balance between the product, geographical and functional elements of their business, but considerable diversity persisted in corporate responses to these common challenges (Humes 1993: 137–41, 206–11, 347–51).

The extent of the geographical and functional integration of MNEs continued to differ considerably between industries, and within industries. In automobiles, Ford and General Motors moved furthest towards globally and regionally integrated companies. Ford attempted to produce a world car – the Escort – in 1981, but the plan failed because it did not establish a single organisational structure for product development and design. From the mid-1980s Ford developed a new 'world car' designed to be sold around the world, which was launched in Europe as the Mondeo in 1993. This time Ford closely integrated the design and production worldwide. In 1995 Ford merged its North American and European units into a single operating unit designed to achieve common governance of product, manufacturing, supplier and sales activities along global product lines. However, even in automobiles, Ford's structure was exceptional. Neither the Japanese nor the European automobile MNEs have sought as yet to match this degree of global integration (United Nations 1993: 150–1; United Nations 1994: 150).

The organisational structures of the MNEs engaged in such complex

*Table 4.2* Growth in international strategic alliance formation in manufacturing, 1980–9

| Industry | Number of alliances | |
|---|---|---|
| | *1980–4* | *1985–9* |
| *Automobiles* | 26 | 79 |
| US-Europe | 10 | 24 |
| US-Japan | 10 | 39 |
| Europe-Japan | 6 | 16 |
| *Biotechnology* | 108 | 198 |
| US-Europe | 58 | 124 |
| US-Japan | 45 | 54 |
| Europe-Japan | 5 | 20 |
| *Information technology* | 348 | 445 |
| US-Europe | 158 | 256 |
| US-Japan | 133 | 132 |
| Europe-Japan | 57 | 57 |
| *Chemicals* | 103 | 80 |
| US-Europe | 54 | 31 |
| US-Japan | 28 | 35 |
| Europe-Japan | 21 | 14 |

*Source:* United Nations 1994: 139

integration were very different from those of the mid-twentieth century. Within MNEs, functional integration made affiliates resemble a network rather than a hierarchy. The network of affiliates was in turn connected to other corporate networks through a variety of linkages such as subcontracting. There was also a proliferation of strategic alliances which brought large competitor enterprises together for specific purposes. During the 1980s numerous cross-border alliances were signed between manufacturing companies. Table 4.2 provides an estimate of their numbers in several of the main industries affected by this trend.

These strategic alliances took numerous forms, from international joint ventures to non-equity arrangements, which were more common. While in the post-1945 decades US MNEs in particular had often used joint ventures as a second best alternative to wholly-owned subsidiaries, the strategic alliances of this era were distinguished by their dynamic use as a tool to promote global product and marketing strategies. They were often intended to be ongoing and long term. The agreements were heavily concentrated in a number of technology-intensive industries – computers, motor vehicles, electricals, telecommunications, biotechnology, chemicals, aerospace – characterised by high entry costs, globalisation, scale economies, rapidly changing technologies and substantial operating risks. The concentration of alliances in the world's fastest growing and most advanced industries differentiated them sharply from the interwar cartels. Strategic alliances enabled MNEs to share the risks of new research and to get faster access to changing technologies, as well as opening up the prospect of technological cross-fertilisation (Morris and Hergert 1987; Lorange and Roos 1992).

The formation of strategic alliances represented a radical shift in strategy by the world's largest MNEs which had spent much of the previous century seeking to maintain control of their proprietary technology and brands. During the 1980s IBM, traditionally highly reluctant to collaborate with other firms, entered alliances with more than forty partners around the world, pooling technology and customer bases. In the international food industry, where the protection of brands among other factors had traditionally encouraged firms to prefer wholly-owned subsidiaries, strategic alliances proliferated from the late 1980s between the largest MNEs. Nestlé entered major alliances with General Mills and Coca-Cola, and Unilever with Pepsi Co. and BSN.

The growing importance of networks rather than hierarchies in multinational manufacturing was striking. As in the case of the interwar cartels, these collaborative arrangements were in a constant state of flux. It was possible that at least one-half of strategic alliances performed unsatisfactorily in some sense. Alliances were hard to sustain if circumstances changed radically, which they frequently did, not least because many of them were specially designed to develop new technologies or products. There were sometimes acute problems caused by differences in national or organisational cultures between firms. Nonetheless, as the twenty-first century approached, it was evident that the boundaries of firms were increasingly hard to discern in the world's fastest growing manufacturing industries, just as they were in the resource industries. Innovation often occurred at the places when boundaries overlapped with one another. Competitive advantages were being generated as much by relationships between hierarchies as within a hierarchy itself. It was in these relationships – rather than in the size and scale of firms – that the sources of success or failure in international business were increasingly found.

## SUMMARY

Since the nineteenth century MNEs have occupied an important place in the international diffusion of manufacturing technologies, processes and products. After starting early in the century, multinational manufacturing grew rapidly between the 1880s and 1930, despite the disruption caused by the First World War, but the Great Depression halted this growth by creating conditions that favoured the alternative of international collusion. Multinational manufacture was prominent in industries in which proprietary technology, brand names and other intangible assets were important. High transaction costs encouraged the exploitation of these assets through direct investment rather than market-based arrangements. Tariffs, patent legislation, market size and competitive behaviour were important locational determinants.

After the Second World War US MNEs were pre-eminent in multi-national manufacturing. They were world leaders in many technologies and possessed considerable international competitive advantages. European and Japanese companies were initially preoccupied with the reconstruction of their domestic economies, and then took advantage of falling trade barriers by exporting rather than investing abroad. From the late 1960s the firms from these countries resumed multinational manufacturing strategies. Locational factors, especially related to cost, emerged as increasingly important influences on multinational manufacturing in recent years.

Multinational manufacturing always presented complex management challenges. Inadequate strategies and structures caused failures and poor-performing investments in each generation. Organisational solutions varied over time and between nationalities. By the middle of the twentieth century multinational manufacturing had become dominated by large managerial enterprises which presided over foreign subsidiaries which were given considerable autonomy. Subsequently a process of geograph-ical and functional integration led to the growth of global manufacturing, yet the boundaries of the MNEs undertaking this integration became far more flexible as outsourcing and strategic alliances redefined the core competences of firms.

# Chapter 5

# Multinationals and services

## INTERNATIONAL BUSINESS AND SERVICES

International business in services made possible much of the multinational investment in natural resources and manufacturing. In the nineteenth century, the transportation, information, energy and financial infrastructure of large parts of the world was put in place not by governments, but by international business. The financing, insurance and transportation of world trade in manufactures and resources was undertaken by MNEs. In subsequent generations, service sector firms retained and expanded their role as enablers of international business. In some cases, they assumed central roles as the owners and co-ordinators of cross-border investments in manufacturing and resources.

The service sector is a highly diffuse one, and the term is often used as a residual to include everything which is not manufacturing or resource exploitation. It includes trade, finance, personal and business services, construction, transportation, communication and public utilities. Not only do these different services have different characteristics, but in many cases they consist of sub-sectors which also differ considerably from each other. This makes generalisations about multinationals in services especially difficult. A further complication is the distinction between FDI in services and FDI by service sector companies. Since the nineteenth century both manufacturing and petroleum companies have diversified into distribution and transportation, while service MNEs have diversified far beyond services.

The impact of multinational investment in services was as significant as that of its equivalent in manufacturing and natural resources. Service MNEs have been transferors of organisational and technological systems across borders. They were large employers. They led the international transfer of consumption patterns and lifestyles.

## ORIGINS AND GROWTH

The range of international business in services in the nineteenth century was striking. Table 5.1 shows some of the enterprises engaged in multinational investment before 1914.

*Table 5.1* International business in services before 1914: illustrative cases

| Company | Nationality | Principal business | First FDI | Countries/ operations c. 1914 |
| --- | --- | --- | --- | --- |
| Mitsui Bussan | Japanese | Trading company | 1877 | 30+ branches in Asia, Europe, Australia, US; manufacturing in China |
| Bank of Australasia | UK | Bank | 1835 | 200+ branches in Australia and New Zealand |
| New York Life | US | Insurance | 1858 | Branches in Europe, Asia, Australia, Latin America |
| Imperial Continental Gas Association | UK | Utilities | 1825 | Electricty and gas utilities in Austria, Belgium, France, Germany, Hungary |
| Brazilian Traction, Light & Power | Canadian | Utilities | 1898 | Electricity, gas, tramway, telephone, utilities in Brazil |

### Trade and distribution

The extensive multinational investments in trade and distribution in the nineteenth century came from many sources. US and European manufacturing firms made numerous investments in sales and distribution companies in foreign markets to assist their exports. These investments often proved a first stage of multinational involvement, and were followed in time by assembly or production facilities. In a number of exceptional cases, such as that of Singer Sewing Machines, the foreign marketing investments reached enormous proportions. In the petroleum industry, the initial international expansion of Standard Oil and, to a lesser extent, the European oil companies, was far more concerned with marketing and distribution than the exploitation of foreign oilfields.

The nineteenth century also saw the growth of international trading companies which offered an alternative organisational form to the vertical integration of manufacturers or petroleum companies. Trading companies of various types had existed for a considerable period of time. The large

European trading companies, which were active mostly between the sixteenth and eighteenth centuries, were chartered by European governments and given monopoly powers to trade within their regions of specialisation. These ventures, which included the Muscovy Company, the English, Dutch and French East India Companies, and the Hudson's Bay Company, had some striking resemblances to modern multinationals (Carlos and Nicholas 1988), but seldom outlived the withdrawal of their monopoly privileges. By 1914 the only survivor of these giants was the Hudson's Bay Company, which had evolved into a successful retailing business – though it was only in 1991 that it stopped trading in fur.

The eighteenth and nineteenth centuries saw a proliferation of international merchant enterprise. This usually involved the movement of individuals, rather than firms, across borders, and it developed in a world where modern concepts of 'nationality' were not fully formed. The merchants engaged in international trade at the world's ports were of varied ethnic origins, and have been described as 'a cosmopolitan bourgeoisie' (C. Jones 1987). Over the course of the nineteenth century a process occurred whereby some European (and occasionally American) merchants involved in selling Western goods and buying local products in Asia, Latin America and elsewhere, evolved into trading companies. The companies of the major European colonial powers were especially prominent, but Swiss and Danish trading firms also became important international players.

The trading companies were important elements in the expansion of world trade flows in the late nineteenth century. They handled the flow of manufactured goods from the developed world to the developing regions and the reverse flow of commodities. Their trading interests also led them to diversify into other activities, leading to their evolution as 'investment groups' (see Chapter 2). The creation of Malaya's rubber plantation industry in the 1900s by the British 'agency houses' was paralleled by diversification strategies in other regions. The British trading companies active in the British colony of Hong Kong and the coastal regions of China – known locally as the 'hongs' – included Swires and Jardine Matheson. The former developed extensive shipping-related activities and sugar refining in China. The latter also diversified into shipping and sugar refining, but additionally established silk, cotton, ice and other factories in China and Hong Kong. It built China's first railway line, controlled Hong Kong's dockyards, invested in electricity generation and undertook land investments (Sugiyama 1987).

There were many trading companies active in Latin America. The British-owned Balfour Williamson was formed in 1851 and opened an office in Chile in 1852, followed by one in San Francisco in 1869, which handled California wheat and other produce exports and imported merchandise for sale in California. Over the next fifty years Balfour Williamson diversified its activities on the US Pacific Coast to include land investment, vineyards, fruit farms, mortgage lending and oil production (Wilkins 1989: 136, 285, 318). In Chile it had investments in nitrates production, while in Peru it owned and controlled an oil company (Miller 1982). W. R. Grace & Co, a trading company which owed its origins to an Irish partner of a British firm active in shipbuilding and the guano trade in mid-nineteenth century Peru, developed diversified activities in plantations and railroads in Latin America, acquired an American character, and from the 1880s was head-quartered in New York (Clayton 1985).

European trading companies became important in Africa from the late nineteenth century. They first appeared in the guise of state-chartered companies. European governments gave such firms special quasi-governmental privileges in the context of imperialist rivalries. These state-chartered companies had mixed fortunes, and were mostly super-seded as formal colonial control was extended over Africa, but a number survived for longer. After the loss of its royal charter in 1900, the Niger Company in West Africa was able to make use of its established position to develop and expand its trading activities (Pearson 1971). It was eventually acquired by Lever Brothers in 1920, and nine years later merged with its major British competitor in the region to form the United Africa Company (UAC), which became a wholly-owned subsidiary of Unilever. It was the largest business enterprise in the West African import and export trade, and also operated in the French West African colonies, but two large French-owned trading companies were active there also, the Compagnie Française de l'Afrique Noire and the Société Commerciale de l'Ouest Africaine (Hopkins 1976a: 38–41; Coquery-Vidrovitch 1975).

The European trading companies were powerful agents in the shaping of the West African colonial economies. They were active in all exporting and importing functions in West Africa, and developed an infrastructure to collect export crops from the small-scale and widely scattered cultivation of the region. They penetrated into the interior of this region from their coastal bases using modern transport technology of steamers, trains and trucks. This operation expanded along the rivers from around 1880; followed the railroad systems from 1900; and from the 1920s involved the use of motor transport on the newly built roads. The firms undertaking river-based trade were required to make particularly large investments in fixed capital, because they (unlike those using the railroads) had to invest in the means of transport. Their operations required not only vessels, but ancillary facilities such as fuel dumps, warehouses and buying stations (Van Der Laan 1981; Hopkins 1976b: 277–8).

In Japan, trading companies assumed an unusually important role. After the Meiji Restoration in 1868 several dozen trading companies were founded. These were mostly 'speciality' trading companies which traded in one or a few goods, usually with one or perhaps two regions. The first one was Maruzen, established in 1869, which specialised in the import of books and fancy goods from Europe and the United States. Mitsui Bussan, the first Japanese general trading company or *sogo shosha*, was founded in 1876. This differed from the 'speciality' trading companies because it came to trade in many products in many regions. It opened its first overseas branch – in Shanghai – in 1877, for the purpose of selling Japanese coal in China. By the eve of the First World War Mitsui Bussan had more than thirty foreign branches and offices in Asia, Europe and the United States, and it traded more than 120 different kinds of goods. It handled around 20 per cent of Japan's total exports and imports. In the 1900s the firm also invested in Chinese cotton textiles production, and opened a flour mill in Shanghai. The growth of *sogo shosha* is discussed in greater detail below (see pp. 181–7).

Trading companies were a dynamic form of international business, whose functions changed over time as they pursued diversification strategies. There was a general trend from trading activities towards production, which seems to have increased over the first decades of the twentieth century. In Latin America, W. R. Grace diversified after the First World War into sugar plantations, nitrates exploitation and many other market and supply-oriented activities. At the end of the 1920s it established a joint venture airline with Pan American to link Argentina and the West Coast of South America with the United States (Clayton 1985: 302–50). In Southeast Asia, the British agency houses diversified further in the interwar years into tea and oil palm plantations, and into altogether new ventures, such as motor car distribution and industrial chemicals (Drabble and Drake 1981: 309–11; S. Jones 1986: 214–15; Brown 1994: 43–65).

### Shipping

Down to 1914 Britain owned more than the rest of the world's shipping tonnage put together. British shipping companies had worldwide activities, and carried a high proportion of the world's trade, including perhaps as much as a half of the foreign trade of the United States (Wilkins 1989: 519). The international shipping activities of other countries grew in importance from the late nineteenth century. German shipping companies such as the North German Lloyd and the Hamburg-American developed substantial transatlantic business, and acquired (for example) their own docks in New York (Wilkins 1989: 517). From the 1880s Japanese shipping companies began developing international shipping routes, first in Asia and later to the United States. Osaka Shosen Kaisha (OSK) was organised in 1884, and Nippon Yusen Kaisha (NYK) in the following year. NYK inaugurated shipping lines between Japan and the United States and Europe. To facilitate this business, the firm set up offices in major US and European ports (Wray 1984).

Shipping companies frequently diversified into other activities. The Scottish-based Mackinnon 'Group' – in fact a collection of interlinked partnerships – constructed a diversified intercontinental enterprise between the 1840s and the 1890s. Its extensive steamship operations, which included important shipping companies such as British India Steam Navigation Co., extended over four continents, and grew from the 1860s on the basis of mail contracts from British and Dutch colonial governments in Asia. Beyond shipping, the group controlled trading firms in the Arabian Gulf and East Africa, and invested in the production of commodities to be carried on its steamers – including tea estates in Bengal and Assam, coal mining in Bengal, jute mills and a cotton mill in Calcutta, and a meat-freezing factory in Queensland, Australia (Munro 1987, 1988). The merger of the British India Steam Navigation Co. and the P & O Steam Navigation Co. shortly before the First World War created the largest shipping enterprise in the world, which under the leadership of Lord Inchcape expanded further in the interwar years (S. Jones 1986: 56).

Shipping was also an activity into which firms from other sectors integrated. In the oil industry, the earliest tankers were commissioned in the 1870s by the Nobels, the Swedish oil producers in Russia. Subsequently the multinational oil companies came to own and operate large tanker fleets (Ferrier 1982: 534). In agribusiness, the United Fruit Company established a fleet for the bulk transport of tropical agricultural products (Read 1983). Lever Brothers also diversified into shipping as part of its commodity activities (Wilson 1954, I: 160, 237–8).

**Banking and insurance**

Bankers had engaged in the finance of cross-border trade and international lending for centuries, and the history of international banking can be legitimately traced back to the Italian bankers of the Middle Ages, through the bankers of south Germany in the sixteenth century, and the Dutch bankers of the eighteenth century (Cameron and Bovykin 1991). These bankers generally operated internationally through partnerships and family connections rather than direct investments.

Business institutions which were much closer to modern-style multinational banks appeared in Europe in the 1830s, when the first British 'overseas banks' were established. These banks were promoted and owned largely in the United Kingdom, where they had (usually) their corporate headquarters. The first banks went to the British colonies in Australia, the West Indies, and Canada, where they established branches and financed foreign trade. The banks specialised in particular regions or countries. A pioneer was the Bank of Australasia, which was founded in 1835, and was a direct predecessor to ANZ, now one of Australia's largest banks. During the mid-century further British banks were founded to undertake business in the settler economies of Latin America and South Africa, as well as in the trading ports of Asia. By 1913 just over thirty British overseas banks operated almost 1,400 branches outside the United Kingdom, spread throughout Australasia, Asia, Africa and Latin America. These banks were 'free-standing' in organisational form for they did not conduct domestic banking activities in Britain, nor did they have equity links with domestic British banks until after 1914.

The British banks made an important contribution to the creation of modern financial infrastructure in the countries in which they invested. In only a few instances did they enter a completely 'virgin' territory, but they often introduced a degree of stability and financial sophistication which had not previously existed. These banks were concerned to provide trade finance and related foreign exchange business. By the end of the nineteenth century a considerable share of the international trade of the Southern Hemisphere countries and Asia was financed by them. However the finance of trade led them to seek deposits, and over time there was a general tendency for them to become involved in purely local business (Jones 1993a). In modern terminology they diversified from multinational service banking – servicing the requirements of corporate clients and expatriates from the home economy – to multinational retail banking – or serving local customers through the same deposit and loan facilities as domestic banks (Grubel 1977).

Over the course of the nineteenth century and subsequently banks of other nationalities also undertook direct investment abroad. Specialist overseas banks were created in France, Germany and other European countries to operate in colonial territories and in Latin America, while European banks also established branches in other European cities, especially London, the major international financial centre before 1914. Almost invariably, these overseas banks had much closer links with pre-existing domestic banks than in the British case (Meuleau 1990; Hertner 1990).

In contrast to the scale and scope of European multinational banking, both Japanese and United States banks initially undertook little FDI. Japan's first multinational bank was founded by the government in 1880. This was the Yokohama Specie Bank, the predecessor to the Bank of Tokyo, which by 1914 had around twenty foreign branches, spreading from China to Europe and the United States. This was a remarkable achievement for an Asian bank in this period, though its trade finance and other activities were of little significance beyond Japan (Tamaki 1990). US multinational banking was minimal before 1914. Subsequently, the number of foreign branches of US banks soared to 181 in 1920, before falling back to 107 by 1925 (Wilkins 1993a). Citibank, which opened its first foreign branch in Buenos Aires, Argentina in 1914, became the pre-eminent bank. By 1930 it had almost one hundred foreign branches, two-thirds of them in Latin America (Huertas 1990: 250–1). There was, therefore, a considerable contrast between the internationalisation of US manufacturing, resource and utility companies, and the retarded growth of US multinational banking.

Like the trading and shipping companies, multinational banks sometimes diversified outside their core business. The 'mixed' banking system prevalent in continental Europe resulted in far closer links between banks and industry than in the United States or Britain, and this was reflected in their foreign as well as domestic activities. The Deutsche Bank was involved in railroad construction in the Middle East, controlled a Romanian oil company; and – together with other German banks – became extensively involved in public utility investments before 1914. During the 1900s French banks were closely involved in Russian industry via their Russian banking affiliates (Crisp 1976: 111–88). Although the international activities of the German banks were heavily curtailed by the First World War, the French banks continued to make diversified investments in foreign banks and manufacturing in the interwar years (Bussière 1983).

Insurance attracted some early multinational investment. From the late eighteenth century the British-owned Phoenix Assurance Company began opening agencies in other European countries, and later elsewhere. It opened a New York fire and marine agency in 1804. After the end of the US Civil War a substantial number of British companies entered the US market, as well as a number of Canadian and German firms in the 1870s. By 1913 there were almost 90 foreign companies active in fire and marine insurance in the United States, including firms from Britain, Germany, Russia, France, Switzerland, Japan and even Bulgaria (Wilkins 1989: 64, 88, 134, 528–35). British firms provided almost a quarter of the total fire insurance cover in the United States around this date, and over two-thirds of that in Canada (Michie 1992: 160). In life insurance, US companies – notably New York Life, which began selling insurance in Canada in 1858 – joined British, Dutch, German and other European firms in expanding across borders (Wilkins 1970: 64–5, 103–7; Gales and Sluyterman 1993; Schröter 1993a: 37).

From the early twentieth century governments began to regulate foreign participation in insurance markets. There was a widespread concern to restrict the provision of life insurance to national companies, and over time this led to a substantial decline in multinational investment. In addition high European inflation during the First World War also caused major losses to the US life insurance companies, because many of their policies were in gold, while depreciated currencies made the cost of paying them exorbitant. After the war the US companies withdrew from foreign markets other than Canada (Wilkins 1974a: 43–4). However, in fire, accident and other types of insurance, there remained international opportunities, and there were also opportunities in motor insurance, which attracted new entrants into multinational motor insurance in the interwar years (Westall 1992: 294–326).

## Utilities

The nineteenth century saw widespread multinational investment in energy, transport and communication utilities, especially in Latin America and parts of Europe. There was a considerable spectrum of different types of firm involved, from free-standing companies to large utility MNEs, while manufacturing companies, banks and agribusiness firms were also involved in utility investments.

From the 1820s a number of British companies established and operated gas utilities in Continental Europe, drawing on Britain's expertise as the world pioneer of gas lighting. They took the free-standing form and did not manufacture gas in the United Kingdom. In the 1850s and 1860s British companies were formed to build and manage gas utilities in India, China and elsewhere. An early and important example of these ventures was the Imperial Continental Gas Association, which acquired an existing gas works in Ghent, in the Netherlands, in 1825. Subsequently this venture expanded by securing municipal contracts to supply gas lighting to other European cities. At the turn of the century it operated gas utilities in ten major European towns outside the United Kingdom – of which Berlin was the largest operation – and twenty-nine smaller towns, and had a total work-force of almost 8,000 (Hill 1950). Imperial Continental survived the switch from gas to electricity, two world wars and post-1945 nationalisations of utilities in several European countries, and continued into the 1970s as a large public utility operation in Belgium and a number of other countries.

By the middle of the nineteenth century a worldwide boom was underway in building railroads. Foreign capital financed much of the construction of the world's railroads, though it was largely portfolio in nature. The government controlled the large railroad systems built in both Russia and British India, which were financed in part by bonds issued abroad. In the United States, the railroad system was a private sector one, owned and managed almost entirely by American companies, though American railroad securities were widely held abroad. Railroads were by far the largest single sector to attract foreign investment in the United States between 1875 and 1914, when the total foreign investment in American railroads was over $4 billion. But the only clearly identifiable FDI in this huge sum was that of Canadian railroad companies, principally the Canadian Pacific and the Canadian Grand Trunk, which crossed the United States border to complete their own systems, though sometimes other foreign portfolio holdings were so large that some managerial control could be exercised (Wilkins 1989: 190–228).

In contrast, foreign investment in Latin American railroads often took the form of FDI, though its significance changed over time. Beginning with the Panama Railroad Company, a New York chartered venture which built a railroad across the Panama Isthmus in 1851 (Wilkins 1970: 22–3), there was US FDI in the railroad systems of Mexico and central America, as well as Canada. By the end of the century the largest amount of US FDI in Mexico was in railroads, though subsequently the government bought out much of the American investment, and control of the system passed into Mexican hands. Elsewhere in Latin America, foreign owner-ship of railroads became considerable in the late nineteenth century, and then tended to decline, though the foreign role was persistent in Cuba and Argentina (Lewis 1983b). In the latter country, British-owned and managed railroad companies became dominant in the wake of the Baring Crisis, a disastrous financial crisis in 1890, when the state-owned railroads were privatised. Between 1900 and 1914 total route mileage doubled, almost entirely in British-owned railroads, although three French-owned railroad companies were also active (Lewis 1983a; Regalsky 1989).

FDI in railroads was often related to investment in other public utilities. By 1914 British-owned and managed gas, electricity, tramway, bus, and dockyard companies were found all over Latin America, and especially Argentina, Brazil, Chile and Uruguay (Rippy 1959). They were often dominant influences on their local economies. The supply of both gas and fresh water to Montevideo, the capital of Uruguay, was the monopoly of two British utility companies, while one of the two companies which operated electric tramways in that city was also British, as was the larger of two companies providing a telephone service (Finch 1985: 257).

Canadian companies undertook important direct investments in Latin American utilities from the 1890s. Southeast Brazil was the scene of some of the most significant Canadian investment in electricity and tramways. The Sao Paulo Tramway, Light and Power Company was formed in 1898, followed by the Rio de Janeiro Tramway, Light and Power Co. Ltd six years later. These linked enterprises were large electricity generators, and created integrated, electrified tramway systems in their cities. Water, power, gas, and telephone enterprises were also operated. In 1912 a Toronto-based holding company, the Brazilian Traction, Light and Power Co. Ltd, was formed which owned the shares of both companies (McDowall 1988). Another Canadian company, the Mexican Light and Power Company, which was founded in 1902, operated a large-scale hydroelectric system and an urban tramway system in Mexico City (Armstrong and Nelles 1988).

The 'nationality' of these Canadian utilities was truly ambiguous. An American engineer was the most influential individual behind the Brazilian and Mexican ventures, providing both entrepreneurship and technical expertise. The tiny Toronto and Montreal headquarters of the companies consisted of a handful of financiers. The key purchasing functions – the acquisition of the capital goods required to build the hydro-electric and tramway systems – was located in New York, while most of the stock was issued on the London capital market.

Belgian utility companies were internationally active from the 1870s, usually taking the form of large holding companies. An example was the Société Générale des Chemins de Fer Economiques, founded in 1880 by several banks including one of the Belgium's largest, the Banque de Bruxelles. By 1914 this enterprise owned and controlled tramway companies in many cities of Italy, Spain, Egypt and elsewhere (Van der Wee and Goossens 1991: 126–7). Belgian FDI in utilities was prominent in Russia, where Belgian companies began to secure concessions from Russian municipalities in the early 1880s to operate horse-drawn tramways, and later electrically powered ones. By the eve of the First World War there were twenty-three Belgian tramway companies active in Russia (McKay 1970: 100).

The building and operation of utilities in the nineteenth century was undertaken not only by specialist enterprises, but also by firms engaged in other types of business. United Fruit invested in railroads and other utilities in central America to facilitate its tropical fruit business. Mining and petroleum companies frequently ran utilities in their area of operation. Trading companies became involved in establishing and managing utilities, sometimes for extended periods, in Latin America and Asia.

There were also large investments in Latin American, Italian, Spanish and Russian public utilities by German electrical engineering firms in the late nineteenth century. These firms obtained concessions to build electrical installations or plants. Subsequently they created companies to which such concessions were transferred. These companies then ordered equipment from their German parents. The German electrical producers also purchased existing horse tramway companies, and electrified them, again using their own products. The outcome of this strategy – which contemporary German observers called *Unternehmergeschäft* – was to create a large market for electrical products by promoting the electrification of a whole region.

There was a problem with such a strategy in so far as it left the electrotechnical companies holding a large portfolio of shares of utility companies. A solution was found when AEG and Siemens participated in financial holding companies along with German, Swiss and other banks. These *Finanzierungsgesellschaften* – such as AEG's Bank für elektrische Unternehmunger established in 1895 – acquired the equity of the utility companies, which they held during the critical development period, and then sold to the public, retaining only a minority equity stake. The financial holding companies were generally headquartered in Belgium or in Switzerland: politically 'neutral' countries with well-organised financial markets and favourable company legislation. They developed sub-holding companies to control regional groupings of utility operations. The AEG group had a number of such sub-holding companies, including one for Italy – the Società per lo sviluppo delle imprese elettriche in Italia – and another for Argentina, Chile and Uruguay – the Deutsche Überseeische Elektrizitäts-Gesellschaft or DUEG (Hertner 1986; 1987b; 1993). DUEG's shareholders included AEG and Deutsche Bank, which held 16 per cent of the equity each, together with eight German and Swiss banks. With assets of $73 million in 1914, this holding company was the biggest German FDI before the First World War (Jacob-Wendler 1982: 72; Schröter 1993a: 29).

Swiss, Belgian and French electrical companies also followed this strategy. In 1895 the Swiss company Brown Boveri formed the Motor für angewandte Elektrizität (shortened to Motor) in alliance with a Zurich bank and several German companies. It specialised in Italy, but also had shareholdings in electrical plants in Switzerland, Norway, France and Germany, and in 1911 founded an Argentinian subsidiary with several partners, including the Italian firm Pirelli. In 1904 the Belgian electrical group Empain founded the Compagnie Générale de Railways et Electricité, which acquired diverse interests in electricity and electrical transport in France, Belgium, Italy, Portugal, Russia and elsewhere. French-owned Schneider et Cie also promoted a Swiss holding company at the end of the 1890s, but did not exercise such exclusive management control as in the other cases (Hertner 1987b; Lanthier 1989: 143–7).

In the late nineteenth century telephones began to attract direct investment. Telephones were an American invention, and in the 1880s US interests – American Bell and Edison – sought to introduce telephones in Europe and elsewhere, often taking minority interests in companies operating franchises for particular cities (Wilkins 1970: 50). Subsequently US and European firms established a series of direct investments in telephone utilities in Latin America and other developing regions. In the 1900s Swedish-owned Stockholms Allmäna Telefon (SAT), in alliance with a syndicate of European banks, secured concessions to operate the telephone systems of Moscow and Warsaw, Poland. Russian and Polish subsidiaries were formed controlled by SAT. SAT and its Swedish competitor Ericsson also secured a concession to operate telephone systems in Mexico (Lundström 1986a: 144–5).

Telephones were one important element behind a surge of US FDI in utilities between 1919 and 1929, which grew as a share of the total stock of US FDI from 4 to 14 per cent of total US FDI (Wilkins 1974a: 55). This period saw the fast international growth of the International Telephone and Telegraph Corporation (ITT). This was a 'free-standing' firm in the sense that it did not operate a business inside the United States, although it was headquartered and managed there. It was founded in 1920 by the merger of two small telephone companies in Puerto Rico and Cuba, the former acquired as a result of a bad debt. Under the leadership of Sosthenese Behn, ITT borrowed extensively on the US capital markets to finance the purchase of foreign telephone companies and the foundation of new ones. In 1925 ITT acquired the international division of Western Electric, the largest US producer of electric products, and with it a network of subsidiaries manufacturing electrical products and telephone apparatus in Europe, Argentina, Australia, Japan and China (Wilkins 1974a: 70–1). By the end of the decade the firm operated telephone and telegraph in several Latin American countries, and had extensive cable and radio investments. Its total worldwide employment, almost entirely outside the United States, approached 100,000 (Abo 1982: 104–13).

The growth of another US utility, the American & Foreign Power Company, was almost as striking. This enterprise was formed in 1923 out of a General Electric subsidiary, although equity links (but not cross-directorships) were subsequently severed. It undertook substantial FDI, especially in Latin America, but also in China, where a major acquisition in 1929 in Shanghai gave it the largest power station in that country. The firm manufactured and sold electricity and gas, ran tramways and even supplied telephone services (Wilkins 1974a: 131–4).

By the standards of the dynamic US utility investments of the 1920s, the European companies appeared to be a spent force. The once extensive Belgian FDI in Russian utilities was eliminated by the Communist Revolution. In postwar Latin America, the British-owned utilities in electricity and telephones often fared badly from competition from US, Italian and Spanish firms, which offered consumers more up-to-date services. Some companies sold out to the Americans (Finch 1985: 259; Miller 1993: 187). Yet there were also signs of adaption to new circumstances. The British railroad companies in Argentina diversified in the 1920s into oil production and exploration, initially to find a reliable source of supply for their engines, and also into urban utilities and tourism, and even fruit marketing (Lewis 1985: 221–2). The system of financial holding companies for electrical utilities was changed rather than entirely destroyed by the First World War. By the early 1920s the holdings of the German electrical companies Siemens and AEG had passed under the control of Swiss banks. Under new ownership, the *Unternehmergeschäft* strategy was continued, with the ownership links in the holding companies being used to generate orders for the Swiss electrical companies (Segreto 1987, 1992, 1994).

**Other services**

There were cross-border investments in a diverse range of other services in the nineteenth and early twentieth centuries. Coinciding with a growth in British takeovers of US industries, British accountancy firms opened

US offices. Deloittes and Price Waterhouse opened New York and Chicago offices at the beginning of the 1890s, and they were followed by other British firms (Wilkins 1989: 536–46). Multinational news agencies originated in the nineteenth century. The French company Havas (later Agence France Presse) was founded in 1835. Reuters originated in 1851, and United Press Associations (later UPI) started in 1907 (Boyd-Barrett 1989). British and German wireless companies were first movers in transoceanic radio communication. The leading enterprise was the British firm Marconi, which established a US affiliate in 1899. The firm specialised in ship to shore and ship to ship transmissions, but shortly before the First World War it also began commercial transoceanic transmissions (Wilkins 1989: 520–2).

There were examples of the provision of construction and engineering services across borders. A cluster of French civil engineering firms were involved in major infrastructure projects in a growing number of countries from the middle of the nineteenth century. After initially undertaking projects in neighbouring Belgium and Switzerland, they invested more widely in the Mediterranean region and Eastern Europe. From the 1900s French firms secured large orders for the construction of railroads, urban sanitation systems and harbour facilities in a number of Latin American countries (Barjot 1986). The French firms excelled at harbour facilities and tunnel construction, but in these and other areas they faced competition from other European firms, especially British contractors such as S. Pearson, whose successful diversification into Mexican oil was discussed in Chapter 3 (see p. 71).

**Organisation**

The managerial challenges faced by service MNEs were as formidable as those encountered in other industries. The control of diversified international trading companies, multinational bank branch networks, or complex utility operations, involved the co-ordination of activities over large distances. Given that many of these investments were in the developing regions, including Eastern Europe, the strategy of reducing managerial problems by investing in geographically 'nearby' countries could not be employed.

There is more evidence of investment strategies reflecting culturally or politically 'nearby' factors. French banks and other firms were attracted to Russia in part because of the political alliance between that country and France before the First World War. A substantial proportion of service sector FDI was located in colonial regions, and the nature of the colony greatly influenced business strategies. The British overseas banks confined their involvement in local – or retail – business almost entirely to countries which were settled by British emigrants, such as Australia, in which large branch networks were established. In these colonies, the British banks were, initially at least, hardly 'foreign' at all, even if their headquarters were far away in London. Elsewhere, they focused largely on trade finance and related exchange business, undertaken at a small number of branches located at ports and trading centres. In some regions the European banks had extensive transactions with the indigenous banking and business communities, typically conducted by the use of inter-mediaries of various kinds, such as *compradores* in Chinese-speaking regions (Jones 1993a). More generally, the British Empire included a number of ports – Bombay, Penang, Singapore, Hong Kong – where the creation of a physical and legal infrastructure under the security of British rule led to their growth as international service centres. Not only British, but other European, American, overseas Chinese and other enterprises, used these centres as bases for trading and banking activities in surrounding regions.

Given the diversity of the enterprises involved, it is not surprising that a variety of organisational structures were found in services. There were examples – as in accounting – of firms expanding across borders in 'classic' multinational fashion. In such cases, direct investments were controlled by the extension of pre-existing managerial structures.

There were also other organisational solutions not involving complex layers of managerial hierarchies. European trading and shipping compa-nies functioned as networks of nominally autonomous units joined by interlocking directorships, equity stakes, and family connections. There was no large group of managers at a corporate 'centre' controlling operations. These organisational structures were far removed from US-style integrated corporations, but they appear to have functioned well in the areas of financial and risk management, and to have permitted diver-sification into related activities without incurring managerial diseconomies. Given the volatile and unpredictable environment often faced by trading companies, it may have been rational to have located much decision-making at the level of individual subsidiaries rather than a single corporate centre (Casson 1994b).

The nature of their environment helps to explain also why European banks and traders opted for Ouchi-style clans rather than bureaucratic hierarchies as a solution to agent/principal problems. In British banks, trading companies and utilities, control over managers at far-flung offices was exercised by socialisation strategies, especially the creation of strong corporate cultures based on the recruitment of a culturally and socially homogeneous managerial corps which enjoyed lifelong employment. London head offices played key roles in these strategies by devoting great attention to the recruitment of staff with the right character and background, who could be trusted to function honestly and in accordance with the enterprise's general policy even without constant bureaucratic supervision. Head offices retained a monitoring role by deciding on matters such as individual salary levels, awarding or denying permission to marry, vetting prospective wives, and congratulating or admonishing individual performance. This system worked well at a time when transport and communication difficulties made formal hierarchical methods of control difficult (Munro 1988; Jones 1993a: 40–53). The British appear to have made particular use of socialisation strategies – which in part rested on aspects of that country's class system and the values promoted in its fee-paying 'public' schools – but there were considerable similarities to be found in other European enterprises.

The use of 'clan' methods of control in the nineteenth century meant that the effectiveness of European overseas banks, trading companies and other ventures was not necessarily reflected in the size of their managerial hierarchies. Small head offices did not mean that managerial control was not being exercised over overseas operations. In the 1900s the London office of the British-owned Imperial Bank of Persia – which was the state bank of Iran and operated around twenty branches over the whole of that country – consisted of part-time directors, four or five permanent staff, and a small and changing population of young British men receiving a few months on-the-job training before transfer to the Iranian branches. Nevertheless the bank functioned effectively in difficult circumstances (Jones 1986c: 158–9).

It needs to be added that – as in manufacturing and resources – there was nothing inevitable about the growth of service MNEs. There were constant reorganisations in search of more effective structures, and numerous failures. Trading companies and overseas banks needed considerable skills in order to survive. Although the British overseas banks were a rather stable form of multinational business, there were some failures during the periodic banking crises in the nineteenth century, while a few large banks failed. These included the Oriental Bank, which was founded in the 1840s and controlled a widely dispersed branch network in Asia, Australia and Africa before failing in 1884, in part as a result of a collapse of coffee prices in Sri Lanka. Subsequently in the early 1930s the largest British overseas bank by asset size, the Anglo-South American Bank, was terminally weakened by over exposure to Chilean nitrates, though the Bank of England was able to promote the bank's rescue and eventual merger into a competitor (Jones 1993a).

### Significance

Multinational service investment played a strategic role in the creation of the worldwide economy which developed by the late nineteenth century. Service MNEs were the facilitators of trade flows and often built the infrastructure which made the trade possible. They were important elements in the incorporation of peripheral regions into the global economy. They spread technologies – from banking techniques to energy systems – worldwide. They facilitated the more rapid dissemination of information which enabled firms to sustain direct investments in foreign countries.

The amount of FDI involved in these activities serves as a poor proxy for their significance. This is partly because the provision of many services is not a capital-intensive process. The establishment of distribution and sales facilities can have a considerable impact while costing far less than a mine or a factory. In addition, the service MNEs of this era were sometimes more co-ordinators and mobilisers of local resources than investors of foreign capital. This function can be seen in the case of the European overseas banks. Although the British overseas banks in the nineteenth century used their equity capital to initially finance a new branch, once a business was established, the strategy was to finance local lending by deposits raised locally or – where permitted – the issue of bank notes. These banks sought to avoid putting their 'capital' at risk by employing it in foreign currencies whose exchange rate might depreciate against their own. Indeed, once the banks were established, there was sometimes a reverse flow of funds back to Europe. If they collected more deposits than they could 'safely' lend, these would be transferred to Britain and invested on the London money markets (Jones 1993a: 30–40, 60).

The European trading companies also drew heavily on local sources of funds to finance their activities. In Southeast Asia, the networks of rubber plantations and other companies controlled by the British agency houses included British-registered free-standing companies, but also locally-registered companies, whose capital came from European residents in the East, overseas Chinese and others (Brown 1994: 43–65). British managed enterprises in Asia (and elsewhere) drew on a pool of capital – the profits of past commercial activities by European expatriates – which might never be remitted to the United Kingdom, but existed as a 'self supporting, closed world' (Tomlinson 1989: 99). Neither the scale nor the significance of the trading companies can be understood if they are regarded simply in terms of being engaged in the export of capital from Europe.

## DETERMINANTS

There were multiple determinants of the growth of multinational investment in services. A distinction can be made between trade-supporting, location-bound services, and foreign-tradable services, though the same firm could be involved in the provision of different types of service.

### Trade-supporting services

A great deal of multinational service investment involved the servicing of international trade. Many of the activities of trading and shipping companies, banks and insurance companies, and utility and contracting firms, were related to the facilitating of trade flows in one way or another. The unprecedented growth of world trade in the nineteenth century, and the integration of new countries and regions into the world trading system, provided many opportunities for such trade-supporting investments.

The importance of Europe as a market for commodities and as an exporter of manufactured goods before the First World War is an important part of the explanation for the prominence of European firms in trade-supporting investments. Even though the American share of world trade grew during the nineteenth century, it was dwarfed by that of Europe, which still accounted for around three-fifths of world imports and exports by 1913. Two-thirds of Latin America's trade was with Europe, and even higher shares of the trade of Africa and Australia. Within this wider picture, the British economy was especially important. Its major industries were extremely export dependent. The British accounted for over two-thirds of all world exports of cotton piece goods before 1913, and overall that country still accounted for over a quarter of total world trade in manufactured goods. The European trading, shipping, banking and other enterprises which serviced these trade flows derived ownership advantages from the importance of their home economies in world trade, and from their knowledge about markets and suppliers.

Intermediaries such as trading companies were used to facilitate trade flows because they reduced search, negotiation and transaction costs in unfamiliar and risky environments. European manufacturers in the nineteenth century did not use international trading companies when buying and selling elsewhere in Europe or North America, but trading companies were active in Asia, Latin America and Africa where the business cultures, institutions and languages were very different from Europe (Yoshihara 1987). The risks of dealing in these areas were particularly high because much of the trade involved primary commodities, which were subject to price fluctuations and to interruptions in supply because of climatic or other natural factors. Without trading companies, the high costs of acquiring knowledge about foreign markets would have been indivisible, and would have fallen totally on individual exporters.

Trading companies reduced risks by gathering information, and by forming relationships with other enterprises. Japan's trading companies were joined in numerous transactions with other Japanese service sector ventures in banking, shipping and insurance (Wilkins 1986b). The British trading companies came to control wide networks of firms. The drive to reduce risk – or lower transaction costs – led sometimes to vertical integration. The process can be seen in the Thai teak industry, which came to be completely dominated by British trading companies before 1914. These companies exported teak from Bangkok, and invested in sawmills in Thailand to facilitate the quality and reliability of supply. This led them to secure more assured sources of supply, which fluctuated from year to year as it was dependent on the success of the rains for floating timber. The diversified activities of the trading companies in turn reduced the dangers if there were a series of 'bad' years (Falkus 1989).

Diversification strategies enabled trading companies to obtain economies of scope from operation in several fields. The agency houses in Southeast Asia not only earned profits from their diversification into rubber plantations, but this also widened the scope of their business. Their emergence as producers of a major industrial raw material provided major new export opportunities. The subsequent rapid increase of population, caused by the growth of the rubber industry, increased imports into Malaya, much of which were handled by agency houses. Increased trade meant more shipping and more insurance – and more business for agency houses in their role as agents for shipping and insurance companies.

The vertical integration of oil companies and agribusiness firms from the late nineteenth century into the provision of shipping services needs explanation because this strategy was not followed by enterprises in other resource industries or in manufacturing. Both oil and agribusiness had certain characteristics which favoured integration into shipping. The rate of production was difficult to vary in the short run and beyond a certain point, the marginal cost of storing products was very high. Consequently the co-ordination of shipping and transportation in these industries relied heavily on forward planning. Long-term chartering of fleets was a theoretical alternative to ownership in such circumstances, but the transport of both oil and agricultural products required special technologies which were embodied in the design of ships. For various reasons, established shipowners were reluctant to invest in such dedicated ships (Casson, Barry and Horner 1986: 355–9). In addition some enterprises sought to own their own fleet rather than face potential exploitation by large shipping companies, which often acted in collusion with one another (Wilson 1954, I: 237; Kindleberger 1985).

Much of the FDI in public utilities fell into the trade-supporting category also. The utility investments undertaken by German electrical manufacturers were a means of creating overseas markets for their goods. A surge of Belgian FDI in Italian tramways and other utilities in the 1880s resulted from a search for markets by Belgian metallurgical producers (Dumoulin 1990). Although British FDI in utilities never originated from British manufacturers, British merchants and land companies were prominent. In Latin America – and elsewhere – railroad ventures and other utilities were promoted by British merchants and landowners already active in the region. They sought expanding market opportunities for their crops and animals, and often invested in several companies. There were many links at director level between British companies in Latin

America active in railroads, other utilities, banks and shipping. There was sometimes quasi-integration to provide services from the agricultural estate to the port of export (Lewis 1983a).

The main locational determinant of this kind of investment in utilities was the absence of adequate infrastructure to support accelerating trade flows. It flourished where trading opportunities existed, and where either governments or local entrepreneurs did not invest in infrastructure. In some contexts, mining or tropical fruit MNEs had little alternative but to make utility investments in order to engage in the successful export of their commodities. The foreign-owned utility companies derived ownership advantages from access to capital and technology, and from links with other foreign enterprises in the host economies.

## Location-bound services

The existence of FDI in location-bound services is at one level straightforward to explain in terms of entrepreneurial perceptions of profitable opportunities in supplying services where consumption could not be separated from production. The investments were undertaken for offensive, profit-seeking motives. Part of the public utility FDI fell into this category. Belgium tramway companies in Russia or the British gas companies in Europe were not a 'trade-supporting' investment. The gas companies sought profitable opportunities in the provision of gaslighting in European cities. This service had of necessity to involve production near the point of consumption because, unlike the natural gas era after 1945, 'town gas' was manufactured from coal, and was not transportable over long distances.

Foreign enterprises engaged in location-bound services held similar ownership advantages to firms undertaking market-oriented manufacturing FDI. They usually possessed organisational skills, including access to new technologies, which could be exploited in foreign markets. Access to capital was important. The Canadian utility companies in Latin America were able to derive advantages in capital raising by using imperial connections to facilitate access to the London capital markets. From soon after the foundation of Canadian companies active in Brazilian and Mexican utilities it was evident that the restricted Canadian capital market could not absorb all their securities. Instead funds were raised on a large scale in London, using some of the most prestigious British financial houses, and later on other European capital markets also (McDowall 1988).

The identification of the ownership advantages possessed by firms needs to be placed firmly in the historical context. In much of the developing world in the nineteenth century, these enterprises were first movers with no indigenous competitors. As a result, a search for advantages held by such firms which enabled them to compete with local rivals is misleading.

A lack of indigenous competitors also sometimes made diversification strategies attractive and feasible. Firms which possessed knowledge about a particular host economy would be alert to further profitable opportunities, and to ways to exploiting them. These enterprises needed compensating advantages only when, over time, local rivals developed.

### Foreign-tradable services

For services for which a choice of exporting or direct investment existed, the problem is to explain why one mode of servicing a foreign market was chosen rather than another. The finance of international trade is an example. British trade with the United States and continental Europe was financed using 'correspondent' relationships between independent banks. On the British side, much of this business was undertaken by the so-called 'merchant banks' (such as Rothschilds, Barings and Schroders). They acted as the London bankers for foreign banks in return for equivalent services in their countries. In contrast, much of Britain's foreign trade with developing regions passed through the British overseas banks.

Internalisation theory helps to explain why different modes were chosen for different geographical regions. International trade finance required detailed creditor information and debt collection facilities. The established and reliable domestic banking systems in existence in the United States and Europe meant that these functions could be undertaken using independent banks in other countries as correspondents. However, in most of the countries in which British overseas banks invested from the 1830s, it was hard to find local banks which could be trusted to act as correspondents, given that the banking systems were non-existent or in their infancy. The transaction costs involved in the use of the market were likely to be high, and it was rational to internalise trade finance by establishing a multinational branch network.

Differential regulation was an important influence on the choice of modality in international banking. Before 1914 the development of US multinational banking to provide international trade finance and other services for US business was constrained by federal and state regulatory restrictions on branch banking in general, combined with the specific prohibition on the opening of foreign branches by national banks, which included the largest American banks. There were even regulatory restrictions on the participation of American banks in international trade finance (Carosso and Sylla 1991). Canadian banks were sometimes able to take advantage of this situation by servicing US corporations in the West Indies and elsewhere (Quigley 1989). Foreign multinational banking within the United States was also made very difficult by US regulations. By the beginning of the twentieth century foreign banks were prohibited from opening branches in most US states, or else – as in New York – limited to opening 'agencies' which could not take deposits (Wilkins 1989).

## EQUITY AND NON-EQUITY STRATEGIES IN A REGULATED ENVIRONMENT

### The changing structure of service sector FDI

There were important changes in international business in services from the 1930s. In contrast to manufacturing and resources, there was not a spread of international cartels as a result of the Great Depression, though shipping was a major exception. From the 1870s the British shipping companies began to combine to set uniform rates on shipping lines. These 'conferences' became important instruments for the organisation and control of shipping routes, especially in the 'liner' trade, which consisted of general-purpose ships carrying small consignments sailing on fixed routes to scheduled timetables. During the 1930s such conferences spread to cover each major route. They were exempted from US antitrust law, except that conferences serving US foreign trade had to have free entry for new members, while elsewhere would-be new members had to fight for membership. The conference system remained firmly in place after the Second World War, though governments of developing countries secured new entry for their own ships. There was also a growth in importance of 'tramp' shipping – ships which did not follow fixed routes or schedules, but sailed from port to port, picking up bulk cargoes placed with them through open markets. New entry into tramp shipping was much easier than liner shipping, and in the postwar period ships from Eastern Europe and Southeast Asia successfully challenged the former dominance of international shipping by Western European countries (Casson, Barry and Horner 1986: 349–51).

Apart from shipping, service MNEs often participated in domestic cartels. During the interwar years and until the 1970s, domestic banking markets were usually cartelised, often with the support of governments and central banks which sought monetary control and banking stability. The European overseas banks were typically full participants in such domestic cartel arrangements. In addition, while antitrust pressures after the Second World War helped to eliminate most international cartels in manufacturing, governments encouraged their growth and facilitated their survival in strategic international services such as air travel and telecommunications.

There was a significant shift in the nature of services provided by MNEs. Beginning in the 1930s, there was a sharp fall in investments in utilities while, especially after 1950, there were new waves of activity in business, trade, hotel and restaurant services, and a renewed importance for trade and finance-related activities. There was also a marked shift in the location of service sector FDI from developing to developed economies. Large parts of the multinational investment in services in the developing world before the Second World War disappeared. By the 1970s almost three-quarters of the total stock of service investment was located in the developed economies. In developed economies, financial, business and professional services were particularly important, while in developing economies trade, tourism and basic financial services accounted for a higher proportion of FDI. In certain service industries like retail trade or communications, there was little investment outside advanced economies.

## The impact of government intervention:
## utilities, airlines and insurance

The growth of government intervention in, and regulation of, many services was a decisive influence on the changing geographical and sectoral distribution of multinational investment in services. This had the effect of closing certain sectors altogether to MNEs, while in others the nature of multinational investment was strictly regulated. Utilities, airlines and insurance illustrate the impact of this government intervention.

From the 1930s foreign-owned utilities faced mounting political difficulties, especially in Latin America, whose effects were exacerbated by the general economic conditions of the period. Currency depreciations had a particularly adverse effect on utilities whose rate structures were controlled by host governments. The mushroom growth of ITT and the American & Foreign Power Company – both heavily exposed to Latin America – was halted and both enterprises had a struggle to survive. ITT was particularly badly affected by the Spanish Civil War (1936–9), as around a quarter of its total income had come from Spain (Abo 1982: 524–9).

The 1930s were also dismal for the European railroad companies in Argentina. The onset of the Depression and the contraction of Argentinian foreign trade caused a sharp decline in their freight traffic, but the government prohibited them from dismissing workers or cutting their remuneration. Currency depreciation and the introduction of exchange controls from 1931 interrupted the repatriation of profits. In addition, the government launched an extensive road-building programme which facilitated competition from motor transport. The profitability of the foreign companies was virtually destroyed and they were unable to pay dividends to their shareholders through the 1930s (Heras 1987: 41–67). While the British companies would not invest in such circumstances, there was mounting criticism of their failure to provide adequate infrastructure for the Argentinian company. The denouement came after Juan Perón became president in 1946. Over the next three years the Argentinian government purchased both the British and the French-owned railroads in Argentina (Wright 1974: 254–62). The remaining British railroad companies in Brazil were sold shortly afterwards (Abreu 1990: 461).

After the Second World War political pressures against foreign utilities intensified. The American & Foreign Power Company had its large operations in China and Cuba expropriated in 1949 and 1960 respectively, and was obliged to relinquish control over its Indian properties following Indian independence. Throughout Latin America, electric power was a political issue which led to the foreign utilities either facing nationalisation or extensive controls over their rates and profit remittances. The US utilities responded by diversification beyond utilities, to such an extent that they could no longer be regarded as international utilities. ITT diversified into car rentals (with the purchase of Avis in 1965) and hotels (with the purchase of Sheraton in 1968) (Wilkins 1974a: 361, 395). By 1970 public utilities comprised a mere 4 per cent of the total book value of US FDI (Wilkins 1974a: 55, 329).

In some cases, foreign utility companies were able to survive. While the Canadian-owned utilities in Mexico were taken over by the government in the late 1940s, Brazilian Traction was able to resist the movement in that country towards national control. In part this was because of its sheer size: in 1946 the Canadian company produced 60 per cent of Brazil's total power, supplied 75 per cent of the nation's telephones, and was the largest private sector employer, with 50,000 Brazilian workers. Incumbency advantages were reinforced by a strategy of adjustment to political circumstances. During the 1950s Brazilian Traction shifted the domicile of its subsidiaries to Brazil, and adopted other Brazilianisation measures. After 1964 – when the government purchased American & Foreign Power's Brazilian business – it was the sole foreign utility in the country. It was not until 1979 that the Canadian utility sold its Brazilian assets to the national power company, in an amicable agreement (McDowall 1988: 382–99).

Telecommunications became an industry in which MNEs could play little role in most of the world. Telecommunications monopolies in many countries – usually state-owned – blocked the entry of foreign operators. These monopolies co-operated in cartel agreements which set the prices of international telephone calls. As the television industry spread in the 1950s and 1960s, almost every country in the world blocked foreign ownership of broadcasting media. There were also numerous restrictions on the country of origin of programmes, often prompted by a desire to protect national cultures.

Air transportation also became rife with government restrictions against foreign companies. Multinational strategies were used in the first stage of the commercial industry's development in the interwar years. The US pioneer was Pan American Airways, which began a service between

Florida and Cuba in 1927, and over the following decade expanded its route network over Latin America, and subsequently began transatlantic and trans-Pacific services. Pan American purchased Mexican and Colombian airlines as part of its expansion strategy (Wilkins 1974a: 134–5). The airlines of European colonial powers, such as KLM of the Netherlands and Imperial Airways of Britain, developed long-haul operations to colonial territories. Direct investment strategies were employed in certain cases. The Singapore to Australia service was operated by a joint venture between Imperial Airways and the Australian airline Qantas. The joint venture was registered in Australia and managed by Qantas, but 51 per cent of the equity was held by Imperial Airways and its operations were co-ordinated with the Imperial Airways' London to Singapore services (Dierikx 1991: 345–6).

The potential for substantial FDI in airlines was greatly constrained by governments. From the beginning civilian aviation was regarded as a matter of national prestige, as well as strategic concern. Airlines were used as instruments of national diplomacy. Pan American was given a range of government subsidies to encourage its spread in Latin America (Wilkins 1974a: 257–8). The European airlines were often government-owned and always in receipt of large subsidies (Dierikx 1991: 333). After the Second World War the airline industry became highly cartelised with rigid government controls on entry, capacity and tariffs. Flights between countries were a matter of intergovernmental negotiation. Traffic rights were negotiated on a bilateral basis, and as a rule only one 'national flag' operator was recognised per route. Foreign ownership of airlines was almost never permitted. As a result, from the 1950s international airlines expanded dramatically, but their direct investments were limited to offices and inventories abroad which did not involve large sums of money (Wilkins 1974a: 392). This situation only started to change with the deregulation of the airline industry which began in the United States in the late 1970s, but the pace of change was slow.

Insurance companies faced substantial regulatory barriers. Foreign insurance companies were nationalised in many developing countries after the Second World War, while a number of developed economies – such as Japan, France and Germany – all but closed their markets to foreign participation. A growing insistence by governments that insurance companies should maintain reserves in each of the countries in which they operated undermined the competitive advantages of large international insurance companies *vis-à-vis* smaller rivals. A variety of other restrictions included obliging foreign insurers to provide larger deposits or satisfy stricter solvency conditions than those required from local insurers (Michie 1992: 166).

Government regulation was an important influence on the differing degrees of internationalisation in different segments of the insurance industry. Multinationals were least active in the heavily regulated life insurance sector. There was more multinational investment in non-life insurance, in which a number of US, British and Swiss firms were especially active internationally. This national pattern was partly explained by the extensive multinational investments of those countries, as non-life insurance companies followed their corporate clients abroad to cover their risks. The most internationalised sector was reinsurance, in which companies based in Germany, Switzerland and the United Kingdom were prominent. Reinsurance was less heavily regulated than other types of insurance, and benefited from restrictions on other segments, because as more insurance was preserved for local companies, they found it necessary to take out reinsurance in order to cover themselves against catastrophes (Goodman 1993).

## Equity and non-equity modes

In many other services international business strategies were less hampered by government regulation. In these services, a range of different modes were employed. A summary is given in Table 5.2, which identifies the 'typical' mode employed to operate in foreign countries. It also gives, for illustrative purposes, a prominent firm engaged in international business in that service.

Advertising agencies were a service in which FDI strategies were employed. Given the development of advertising and marketing methods in the United States, it was American firms that led the way. They had opened offices in Europe even before the First World War, and in the interwar years they expanded further as agencies such as J. Walter Thompson, Lord & Thomas, and Paul E. Derrick opened foreign offices to service the accounts of their large domestic advertisers who had become MNEs. During the 1920s Walter Thompson had an agreement with

*Table 5.2* International business in services: organisational modes

| Service | Illustrative firm | Mode |
|---------|-------------------|------|
| Advertising | J. Walter Thompson | FDI (100%) |
| Accounting | Price Waterhouse | Partnerships |
| Construction management | Bechtel | Transitory FDI, but permanent offices |
| Hotels | Holiday Inn | Franchising/management contracts |
| Fast food restaurants | McDonald's | Franchising/management contracts |
| Retailing | Sears, Roebuck | FDI (100% and joint ventures) |

General Motors that it would open an office in every country where the car firm had an assembly operation or distributor, and this drove its expansion in Europe and elsewhere. Once established in a country, however, the US advertising agencies developed local client bases (West 1987).

US agencies dominated the world industry after 1945. They were the pioneers of market research, new advertising techniques, and a succession of other innovations. By the end of the 1970s they were operating in every non-communist country in the world except Curaçao, Egypt, Malta, Morocco, Paraguay and Turkey. The competitive advantages of the US firms rested on the importance and strategies of US MNEs. Their presence in a market was directly correlated with the overall US business presence (Terpstra and Yu 1988). Especially after 1945, US MNEs often preferred to appoint one agency to deal with their entire international business. European-owned agencies were disadvantaged in this respect as their MNEs for much longer treated each country in which they had a subsidiary separately, and encouraged subsidiaries to appoint local agencies (West 1988). It was not until the 1980s that a number of British and Japanese advertising agencies began to challenge the US pre-eminence in the industry.

The use of FDI strategies by advertising agencies rested on considerable internalisation advantages. The companies had a strong brand name and image, and there was a high cost of quality control if alternative strategies were employed. Yet locational factors, such as the need for on-the-spot contact with clients and adaptation to local tastes, made the export of the service difficult. Similar factors dictated the use of FDI strategies in a number of other professional business services, including market research and executive search agencies (Dunning 1989).

In many professional business services cross-border activities were more typically conducted by informal networks of independent firms. This organisational form became pre-eminent in accounting, engineering, architecture and surveying sevices, and legal services. These services not only required local specialised knowledge, but products required specific customisation. A high degree of knowledge of local laws, standards and procedures was also required. International networks of independent national firms provided the advantage of a presence in all major markets without incurring the costs of co-ordination through ownership ties. These firms often used a common name, enabling local firms to gain in reputation. Various techniques were available to monitor behaviour so as to prevent damage to the reputation of the firm: these included maintaining minimum standards of professional work and periodical quality reviews throughout the organisation (Aharoni 1993: 121–42).

The growth of international accounting partnerships provides an important example of this strategy. Before the Second World War a number of US and UK accountancy firms had operated under the same names in both countries, and these arrangements were formalised after the War. In 1945 Price Waterhouse established a separate international firm on a world-wide basis through the integration of its existing national practices. A series of other mergers at international level followed. In 1957 an Anglo-US-Canadian merger created Coopers & Lybrand, and three years later a similar tripartite international merger produced Touche Ross.

The merger of accounting firms at international level enabled them to enter previously unserved national markets. The leading firms entered national markets through mergers with established national practices, and over time comprehensive international networks were built up. If no suitable practice existed for a merger, new firms were sometimes established, while in other cases national firms were recruited as representatives or correspondents rather than being integrated into the international firm. By 1975 Price Waterhouse had offices in seventy-six countries, Coopers and Lybrand in seventy-three and Peat Marwick Mitchell in sixty-eight. Although these international firms were partnerships, in most cases the partners from the US arm of the practice were particularly prominent (Daniels, Thrift and Leyshan 1989: 86–97).

The major exception to the partnership strategy in international accounting was that employed by Arthur Andersen, the US-based firm. Before 1945 this firm did not open any overseas offices in its own name, but entered into agreements with foreign firms that would represent it in particular countries. From the 1950s Arthur Andersen severed all its existing agreements with national practices, and began to open offices in foreign countries in its own name.

While considerable numbers of firms engaged in international construction management, a few large firms accounted for a large proportion of all overseas work done. United States firms became particularly prominent overall, replacing the earlier lead of European companies. During the interwar years firms such as Ulen & Company and J. G. White began construction work abroad, usually in Latin America, while other companies had undertaken contracts in China (Wilkins 1974a: 135–6). After the Second World War US companies took by far the largest share of international construction contracts. They held considerable advantages in terms of specialist expertise, skilled personnel and reputation, and benefited in many developing countries from US government links on defence and political matters. The firms of other countries tended to have regional specialisations. French contractors were powerful in Africa, probably because of past colonial links and the willingness of the French government and banks to finance projects in certain countries. During the 1970s South Korean firms acquired a substantial share of the Middle East market – where they concentrated on labour-intensive projects in which they could exploit their advantage in low-cost skilled labour (Enderwick 1989: 135–7).

There were multiple modes of market servicing, depending on the type of project. Licensing was used for process plant projects whose proprietary technologies existed, and was generally employed in developed market economies. Management contracts and turnkey arrangements were used by firms engaged in industrial plant and heavy civil work, especially in developing economies lacking suitably qualified management. Turnkey projects involved contracts for the construction of operating facilities which were transferred to the owner, for a fee, when the facilities were ready to commence operations. Turnkey contracts in remote areas of developing economies sometimes involved building entire infrastructures – reminiscent of the early, pioneering days of international business. The larger companies also maintained permanent offices in some of the countries they served, though the main part of their business was of a transitory nature (Enderwick 1989: 132–51).

The Bechtel group of companies was one of the largest engineering and construction enterprises. Beginning in the United States as a railroad construction business in 1898, its first international project was in 1940 when it was involved in a joint venture to construct a pipeline system in Venezuela. Subsequently it undertook projects all over the world, specialising in the provision of engineering, procurement and construction services for nuclear, fossil fuel and geothermal power generating plants; the design and construction of petroleum refineries and petrochemical plants; and oil and gas field development including long-distance transportation systems. By 1979 the firm had offices in twenty countries, and one-fifth of its 35,000 permanent, non-manual workers were based outside the United States (Stephenson 1984: 118–21).

Although much of Bechtel's overseas investment was 'transitory', the firm was an important agent of technology transfer. During the 1950s and 1960s Bechtel's projects were generally performed on a turnkey basis, with most of the engineering done outside the host country. Technology transfer took the form of on-site training activities for basic construction crafts, plant operations and maintenance office staff skills. Subsequently, contractors were increasingly required by host governments to transfer more advanced technology in the course of accomplishing contracted work. To achieve this, Bechtel incorporated host nation engineers in its project teams, both in the United States – where initial project conceptual engineering was usually done – and in the host nation. Over the length of the project design, Bechtel aimed to transfer the principal leadership role from the company to the host nation. These processes involved the transfer of its firm-specific advantages to the client, but as technologies and products were constantly evolving, Bechtel could continue to provide needed services (Stephenson 1984: 124–71).

In the hotel and fast food restaurant sector, franchising and management contracts became the predominant modes used in international business.

The hotel industry had been primarily national before the Second World War, although Swiss companies were among those that had made direct investments in foreign hotels even before 1914 (Wavre 1988: 94). Subsequently, international business in hotels expanded alongside the improvements in transport and the growth of international tourism. A number of major US hotel groups – Holiday Inn, Inter-Continental, Hilton and Sheraton – emerged, alongside a smaller number of French and UK hotel firms, such as Club Méditerranée and Trust House Forte. The importance of these three home economies may have reflected the fact that their domestic industries were characterised by chains of hotels, which gave them experience in multi-plant operations. The great majority of these hotel MNEs were independent hotel chains, but a number were also associated with tour operators, specialist hotel development companies, or airlines. In the 1970s this latter group included Inter-Continental and Hilton International – owned by Pan Am (until 1981) and TWA (until 1987) respectively.

International hotel groups were active in both developed and developing countries but there were distinct country-specific patterns. Canada's position as a major host for foreign-owned hotels reflected the extension of US chains across the border. In the developing world, there was a high concentration on Asian newly industrial countries (NICs), notably Singapore, Hong Kong and Thailand, which had heavy tourist and business demand.

The use of management contracts and franchising arrangements enabled hotel companies to exploit a number of ownership advantages in foreign countries – including their brand name which guaranteed a quality of service as well as access to international reservation systems – without the need for equity investments. The performance requirements of the international hotel group could be satisfactorily codified in a management contract or franchising agreement. Moreover, although most customers for hotels outside North America were foreigners, local knowledge of such things as decor, ancillary services and local inputs often made a substantial local managerial presence desirable (Dunning 1988a: 242–67).

The fast food industry, whose multinational growth dated from the 1960s, also typically employed franchising and management contracts. Although the concept of 'fast food' is strongly identified with the United States, one of the first movers in international business was British-owned J. Lyons. This firm acquired the international franchise of the Wimpy Bar, an American hamburger operation, and while the US venture remained modest, the British firm exploited the Wimpy concept on a large scale, first in Britain and then, by the 1960s, elsewhere in Europe, in Australia, South Africa, Thailand, Congo and Hong Kong. Lyons, itself a licensee, in turn licensed its foreign operations (Hollander 1970: 68).

However it was US-owned firms which subsequently came to dominate the industry. McDonald's opened its first foreign restaurant in Canada, in 1967, and in 1970 large-scale foreign expansion began. It entered most foreign countries through forming 50/50 joint ventures with local partners who ran the foreign operations. Each national company marketed McDonald's well-defined fast food menu and operating system, but the marketing strategy was tailored to different national situations. In some countries the joint venture company owned and operated the restaurants, while in others they licensed to local franchisees, as in the United States. The scale of McDonald's international expansion was remarkable. Its Japanese joint venture, started in 1971 and controlled by the Japanese partners, was a rapid success, despite ostensibly wide cultural differences in food tastes. By the early 1990s the company operated more than 2,500 restaurants in fifty foreign countries. It formed a cluster of multinational fast food chains including Kentucky Fried Chicken and Burger King. The latter passed into British hands through acquisition. Few consumers of their hamburgers were aware that the firm's owner was a British conglomerate, Grand Metropolitan.

Franchising strategies were found in retailing outside the fast food sector, though FDI was more widely employed. Multinational retailing has a long but erratic history. F. W. Woolworth, Singer and Eastman Kodak were among the US firms which undertook multinational retailing investments in the nineteenth century. But, until after the Second World War, most US mass merchandisers had little foreign involvement. The largest US merchandiser, Sears Roebuck, did not expand abroad significantly until 1942, when it opened a small store in Cuba. Subsequently it opened stores in Canada, Latin America and Europe (mainly Spain) (Hollander 1970: 26; Truitt 1984). Safeway Stores, which had Canadian shops from the 1920s, began opening shops in the 1960s in Britain, Germany and Australia (Wilkins 1970: 393). Postwar multinational retailers also included dealers in luxury goods – who often established branches in the leading metropolitan centres of New York, Paris and London – department stores, variety and discount stores, mail order firms, and food and clothing specialists.

Multinational retailing was a market-oriented phenomenon. It was the rising incomes, increased urbanisation and growing consumer spending in Europe from the 1950s which encouraged US firms to open stores in that region, and European firms to cross national boundaries. In the luxury sector, prestige considerations encouraged firms to open in fashionable cities. Firms such as the US supermarket chains had – or believed they had – ownership advantages in retailing techniques. Yet there were frequent failures in multinational retailing, as firms underestimated the problems caused by consumer resistance to change, the competitive response of local retailers, and operating difficulties in foreign environments (Hollander

1970: 102–40). As a result, although cross-border retailing grew in the post-war period, most firms remained oriented towards their domestic markets.

The fast changing consumer markets of developed countries left little scope for first-mover advantages in retailing. F. W. Woolworth built a large multinational retailing operation on the basis of the 'five-and-dime' variety store concept on which it was founded, but from the 1960s a trend towards more specialised retailing caused growing problems, especially as the US firm was very slow to adjust its strategy. For a time its overseas stores subsidised the ailing US operation, but in the 1980s it had to sell its British general merchandise stores. During the same decade Sears Roebuck divested from Spain and Latin America, and Singer sold its worldwide chain of sewing machine shops.

In contrast, a new generation of multinational niche retailers emerged. IKEA, the Swedish pioneer of flat-pack furniture, expanded rapidly in Europe from the middle of the 1970s, and opened its first store in the United States in 1985. The US speciality retailer Toys 'R' Us began a rapid international expansion after 1984, when it opened its first non-American stores, and within a decade owned over 200 stores in fifteen countries outside the United States. In the same period, Japanese retailers such as Sogo, Takashimaya and Yaohan opened stores in Singapore, Hong Kong and Thailand, before making their first investments in Western countries.

## The international traders

In many ways the most surprising aspect of the history of the European trading companies is not that they were important in the heyday of colonial empires and rapidly expanding world trade, but that they persisted subsequently. The Depression of the 1930s, the Second World War, decolonisation, and state intervention in commodity marketing fundamentally altered the business environment they faced, yet the European trading companies proved remarkably resilient. They remained influential business enterprises in a range of political and economic conditions.

In Asia, the British trading companies based in Hong Kong – the 'hongs' – were badly disrupted by the Pacific War and the 1949 Communist Revolution in China, after which they lost all their considerable assets in that country. Yet they survived, expanded into new regions of Asia and elsewhere, and became active participants in Hong Kong's rapid economic growth from the late 1950s. Both Swires and Jardine Matheson remained under the control of their founding British families, but this did nothing to prevent entrepreneurial diversification – Swires were major share-holders in Cathay Pacific, one of Asia's most successful airlines – and, in the 1980s, the assumption of a dynamic role in China's modernisation. While West Africa's economy provided a considerable contrast with that of East Asia, Unilever's UAC also remained remarkably durable. During the 1950s it diversified into retailing. After Nigerian independence in 1960, it remained Nigeria's largest business enterprise, and survived the growing hostility to foreign companies in that country. UAC undertook further diversification, entered joint ventures with manufacturing MNEs, and prospered through a civil war, half a dozen military coups, and severe boom and bust cycles of Nigeria's oil dominated economy. It was only in 1994 that UAC Nigeria passed – amicably – into local ownership (Biersteker 1987; Fieldhouse 1994).

A number of factors explain the survival of the trading companies. They benefited from incumbency advantages. They also showed a continued ability to diversify into new activities and to adapt. Over time managerial and organisational structures evolved. After the Second World War the cluster of trading, shipping and other firms linked together in the Inchcape group was moulded into a public company, which then acquired a series of other long-established British trading companies. By the 1980s Inchcape had emerged as the closest European equivalent to a Japanese *sogo shosha*, with global trading interests in several thousand commodities (S. Jones 1986). Finally, the European trading companies displayed considerable political skills in dealing with host governments in Africa, Asia and elsewhere. In some cases – such as that of British-owned Lonrho in Africa – the development of close working relationships with the political elites of newly independent countries provided a major ownership advantage (Dumett 1988: 507–8).

New forms of international trading companies grew in importance after the Second World War. Previously a number of European commodity traders such as Louis Dreyfus et Cie had been active in the international grain trade, but postwar changes in the nature of commodity markets led to a rapid expansion of this business. The most important changes were the intervention of the state, especially in the creation of monopoly marketing boards and the nationalisation of mines and plantations in many developing countries, and the emergence of genuine world markets, as indicated by the prodigious growth of the leading world commodity exchanges, such as the Chicago Board of Trade, the New York Sugar and Coffee Exchanges, and the London Metal Exchange.

During the 1950s the large US-based commodity firms entered the world markets. Cargill, one of the leading US grain traders, established an international company initially based in Canada, which in 1956 was shifted to Switzerland. This company – Tradax – became the basis for the group's international expansion, developing as one of the largest grain companies in the world (Broehl 1992). Subsequently Cargill diversified into the production, processing and marketing of an extremely diversified range of food products, as well as coal mining and steel production, on almost a worldwide basis.

The core business of the commodity traders was the purchase of commodities in one country and their sale in another, but this process involved a range of risks because of fluctuations in prices, exchange rates, freight rates and so on. The companies sought to control these risks by owning their own shipping fleets, some of which became very substantial in the 1960s and 1970s, although this strategy was reversed subsequently. They also developed specialist skills in financial management, to such an extent that there was a convergence between some commodity traders and financial institutions in the 1980s. The overall size of the commodity groups was difficult to ascertain because they remained in family ownership and/or were private companies, but the largest of them (such as Cargill and Philip Brothers) were reliably ranked among the thirty largest industrial enterprises in the world (Chalmin 1987: 160–5).

The commodity traders dominated world trade in many commodities. The world grain market was substantially in the hands of six large enterprises: Cargill and Continental from the United States, Louis Dreyfus (France), Bunge and Born (Argentina), André (Switzerland) and Tuppfer (Germany). In the 1970s these six firms accounted for 96 per cent of US wheat exports, 80 per cent of Argentinian wheat exports, and 90 per cent of European wheat exports (Chalmin 1985: 190). There was a similar concentration in international trade in commodities such as sugar and coffee, cotton and metals. Changes in the structure of commodity markets and the high risk nature of commodity dealing provided opportunities for new entrants to grow rapidly. The Swiss-based Marc Rich & Co. (renamed Glencore International in 1994), was only founded in 1974, but twenty years later it was one of the world's biggest traders in oil, aluminium and alumina, as well as a diversified range of minerals and agricultural commodities. The group's estimated annual turnover of $25 billion to $30 billion made it Switzerland's second biggest corporation after Nestlé.

### Significance and renaissance

Between the 1930s and the 1970s multinational investment in services was constrained by regulatory controls and other government policies. Nevertheless international business in services had remained important. The spread of accounting and advertising agency firms across borders had facilitated the growth of other MNEs. Construction management firms had not only built infrastructure but transferred technology. Multinational retailers spread modern marketing concepts and the technical and managerial skills necessary to implement them (Truitt 1984: 53). Retailers, fast food chains and hotels had impacted the lifestyles of millions of people. Although government intervention constrained many multinational services, it was a factor in the growth of the commodity trading companies. To some extent, these traders replaced the resource MNEs as the controllers or allocators of world resources.

From the 1980s many of the government-imposed restrictions on multinational involvement in services began to be swept away in developed economies and, at a slower pace, in developing ones also. The twin trends of deregulation and privatisation reopened opportunities for service MNEs which had existed before the 1930s. Air transportation was a major example of this trend. From the late 1980s there was a considerable growth of both FDI and strategic alliances in this sector, which had long been closed to foreign participation. The privatisation of Latin American and Eastern European airlines opened up opportunities for foreign airlines. The United States emerged as the major host economy for FDI in airlines following the deregulation of the industry from the late 1970s, and more especially after the raising in 1991 of the permitted ceiling from 25 per cent to 49 per cent of the share of the equity of a domestic airline which a foreign airline could hold.

Telecommunications and public utilities also re-emerged as a sector in which multinational investment was possible. The privatisation of telecommunications and utility monopolies in developing countries was accompanied by the liberalisation of FDI rules. The former socialist Eastern European countries and many developing countries looked to foreign companies to modernise outdated facilities. Technological change and the growing strategic importance of telecommunications undermined government monopolies, and made governments more receptive to using foreign companies to access the latest technologies. The upshot was an accelerating growth of FDI in world telecommunications in both developed and developing countries. United States FDI stock in telephone and telegraph communication industries in the world grew at an annual rate of over 140 per cent between 1989 and 1992, the highest rate of growth among all industries (United Nations 1994: 53).

During the 1980s two services – trade and finance-related activities – accounted for two thirds of the total service sector FDI in developed countries. The following two sections examine the development of international business in these two key sectors in more detail.

## SOGO SHOSHA

Japan's *sogo shosha* merit special attention because of their large share of Japan's foreign trade, their great importance in the world economy, especially after 1950, and their significance in the internationalisation of Japanese business as the most significant Japanese direct investors abroad until the 1970s.

The initial emergence of *sogo shosha* was related to the specific historical circumstances faced by Japan which heightened the risks that country faced when trading with the international economy in the middle of the nineteenth century after two centuries of isolation. The country had a severe lack of information about foreign markets and a severe shortage of people with requisite language and trading skills to undertake foreign business. *Sogo shosha* used such scarce human resources most effectively by employing them in diverse goods, areas and functions. A shortage of knowledge about foreign countries also explains why most Japanese manufacturers did not integrate vertically by establishing their own distribution facilities abroad. Extreme ignorance of foreign markets, laws and languages made such a strategy costly. It was rational, in the Japanese context, to rely on trading companies (Yoshihara 1987). Their use was also appropriate to the industrial structure of Japan, which – with the significant exception of textiles – consisted of industries where economies of scope were more achievable than economies of scale. Trading companies had the 'capabilities for maximising economies of scope by carrying and moving a number of products quickly through the distribution pipeline' (Fruin 1992: 113–6).

The growth of the first *sogo shosha*, Mitsui Bussan, was facilitated by two other factors. The Japanese government, anxious to reduce Japan's dependence on foreign merchants, was an important initial source of business (Yamazaki 1987: 37). Mitsui Bussan was also part of the Mitsui *zaibatsu*, one of the diversified family-controlled holding companies which were important features of the Japanese business system before the Second World War. Much of Mitsui Bussan's business involved dealing in commodities such as raw silk, raw cotton, cotton yarn, coal, machinery and sugar, which were produced by enterprises which also belonged to the Mitsui *zaibatsu*, or else were financially supported by Mitsui Bank. Mitsui Bussan was given sole-agency status with many other Mitsui companies, most of which dominated their respective industries (Yamazaki 1987). Mitsubishi – which founded its own *sogo shosha* in 1918 – was another of Japan's big *zaibatsu*.

The subsequent growth of the *sogo shosha* was far from smooth. During the First World War Japan's position as a member of the Allies, but located thousands of miles away from the battlefields in Europe, worked to the advantage of the trading companies. There was rising demand for Japanese products overseas – such as textiles – as European supplies were cut off. The trading companies diversified the range of commodities they handled and their geographical coverage. In contrast, the subsequent postwar recession, and the further disruption caused by the devastating Tokyo earthquake of 1923, created a more difficult environment for the trading companies, especially as Japanese foreign trade was stagnant throughout the 1920s. A number of trading companies failed, culminating with the bankruptcy in 1927 of Suzuki Shoten, which had developed into a *sogo shosha*.

Survival in this environment depended on effective management and adaptive business strategies. Mitsui Bussan evolved risk management strategies, which included financial control systems which enabled the calculation of income and expenditure for every commodity, and it avoided the speculative activities which were common among trading companies. The firm developed a high-quality managerial *cadre*, beginning to recruit graduates from a special training school as early as the 1880s, and it steadily expanded its numbers of graduates from then on, starting to recruit staff from the elite Tokyo University after 1905. The wartime growth of industrial production in Japan was a potential threat to Mitsui Bussan, which had been strongest in importing. Manufacturers sometimes undertook their own distribution, while other trading companies competed for the business of manufacturers. Mitsui Bussan responded by investing in a sizeable number of manufacturing companies and putting directors on their boards (Sakamoto 1990: 73–4).

During the 1930s the *sogo shosha* benefited from a more favourable environment as Japan's exports grew rapidly. The trading companies expanded the range of commodities in which they traded, and opened up new markets in Latin America, the Middle East and the Soviet Union. These 'global sales networks' enabled them to develop third country trade (Kawabe 1990: 174). In the United States, the branches of Mitsui and Mitsubishi diversified the products they handled, selling a range of products from fertiliser to pottery and canned crab meat. The *sogo shosha* also expanded their activities in the Japanese colonial empire, which included Korea and Taiwan, in Manchuria which was occupied in 1931, and in China, the victim of Japanese military aggression. The trading companies became engaged in both manufacturing and natural resource exploitation in these occupied regions (Kawabe 1989: 182–3; Kawabe 1990: 175–8).

Although the emergence of *sogo shosha* can be understood by reference to Japan's historical circumstances, the survival and growth of these institutions after the Second World War requires further explanation. The dissolution of the *zaibatsu* after the war was accompanied by the break-up of the *sogo shosha*. Mitsui Bussan was broken into 233 companies and Mitsubishi Shoji into 139 companies. But subsequently most of these companies came back together. They were joined as *sogo shosha* by a number of other firms, which had formerly been speciality textile, steel and machinery trading companies. A total of ten (nine after a merger in 1977) *sogo shosha* accounted for over 80 per cent of Japan's total imports and exports during the 1960s, and although this percentage fell over time, even in 1990 they handled more than half of Japan's imports.

The re-emergence of the *sogo shosha* took place in the context of the system of horizontal enterprise groups which replaced the dissolved *zaibatsu*. These groups – *kigyo shudan* – emerged from former *zaibatsu* or from new groups of firms around Japan's banks. The *kigyo shudan* consisted of considerable numbers of firms in a wide range of industries joined by webs of cross-shareholding. They must be distinguished from the vertical supplier *keiretsu* seen in the automobile and other industries, though an individual firm might belong to both types of grouping (Fruin 1992: 23–4). Each *sogo shosha* was a member of one (or sometimes two) *kigyo shudan*, and played a central role within it.

The primary function of the *sogo shosha* in the postwar decades remained trade intermediation. They traded in almost everything, handling between 25,000 and 40,000 different products, although the companies differed quite considerably in their product profiles. They earned the bulk of their profits from the movement of bulk commodities, assisting their clients on a commission basis in finding buyers or sellers. Japan's rapid industrialisation from the 1950s made the country a leading importer of many primary commodities, providing the *sogo shosha* with enormous business opportunities in the area of procuring raw industrial materials and energy resources from overseas. They were also major participants in Japan's export growth. They performed the export function for many small manufacturers who were too small to engage in the export business themselves, and to whom they also provided credit.

The prominence of the *sogo shosha* in Japan's foreign trade rested on their continued ability to handle transactions of certain products at a low cost. The main product characteristics in which they held such advantages were standardised products, products handled in large lots or repetitively, products which were handled several times through the production cycle, and products where the achievement of economies of scale in trading were conditional on access to world markets (Roehl 1983). A considerable proportion of trade transactions were with other members of their *kigyo shudan*. The *sogo shoshas* developed advanced information-gathering capabilities. They sought to acquire and process worldwide economic – and other – information, which was provided free to clients. As computers and facsimile machines became available, these information activities grew in scale, and in their significance as a source of competitive advantage for the *sogo shosha*.

The *sogo shosha* were also Japan's leading multinationals, not only in overseas trading, but also in manufacturing, resource extraction and other non-trading ventures. The Japanese trading companies lost all their overseas assets after the Second World War, and it was not until 1949 that they were allowed their own overseas offices. Thereafter the trading companies rapidly re-established their international networks of offices. Towards the end of the 1950s there was a shift in strategy as the *sogo shosha* began to form joint ventures or affiliate firms abroad. The change of strategy was at least partly a defensive reaction to the FDI undertaken by Japanese manufacturers. When Japanese cotton textile companies invested in Brazil and other Latin American countries in the 1950s, the *sogo shosha* lost their export markets. Threatened by this loss, the *sogo shosha* began to participate in overseas investments with the intention of protecting their foreign business. They developed an innovative system of organisation involving the setting up of separate joint ventures with selected partners (Yasumuro 1984: 78–9).

The graph in Figure 5.1 shows the growth in *sogo shosha* joint ventures from the early 1960s.

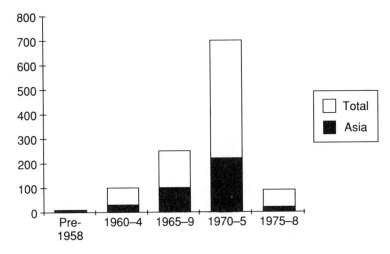

*Figure 5.1* Foreign joint ventures of *sogo shosha* before 1978
*Source*: Yasumuro 1984: 78

The number of *sogo shosha* joint ventures grew rapidly during the 1960s, before falling back after the oil crisis of the early 1970s. The focus of attention was Asia, which attracted by far the largest number of investments, followed by Brazil. Different forms of joint venture ownership were employed in different contexts. Joint ventures in developed countries were often wholly owned by two Japanese partners, typically a *sogo shosha* and an industrial enterprise. These were usually concerned with marketing and servicing, and were usually designed to promote the export of manufactured goods from Japan. The most frequently used structure in developing countries were joint ventures with three partners, such as a *sogo shosha*, a Japanese industrial enterprise (or occasionally another *sogo shosha*) and a local firm. These were often involved in manufacturing and raw materials, and they proved an effective means of undertaking business in unfamiliar foreign countries. The scale of involvement in manufacturing and natural resources was much higher than before the Second World

War, and *sogo shosha* also became active in large-scale construction projects. A list of the main overseas projects of Mitsui Bussan in the early 1960s included aluminium refining, oil and natural gas and forestry development in the United States, iron ore production in Australia, textiles and cement production in Indonesia, fertiliser production in Brazil, and liquid natural gas in Abu Dhabi. In such big development projects, the *sogo shosha* often served as 'systems organisers', orchestrating the roles and participation of other firms in the same enterprise group. In this role, they were able to draw on their global information and sales networks (Kawabe 1990: 190–2).

The *sogo shosha* co-existed with other Japanese enterprises engaged in international trade. There continued to be large numbers of smaller and more specialised trading companies which dealt with narrower product ranges or geographical areas. Of greater long-term significance were the in-house trading companies established by the Japanese consumer electronics and automobile manufacturers, which established their own sales organisations in the United States from the 1960s. *Sogo shosha* had fewer advantages in trading in goods characterised by high technology, aftercare services and by brands, and the manufacturers of these products did not require their assistance to sell or invest abroad. The result of the expansion of the sales and service networks of Japanese manufacturing companies in the developed market economies was a fall in the share of the *sogo shosha* in Japan's foreign trade. By the 1970s some argued that the *sogo shosha* had entered their 'winter' period, although new opportunities presented themselves in third-country trade, counter-trade and – from the 1980s – in the emerging Chinese market. Moreover, the *sogo shosha* began to restructure themselves away from trade, and into information and financial enterprises. Their international investment strategies were modified as circumstances changed. The *sogo shosha* shifted to market relationships – using long-term contracts – in many of their overseas resource activities, while continuing to make equity investments when engaging in more unfamiliar or risky activities involving new technologies.

Although the sheer size of the *sogo shosha* and their role in the postwar Japanese economy has often led to them being regarded as 'unique' to that country, the extent of such uniqueness needs careful definition. There were parallels with the European trading companies, especially as they engaged in geographical and industrial diversification from the 1950s (Chalmin 1985: 64). By the 1980s British-owned Inchcape had emerged as very similar to a *sogo shosha* in terms of product, regional and functional diversification (Cho 1987: 16–23). The main difference was that a firm like Inchcape was much less concerned with the foreign trade of the United Kingdom than the *sogo shosha* were with Japan. An analysis of the 'principals' for whom Inchcape acted as selling agent in the mid-1980s showed that under one-third were British, while over a fifth were US firms (S. Jones 1987: 133).

During the 1970s the example of the *sogo shosha* encouraged the governments of certain developing countries to establish similar institutions. Beginning in 1975, the Korean government began to designate the title of general trading companies as a strategy to increase the competitiveness of Korean exports. The designated companies – of which the Samsung Trading Company was the first in 1975 – received subsidies and were in turn set export targets. The Korean general trading companies accounted for 50 per cent of total Korean exports by the mid-1980s, although they did not emulate the extensive diversification of the *sogo shosha*. There were less extensive attempts to copy the Japanese model in Thailand, Taiwan and elsewhere (Cho 1984: 43–83; Yamazawa and Kohama 1985).

## MULTINATIONAL BANKING

Multinational banking has grown enormously in scale, complexity and importance over the last forty years, but the nature of banking makes it difficult to make comparisons with manufacturing or even other services. The assets of financial institutions are not comparable to those of non-financial institutions, which is why they are excluded from rankings of the largest MNEs. Banking consists of quite distinct types of activity – retail, service or wholesale – which need to be explained by different factors (Grubel 1977). Moreover, the nature of the industry was revolutionised in the 1960s and a very considerable proportion of the activities undertaken thereafter were without precedent.

The structure of multinational banking as it had developed in the nineteenth century remained in place until the 1960s. The European overseas banks survived the Great Depression and the Second World War. British overseas banks – in some of which Britain's domestic banks had acquired shareholdings after the First World War – owned several thousand branches in Australia, New Zealand and South Africa, and parts of the developing world, where they provided a mixture of retail and trade finance services. There were smaller branch networks owned by French and other European banks in developing countries, mostly former colonies or Latin America. In the developing world, the banks tended to confine their business to the westernised business sector and maintained a limited number of branches at commercial centres.

The US dominance of international business after the Second World War was not reflected in multinational banking. US banks divested from many of their foreign branches in the 1930s, and did not return after 1945. In the late 1950s only seven US banks had any overseas branches. In the same period foreign banks had virtually no business in the United States.

There was also virtually no multinational banking in Europe. German banks followed the example of their manufacturing clients and avoided multinational investment. Germany's expanding foreign trade was financed through correspondent relationships, and it was not until the 1970s that German banks began to open branches abroad (Tilly 1993).

The main problem for multinational banking was the lack of growth opportunities. From the interwar years, and especially after the Second World War, banking became a highly regulated industry. Product innovation, even by locally owned banks, was difficult. Central banks assumed many of the tasks once undertaken by private banks. Exchange controls and restrictions on currency convertibility provided few opportunities for international banking. From the 1940s there was a spread of restrictions on foreign banks. The prohibition of branch expansion by foreign banks became particularly common. In a number of developing countries foreign banks were nationalised, while in others they were subject to crippling discrimination. It became common for government and public corporation accounts to be given only to locally-owned banks (Jones 1993a: 291–4). In contrast to the manufacturing sector, there were also major obstacles to multinational banking in developed country markets. In the United States, foreign banks were virtually excluded by regulations. In Europe, they were either completely excluded or extremely constrained, while foreign acquisitions of domestic banks were almost impossible.

During the 1960s multinational banking underwent a transformation. The key development was the emergence – or re-emergence – of an integrated international money and capital market. The development of the Eurodollar market owed its birth in the late 1950s to restrictions on interest paid on deposits (Regulation Q) within the United States. The unwillingness of Eastern European governments to hold their dollars in the United States, and British government restrictions on sterling lending by its banks, helped to create the conditions where a market for dollars outside the United States – or 'Eurodollars' – emerged in London. The market grew in London, partly because of the large financial infrastructure associated with its traditional role as an international financial centre, but especially because of the lightness of regulatory controls. There were no liquidity ratios, and there was freedom of entry and exit in London's Euromarkets. This made London an attractive location compared to the other more tightly regulated European financial centres such as Paris and Frankfurt, as well as Tokyo, which remained very heavily regulated until the 1980s. London's ability to attract transactions in non-sterling currencies enabled it to become and remain the world's largest international financial centre, even though the United Kingdom no longer had its nineteenth century role as a net overseas lender, and even though the British currency was only a minor international medium of exchange.

The Eurodollar market was able to capture a rising share of financial intermediation from sheltered and conservative domestic banking markets. It was regulated neither by the host country nor according to the currencies being transacted. In large transactions for corporations and governments – or wholesale banking – multinational banks could offer higher deposit rates and charge lower loan rates on business transacted in London. The emergence of Eurobonds in 1963 resulted in a similarly unregulated capital market. The nature of international banking was transformed. Formerly it had been closely tied to international trade flows and related exchange operations. Over time, the Eurocurrency, Eurobond and foreign exchange markets became largely uncoupled from international trade. Multinational banks became the dominant players in these new financial markets, while lending to MNEs and to governments was undertaken on a dramatically enhanced scale. This lending was especially centred on a number of financial centres which combined the right mixture of regulatory and fiscal conditions, together with political stability. The 'hierarchy' of such financial centres had London as its apex, followed by New York and later Tokyo, extending down to major regional centres such as Singapore and Hong Kong in Asia, and at its base had 'offshore' centres such as the Cayman Islands and Panama, through which transactions were passed mainly for fiscal reasons (Reed 1981; Jones 1992b).

A distinguishing characteristic of the global markets was their continued growth even after the original causes of their emergence were removed. During 1973 and 1974 the United States abolished Regulation Q and controls against capital outflows, but the oil price rises of the period provided a further stimulus to the system. There was a massive inflow of funds into the Eurodollar market from the oil producing countries, while many non-oil producing countries borrowed from the market to finance their deficit balance of payments. The world debt crisis, which began in 1982 when Mexico announced its inability to service its large debt, revealed the poor quality of much of this international bank lending.

Multinational banking underwent great changes after 1960. There was a rapid growth of international banking, led by American banks. By 1975 126 US banks had over 700 foreign branches, and by 1985 the number had risen to over 860. US banks fuelled the growth of the Euromarkets through rapid product innovation, developing new lending instruments such as floating rate loans and syndicated credits. While in 1960 foreign operations were of marginal concern to US banks, by the mid-1980s the total assets of their foreign branches amounted to 20 per cent of the total assets of all US banks. The primary activity of these branches was Euromarket operations. In 1980 the fifty-seven US bank branches in the United Kingdom accounted for almost 40 per cent of total US bank assets abroad, with other significant shares being held by financial centres such as Singapore, Hong Kong, and the Cayman Islands (Goldberg and Johnson 1990: 128–31).

The determinants of much of this multinational banking lay in the advantages of direct representation in a virtually unregulated 'supranational' financial market. Banks sought to escape from regulated national markets in order to secure the higher rates of return on equity that are associated with operations in an unregulated market. In these markets, multinational banks competed with other giant banks in a large, wholesale banking market. The sheer size of the parent bank was a precondition for entry into this market, but net ownership-specific advantages were not needed since there were no indigenous banks in the supranational market (Gray and Gray 1981: 47–52).

This type of multinational banking – which was entirely a post-1960 phenomenon – coincided with more traditional forms of multinational service and retail banking which were broadly similar in nature (if not scale) to that undertaken in the nineteenth century. The multinational bank branches located in financial centres operated in both the supranational financial markets and their national financial markets. There was a particular link with servicing the requirements of their parents' clients. During the 1960s US bank branches in London serviced the British subsidiaries of US non-bank corporations. There was a direct correlation between the growth of US FDI in general in the 1960s and the expansion of US multinational banks, with the multinationalisation of manufacturing firms creating a derived demand for the multinationalisation of banks as well. Over time US banks also lent to local corporate clients (Kelly 1977).

Multinational retail banking also continued to be undertaken. During the 1960s Citibank began to diversify from servicing large corporations in foreign markets to retail banking. It opened branches to attract household deposits, undertook consumer lending, and acquired a number of foreign consumer finance companies (Cleveland and Huertas 1985: 264–5). Foreign banks could exploit ownership advantages in management, product differentiation and technology in foreign retail markets, though these rarely compensated for the disadvantages of foreign banks at the local level, which usually limited the success of multinational retail banking. A number of the descendants of the European overseas banks also continued to undertake multinational retail banking as well as trade finance, especially in Asia and Africa. The most noteworthy survivor of this *genre* was the Hongkong Bank. This bank, which was British managed but based in the British colony of Hong Kong until 1993 when the parent holding company shifted domicile to Britain, was favoured by its entrenched position in that fast growing and low tax economy. The purchase of banks in the United States and Britain in the 1980s and 1990s made it (in 1994) Europe's largest bank by market capitalisation, and the nearest European equivalent to Citibank as a 'global bank' (King 1991; Jones 1993a: 343–9).

The growth of multinational retail and other types of banking was facilitated by the progressive deregulation of financial services which took place in developed economies from the 1970s. This deregulation, which partly reflected the impact of the Euromarkets in undermining national regulatory controls, facilitated the entry of foreign banks into previously closed markets such as those of the United States, Canada and Australia. Foreign acquisitions of banks became feasible, though hostile takeovers continued to be ruled out by regulators. British and Japanese banks purchased several large American banks to facilitate their entry into the American market. Regulatory barriers between different financial services – such as commercial investment banking, and banking and insurance – also began to be dismantled.

During the 1970s German, French, Italian and other European banks began to expand abroad, but the most striking growth was of Japanese banks. It was not until that decade that the liberalisation of Japanese regulatory constraints enabled its banks to make their first substantial foreign investments. The major commercial banks – including Dai Ichi Kangyo, Fuji, Sumitomo, Mitsubishi and Sanwa – and the 'Big Four' securities houses – Nikko, Yamaichi, Nomura and Daiwa – established offices in the major European financial centres, as well as the United States (Mason 1992b). In the following decade their international growth accelerated. The Japanese share of international bank assets rose from 23 to 35 per cent between 1984 and 1990. The share of US banks fell from 26 to 12 per cent over the same period, a consequence – in part – of their particularly large exposure to Third World debt.

The rapid international expansion of Japanese banks was driven by a number of factors apart from the relaxation of Japanese controls over outward FDI. It was partly the result of following their own clients as they went abroad, and initially much of the business of their foreign branches was with Japanese-owned firms, although in the United States and elsewhere they also developed a domestic client base (Seth and Quijano 1991). It was less evident that the rapid international growth of Japanese banks reflected large ownership advantages in management or innovation over foreign competitors. In part it was the result of continuing regulation of domestic banking in Japan, which encouraged the banks to use financial centres such as London and New York to fund their domestic operations (Terrell, Dohner and Lowrey 1989). The phenomenal growth of Japanese bank assets in the 1980s which drove their international expansion reflected the inflationary surge of land and stock prices in Japan between 1985 and 1990. The subsequent collapse of this 'bubble economy', combined with new international rules on capital adequacy, resulted in the retrenchment of Japanese financial activities abroad.

In the twenty-five years after the advent of the Eurocurrency markets, multinational banking evolved more like other sectors of international business. United States and then Japanese-owned institutions became very important. Multinational banking activities became more focused on developed economies. The isolation of the United States from world banking was ended (Darby 1986). In the 1960s foreign banks held an insignificant share of the American market. By 1983 they had acquired 18 per cent of the commercial and industrial loan market. By 1992 non-US banks accounted for 45 per cent of the loan market, which made commercial bank lending a more foreign-dominated business sector in the United States than the automobile industry. It was a radical transformation.

A general deceleration in multinational bank branching became noticeable from the mid-1980s. This reflected partly a fall in international bank lending due to the debt crisis, and the growing importance of securities markets rather than banks in the financial system. Many large banks abandoned strategies based on having a 'global' presence in favour of a more selective concentration on products and markets in which they had a sustainable advantage. United States and British banks, both severely weakened by the world debt crisis and subsequent real estate lending, divested from many foreign operations. The total number of overseas branches of US banks fell from 860 in 1985 to just over 700 in 1992. While US overseas bank assets expanded rapidly during the 1970s both in absolute terms and as a proportion of total overseas assets, from the early 1980s bank assets fell as a proportion of the total US private assets abroad.

Multinational banking can be compared to automobiles and electronics as one of the industries where competitive advantage has shifted markedly between countries. Rankings of the world's largest banks and their share of worldwide sales in the 1960s showed US banks as pre-eminent. Thirty years later Japanese banks had taken their place (Franko 1991). In 1994 the world's ten largest banks by total assets consisted of eight Japanese banks, followed by a French and a Chinese bank. Citibank, the largest US bank, was ranked twenty-sixth, and only five US banks were counted in the top fifty banks. These rankings reflected both the new international importance of Japanese banks and the consequences of the poor lending of US banks in recent decades, but the range of products and markets included in the banking sector, and the nature of financial assets, makes direct comparisons with manufacturing misleading. In certain products US banks remained highly internationally competitive (Hirtle 1991), while US – and European – banks continued to possess more extensive global networks than the Japanese (Dicken 1992: 369).

The development of the global currency and capital markets outside the control of governments gave banks and their products an unprecedented importance, and transformed the means by which MNEs in all sectors financed their activities. There was a growing convergence between industrial and financial corporations, as the Euromarkets permitted the development of the global treasury function at large MNEs, with firms seeking or transferring funds around the world in search of the lowest cost or best return. Financial services were an industry driven by innovation, deregulation and technological advance. In the 1990s these factors drove the expansion of transactions in derivative instruments such as financial futures, swaps and options. As these operations grew in scale and significance, so did the risks of doing business in them.

## SUMMARY

Multinational service companies flourished in the borderless world of the nineteenth century. Multinational trading and shipping companies, banks and utilities facilitated the expansion of world trade, helped construct the infrastructure of a global economy, and spread technologies. Trading companies developed a long-term role as co-ordinators of economic activities in the resource and manufacturing sectors. Much of this multinational investment was related to servicing trade between the developing and industrialised countries.

As the twentieth century progressed, and especially from 1930, government intervention ruled out multinational investment in some services and constrained its growth in others. Foreign-owned utilities, banks, insurance companies, and airlines were seldom permitted. Yet there remained new opportunities, mainly in developed economies, in professional business services and the provision of consumer services such as fast food restaurants and hotels. Moreover, the changing nature of trade flows and increased government intervention did not make trading intermediaries redundant. After the Second World War, the *sogo shosha* and the commodity trading companies grew rapidly, and increased their significance in the world economy.

Multinational banking underwent an unprecedented growth from the 1960s, but its significance was wider still. A great deal of the growth of multinational banking was related to escaping from national regulatory controls. The deregulation of financial services which followed helped undermine government intervention elsewhere. The global money and capital markets, often operating in a wholly unregulated environment, became of central importance in international business. The spread of deregulation and liberalisation and the return of the borderless world provided the conditions for the rapid relative rise in the importance of services in international business. As the 1990s progressed a half of total world FDI was located in services, and the proportion showed every sign of growing.

# Chapter 6

# The competitiveness of firms and nations

## COMPARATIVE HOME ECONOMIES

As companies were transformed from national firms to international producers, and then to global enterprises, they did not become nationless. Rather, their national origins continued to exercise a strong influence on when, where and how they invested abroad. This chapter explores the relationship between MNEs and their home economies. It begins by summarising and drawing together material presented in earlier chapters on the major long-term national differences in the ownership, timing, propensity to invest, industrial and geographical distribution, and organisation of international business.

The number of major home economies has always been small. Before the First World War at least four-fifths of world FDI was based in Western Europe. Within this region there was a dispersion of ownership between individual economies, although the United Kingdom had by far the largest slice. Between the First World War and 1980 three countries – the United States, the United Kingdom and the Netherlands – accounted for between two-thirds and three-quarters of total world FDI. From the 1980s the number of major home economies rose again. By 1993 the share of the United States, the United Kingdom and the Netherlands in the world stock of outward FDI was down to 45 per cent, but if the shares of France, Germany and Japan were added, these six countries alone accounted for three-quarters of total world stock.

This ownership pattern reflects strong national differences in the timing of international business activities. In the broadest terms, European enterprises seemed pre-eminent in the nineteenth century, US enterprises took this position for much of the twentieth century, while Japanese enterprises grew rapidly in importance from the 1970s. However this is a considerable oversimplification. In terms of stock position, if not flows, Western European companies remained the largest holders of FDI until the Second World War, lost that position to the United States in the 1950s and 1960s, and regained it thereafter. Although the flows of new Japanese

FDI were very large over the last two decades, the cumulative nature of multinational investment meant that Japan's stock position only passed that of the United Kingdom in the early 1990s.

There were marked national differences in propensities to engage in multinational investment. The United States has been a persistently large outward investor since the nineteenth century. Even more striking was the long-term British propensity to engage in international business, which survived that country's relative economic decline after the Second World War. A trio of three small European economies – the Netherlands, Sweden and Switzerland – have also been persistent long-term foreign investors. For much of the twentieth century, their stock of FDI was very large given their size, and if compared to the larger European economies. In 1967 Dutch outward FDI was equal to that of Germany, France and Italy combined. It was only around 1980 that the stock of Dutch FDI was surpassed by that of Germany, even though the population of the latter country was four times larger. There was also a striking contrast with other small Western European economies – Belgium (at least since 1914), Austria and Norway – which have been persistently low outward investors. In 1990 the stock of Swiss FDI was forty times larger than that of Austria.

In contrast, some economies were erratic multinational investors. France and Germany were major participants in the great world boom in international business between the late nineteenth century and the First World War. Thereafter both countries experienced a prolonged period of subdued international investment, before their outward FDI began to rise rapidly again from the 1970s. Japan also falls into this category. By the interwar years the worldwide activities of Japanese trading and other service sector companies, as well as investments by Japanese cotton textile and mining companies in the markets and resources of Asia – especially China – resulted in the creation of a complex international business system. Although the stock of Japanese FDI probably never reached 3 per cent of the world total, in 1930 it may have amounted to between 11.5 and 13.6 per cent of Japan's gross national income. After the Second World War Japanese outward FDI remained at low levels until the resumption of growth from the 1970s, but even in the mid-1980s the ratio of Japanese outward FDI to its national income was only 5.9 per cent (Kuwahara 1990).

Finally there was a group of genuine latecomer multinational investors. These were the Asian and Latin American newly industrial countries (NICs), particularly Hong Kong, Singapore, South Korea, Taiwan and Brazil, whose outward FDI began on a small scale in the 1960s and 1970s and then grew rapidly from the 1980s. By the end of that decade the estimated stock of FDI from developing countries – mostly these NICs – was around 8 to 10 per cent of the world total (United Nations 1993: 14). South Korea and Taiwan became net outward investors in 1990 and 1988 respectively.

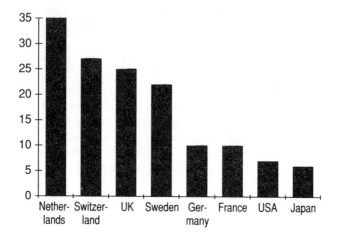

*Figure 6.1* Ratio of outward FDI stock to GDP of major home economies, 1990 (%)
*Source*: Dunning 1993: 288

These differences in the timing and propensity to invest are reflected in continuing and substantial variations in the relative importance of multinational investment between home economies. Figure 6.1 gives the ratio of outward FDI stock to each country's gross domestic product (GDP) for eight major home economies in 1990, which together accounted for 92 per cent of the total developed market stock of FDI in that year.

Figure 6.1 shows the considerably higher relative importance of outward FDI in 1990 to the economies of the Netherlands, Switzerland, Sweden and the United Kingdom compared to those of Germany and France, even after the fast growth of multinational investment from those economies over the previous twenty years. In contrast, although the United States held the largest absolute stock of FDI of any single home economy, it was much less important compared to the total size of the American economy, and close to the Japanese ratio.

There were strong, long-term national differences in the industrial distribution of multinational investment. In terms of broad economic sectors, the United States, the United Kingdom, France and the Netherlands have had substantial investments in natural resources, although over time the relative importance of this sector has declined in importance. In 1897 as much as 46 per cent of total US FDI was in natural resources. By 1940 this proportion had fallen to 35 per cent, and by 1977 to 14 per cent (Wilkins 1970: 110; Wilkins 1974a: 182–3; Lipsey 1988). In all countries the petroleum industry became progressively more important over time than mining and agriculture, and especially from the 1930s. Over the long term, much less German and Japanese FDI was located in natural resources, although this needs some qualification. There were major German multinational activities in petroleum and metals before the First World War, while Japanese companies made important resource investments in interwar Asia, and again in the 1950s and 1960s.

Japan provides the most significant example of a home economy in which the service sector has formed a large component of outward FDI over a long period. From the nineteenth century until the 1970s services were the most important sector. In 1971 they comprised around 50 per cent of the total Japanese stock of FDI. This proportion subsequently rose – as was the norm everywhere – and it remained higher than in other home economies (United Nations 1992: 18). At the other extreme, service industries have not figured largely in Swedish, Swiss or German multinational investment, although this generalisation probably does not hold true for the latter before 1914 or from the 1970s. The British and the Americans always had a significant proportion of their outward FDI in service activities, though with considerable shifts over time in the relative importance of particular service industries. In the American case, the foreign expansion of US utility companies in the 1920s resulted in over a fifth of the total stock of US FDI being in that industry in 1940, but after the Second World War this proportion fell rapidly. In contrast, the internationalisation of US banks raised the relative importance of finance in total US FDI from 4 to 14 per cent between 1957 and 1982 (Lipsey 1988).

Within manufacturing, strong national differences are apparent, though once more with substantial changes over time. In the case of the United States, the machinery and electrical industries were the most active outward investors before 1914, followed by the food and automobile industry in the interwar years, the chemical industry from the 1950s, and the computer and electronics industries subsequently. These industries remain the main areas of US multinational manufacturing (Mataloni and Goldberg 1994). The British had a bias towards branded consumer goods from the nineteenth century, and this grew in relative importance until – in the 1950s and 1960s – about one-half of all British overseas assets in manufacturing were in food, drink and tobacco. This bias has remained – in the 1980s these industries represented 30 per cent of Britain's stock of manufacturing FDI (Balasubramanyam 1993: 149) – although chemicals, pharmaceuticals and engineering also became considerably more important.

Among other home economies, similar patterns of specialisation are apparent. From the nineteenth century the chemicals and electricals industries have been the most prominent in German FDI – accounting for one-fifth and one-tenth of the total stock in the mid-1970s. German FDI in automobiles became significant from the 1950s. In the Dutch case, food and, from the interwar years, chemicals and electrical engineering have been the most important manufacturing sectors. Swedish manufacturing

FDI has always been concentrated in engineering and machinery. Swiss manufacturing FDI first occurred in textiles, and later textile machinery, followed from the late nineteenth century by branded food products, chemicals and pharmaceuticals (Jones and Schröter 1993a). Japanese manufacturing FDI was concentrated in textiles through the twentieth century until the 1970s. This industry still comprised around 20 per cent of Japan's total FDI in the postwar decades, a much higher percentage than any other country. It was only subsequently that the international expansion of the electronics and automobile industries reduced the overall significance of textiles.

The shifting geographical location over time of the multinational investments of different countries reflected overall trends in international business. Those economies which undertook extensive FDI in natural resources and related services had a considerable proportion of this investment in developing countries before the Second World War. Subsequently, this proportion fell as multinational investment became more focused on manufacturing and services in the developed economies. Since the 1970s the growth in importance of the United States as a host economy has been strongly reflected in the distribution of European and Japanese FDI, while Western Europe has grown in significance as a host for US and Japanese FDI.

Within these general trends, distinct geographical patterns can be discerned. The distribution of US and Japanese FDI was skewed towards the Americas and Asia respectively. In the case of the United States, almost three-fifths of US FDI in 1914 was found in Canada (23 per cent), Mexico (22 per cent) and Cuba and the West Indies (11 per cent). Subsequently, Mexico and Central America generally became much less important for American investors compared to South America, but Latin America as a whole accounted for 40 per cent of total US FDI in 1950, though this ratio fell sharply thereafter. Canada's share of US FDI was between 25 and 30 per cent from the late nineteenth century until the 1970s, when it began falling in favour of Western Europe (Wilkins 1970, 1974a; Mataloni and Goldberg 1994). Nonetheless, Canada alternated with the United Kingdom into the 1980s as the single most important recipient of US FDI, while in the 1980s around two-thirds of all FDI in Mexico was from the United States.

In the case of Japan, the amount of FDI in East Asia – primarily China – far exceeded that elsewhere before the Second World War, even though significant service sector investments were made in the United States (Wilkins 1990b). In the postwar decades Japanese FDI was heavily skewed towards Southeast Asia and other developing regions, notably Latin America, and this remained the case until the growth of Japanese manufacturing FDI in the United States and Europe from the 1970s. In 1990 North America accounted for 50 per cent of Japanese manufacturing FDI,

Asia for 25 per cent, and Europe for about 12 per cent (Strange 1993: 71). The MNEs from the Asian NICs followed the Japanese pattern of initially focusing on 'nearby' Asian economies, before – recently – shifting attention to North America and Europe (United Nations 1994: 76).

The geographical distribution of European FDI was heavily influenced by a tendency to make manufacturing investments in 'nearby' European countries. In countries whose FDI was mainly in manufacturing – such as Sweden – the rest of Europe was the primary location for investments over a long period, although some investments were made also in the United States (Olsson 1993). The United States was probably the single largest host economy for German FDI before 1914, even though the majority of German FDI was in Europe, but thereafter until the 1970s, German FDI in the United States was much less than in Europe. From the 1970s almost all European countries saw large-scale investments in the United States, but intra-European investments remained of major importance. By 1990 Germany had 48 per cent of its FDI in Europe and 27 per cent in the United States. The equivalent French proportions were 57 per cent and 24 per cent, and those of the Netherlands 41 per cent and 34 per cent (Jones and Schröter 1993b; Dupuy, Milelli and Savary 1991: 35). Italy had three-quarters of its total FDI elsewhere in Europe in the same year.

The main deviation from this European 'nearby' pattern occurred in the countries with colonial empires. Almost three-quarters of Dutch FDI was located in the Dutch East Indies in 1914, and around one-half in 1947, the date of Indonesian independence (Gales and Sluyterman 1993). From the interwar years French colonies became the location of most French international business in the resource and service sectors. Even in the early 1970s around 30 per cent of total French FDI was located in former colonies – primarily in Africa – though by 1980 the proportion had dropped dramatically to less than 5 per cent (Michalet and Chevallier 1985: Savary 1984: 49–50, 53).

In the British case, the influence of empire and of the United States was sufficient to very considerably reduce the relative amount of FDI located in geographically 'nearby' European countries. Before the First World War around two-fifths of total UK FDI was located in the Empire, with the remainder widely spread over Latin America, the United States and elsewhere in Europe (Corley 1994). During the interwar years the Empire grew in relative importance, and between 1945 and 1960 around four-fifths of new UK FDI went to the developed market economies of the former Empire, mostly Australia, Canada and South Africa. By 1962 around 55 per cent of the stock of UK FDI was in the former empire, while only 13 per cent was located in Western Europe and under 10 per cent in the United States. Thereafter, UK FDI shifted rapidly towards Western Europe, and – especially – the United States, which by 1990 accounted for half of the total stock of British FDI (Jones 1994: 190–3).

Finally, strong national differences can be observed in the ways companies sought to control and organise their foreign operations. At least three areas of difference can be identified. These were, first, the presence of a large number of free-standing companies in British and Dutch FDI before 1930, which contrasted with the preference for the 'classic' MNE structure in the United States and other European countries. Second, over the last one hundred years European and Japanese companies have often been embedded in networks, while US firms were much less frequently involved in international collaborative activities. Third, European (and Japanese) enterprises have demonstrated a greater use of clan – or at least more personalised – methods of managerial control than their US equivalents.

## THE HOME ECONOMY IMPACT ON MNEs

This section identifies some characteristics of home economies which influence national variations in multinational propensities and timing, industrial and geographical distribution, and organisation and control.

### Evolutionary models

There have been a number of attempts to relate the national differences in multinational investment to the stage of a country's economic development. These models are potentially of particular importance in explaining the differences in the timing of flows of outward FDI from different countries. In the investment development path model proposed by Dunning, a country's international investment position is related to its level of development as measured by its GNP per capita. A developing economy passes through four stages. In Stage 1 of pre-industrialisation there is no inward or outward FDI. In Stage 2, if the economy has developed, the country will begin to attract inward FDI as domestic markets increase and the variable costs of servicing those markets are reduced. In Stage 3, a country's net inward investment per capita begins to fall. This may be because the original ownership advantages of foreign firms have declined, or because local firms have begun to improve their competitive capacity, or because local firms have developed their own comparative ownership advantages which they have begun to exploit through FDI. In Stage 4, a country is a net outward investor, with its investment flows abroad exceeding those of foreign-owned firms in its own country. This reflects the development of strong ownership advantages by its firms and/or an increasing propensity to exploit these advantages internally from a foreign rather than a domestic location (Dunning 1981).

This investment development path model is helpful in providing a dynamic link between economic development and FDI flows. In Wilkins' words, 'the more industrialised, the more economically advanced the country, *ceteris paribus*, the more likely for it to be a headquarters for business abroad' (Wilkins 1988b: 11). Historically, the surges of economic development first in Western Europe, then in the United States, and then in Japan have been followed by accelerating FDI flows from those regions. From the 1960s, as the Asian NICs progressed rapidly along the development path, their international investment positions also moved in the direction suggested by the model.

Yet there are numerous problems in applying the Dunning model historically and to individual countries. The European first movers in international business – notably the United Kingdom – built up large stocks of outward FDI during the first stages of economic development. The growth of inward FDI into the United States over the last two decades to a level when it approached the level of US outward FDI is hard to reconcile with 'Stage 4'. The stages are not helpful in explaining inward FDI flows into crude oil production, mining and agriculture. Finally, different countries at the same stage of their development path have displayed distinctly different FDI propensities.

The influence of country-specific factors forms one part of the product cycle model proposed by Vernon in the mid-1960s. It was argued that firms based in the US had a greater propensity to develop new products because of high per capita incomes and high unit labour costs in their home economy. The model suggested that when a new product was developed in the US, a firm normally chose a domestic production location, partly because of the need for close contact with customers and suppliers. As a product matured, long-run production with established technology became possible. When it became economic to invest abroad, Western Europe was the preferred choice of location since demand patterns were close to the US and (at that time) labour costs were relatively low. When the product entered its standardised phase, the lowest cost supply point became a priority, and production could be transferred to developing countries (Vernon 1966).

The product cycle hypothesis provided an explanation for the large flows of US manufacturing FDI into postwar Europe, but as the international pre-eminence of the United States declined, the model needed modification. In later formulations, Vernon reduced the role of the US as a source of new products, but the modified model continued to stress the role of home economies in innovatory activities of their firms. Historically, 'US firms have developed and produced products that were labour-saving or responded to high-income wants; continental European firms, products and processes that were material-saving and capital-saving; and Japanese firms, products that conserved not only material and capital but also space' (Vernon 1979: 256).

The product cycle theory works best as an explanation for US manufacturing investment in postwar Europe, and it also provides insights on the determinants of Japanese manufacturing FDI in the United States and Europe after 1970. Goods requiring resources and capabilities in which Japan had created a comparative advantage were first exported by Japan to countries with similar income levels. Then, when it became more profitable to produce these goods in these markets – or barriers were placed on Japanese exports – production facilities were shifted (Dunning 1994). However, as in the case of the Dunning model, a great deal of international business activity is left unexplained by product cycle theory.

The view that outward industrial investment is associated with technology leaders is supported by considerable historical evidence. There is a strong correlation between the innovatory competitiveness of countries in particular sectors and the propensity of their firms to engage in multinational activity. Since the nineteenth century new waves of outward FDI in manufacturing have originated from technologically leading firms clustered in specific home economies which were either present or former world technology leaders (such as the United States and the United Kingdom) or else highly technologically developed (such as the Netherlands, Switzerland and Sweden). The home country distribution of outward FDI has reflected the fact that countries differ in their technological capabilities, and that these differences – and differences in the patterns of technological specialisation among countries – have been stable over long periods of time (Pavitt and Soete 1982; Cantwell 1989; Cantwell and Bellak 1994). This pattern is a continuing one. The internationalisation of Japanese firms followed the emergence of Japan as a world technology leader, while the subsequent growth of Third World manufacturing MNEs can be similarly related to technological accumulation in the Asian NICs (Tolentino 1993).

As shown in Chapter 1 and subsequently, the causes of such technological differences have to be placed in a wider organisational context. The firms of different countries have differed in their organisation and these differences have translated into differences in innovation. There have been various attempts to model these differences in a dynamic fashion. Chandler demonstrated the advantages of US-style managerial capitalism over British-style personal capitalism in the new capital intensive industries of the late nineteenth century (Chandler 1990). Lazonick developed a model of changes of international competitive advantage which highlights the impact of institutional structures on the ability of firms to develop and utilise the productive resources that they control. Lazonick identifies major competitive shifts with the shift in advantage from British-style 'proprietary capitalism' to US-style 'managerial capitalism', and then to Japanese-style 'collective capitalism' (Lazonick 1990, 1991).

While neither Chandler nor Lazonick are specifically concerned with international business, Kogut has specifically related national differences in trade and FDI patterns to a country's technological and – especially –

organising abilities. Given the evidence that the pattern of technological specialisation among developed countries is stable over long periods of time, Kogut argues that technology accumulates in a country in the same way as it accumulates in firms. This can be explained by persistent variations in organisational and institutional capabilities between countries. These 'organising principles' – whose effectiveness is regarded as the critical factor in explaining changing patterns of international competitiveness between countries – diffuse more slowly than technologies across national borders. The capabilities of firms which they exploit in foreign countries are in part derived from the 'diffused skills and institutional strengths of their countries of origin'. In this framework, the international importance of the United Kingdom in the nineteenth century rested on the expansion of organised industrial production, the subsequent US pre-eminence was built on mass production and the principles of scientific management, while the growth of Japanese industrial competitiveness reflected the evolution of lean or flexible production (Kogut 1991).

This model – like those of Chandler and Lazonick – is valuable for examining changes over time in the sources of outward FDI in manufacturing, especially in capital goods sectors employing frontier technologies. However these models are not readily transferable to other parts of manufacturing, or to the service and resource sectors. Moreover there is a considerable divergence between 'country leadership' as defined in these studies and patterns of international business. This is evident in the case of the United Kingdom, whose treatment in Chandler, Lazonick and Kogut as the exemplar of outdated management and production methods belies its continued extremely high propensity to engage in FDI.

## Factor endowments, business structures and regulatory influences

The factor endowments, business structures and regulatory characteristics of home economies influenced the international business activities of their firms in numerous ways. These characteristics sometimes changed considerably over time, and it is important that the relationship is seen in a dynamic rather than a static context.

Capital availability was important. The leading European capital exporters of the late nineteenth century – the United Kingdom, Germany and France – were also leading homes to multinationals, while the development of the United States as the world's largest creditor after the First World War was accompanied by that country's emergence as the largest home economy in terms of FDI flows. The phenomenon of the free-standing company in particular appears linked to capital availability, even though only certain capital exporters developed this institutional form. But the fact that multinational investment can only partially be explained in terms of capital exports means that the correlation is not complete.

The United States, Sweden and Japan grew as direct investors before 1914 while their economies were net capital importers, while the United Kingdom remained a major outward investor long after it ceased to be a net capital exporter.

The existence of natural resources in home economies helps to explain the industrial distribution of the FDI of different countries. It was shown in Chapter 3 that the existence of natural resources provided resource MNEs with access to skills which could be exploited abroad. This was one significant factor behind the prominent American position in international petroleum and mining. The British had a traditional mining industry whose resources were largely depleted over the course of the nineteenth century. This gave them both a reservoir of skills in mining, and a strong need to locate new sources of supply. Resource availability was an important source of ownership advantage in manufacturing. Examples included the group of Swedish MNEs which grew out of Sweden's raw material base of iron ore and forest products, and the Swiss MNEs which reflected the importance of that country's dairy products industry.

Created resource endowments were also important. Germany had few natural resources, but from the late nineteenth century made extensive investments in scientific and technical education. The development of Germany's competitive strengths in chemicals and electricals rested in part on this educational system (Chandler 1990: 425–6; Locke 1984). Subsequently, extensive training and apprenticeship systems were developed in Germany which provided the basis for the highly skilled workforce required by those industries. Likewise Sweden's strengths in advanced engineering products reflected the heavy investment in technical schools and literacy in that country even when – in the nineteenth century – it was still a very poor economy. This helps to explain why Swedes were so able to absorb new technologies and apply them in modern industrial production (Olsson 1993: 100–1).

The ability of US corporations to grow to a large size, create managerial hierarchies, and expand across borders rested in part on the close links which developed between American higher education and industrial enterprises, especially after 1900. Corporate research departments were able to recruit electrical and chemical engineers and managers from the Massachusetts Institute of Technology and other institutions. US educational institutions were the first to develop degrees in business education. In 1900 Dartmouth's Amos Tuck School of Administration and Finance became the first US school of business to enrol graduate students. In 1908 Harvard Business School was founded. These schools provided a supply of first-class managers to administer US MNEs (Chandler 1990: 82–3). At the other extreme, British higher educational institutions did not develop significant business education programmes until the 1960s, and few companies recruited university graduates until the same period. The

British managerial class was – and remains – less formally educated than elsewhere in Europe and the United States, with many managers receiving a training in accounting rather than possessing an engineering or business degree (Keeble 1992, Lane 1989). This did not prevent British companies investing abroad, but it may explain in part their bias towards certain services and consumer goods rather than industries involving complex production technologies, as well as their use of clan methods of control rather than the creation of extensive bureaucratic hierarchies.

The overall size of home economies influenced international business. The growth of the United States as a large, mass consumption society by the late nineteenth century provided the environment for US firms to pioneer the introduction of low cost, standardised, mass-marketed products in many industries. After the Second World War, the size of the American market and the importance of US defence spending in the Cold War gave US firms in computers and electronics great advantages over their competitors. The type of home country market could also be important. In Japan, there was a long-term tradition that consumers had an idiosyncratic demand for consumer durables with the latest up-to-date features. This aspect of the home market stimulated Japanese firms after the Second World War to pioneer flexible manufacturing and marketing processes (Yasumuro 1993a).

The relative importance of the Netherlands, Switzerland and Sweden as home countries raises the possibility that a 'small economy' effect is significant in explaining FDI propensities. Enterprises from those countries were often driven abroad from the nineteenth century onwards because their home markets were so small (Gales and Sluyterman 1993: 91; Olsson 1993: 102). However, the co-existence of these cases with neighbouring small countries with low propensities to invest suggest that variables other than size need to be considered.

The industrial structures of the economies was probably among the most important. Small countries have more 'unbalanced' industrial structures than large ones – some industries proportionately large, others missing. Depending on its particular complement of industries, it can therefore be predicted that a small nation will have either a very large amount of FDI or a very small one (Caves 1982: 59). The industrial structure in turn resulted in differences in concentration levels. It was the small economies with high concentration levels which were the most active in outward FDI. In contrast, low European investors such as Denmark and Norway were countries in which the role of small and medium-sized companies was considerable (Jones and Schröter 1993b: 23).

The significance of concentration levels is not limited to the small economies. The United Kingdom's continued prominence as an outward investor may be in part explained by the growing importance of large firms in its economy. Beginning in the interwar years, and gathering pace in the 1950s and 1960s, concentration levels in British industry rose rapidly. By 1970 the share of the 100 largest enterprises in manufacturing net output was considerably higher in the United Kingdom than in the United States, while the small or medium-sized enterprise sector had shrunk (Channon 1973). Among other influences, British MNEs may well have possessed considerable advantages in capital-raising derived from their large size, as well as the sophisticated nature of the British capital market (Clegg 1987: 102). In contrast concentration levels remained lower in Germany, France and – especially – Italy.

The extent to which a country's firms were internationally active in mining and petroleum – and especially the latter – was a distinctive factor behind national variations in size of FDI. The capital-intensive nature of mining and petroleum translated into large stocks of FDI. As oil replaced coal as the world's most important source of energy, the international oil companies grew in their relative importance. Their size reflected both their ownership of world oilfields before the nationalisations of the 1970s and their extensive investments in refining, transportation and distribution. Significantly, the homes of the world's largest oil companies – the United States, the United Kingdom and the Netherlands – were the same countries which were the pre-eminent home economies for world FDI as a whole between the First World War and the 1970s. The petroleum industry accounted for between one-quarter and one-third of total US FDI in the 1950s and 1960s (Wilkins 1974a: 384–90), and was at least as prominent in British and Dutch international investment.

Home country laws have exercised important influences on international business. US antitrust laws discouraged over a long period much of the collaborative behaviour which was frequently seen in the international operations of both European and Japanese firms. On a number of occasions, antitrust rulings have seriously impacted the competitive positions of major US MNEs to the benefit of their competitors, foreign and American. Thus the dissolution of American Tobacco before the First World War led to the shift of BAT to British control (see p. 109). After the Second World War the antitrust ruling against Alcoa led – among other things – to its former Canadian affiliate, Alcan, becoming a major MNE in its own capacity (see pp. 83–4). Antitrust laws proved a major constraint on the development of collective industrial research by US firms, with the result that it lagged markedly behind that undertaken in Europe and Japan. It was not until 1984 that Congress passed the National Co-operative Research Act which eased antitrust laws and permitted collaborative research among competing firms.

Home country regulations on inward investment and trade barriers – discussed in more detail in the following chapters – had important influences on outward multinational investment. After 1945 the considerable advantages derived by US firms from the US defence budget were bolstered by the fact that foreign-controlled firms were not eligible for the security clearance required to bid on US defence contracts (Safarian 1983: 38–9). In the same period, the Japanese consumer electronics and automobiles industries grew to a large scale within a Japanese market protected by both import controls and strict limits on inward FDI. This home country protectionism was an important source of ownership advantage for these US and Japanese industries, even though there were other important factors behind their growth.

The continuing significance of the home country environment in even the most globalised of industries is the theme of Michael Porter's 'diamond' model of the sources of international competitive advantage. Porter argues that four sets of attributes of a home economy are critical for the competitiveness of its firms: the quantity and quality of demand by domestic consumers; the level and composition of natural and created resources; the extent to which its firms are able to benefit from agglomerations or external economies by being grouped in clusters of related activities; and firm strategy, structure and rivalry. The importance of such fierce competitive rivalries at home for shaping competitiveness abroad is a special theme of Porter's work. He is able to show conclusively that many of the most internationally competitive firms – such as Japanese consumer electronics and automobile companies – emerge from industries which are characterised by fierce rivalries between firms in their domestic markets (Porter 1990).

This model does not seek to explain patterns of multinational investment, but by identifying factors behind national strengths in particular industries, it is of considerable relevance (Dunning 1993: 102–27). The model is particularly valuable in stressing that the four sets of attributes are interlinked and interact with one another in a 'diamond'. Although the influence of the home environment of MNEs is pervasive, this influence is felt in multiple directions.

## The role of culture

There is considerable evidence that culture is a pervasive influence on international business. As the research of Hofstede (1980, 1991) and others has shown, countries differ widely in the organisation of their firms and the behaviour of their managers, and these differences can be said to derive in part from different cultural values. Although the influence of culture is pervasive, it is also diffuse and much harder to demonstrate than more tangible phenomenon such as factor endowments or legal systems. This makes a discussion of the home country cultural influence on MNEs more speculative than conclusive.

The impact of culture can be seen in several different areas. Differences in levels of outward investment may reflect wider differences between outward and inward-looking cultural orientations. The colonial and mercantile traditions of the United Kingdom and the Netherlands stimulated a strong outward looking commercial tradition. Switzerland and Sweden had no colonies, but a long tradition of international trade and exposure to foreign cultures. Both countries became noteworthy for their multilingual abilities. Switzerland was composed of three language groups – German, French and Italian – while in Sweden, German and later English were widely understood. Outward orientation was often reflected in migration flows. The United Kingdom, the Netherlands, Switzerland and Sweden were major sources of emigrants in the nineteenth century. The United States – to which most of these people emigrated – had almost by definition an outward cultural orientation, as it was a country of immigrants.

The pre-eminence of the English-speaking economies in the development of international business was a continuation of the expansive drive which led to the settlement of large tracts of lands in earlier centuries, but this was also a self-reinforcing process. The fact that English was the common language of the United States, the United Kingdom, and the large number of countries which came under British colonial influence, encouraged cross-investments by reducing the perceived risks of international investments. This was perhaps the most important example of the 'nearby' phenomenon.

Cultures developed more inward-looking orientations for several reasons. Japan emerged from the long Edo era of national seclusion with little knowledge of the rest of the world, and a strong sense of the uniqueness of Japanese culture. Modern Japan developed as outward looking in some respects – for example, in the acquisition of foreign technology – but with a distinctly arm's-length attitude to the people and firms of foreign countries. France was unlike Japan in that it had an extensive colonial empire, but it was also the only European country in the nineteenth century to experience net immigration. An extreme confidence in the cultural superiority of France produced an inward-looking culture with some parallels to that of Japan. The subdued level of French FDI for much of the twentieth century may have reflected this.

Buckley and Casson suggest that MNEs personify the entrepreneurial cultures of their home economies – which can be contrasted with the less entrepreneurial cultures prevailing in many developing economies. An entrepreneurial culture has a number of features – particularly a scientific outlook, a certain kind of individualism combined with an acceptance of the need for voluntary association, and sufficiently high levels of trust to prevent high transaction costs (Buckley and Casson 1989; Casson 1991a). This theory is most readily applicable in explaining why outward investment has been so concentrated in the hands of Western Europeans and North Americans, and more recently, of East Asian countries. However, it is in need of greater refinement before it can explain the significant differences between Western European countries.

The most important attempt to relate perceived differences in the organisation of firms between countries to culture has been the research of Hofstede. Hofstede identified four dimensions of culture which differed between countries: their readiness to tolerate inequality (Power Distance); their tolerance for uncertainty (Uncertainty Avoidance); their relationships between the individual and the collective (Individualism); and their attitudes towards gender roles (Masculinity). On the basis of over 100,000 answers to a questionnaire of IBM's workforce in 1967 and 1973, Hofstede identified major differences in countries in these dimensions. He related such cultural differences to national organisational differences – such as whether firms had tall or flat hierarchies – and concluded that 'organisations are culture bound' (Hofstede 1980, 1991).

Hofstede's research is not specifically addressed to MNEs – though it carries the strong implication that MNE parents would be ill-advised to transfer their management systems in their entirety to foreign affiliates – but it may provide one explanation for different national propensities to engage in multinational investment. The ownership of world FDI has historically been correlated with cultures identified by Hofstede as being very individualistic, with a preference for equality (low Power Distance) and a willingness to tolerate uncertainty (low Uncertainty Avoidance). The United States, the United Kingdom and the Netherlands shared these characteristics. This might explain differences between neighbouring European countries in their investment propensities, for Belgium differs greatly from the Netherlands in terms of Hofstede's cultural dimensions, as does France from the United Kingdom. It might be hypothesised that international business, as it is more risky than domestic business, would be favoured by cultures which were more individualistic and less risk-averse than others. The particularly prominent role of English-speaking countries as sources of FDI in natural resources might be explained in such cultural terms. Mining and petroleum were and remain high-risk business activities. Cultures in which entrepreneurs were willing to act independently and take risks provided a competitive advantage in such an environment.

Cultural differences can also explain the modes employed by firms when they operate abroad. This is because choices between markets and hierarchies take place in a cultural context, and the transactional preferences can be determined by cultural factors (Boisot 1986). Casson identifies the level of trust in a culture as a crucial factor. The case of Japan, a 'high trust' culture, can be contrasted with the United States, a 'low trust' culture. In the former, there are very few lawyers, while in the latter litigation is a way of life. Morality can overcome problems that formal procedures – based on monitoring compliance with contracts – cannot (Casson 1991a). High trust cultures provide a more supportive environment for network-like arrangements to operate than low trust cultures, where the problems of sustaining collaborative links can be considerable (Powell 1990: 326–7).

A number of studies have applied cross-cultural theories to understanding national differences in the market entry strategies of the MNEs. It has been hypothesised that the MNEs of countries culturally similar to the United States – such as other English-speaking nations and Scandinavia – are more likely to invest in the United States using wholly-owned subsidiaries, while direct investors based in countries which are more culturally distant – such as Japan – are more likely to employ joint ventures. This is because joint ventures enable the delegation to the local partner of matters such as the management of the labour force and negotiations with suppliers and customers. Kogut and Singh (1988), using a sample of firms based in more than a dozen countries which invested in the United States in the 1980s, and employing Hofstede's four cultural dimensions, found evidence that greater cultural distance increased the probability of greenfield joint ventures being chosen to enter the United States. However there are considerable problems in establishing controls for other factors that affect the choice of entry mode. This methodological problem has resulted in other studies both refuting (Kim and Daniels 1991) and supporting (Hennart and Larimo 1995) a cultural impact on MNE entry strategies into the United States. There remain no long-term historical studies of this phenomenon.

These linkages between culture and international business are suggestive rather than conclusive. There are serious problems in separating the impact of national culture from other factors, while MNEs are influenced by several different types of culture – corporate, industry and national – which overlap. There is the major problem of 'cultural shift'. It is by no means evident that Hofstede's four dimensions of culture – based on answers to a questionnaire at a specific moment in time – are useful for describing cultures one hundred years previously, or in the 1990s, even though there is reason to believe that underlying cultural orientations may change rather slowly, unless subject to major external manipulation. It is not evident that Hofstede's dimensions are the optimal way of describing national cultural differences. They do not identify some key differences – such as attitudes towards time – while some of them may be misleading. Triandis (1993) has argued that individualism and collectivism co-exist and are simply emphasised more or less in each culture depending on the situation. In short, while culture appears to be an important influence on international business, further research is needed in the theory of cross-cultural management before the nature and extent of this influence can be conclusively demonstratated.

## Wars and chance

Major exogenous upheavals in home economies such as wars have been shown to have exercised a major long-term influence on the development

of international business. The low level of German FDI between the First
World War and the 1970s, and the low Japanese FDI between 1945 and
the 1970s, can only be understood in the context of the sequestrations of
those countries' foreign assets as a result of the world wars, even if other
important variables were also at work. It would appear that a rise in risk
aversion was more important than the loss of capital in explaining the
long-term consequences. The high perceived risk of FDI encouraged
entrepreneurs to consider alternative modes and locations for operating
abroad.

In contrast, the high propensity of Sweden and Switzerland to invest
abroad can be related to their neutral status during the First and Second
World Wars, while the Netherlands was neutral in the First World War.
Neutrality left their foreign assets intact – though Swedish firms suffered
from the destruction and loss of property in Russia following the
Communist Revolution and Eastern Europe following the Second World
War – while their business at home was spared the destruction seen else-
where in Europe.

It remains true that both the British and the Dutch were persistent
foreign investors in spite of heavy losses of assets. The Second World
War, decolonisation and the growth of nationalism in developing countries
had a serious impact on both countries. The United Kingdom may have
lost 40 per cent of its total overseas business assets between 1938
and 1956 through sequestration, wartime destruction of property and
obligatory sales. The latter included the enforced wartime sale of the
largest British-owned industrial asset in the United States – the American
Viscose subsidiary of Courtaulds (Coleman 1969; Houston and Dunning
1976). Dutch FDI was hit hard by the demise of the Dutch colonial
empire in Asia, which was followed by the nationalisation of Dutch
property at the end of the 1950s. Yet in both the British and Dutch cases,
such massive external shocks did not result in a dimunition of the desire
to invest abroad.

## Firms, nations and time

The influence of home economies on MNEs is pervasive, but needs to be
kept in perspective. There are strong country commonalities in the
strategies pursued by firms from the same country, but firms of a particular
nationality do not share equally the resources of their home countries,
and there is a wide range in performance among firms headquartered in
the same country. It follows that home country characteristics provide
only a partial explanation of the dynamics of international business.

The growth of the largest MNEs of the twentieth century – Shell
and Exxon, Ford and General Motors, Unilever and Nestlé, Matsushita and
Sony – reflected idiosyncratic firm-specific experiences which differentiated

them from numerous less successful national competitors. These experiences ranged from individual entrepreneurial decisions at crucial moments, to the development of a particular management or production system which turned out to be very effective. The growth of these giant MNEs can be regarded as resting on certain aspects of their home economies, but their individual histories demonstrate great diversity in management, strategy, culture and performance.

Finally, the stock of multinational investment of a country is the result of a cumulative process. It reflects past factor endowments, laws, national 'diamonds' and cultural values at least as much as contemporary ones. MNEs can continue to be prominent in an industry long after their home country lost the comparative advantage which stimulated their growth initially. The role of first mover and incumbency advantages has been especially critical in the service and resource industries.

## MNEs AND NATIONAL COMPETITIVENESS

The relationship between MNEs and the competitiveness of their home economies is complex. The very concept of national competitiveness is regarded by some writers as misleading (Krugman 1994), and the term certainly carries a range of possible meanings. In this section the concept of national competitiveness is used loosely to demonstrate the general point that in an open economy with substantial outward and inward FDI, both the interests and performance of firms and countries can diverge considerably.

### MNEs as measures of competitiveness

In a general sense, both the ability and the incentive of firms to produce outside their national boundaries is related to the competitive advantages held by their home economies. However the correlation between the amount of FDI possessed by a country and its competitiveness (however defined) is not straightforward. This is partly because of the cumulative nature of FDI. And it is partly because countries exploit international competitive advantage as much by exporting as by direct investment. Indeed, major studies of international competitiveness often use national shares of world exports as the key measure of a country's competitiveness (Porter 1990). The post-1950 economic growth of Japan, Germany and France rested precisely on exporting rather than on multinational investment.

The link between international business and home country competitiveness can work in several ways. While home economies can provide competitive advantages for their firms, it is also possible that MNEs can be motivated to escape from unattractive homes and relocate production in more attractive economies. This mechanism may provide one explanation for the high propensity of British firms to produce abroad after the Second World War. They sought to escape from the relatively slow growing British economy by investing in more dynamic markets overseas (Hamill 1988, 1991).

The ability of MNEs to escape from unsatisfactory homes illustrates the possibility of a divergence between the competitiveness of MNEs and of their home economies. The significance of this issue can be seen in the case of the United States. The advent of a merchandise trade deficit in 1971 suggested that the country was becoming less internationally competitive. Porter's examination of shifts in world export share over the 1970s and 1980s indicated that the United States was losing competitive advantage in a wide range of sophisticated industries, including automobiles, semiconductors and consumer electronics, even though its performance in others – such as computers, biotechnology, and consumer packaged goods – remained very strong (Porter 1990: 507–8). This evidence prompted debates about the causes of the declining US competitiveness. It was widely believed that among these causes were various managerial failings, including the problems of excessive diversification through mergers and acquisitions, short-term investment horizons caused by preoccupation with dividend payments to shareholders, and the diversion of some of America's best managerial talent into highly paid jobs in financial services away from manufacturing (Porter 1990; Chandler 1994).

The scale of US MNE operations overseas suggests that some aspects of this story need to be qualified. Figure 6.2 provides estimates of the world market shares of manufacturing exports of the United States and of US MNEs between 1966 and 1990.

While the United States experienced a considerable decline in its share of world export markets for manufactured goods from the mid-1960s, the share of its MNEs, exporting both from the United States and from overseas production, rose. United States MNEs performed better than the United States as they shifted production to more competitive locations. The share of majority-owned affiliates in the total exports of US MNEs (parents and affiliates combined) rose from 38 to 54 per cent between 1966 and 1990. A similar phenomenon can be observed in the case of Sweden over these decades (Lipsey and Kravis 1987; Blomström and Lipsey 1989; Blomström 1990).

This evidence throws into question very general criticisms of the entire US management system, for it would seem that US firms were able to retain or expand their market share. It needs to be stressed that aggregate data of this kind is hard to interpret, and that other measures of corporate performance do not necessarily point in the same direction. An analysis of the number of firms and percentages of consolidated worldwide sales accounted for by the twelve largest companies in major industries between

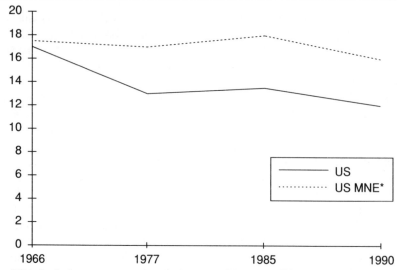

*This includes parents and majority-owned foreign affiliates

*Figure 6.2* US and US MNE share of world exports of manufacturers, 1966–90 (%)
*Source*: Lipsey 1994

1960 and 1990 confirmed the diminishing importance of US-owned firms in a range of industries, especially chemicals, electrical equipment, tyres and banking, which illustrates their continued pre-eminence in others, such as aerospace and electrical equipment (Franko 1989, 1991). The evidence from US MNEs does not 'prove' that the United States was not experiencing relative decline, but it does demonstrate the importance of distinguishing between location-based measures of competitiveness – the performance of firms exporting from the United States, which will be both American and foreign-owned – and ownership-based measures of competitiveness – the performance of US-owned firms in both the United States and foreign countries.

## MNE effects on home economy competitiveness

Outward investment by MNEs has an impact on the competitiveness of their home economies. The remittance of dividends, royalties and income generated abroad should have a positive impact on a home country's income per capita, but there are also potential 'losses' arising from the ability of MNEs to transfer resources from their home economies to other economies. The methodological issues involved in measuring these impacts are acute, and the amount of research undertaken on them is surprisingly small. Appropriate FDI data for testing hypotheses is only in existence from the 1960s, and even then only a few countries – notably the United

States – have sufficiently detailed data for some of the key issues to be examined. As a result, it remains impossible to provide firm generalisations. The following discussion confines itself to a review of the issues, and a discussion of the limited and partial empirical research which has been done on them.

The fact that MNEs operate abroad through FDI has given rise to debates about the extent to which foreign investment 'crowds out' domestic investment. This issue has a long pedigree. The huge British capital exports before 1914 aroused considerable concern, and in the interwar years Lord Keynes, the famous British economist, was among those who suggested that Britain would have earned higher social returns by domestic investment (Hood and Young 1979). In the post-1950 period, the coincidence of extensive British outward FDI and the slow-growing British economy – caused, in part, by low levels of investment – resulted in a number of major studies, all of which concluded that investment overseas could not be regarded as a substitute for investment in Britain. This was partly because in most cases investment in Britain was not a feasible alternative to investment overseas, and partly because FDI was largely financed by overseas borrowing and retained earnings (Reddaway 1968; Shepherd, Silberston and Strange 1985). This was a general feature of all multinational financing after 1945 – and almost certainly much earlier – and is an important reason why a crude view that MNEs 'damage' their home economies by exporting capital is not supportable.

Nonetheless, there is some case study evidence that lends some support to an argument that there might be some kind of trade-off between domestic and foreign investment. An examination of the domestic and foreign fixed investment expenditures of seven US MNEs between 1960 and 1980 found a considerable interdependence between foreign and domestic investment. A one per cent exogenous rise in foreign demand or in a firm's overseas output reduced the parent firm's US fixed investment by amounts ranging from 0.3 to 0.8 per cent in most of the firms (Stevens and Lipsey 1992). A study of Dutch MNEs in the food and metal/ electronics industries between 1978 and 1984 also found that there was an interdependence between domestic investment and FDI. If the Netherlands became less advantageous relative to foreign locations, Dutch MNEs allocated more capital abroad and invested less domestically, and vice versa (Belderbos 1992). However a great deal of further research needs to be done before such research can be generalised.

A second major area of debate concerning the impact of MNEs on their home economies concerns their effects on trade. The central problem concerns the extent, if any, to which foreign production is a substitute for home-country exports. During the 1960s the balance of payments problems of the United States and the United Kingdom resulted in major econometric studies of this issue by Hufbauer and Adler and Reddaway respectively. These studies pointed to either no effect or else a positive effect of overseas production on the home economy, though the result depended on the assumptions made. The British study assumed that in the absence of British foreign affiliates, their markets would have been supplied not by British exports but by local or other foreign suppliers. This assumption of a near-zero export displacement effect was unrealistic. In the US study, Hufbauer and Adler used a number of alternative assumptions, which showed that once the possibility of significant export displacement is allowed, negative net balance of payments results were possible (Hood and Young 1979: 311–16).

Subsequent research on US MNEs has reinforced the conclusion that their non-US production has had little effect on exports from the US by parent firms or by all US firms as a whole. A series of econometric studies have suggested that, in the US case, complementarity – the stimulus to home exports of intermediate and other related products – has been more important than substitution effects. This has also been the conclusion of several major studies on Swedish MNEs over recent decades (Lipsey 1994; Blomström and Kokko 1994). Blomström concludes that the 'common belief in the home economies ... that outward foreign direct investment substitutes exports and undermines the industrial base of the home countries ... has very little support' (Blomström 1990), but the extent to which this conclusion is applicable over a longer time period and between all home economies is unknown.

A related area of debate has been the extent to which foreign production affects the level of demand for labour in home economies. In crude terms, MNEs may appear to 'export jobs'. The growth of unemployment in most developed economies over the last decade suggested a correlation with outward investment, especially when in certain industries MNEs had a clear strategy of shifting manufacturing production to countries with lower wages and labour standards. Although considerable research has been undertaken on this issue for the last thirty years, it has proved very difficult to reach any overall generalisation. The balance of the evidence suggests that the overall impact of outward MNE activity on home country employment has been marginally positive, partly because of the growth of exports from the parent to the new foreign affiliates. In the US and Swedish cases, a change in the skill mix within the investing industry has been observed. There was a shift in labour demand favouring white collar employees at the expense of blue collar workers, because MNEs tend to export production activities, while concentrating management, marketing and R & D at home (Dunning 1992: 362–6; Blomström and Kokko 1994).

There is no reason to assume that this general conclusion holds true across all countries, given the nation-specific differences in corporate strategies. In the 1980s British MNEs performed a far higher percentage of their research outside the United Kingdom than US MNEs undertook outside the United States (Casson 1991b). Changes over time in the nature of international business mean that the employment effects of outward investment will have varied. The extensive resource and service sector multinational investment which predominated in international business before the 1950s can be assumed to have generated substantial home economy employment through head offices, as well as distribution and processing facilities. The negative employment effects of manufacturing FDI may have been greater historically than more recently, when the growth of strategic asset-seeking through cross-border mergers and acquisitions has sharply reduced the usefulness of thinking in terms of employment at home and employment abroad as alternatives.

MNEs may impact the innovatory capacity of their home economies. It can be argued that MNEs can have a negative effect on their home economy's competitiveness through technological exports which improve the international competitiveness of firms in host economies. In so far as international business has been associated with the diffusion of technical knowledge, a process which has included the leakage of proprietary knowledge from the control of MNEs, this argument has validity. However, there is case study evidence from the interwar years (Jones 1986b; Cantwell 1992: 36) and subsequently which has demonstrated that technical feedback from outward FDI can be considerable (Dunning 1992: 331–48). By investing abroad, MNEs gain access to tangible and intangible resources – not only technology, but also management systems and natural resources – which will enhance their competitiveness, and through transfer back to the home economy, can enhance its competitiveness also.

The important contribution of MNEs in providing home economies with access to resources which they lacked is evident in resource-based outward FDI over the last century. Although the United Kingdom lacked a domestic supply of petroleum until the 1970s, when the North Sea oilfields were discovered, the activities of British oil companies abroad provided that country with preferential access to oil supplies and the basis to build a large refining industry. Both in the interwar years and subsequently, FDI strategies were employed by resource-scarce Japan in search of resources from elsewhere in Asia. Another example of this phenomenon is provided by the international sourcing of labour-intensive intermediate and final products from developing countries by MNEs over the last three decades. In semiconductors, the strategies of US and Japanese MNEs in producing labour-intensive components in cheap labour countries and then importing back to the home economy factories ensured a slower rate of increase in the costs of production in the United States and Japan, and thus led to a greater competitiveness of their products in world markets (United Nations 1992: 212–3).

These issues can be discussed in terms of the benefits of 'economic restructuring' versus the threat posed by 'hollowing out'. MNEs contribute to the restructuring of economies by shifting low value-adding activities abroad out of their home economies, permitting the upgrading of the use of domestic resources. The economic development of East Asia over the last forty years illustrates this process. In the 1950s and 1960s Japan's manufacturing investments in other Asian economies were in labour-intensive activities in which it was losing its comparative advantage, such as textiles and toys. These investments expanded those sectors in the host economies of what became the Asian newly industrial countries (NICs) and assisted them to capture large shares of world markets for their products. The subsequent rising wage rates and trade surpluses in the NICs undermined their comparative advantage in labour-intensive sectors, and they themselves transferred those activities through FDI to less-developed neighbouring countries. At the same time, Japan trans-ferred higher-value manufacturing goods and services to the Asian NICs as the dynamic restructuring process continued (United Nations 1992: 256–7; Ozawa 1992). However, it is not evident that this East Asian experience is generalisable either for other regions or earlier time periods, for it was made possible by the growing ability of MNEs to organise and manage value-adding activities in an integrated manner across national borders.

The phenomenon of 'hollowing out' refers to almost the opposite process whereby innovatory capabilities and manufacturing capacity are transferred out of a home country without any compensatory upgrading of the remaining resources. This mechanism might lead to a country losing key components of its competitiveness. The suggestion that British MNEs – at least after the Second World War – have been motivated to invest abroad by a desire to 'escape' from their economy might suggest that a hollowing out process was at work. British MNEs appeared to be shifting a higher proportion of their more sophisticated or higher value added products – and their R & D – to the United States and elsewhere in Europe where income levels were higher. In a country with a high level of outward FDI such as the United Kingdom, this process has the potential to become self reinforcing, and lead to a spiral of downgrading rather than upgrading (Panic 1982). On the other hand, one of the advantages of outward FDI is that exposure to international competition can pressure MNEs to increase their efficiency, which can in time lead to an upgrading in the use of their domestic resources. This appears to have happened in the British case. In the early 1960s US MNEs were considerably more profitable in their foreign operations than British firms, but over the following two decades the profitability of British firms abroad rose sharply relative to those of other nations, as well as compared with British firms operating only in the United Kingdom (Dunning 1970, 1988b: 225).

The impact of MNEs on the competitiveness of their home econ-omies remains a subject full of uncertainties. While the main issues can be identified, it is hard to reach conclusions, and harder still to arrive at a net overall effect. Casual empiricism demonstrates that economic success has not in the past depended on extensive multinational investment. The 'economic miracles' of Germany, France and Japan after the Second World War, and the subsequent export-led miracles of the Asian NICs, provide powerful examples. However these cases arose in a period of falling trade barriers. Production abroad may well be a 'superior' strategy for enhancing a home country's competitiveness in the different circumstances of the 1990s. Existing research suggests that it is unlikely that the twentieth century's leading long-term multinational investors – notably the United States, the United Kingdom and the Netherlands – have suffered a serious loss of competitiveness because of this investment, but the extent to which these economies have actually benefited is also hard to demonstrate.

## POLICY AND OUTWARD INVESTMENT

Despite the long history of international business and its significance in the case of major home economies, government policies towards outward investment have remained rather limited although certainly not without significance.

From the nineteenth century governments were very aware that national diplomatic influence and national economic influence were related. This led European and US governments to support their nationals generally – by seeking to secure their access to, and safety in, foreign markets – and more specifically, when military interventions were made in developing countries to protect business interests. In countries of great strategic interest – such as China before the First World War – European governments and their business interests worked closely with one another. Certain natural resources – notably petroleum – were of such strategic interest that the industry became thoroughly political. The interwar Middle Eastern oil industry was a prominent example of a situation in which diplomatic and corporate rivalries overlapped and reinforced one another. The oil industry was unusual because European governments came to own (in whole or part) national oil companies such as the Anglo-Persian Oil Company and Compagnie Française des Pétroles. The use of subsidies and other forms of assistance to support shipping companies, airlines and other symbols or sources of influence in foreign countries was also widespread before the Second World War.

By the interwar years governments had identified some of the central issues facing home economies. In the United States, the Republican administration of the 1920s generally encouraged US firms to move abroad, but also expressed worries about the consequences. Worries were expressed about the export of employment and technology to foreign countries, and the dangers of creating competition abroad to US exports. They did not translate into policies to restrict US outward FDI, though some positive inducement was given to US firms in less developed areas, especially in Latin America and China. A series of legislative measures from 1922 exempted investments in federally incorporated 'China Trade companies' from US corporate taxation (Wilkins 1974a: 52–3).

The spread of exchange controls in the 1930s extended the home government impact on MNEs. Capital controls constrained FDI by German firms. After the Nazi regime came to power in 1933, all new FDI had to be approved officially, and only exceptional investments were permitted (Schröter 1993a: 30–2). In contrast, the United Kingdom's introduction of exchange controls after 1929 was designed to curb flows of portfolio investment rather than FDI. MNE investments overseas were not affected, but these British controls may well have limited the creation of new free-standing firms, because the former method of financing new ventures overseas by subscription and the issue of fresh capital was made difficult.

During the 1930s Japanese governments promoted Japanese overseas business activities in the wake of its military aggression against China. Many of the investments made by Japanese industrial firms in China in the 1930s were Chinese plants occupied by the Japanese Army, and turned over to Japanese companies for their management. After the outbreak of full-scale war with China in 1937, Japanese enterprises including the *sogo shosha* were progressively integrated into the tightly-controlled Japanese war economy (Yasumuro 1984; Maeda 1990: 106–9).

Although home governments typically supported their firms in foreign countries if they encountered difficulties, the nature of that support varied enormously with the size and strategic importance of the investment, the nature of the host economy, and the prevailing circumstances. In Latin America, US 'dollar diplomacy' was notorious, though the US government's willingness to support its business interests with military force was not automatic, especially in the 1930s (Wilkins 1974a: 178–80). Yet a case study on ITT in Spain in the 1930s concluded that the firm's ability to survive Spain's political upheavals and civil war was largely determined by its relationship with the US State Department (Little 1979). There were many complexities and conflicts of interest in the relationships between MNEs and their home governments, and the willingness – and ability – of diplomats to render effective support for business varied from case to case.

After the Second World War home country policies towards outward investment continued on a rather low key basis. The US government generally sought to provide a supportive environment for US FDI, which was seen as making an important contribution to world economic welfare. A number of guarantees were offered against currency devaluation and expropriations (Behrman and Grosse 1990: 68–73). The thrust of US policy in the 1950s and 1960s was to encourage US MNEs to invest in less developed countries through guarantees and soft and hard currency loans. In 1962 Congress also passed a measure – the Hickenlooper Amendment – that threatened the withdrawal of US foreign aid to a country if expropriation of US properties was not followed by prompt and adequate compensation (Wilkins 1974a: 328–34).

Beyond the United States, home governments rarely promoted outward investment, though only in a number of exceptional cases did they seek to restrict it. The primary concern of European governments after the Second World War was with the balance of payments implication of outward FDI, and for that reason it continued to be affected by exchange controls until the 1970s and even later in some cases. These regulations usually covered fresh capital funded by parent companies or raised for acquisitions, as distinct from overseas profits reinvestment, and their main impact may have been to influence the method of financing FDI by encouraging the use of overseas borrowing and retained earnings. Probably the impact of such policies was greatest in the immediate postwar period. There is some evidence that British exchange controls were a factor in encouraging British firms to invest in the sterling currency region (Davenport-Hines and Slinn 1992: 232, 234, 338; Bamberg 1994: 313–14).

During the 1960s US payments deficits also led to intervention in outward investment from that country. In 1965 US firms were asked voluntarily to limit the outflow of capital to their affiliates in developed countries, and also to increase the inflow of their dividends. As in the British case, the ability of MNEs to borrow abroad to finance their foreign operations meant that the overall effect on US MNEs was small, beyond increasing such foreign borrowings. The capital controls were liberalised in 1969 and removed five years later (Safarian 1993: 369; Wilkins 1974a: 335–6).

The only major economy which sought to restrict outward FDI on a large scale was Japan. Under the terms of the Foreign Exchange and Foreign Trade Control Law of 1949, the Japanese authorities regulated all overseas investments. Over the following two decades, the government scrutinised every potential Japanese FDI abroad, and denied requisite foreign exchange to those investment proposals that did not gain its approval. The main policy aim was to retain scarce capital in Japan to re-industrialise the country. FDI was not completely suppressed by these controls, but it was heavily dampened. Generally, the policy-makers favoured investment applications that either promoted Japanese exports of manufactured goods or secured Japanese imports of initial raw materials. Proposed investments that threatened Japanese producers at home were unwelcome. It was only in the late 1960s, as Japanese trade surpluses rose, that these capital controls began to be liberalised, a process culminating in 1972 when all remaining restrictions were removed. Not surprisingly, this year came to be referred to metaphorically in Japan as the 'gannen' – the term gannen signifying the first year of a new imperial reign in Japan (Encarnation 1992: 107–12). In 1980 the further revision of the Foreign Exchange and Foreign Trade Control Law greatly eased regulation concerning foreign investment by Japanese financial institutions also.

The abandonment of policies based on balance of payments concerns meant in effect a revision to a neutral policy stance regarding outflows of FDI. In a number of countries, notably the United States and Sweden, strong concerns were sometimes voiced about the export of jobs or technology by their MNEs, but the few measures which were adopted – such as a 1974 Swedish law which blocked capital outflows perceived to be in conflict with the objectives of national economic policy – were ineffective. Governments in general declined to address the issues raised by the potential impact of outward investment on national competitiveness. While many host governments adopted policies to attract inward FDI in the 1980s and 1990s, the promotion of outward FDI has not yet become a policy objective.

In the postwar period, home governments continued to support their businesses overseas, but their ability to take coercive measures in support of their companies declined over time. During the 1950s and 1960s the enormous economic and military importance of the United States supported an international policy regime in which expropriations were rare. The United States was able to use a mixture of sanctions and rewards to maintain this system. But this regime was eroded in the 1970s as US economic hegemony declined, the governments of developing countries gained power, and there were new entrants into international business (Lipson 1985; Rodman 1988).

Home governments became more concerned about certain aspects of the behaviour of their own firms abroad. During the 1970s the use of bribery and corruption by several MNEs raised widespread concern. The most prominent cases included payments by United Brands to Honduran government officials in an attempt to bring down the export tax on bananas, and evidence of widespread bribery by Lockheed of senior individuals in Japan and various European countries. The most celebrated case of all was ITT's attempts to destabilise the Chilean government in 1970–71 in order to protect its interests in the Chilean telephone system (Hood and Young 1979: 348–52). These kind of incidents – which were almost certainly exceptional – led to US legislation on corporate bribery, which obliged disclosure of illegal or improper payments to government officials (Safarian 1993: 376).

These national attempts to develop and legislate standards for MNEs have continued to encounter the problem that national laws can be fully effective only within the limits of national jurisdiction. They could not handle all the international activities of MNEs, and ran the risk of jurisdictional conflicts due to differences in policies or legal approaches. Attempts to define international standards for MNEs, and to construct an international framework for their operation, remained elusive.

## THE END OF NATIONALITY?

In recent years influential studies by Reich (1990, 1992), Ohmae (1990) and others have argued that MNEs are in the process of being denationalised. There are many grounds for supporting such a proposition, especially in the case of the largest MNEs. Although Switzerland's Nestlé – 95 per cent of whose sales are achieved outside Switzerland – is an extreme case, the world's largest MNEs now have a considerable percentage of their output outside their home economies, and have their stock quoted on numerous equity markets. Important headquarters functions – such as R & D, finance and marketing – are now dispersed geographically within large MNEs, and no longer confined to their home countries (Hakanson 1990). Although there are numerous parallels between the borderless world existing before 1930 and that of the 1990s, the denationalisation of international business might be seen as a fundamentally new phenomenon.

For Reich, this trend carries major policy implications. Recognising the distinction between the competitiveness of the American economy and that of US MNEs, Reich argued that issues of ownership, control and national origin were of diminishing importance for policies concerned with the competitive performance of the United States economy. The American economy benefited far more from the operations of a foreign-owned company, which undertook R & D and product design and manufacturing in the United States, than it did from an American company which performed most of these functions beyond the national borders. The policy implication is that the US government should facilitate the entry of foreign companies into the United States, while avoiding protection of US companies, simply because they were American-owned. 'The old notion of national boundaries is becoming obsolete' (Reich 1990: 63).

In practice, the influence of nationality continues to be more persuasive than this analysis suggests. The sources of multinational investment and the direction of investment flows continue to show strong national differences. The boards of directors of almost all MNEs continue to be predominantly of home country origin. The globalisation of international business led to a convergence of organisational structures between large MNEs, but the behaviour of managers within them continues to show persistent national or cultural differences (Laurent 1983; Child and Kieser 1979). And, as Porter's 'diamond' of international competitive advantage demonstrates, the home countries of companies continue to exercise an important influence on a firm's competitiveness.

## SUMMARY

The relationship between MNEs and their home economies is strong but complicated to unravel. The ownership of international business has been concentrated in a small number of home economies, whose firms have differed considerably in the industries and countries in which they undertook multinational investment, and how they organised this investment. Many aspects of the home environment influenced these national differences, including their factor endowments, the size and structure of the economy, the regulatory system and cultural values. The propensity to win, lose or stay neutral in the major wars of the twentieth century has also been of major significance.

The ownership of a large stock of outward FDI cannot be automatically correlated with a highly competitive economy. For a long period in the twentieth century it partly reflected whether an economy happened to possess a large stake in the capital-intensive petroleum and mining industries. It may reflect past patterns of national competitiveness. However multinational investment does need to be taken into account in attempts to measure national competitiveness. MNEs can also exercise a considerable influence on home country competitiveness. MNEs may assist in economic restructuring, but they may also hollow out an economy. They may impact the level of domestic investment, the nature of employment, and a country's trade performance, but a variety of outcomes are possible. There is certainly the possibility of asymmetry between the interests of MNEs and their home economy.

Home governments have generally supported the foreign operations of their firms, especially if they operated in industries regarded as strategic, but they have also sought at various times to restrain, control or monitor outward FDI in the interests of the home economy. On the whole, policies towards outward investment have been and remain less extensive than those towards inward investment.

# Chapter 7

# Multinationals as engines of growth

## COMPARATIVE HOST ECONOMIES

There remain great uncertainties about changes over time in the distribution of inward FDI among host economies.The fact that there have always been far more host than home economies makes the analysis of changes in the size and importance of host economies more complicated than similar exercises for home economies.This section looks in more detail at the evidence on the size and significance of host economies over time, and examines why some economies were more attractive as hosts than others.The following sections discuss the impact of international business on host economies.

### Host economies over time

The broad outlines of the changing geographical distribution of the stock of inward FDI have emerged in earlier chapters. In the nineteenth century and continuing into the interwar years, the majority of world FDI was located in the developing world, especially Latin America and Asia. This investment was overwhelmingly concerned with natural resources and service activities. From the 1950s there was a redistribution of world FDI to the developed world. In 1992 only around 20 per cent of world FDI was located in developing countries, and most of that was found in the small group of fast-growing East Asian and Latin American countries.

Wilkins (1994a) provides a disaggregation of this overall picture on an individual host basis, and her estimates for 1914 and 1929 are given in Tables 7.1 and 7.2.

These tables represent informed guesses, and the 1914 figures are so inadequate that Wilkins declines from quantifying her ranking. Nonetheless it does appear reasonable to view the United States and Canada as among the world's largest host economies at both benchmark dates. Wilkins also ranks a number of Western European countries, led by the United Kingdom, as major hosts. The view of the overall importance of developing countries

*Table 7.1* Inward stock of FDI in 1914: ranking of hosts

|  | Country |
|---|---|
| 1 | United States |
| 2 | Russia |
| 3 | Canada |
| 4 | Argentina |
| 5 | Brazil |
| 6 | South Africa |
| 7 | Austria-Hungary |
| 8–9 | India |
|  | China |
| 10–12 | Egypt |
|  | Mexico |
|  | United Kingdom |

*Source:* Wilkins 1994a

*Table 7.2* Inward stock of FDI in 1929: ranking of hosts

|  | Country | Amount |
|---|---|---|
|  |  | $2.4 billion – $1.4 billion |
| 1 | Canada | |
| 2 | United States | |
|  |  | $1.2 billion – $800 million |
| 3 | India | |
| 4 | Cuba | |
| 5 | Mexico | |
|  |  | $800 million – $500 million |
| 6 | Argentina | |
| 7 | Chile | |
| 8 | United Kingdom | |
| 9 | Malaya | |
|  |  | $500 million – $350 million |
| 10 | Venezuela | |
| 11 | Brazil | |
| 12 | Australia | |
| 13 | South Africa | |
| 14 | Netherlands East Indies (Indonesia) | |
| 15 | Egypt | |
| 16 | China | |
|  |  | $350 million – $200 million |
| 17 | Germany | |
| 18 | Spain | |

*Source:* Wilkins 1994a

*Table 7.3* Inward stock of FDI in 1993: ranking of hosts

| Country | Amount (millions of US$) | % World total |
|---|---|---|
| United States | 440,892 | 20.6 |
| United Kingdom | 186,495 | 8.7 |
| France | 139,953 | 6.6 |
| Germany | 130,650 | 6.1 |
| Canada | 124,468 | 5.8 |
| Spain | 105,094 | 4.9 |
| Netherlands | 91,336 | 4.3 |
| Australia | 82,736 | 3.9 |
| Belgium/Luxembourg | 67,957 | 3.2 |
| Italy | 66,521 | 3.1 |
| China | 55,457 | 2.6 |
| Singapore | 50,802 | 2.4 |
| Indonesia | 44,145 | 2.1 |
| Mexico | 41,912 | 2.0 |
| Brazil | 40,371 | 1.9 |
| Japan | 38,820 | 1.8 |
| Switzerland | 33,362 | 1.6 |
| World total | 2,132,925 | 100.0 |

*Source*: United Nations 1995

as hosts – a view which also rests only on informed guesses – needs to be qualified by the presence of these prosperous developed market economies among the largest hosts before the Second World War.

The post-Second World War decades saw important shifts – as well as strong continuities – in the ranking of host economies. An estimate of the distribution of inward FDI by 1960, by which time the overall share held by developing countries was falling sharply, gave the three largest hosts as Canada (24 per cent), the United States (14 per cent) and the United Kingdom (9 per cent) (Stopford and Dunning 1983:12). This trio have remained among the world's largest host economies, but the rapid growth of inward FDI into the United States resulted in its emergence as by far the world's largest host economy. Table 7.3 gives the stock of inward FDI and their share of the world total for the seventeen largest host economies in 1993, which collectively accounted for 82 per cent of world inward investment.

A number of striking features emerge from Table 7.3. Within the general picture of the concentration of inward stock among the developed economies of North America and Western Europe, it can be seen that over 35 per cent of the total world stock of inward investment was located in the three English-speaking economies of the United States, the United Kingdom and Canada, though the latter had lost its place as the third largest host economy, having fallen behind both France and Germany.

These three countries also accounted for just over two-fifths of the world stock of outward investment. There was no correlation between the size of inward investment and the overall size of the economy. Singapore, a city state of three million people, had a greater stock of FDI than Brazil, and almost as much as the entire continent of Africa ($48,228 million).

The relative unimportance of developing countries is reflected in Table 7.3 by the comparatively small total amounts of FDI stock held by even the largest developing hosts, China, Singapore and Indonesia. Among the developing hosts, Brazil, Mexico and Indonesia featured in the Wilkins' rankings of pre-Second World War hosts, but some other leading developing hosts were inconsequential in 1993. India's inward FDI stock of $2,231 million only amounted to 0.1 per cent in that year. China's stock of FDI had been virtually zero between 1949 and the 1980s, but a subsequent surge of FDI flows into the country gave it 2.6 per cent of the world stock by 1993.

Japan's position as a host economy – or rather its lack of a position – is evident. The total stock of inward FDI into Japan was very small before the Second World War – though not without consequence. Japan may have held 0.4 per cent of world inward FDI in 1938, which had fallen to 0.2 per cent by 1960 (Dunning 1992: 118). Unlike the case of outward investment, there was no large surge of inward FDI into Japan subsequently. In 1993 Japan's stock of outward FDI was over six times greater than its stock of inward FDI.

From a host economy viewpoint, the absolute size of FDI stock only provides the crudest indication of the importance of foreign MNEs. There are a variety of more detailed measures which can be used, though in every case the available data is limited to the more recent past. Figure 7.1 gives the ratio of inward FDI stock to each country's GDP for eight host economies.

Figure 7.1 demonstrates that inward investment was relatively more important for some hosts than for others. While the United States had become immensely important as the world's largest host economy, the relative importance of inward FDI to the American economy was much less than in the case of Canada and the United Kingdom. Calculations of the share of foreign affiliates in employment (and other indicators) point to a similar conclusion. At the end of the 1980s foreign affiliates accounted for less than 4 per cent of US employment, and under 1 per cent in Japan. In contrast, the figure was 16 per cent in Brazil, 20 per cent in France, and 60 per cent in Singapore. While many developing countries were very low in world rankings of hosts, foreign-owned affiliates could still be immensely important in their national economies. Ghana's stock of inward FDI was only $375 million in 1990, but foreign-owned affiliates accounted for 48 per cent of total employment (United Nations 1992: 330–2). On

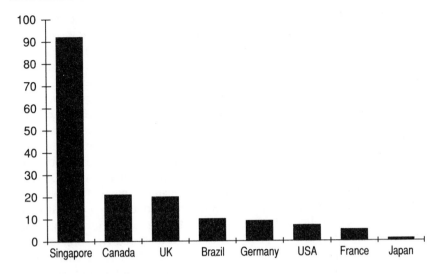

*Figure 7.1* Ratio of inward FDI stock to GDP of host economies, 1990
*Sources*: United Nations 1992: 326–8; Dunning 1992: 20

the other hand, India had a small amount of FDI which was insignificant in the context of the whole economy. The ratio of FDI flows to gross fixed capital formation in India was 0.2 per cent between 1981 and 1985 and 0.3 per cent between 1986 and 1990. The equivalent Brazilian ratios were 6.8 per cent and 3.9 per cent, and those of Singapore 18.1 per cent and 33.9 per cent (United Nations 1994: 421–5).

## Explaining the relative importance of hosts

A number of factors have accounted for the importance of countries as hosts to foreign enterprises. These factors have interacted with one another and are by no means the only influences on individual countries.

The first is the distribution of natural and created resource endowments. The availability of natural resources was clearly a major influence in pre-Second World War investment flows, and was the major locational determinant for developing country hosts. A considerable amount of inward FDI into the United States and Canada was also resource-related. National resource endowments continued to influence FDI flows after 1945, but the growth in importance of manufacturing and service sector investments made created resource endowments of growing significance. This is indicated by the importance of countries such as Singapore and Switzerland, to which foreign companies were attracted because of high levels of investment in human capital and infrastructure.

Second, market size has been extremely important. From the nineteenth century, MNEs sought access to the American market because of its size and income levels. The major Latin American hosts, Brazil and Mexico, were large markets which companies wanted to serve. In some cases countries were used as export platforms to serve other markets.

Third, geographical location has been of considerable significance, given the importance of 'nearby' influences in multinational investment. Canada's importance as a major host economy reflected its situation next to the United States, from whom much of its investment came.

Fourth, cultural factors, including language, legal structures and corporate governance structures, have been a major influence on FDI flows. The high risks involved in international business mean that firms will prefer culturally similar locations to make investments – provided such a decision is not explicitly lacking rationality. The close cross-investment relationship between the United States and the United Kingdom provides a leading example. Throughout the last one hundred years each country has been the single largest inward investor in the other country, though the net relationship has changed, with British FDI in the United States larger than US FDI in the United Kingdom before the 1940s and again from the mid-1980s (Dunning 1988b: 233–50). This relationship rested on a number of the locational factors discussed above, but also on the lower perceived risk of operating in the other country. This lower risk made the United Kingdom the preferred first location for many companies investing in Europe. More recently, the use of English has been an important influence making the United Kingdom a favoured location in Europe for Japanese investors.

A fifth influence on the location of inward FDI has been government policies. In general terms, it can be said that some of the most striking features in these historical rankings of hosts – for example the disappearance over time of once major hosts such as Russia and India – are explicable only by reference to political factors. The importance of host government policies is so great that a full discussion is reserved for the next chapter.

## The importance of sub-national trends

A focus on national economies as hosts can be seriously misleading because multinational investment has rarely been spread evenly in host economies. Multinational investment in mines and oilfields was – almost by definition – concentrated in particular geographical regions.

This phenomenon has also been a strong feature of inward investment into developed economies. When US MNEs established factories in inter-war Britain, they focused especially on the southeast region of England. After the Second World War, much new investment went to Scotland, where a large US-owned electronics industry developed (Bostock and Jones 1994: 113–5). Subsequent Japanese inward investment into Britain also showed a marked geographical concentration, and the same pattern is strong in the case of the United States. Japanese transplants in the United States have been very heavily concentrated in the so-called 'transplant corridor' of the industrial Midwest and upper South (Kenney and Florida 1993: 5). In multinational banking, the geographical concentration is even more dramatic. The role of international financial centres means that London, New York and Tokyo contain a very high percentage of all the offices owned by foreign banks in these respective host economies.

These sub-national patterns are of major significance. The attractiveness of countries as hosts was in part attributable to the attractiveness of particular regions or centres, while the impact of MNEs was frequently experienced most strongly at this regional or city level rather than nationally.

## THE IMPACT ON HOST ECONOMIES

It is evident that since the nineteenth century MNEs have discovered and exploited world resources, created transportation and information infra-structures, and moved production processes between countries. The impact on host economies has been considerable. However it is evident also that given the diversity and complexity of international business, the nature of this impact has varied greatly between individual cases. There are at least seven major areas in which the impact of international business can be disaggregated.

First, the conditions under which international business has operated have changed markedly with time. This is particularly obvious in the natural resource sector, where the distribution of rents between firms and host governments experienced rapid change (to the benefit of the latter) from the 1950s. While the impact of MNEs can be compared over time, the nature of the comparison needs to be carefully specified. The element of time is also extremely important for assessing the impact of individual investments. The contribution of a foreign enterprise may look greatest at the initial stage of an investment, when it introduces new products or processes into a host economy, and may look negative at later stages, when dividends are flowing out to the parent.

Second, the impact of international business has varied considerably between industries. MNEs in manufacturing, service and national resource industries can all bring benefits – or impose costs – on host economies. But the nature of the benefits or costs varies because of inter-industry variations in technology, skill, size, export orientation, etc. A stereotyped contrast can be drawn between FDI directed towards natural resources and to labour-intensive manufacturing sectors supplying relatively simple consumer goods, and FDI in a highly innovatory sector or producing high quality differentiated products. The latter type of investment cannot be automatically regarded as more 'beneficial' than the former – but its impact on a host economy will be different. A crucial question for assessing the impact on a host economy is the kind of value-added activities performed by a foreign firm. If an economy is a host for a large quantity of low value-added assembly operations, it may experience rapid economic growth, but its developmental prospects in the long term may be less good. The quality of FDI, rather than its quantity, may well be the crucial determinant of its impact.

Third, the impact of international business on a host economy has varied between enterprises. Because each MNE has a unique combination of skills and resources, it will have a discrete, firm-specific impact on a host economy. Before 1914 free-standing firms had a different – and maybe less important – impact on their host economies than 'classic' MNEs, which transferred a package of skills first developed at home (Wilkins 1989: 613–15). Nationality of investing firm may be important also. During the twentieth century US and subsequently Japanese firms have been regarded as embodying the best technological and organisational systems. It might be presumed that multinational investment from those countries would be more beneficial to host economies than from 'sub-standard' countries. The relationship between parents and foreign subsidiaries can influence the host economy impact. A study of foreign-owned affiliates active in Canada from the 1880s to the 1950s, showed that among the major features affecting decisions involving transfers of technology were the role played by managers in the affiliated firm in negotiating for these transfers, and the degree of control exercised by the parent company over the Canadian enterprise (Taylor 1994).

Fourth, the mode of entry of foreign firms into a host economy may have had an important influence on their impact. Entry by a greenfield investment or by the acquisition of an existing domestic firm may have different effects on concentration ratios and on technology transfer. It is often assumed that a greenfield investment is preferable to an acquisition from a host economy perspective in that it is more likely to result in new products and processes being introduced. However, the empirical evidence does not support such a clear distinction between the consequences of greenfield and acquisition modes of entry. MNEs have often combined acquisition and greenfield strategies when they entered a foreign market (Wilkins 1974a; Bostock and Jones 1994).

Fifth, the use of different institutional and contractual forms to operate in foreign countries is likely to have had different consequences. The willingness of an MNE to transfer technology or brands to a foreign subsidiary might well be influenced by whether that subsidiary is wholly-owned or a joint venture, although the reasons why the firm entered such an arrangement will be a significant factor. Licensing, franchising and direct investment strategies can be expected to differ in their impact on host economies.

Sixth, the impact of MNEs has depended on the nature of the host economy. The outcome of a multinational investment on a host economy will be heavily influenced by the stage of development of indigenous skills and capabilities, infrastructure and institutions. In manufacturing and some other areas, some of the most positive gains from inward FDI arise from the response of local firms. These responses range from the ability to serve as efficient suppliers in the short term to, in a longer time frame, their ability to absorb and learn the technologies and management skills of foreign competitors. The host country response is sometimes heavily conditioned by the policies of its government. Host governments can improve the ability of their enterprises to absorb foreign technologies by investing in education and infrastructure. They can set the conditions under which foreign firms enter and operate in their country. They provide the overall macro-economic framework under which foreign-owned affiliates function.

A broad distinction can be made between the impact of international business on developed and developing economies. In the former, it could be expected that local enterprises would have more capacity to absorb foreign technologies, or to offer competition to foreign MNEs. Developed country governments are likely to be better placed than their developing country equivalents to negotiate with large foreign companies. The cultural differences between MNEs and developed hosts are likely to be much smaller than those between MNEs and developing countries (Buckley and Casson 1989). It is not evident, however, that in a long-term perspective any clear-cut distinction can be drawn between the effects of MNEs on developed and developing economies, given the diversity of experience within both categories.

Finally, it is difficult to generalise about the overall impact of international business because of the difficulty of defining the 'counterfactual' position. What would have happened if the multinational investment had not been made? This is a fundamental issue in discussing the impact of international business on a host economy, but there are major methodological problems involved in reaching a conclusion. It is possible to make a calculation on a case-by-case basis. Lall and Streeten, in a classic study of the impact of 159 MNEs on six developing countries in the 1960s, compared actual foreign investments with their most likely local replacements using local technology or easily purchased foreign technology (Lall and Streeten 1977). The problem with this kind of study is that the crucial variable is likely to be the availability of entrepreneurship rather than technology, and that is exceptionally difficult to estimate. It is usually a matter of pure speculation whether a particular FDI introduced an activity a local firm would never have done, or alternatively 'crowded out' local firms from engaging in such an activity. An even wider set of uncertainties is introduced if consideration of the 'strategic counterfactual' is introduced: the impact of foreign-owned firms on indigenous entrepreneurship and technological capabilities if different strategies on trade, capability building and foreign entry had been adopted by the host government (Lall 1993: 23). There is every reason to believe that the counterfactual position has differed considerably between individual investments, industries, time periods and countries.

It is important to bear these factors in mind in the following sections concerned with the different ways in which international business has impacted host economies.

## RESOURCE TRANSFERS

### Technology and organisation

The role of international business in technology transfer and creation has been considerable and, given that technology and technological innovation play a central role in economic growth, this represents one of the most important areas in which MNEs can act as engines of growth. By transferring technologies and organisational structures between countries, they have functioned as Schumpeterian-style entrepreneurs in disrupting established practices and introducing innovations (Wilkins 1974a: 437).

It can be readily demonstrated that manufacturing MNEs were important transferors of technology between industrialised economies from the nineteenth century onwards (Wilkins 1974b). Before 1914 foreign-owned enterprises in the United States were significant in transferring technologies in a wide range of producer and consumer goods. In an industry such as chemicals, European companies played a leading strategic role in introducing new products and processes into the United States (Wilkins 1989: 411–12; 621–2). Major technology transfers could be accomplished as much by small – or 'unsuccessful' – foreign investments as by large MNEs. One example was the US activities of a group of British steel firms from the Sheffield district of the United Kingdom between the 1860s and 1950s. Most of their investments in the United States were financial failures or did not prove long-lasting, but they served as 'the focal points for the transmission of nearly all the major breakthroughs in alloy steel technology' (Tweedale 1986: 90). In the interwar years US MNEs were important transferors of technologies in electricals and automobiles to Europe through their foreign investments (Wilkins 1974a).

The existence of widespread technology transfer by MNEs does not automatically imply that it had a 'positive' impact. Available evidence suggests that in a range of manufacturing industries MNEs played a dynamic role in the technological capabilities of host economies, but there were also problems. Host governments sometimes encouraged MNEs to transfer technologies which were 'inappropriate'. The Soviet government of the 1920s had an exaggerated impression of the benefits of Ford technology which led it to purchase thousands of tractors from that company which were not suitable for Russian conditions (White 1986: 91–6). Nor were transferred technologies automatically absorbed and utilised by host economies. Ford's Dagenham factory in interwar Britain was enormous, but physically located away from the principal centres of British car production, which limited technological 'spin-off' to domestic firms (Church 1986: 117).

There is a considerable vacuum of knowledge concerning the role of international business in technology transfers before the 1950s outside the manufacturing sector. Technology transfer is often conceived of in terms of manufacturing, but it can also be highly significant in both the resource industries and services (Shelp 1984; Chen 1994: 5, 24–5). It would seem that technology inflows into developing countries by MNEs in services and natural resources were substantial. Foreign companies provided major channels of mining, engineering, transportation, commercial and financial technologies into host economies. The establishment and maintenance of mines, oilfields, plantations, shipping depots, railroad systems and so on involved the transfer of packages of skills and information, often – in the nineteenth century – to economies which were very backward indeed in technological terms.

The new technologies introduced into countries by international business transformed environments and lifestyles. Plantation agriculture changed the physical appearance of large parts of Central America, Africa and Asia, as well as the lifestyles of their citizens. The foreign-owned enterprises which introduced modern transportation systems, power utilities, and telephones into host economies provided technologies which revolutionised the lifestyles of those affected by them. Access to the safe urban transportation provided in Brazil by tramway utilities such as Canada's Brazilian Traction helped to advance the emancipation of Brazilian women – or at least those of the middle and upper class – who had endured a cloistered existence in the nineteenth century (McDowall 1988: 203). Given the absence of appropriate infrastructure in developing countries, foreign enterprises frequently introduced not only technologies specific to their activities, but also social technologies such as police, postal and education systems.

The historical evidence points often to the positive impact of these transfers on developing countries. In the nineteenth century – and indeed much later – indigenous managerial and entrepreneurial resources in many developing economies were so scarce as to make the idea of indigenous acquisition of technologies through alternatives to multinational investment wholly unrealistic. Similarly, while the introduction of capital-intensive technologies by foreign mining or agribusiness firms might be regarded as 'inappropriate' to indigenous factor endowments, it contributed to major productivity improvements in those sectors. However the flaws in this technology transfer process also stand out. A great deal of supply-oriented investment was enclavist. Mining and plantation economies were frequently self-sufficient operations that developed few linkages with the wider national economy of the host country. In interwar Latin America, US mining operations were often centred on self-sufficient company towns. Oil company towns in particular were often 'closed towns' which strictly regulated those who lived or entered there (Wilkins 1974a: 122–7).

Technological diffusion was also constrained by the nature of the host economies. High illiteracy rates, undeveloped infrastructures and alien business cultures provided formidable obstacles. An examination of why the transfer of technology did not lead to successful development in nineteenth century China found that the country's system of political economy and the attitudes of its officials were major obstacles. Foreign firms were restricted in the activities they could undertake, and the government sought to confine them to coastal ports (Brown 1979).

Research on technology transfer by MNEs to developing countries from the 1950s has highlighted some of the problems which arise in this area. It was sometimes found that the profits, royalties and fees charged to developing economies were high. MNEs often imposed restrictive conditions on exports, imports and other matters when they transferred technologies. Such restrictions had adverse effects on host economies by restricting their export capacities, increasing import costs and restraining the expansion of technology capacity. However these 'indirect' costs of technology transfer associated with restrictive practices have proved extremely difficult to calculate (Hood and Young 1979: 201–2; Chen 1994: 12–14).

The appropriateness of the technology transferred to developing countries has also been an issue. It was apparent that MNEs sometimes used overly capital-intensive technologies in developing countries, that some transferred technologies failed to create local linkages, and that they were used to produce inappropriate products. Empirical research found wide variations between countries, industries and firms in these outcomes. Investigation into whether foreign affiliates used more capital intensive technologies than domestic firms found they did in (for example) India, Brazil and Ghana, but did not in the Philippines, Mexico and Malaysia (Chen 1994: 16). However, as accurate comparison of the technology of MNE affiliates and local companies is very difficult, firm conclusions are hard to draw. Generally, it would seem that MNEs always make some adjustment of technology to local conditions. The initial engineering of a plant is virtually always geared to the characteristics of each site. Once a facility has been established, there is often further adaptation in ancillary activities, though not in the core technology (Lall 1993: 13–14).

A more crucial issue than both the cost and the appropriateness of transferred technology is the extent to which it is utilised and diffused in the host economy, and thus contributes to that economy's own technological capability. The nature of the host economy is crucial in explaining variations in the ability of a country to utilise foreign technology, yet MNE strategies are also important in the technological development process. The fact that MNEs have undertaken technological development mostly in their home economies has limited their impact in this area, especially in developing economies, where very little R & D has been undertaken. Developed host economies have faced the different problem that most R & D undertaken by the foreign affiliates of MNEs has been directed to the adaptation of particular products and processes rather than to basic or fundamental research (Casson 1991b). The location of R & D may also be a regional issue within host economies. Since the Second World War a number of European regions – such as Scotland – have suffered from 'branch plant syndrome', or a concentration of low skill and low value-added activities, while foreign MNEs have located their R & D either at home or in more attractive regions of the host economy.

A strong MNE presence also has the potential to hinder the development of local technological capabilities by driving out local competitors. It was argued by some that Japanese acquisition of US firms in high-technology industries since the 1970s would lead over time to the transfer of more sophisticated R & D activities back to Japan. However, little evidence has been found to support the view that foreign investors shifted their R & D activities from the United States, as many foreign companies wanted to take advantage of the technology centres in that country. Foreign MNEs transferred technology into American industries such as automobiles, steel and rubber, where the United States had been losing international competitiveness (Graham and Krugman 1989: 52–3; 58–9; United Nations 1992: 142–3). This was part of a wider trend towards the emergence of significant levels of geographically-dispersed R & D in MNE strategies, although into the 1990s this trend remained confined to developed host economies (Pearce and Singh 1992).

An important point in the history of technology transfer by MNEs is that it has been achieved by the full spectrum of equity and non-equity modes. Although the assumption that firms sought to protect their proprietary technology by operating abroad through wholly-owned subsidiaries might suggest that this mode has been the most significant for technology transfer, historically joint ventures, international cartels and licensing arrangements have all proved effective transferors of technology on a large scale.

Japan provides a major example of the acquisition of foreign technologies through modes other than wholly-owned direct investments. Despite the low amount of inward FDI received by Japan, international business has played an important part in that country's modernisation. Between 1899 and the 1930s Western manufacturing MNEs made direct investments in Japan in technologically advanced industries, especially machine equipment and electric machinery, in which Japanese business was weak or non-existent. US companies such as Western Electric and General Electric were among the pre-1914 investors, while the US automobile companies invested in the 1920s. In many cases, foreign firms formed joint ventures with Japanese partners, several of which later became leading Japanese enterprises. The first of these joint ventures was the Nippon Electric Company (NEC), established in 1899 with Western Electric as a 54 per cent shareholder (Mason 1992a: 20–47).

There were important technological and managerial transfers into Japan from these foreign affiliates. Mitsubishi Electric, founded in 1921, had become a major manufacturer of heavy electric apparatus by the end of the decade as a result of an affiliation with Westinghouse, through which a large transfer of production and management techniques was made to the Japanese company. There was a rapid dissemination within Japan of techniques learnt from foreign affiliates as companies emulated one another, and as workers changed companies. The latter phenomenon was noticeable in the case of the Japanese rubber industry, which owed its origins to Dunlop's factory in Kobe which opened in 1909. Bridgestone, the first Japanese-owned rubber company to make automobile tyres, was dependent on former Dunlop engineers and skilled workers for its production technology in its early stages. In the same period Toyota's sales organisation was formulated by personnel who had learned American marketing methods while working with General Motors' affiliate (Udagawa 1990: 18–19).

Interwar Japan demonstrates the significance of the host economy in explaining the success (or otherwise) of technology transfers. Although Japanese technological levels were low compared to contemporary Western economies, the business system was well developed, and possessed the organisational capability to absorb and adapt new technologies. A noticeable feature of the transfers into Japan was that the recipient Japanese enterprises typically made some modifications to suit Japanese conditions. Public policy was also an important factor in transferring technology. The Japanese automobile industry originated in the 1920s entirely through the operations of Ford and General Motors, which established assembly operations. The US firms bought parts locally, and a network of suppliers grew up around them. These included Nissan, which started in the motor vehicle industry as a Ford parts supplier. In the 1930s the Japanese government introduced a series of restrictions on Ford and General Motors which finally led to these companies divesting from Japan just before the outbreak of the Pacific War (Mason 1992a: 72–97). Nissan and Toyota were able to take over many former Ford and General Motors suppliers and dealers, as well as key personnel (Wilkins 1990a: 44–8).

After the Second World War, Japanese public policy discouraged wholly-owned FDI, but encouraged the acquisition of foreign technology through licensing agreements. Between 1950 and 1970 the Japanese government approved over 7,800 licensing contracts with durations of more than one year for foreign companies to transfer technology to Japanese enterprises in chemicals, food, machinery, steel and other industries (Mason 1992a: 151, 197–8). These licensing agreements were of major importance to Japan's fast economic growth in the postwar years.

Organisational innovation and improved managerial practices are a major aspect of technological development for enhancing productivity and accelerating growth. The technologies which were transferred by the service and natural resource investors of the nineteenth and early twentieth centuries were embodied in discrete managerial and organisational systems. In the twentieth century, MNEs have facilitated the transfer of entire management systems between countries. At the beginning of the century the European affiliates of US MNEs introduced mass production techniques. Subsequently, they utilised the management methods and systems associated with the M-form of organisation. In post-Second World War Europe, US affiliates employed a wide range of US marketing, accounting and other managerial techniques. Since the 1970s Japanese MNEs have transferred to the United States, Europe and Southeast Asia Japanese-style managerial methods or 'lean production'. In their automobile and electronics affiliates, Japanese companies have employed team-based organisation, just-in-time inventory procedures and quality control production methods. They have transferred aspects of the keiretsu system, as large numbers of suppliers and subcontractors have accompanied the major transplants.

The role of MNEs in diffusing managerial techniques made an important contribution to growth. Management practices were transferred into host economies both within affiliates, and through local suppliers or competitors emulating the foreign entrants. The US companies in post-1945 Europe had considerably higher productivity levels than their European competitors, due in part to their more professional managerial practices in sales and marketing, financial and personnel management. Later, the Japanese affiliates in the United States had higher productivity levels than their US competitors, who subsequently improved their own performance by emulating them. Service MNEs were sometimes important in the transfer of these management skills and practices. US management consultancy firms played a considerable role in the spread of the M-form in postwar Europe.

The international transfer of management and organisation by MNEs is a complex process. New organisational practices, institutional structures and work methods take longer to diffuse across national boundaries than do narrowly-defined technological innovations, while some elements of a national management system appear to be more transferable than others. Despite the example of the US affiliates in their country in the interwar years, British firms were very slow to adopt the principles of scientific management which had become pre-eminent in interwar United States. But after the Second World War the M-form was rapidly diffused from the United States to the United Kingdom (Kogut and Parkinson 1993; Kogut 1991). Japanese managerial practices have similarly only been partly diffused and transferred to host economies. Some practices, such as just-in-time and quality management, have been far more transferable than others, such as lifetime employment.

Host country factors were usually decisive in the transfer of managerial practices. Inherited national traditions of management and organisation were seldom easily changed. Some practices – for example, concerning labour management – were enshrined in national laws. Culture appears an important variable in the transfer of management systems. In so far as organisations were 'culture-bound', in Hofstede's terms, foreign managerial practices which were particularly alien to the host culture were probably the hardest to transfer (Yasumuro 1993b).

**Capital**

The transfer of capital by MNEs can supplement domestic savings and contribute to domestic capital formation. For countries that are capital constrained, this can bring large incremental benefits by providing an addition to domestic investment. In practice, research on MNEs since the Second World War has consistently shown that the provision of financial capital has rarely been significant for host economies. Once established, MNEs relied heavily on local borrowing and retained earnings to finance subsequent growth, though the precise means by which investments were financed has varied. A study of Brazil and Mexico between 1967 and 1989 showed that reinvested earnings by MNEs accounted for between 15 and 90 per cent of annual inflows of FDI (United Nations 1992: 113). The use of local borrowing raises the possibility that MNEs can by virtue of their size or other advantages gain privileged access to local savings to the detriment of local firms (Hood and Young 1979: 184, 198–9).

After the Second World War a number of factors, including the existence of exchange controls, encouraged MNEs not to finance their operations from funds provided by their parents, but this strategy appears to have been widely employed from the early days of international business in the nineteenth century. Firms often transferred funds into a country to start an operation, but future growth was typically financed by reinvested profits (Davies 1976: 79). From the early stages MNEs used the credit facilities of locally based banks to finance their operations. Manufacturing MNEs also raised funds from local capital markets, usually by selling off part of the equity of a subsidiary. In the interwar years this phenomenon became quite common, either because of financial pressures on the parent company, or because of a desire to take a more 'local' appearance to counter criticism of foreign companies.

There have been time periods and host economies in which the role of international business as a transferor of capital to the host economy has been important. The British 'free-standing' investments in the United States in the late nineteenth century was probably one instance. Whatever their other determinants and consequences, the free-standing firms functioned as an institutional means of facilitating capital flows from the world's principal lending economy into the world's principal borrowing economy (Wilkins 1989: 144–67). A hundred years later, after the onset of the world debt crisis in the early 1980s, FDI assumed a greater importance for some host developing countries as a means to augment domestic savings without resort to debt-creating sources of finance (United Nations 1992: 113).

Historically, foreign enterprises have sometimes contributed considerably to more efficient financial intermediation. In the nineteenth century European overseas banks introduced the entire concept and infrastructure of modern banking into some developing countries. In other cases they comprised the most stable element of the banking system, as in late nineteenth century Latin America. By financing their lending through locally raised deposits and the issue of bank notes, they contributed to the financial deepening of their host economies, even if they did not transfer large amounts of capital to them (see p. 163). Later generations of multinational banks made important contributions to financial intermediation. From the 1960s US banks were important in extending banking services, strengthening markets for foreign exchanges, and reducing the risks of financial services. The American banks which opened branches in Europe in this period often exercised a dynamic role on local banking systems by introducing new lending instruments and more aggressive marketing practices (Kelly 1977).

Financial deepening by foreign enterprises involved costs as well as bringing benefits. The European overseas banks in the nineteenth century had lending policies which favoured international trade finance. They focused their lending on European businesses or large-scale indigenous commercial enterprises, and did not lend to the peasant agriculture which was so important in many of their host regions. In Asia (and elsewhere) lending to locally-owned businesses was channelled through intermediaries – such as the *compradore* in Chinese-speaking regions – which increased their cost of borrowing. These practices continued into the 1950s and, although they reduced risks for the banks, they may well have hindered the development of entrepreneurship in these host economies (Jones 1993a). More recently, multinational banks in developing countries have often specialised in serving other MNEs or large domestic clients. While host government restrictions have often encouraged or even obliged such strategies, it has meant that foreign banks have assumed little role in the domestic intermediation process.

**Employment**

Multinationals create employment in host economies. It is quite possible that the importance of international business in terms of world employment was relatively greater historically than today because of the vast numbers of workers who were employed in the labour-intensive service and natural resource sectors, especially in developing economies. The random estimates which have survived suggest that the scale of employment provided by foreign enterprises was considerable. US mining and smelting properties in Mexico are estimated to have employed more than 500,000 Mexicans in 1915. The size of employment in individual mining and oil enterprises was sometimes staggering. At the end of the 1920s the Guggenheims employed 100,000 workers in their Chilean nitrate operations (Wilkins 1974a: 34, 105). Jardine Matheson, the British trading company, employed 250,000 people in China before the Communist Revolution (Keswick 1982). Foreign-owned plantations were massive employers also: Unilever's Huileries du Congo Belge subsidiary had 40,000 workers in the early 1960s (Fieldhouse 1978: 590).

The generation of employment by MNEs is a direct function of the amount of their capital investment and of the labour intensity of the production process. The large numbers of jobs in menial and low-skill occupations in early multinational mining, petroleum, agricultural and service activities provided opportunities and incomes which were marginally higher than those available in the indigenous sector, but the skill mix offered limited opportunities for the upgrading of human skills and competences. A similar problem was to arise later with the location of low-skill assembly jobs in cheap labour economies in Latin America and Asia.

Over time matters such as the preservation of managerial and skilled positions for expatriate staff and the low provision of training facilities in mining and other companies became issues of contention between MNEs and developing countries. During the interwar years MNEs started to promote nationals into supervisory roles, as well as to provide skill training (Wilkins 1974a). Cost-saving provided an important incentive as locally recruited staff were far cheaper than expatriates. Some host governments also put direct pressure on foreign companies to localise and train their staff. However, since most jobs in mining, plantations etc. by definition required little or no skills, there was a limit to the significance of this trend.

Manufacturing MNEs were significant employers in developed countries by the interwar years, although their overall share of the workforce remained small until well into the post-Second World War period. A number of firms were big employers. During the 1920s ITT's workforce in Europe alone reached 30–35,000. Jersey Standard in the early 1920s had 20,000 workers in Canada and another 17,000 in Europe (Wilkins 1974a: 71, 85). Over time the numbers employed in the manufacturing sector and their overall relative importance grew. In 1932 the British manufacturing subsidiaries of US MNEs employed around 65,000 people. In the early 1960s total British employment in US manufacturing affiliates had reached around 450,000. These figures represented 5 per cent of employees in manufacturing industry in the early 1960s, and 1.25 per cent in the 1930s (Bostock and Jones 1994; Jones 1988).

The growth of international business over the last two decades led to a growing number of jobs worldwide in MNEs. The total numbers employed in the world by MNEs grew from forty million in 1975 to seventy-three million in 1992. About 60 per cent of the latter represented employment in the parent companies – primarily based in developed countries – and the remainder (twenty-nine million jobs) employment in foreign affiliates. In absolute terms, this only represented 3 per cent of the world's labour force, while the twelve million jobs in foreign affiliates located in developing countries (of which half were in China) represented a negligible proportion of those countries' total workforces. However MNEs also create a considerable amount of indirect employment through a variety of linkages with subcontractors and suppliers, and this may have raised the total number of jobs associated with MNEs to 150 million in 1992 (United Nations 1994: 164–213).

The quality rather than the quantity of employment provided by MNEs has remained a key issue. The willingness of foreign companies to employ nationals in senior management positions in their affiliates is one aspect but practice has varied considerably between companies, countries and industries. By the interwar years a British managing director had already become a regular occurrence in US affiliates in that country, perhaps because of the linguistic and cultural similarities between the countries (Bostock and Jones 1994: 116–17).

Generally US MNEs exhibited a much greater propensity to employ locals in senior positions than Japanese MNEs, which usually had more expatriates in their foreign affiliates. However in all cases there was a correlation between the number of expatriates and the age of the investment – new ventures typically began with nationals from the parent firm in senior positions – and its condition, as MNEs typically made greater use of expatriates if an affiliate had difficulties. There have been industry differences also. Multinational banks typically appoint their own nationals to senior positions in foreign branches. This reflects the importance of personal contacts in banking services, but it has a distinct impact on the skill mix of the employment available in major international financial centres such as London and New York (Daniels 1986).

Foreign-owned companies often use different employment terms, conditions and practices to those prevailing in the host economy. Though there were always considerable variations between firms, when US manufacturers invested in Europe in the first half of the twentieth century they were often disinclined to negotiate with trade unions or – as in the case of the United Kingdom – to join employers' associations (Jones 1988: 443). After the Second World War US MNEs introduced important innovatory practices into their Western Europe affiliates, notably bargaining at the level of the enterprise or plant and productivity bargaining. Subsequently Japanese MNEs active in Europe and the United States introduced a wave of innovatory labour practices focused on the introduction of flexible work-organisation methods (United Nations 1994: 266–70).

In recent years, the significance of MNEs as employers of women has become important. A large proportion of the labour force employed by MNEs in export processing and free trade zones which have proliferated in Asia and Latin America over the last two decades are young females. In many cases this has provided employment opporties for women who had previously had low levels of participation in paid economic activity because of socio-cultural traditions and overt discrimination. But these jobs are overwhelmingly low paid and low skill, and might be regarded as confirming rather than challenging the lowly status of women in certain countries. From another perspective, the greater employment opportunities (however low income) for women than men disrupted traditional gender roles, sometimes causing acute dislocations in communities.

MNEs from a number of countries, notably the United States, have for decades had a growing and substantial proportion of women in managerial positions. Exposure to women in senior managerial positions in MNEs might be expected to break down stereotypes and social restrictions on the employment of women in senior positions in host economies where female emancipation is less advanced. However, in practice, MNEs have not yet assumed a dynamic role in lessening gender discrimination. Few MNEs have sent female managers abroad, especially to host countries where the representation of women in management is small, on the grounds that foreign prejudice renders them ineffective (United Nations 1992: 186–7). Moreover, while US firms have been in the forefront of equal employment opportunities, Japanese companies have been among the most extreme in their discrimination against female managers, and even some European countries – such as Switzerland – rarely employ women in senior management. As a result, there remains no correlation between MNE activities and enhanced female career opportunities.

## TRADE

International business has a considerable impact on the structure of trade of host economies. Almost by definition, many enterprises which invested across borders have a greater involvement in the international economy than purely domestic firms.

Before the 1930s the trade effects of international business on developing hosts were highly significant given that so much was concerned with primary commodities. The resource MNEs, trading companies, overseas banks and other service companies provided a business infrastructure to exploit and export commodities. The consequences were sometimes, as in the case of petroleum, dramatic. The international oil companies turned one economy after another – Russia and Mexico before 1914, Iran and Venezuela in the interwar years, Kuwait and Saudi Arabia subsequently – into major export economies. MNEs helped to turn other developing countries into major exporters of bananas, sugar, rubber and many other commodities. Some of these countries became dependent on one or a few commodities for almost all of their export earnings. The sharp contraction in the value and volume of world commodity trade in the 1930s began the process of disenchantment about the developmental prospects of such reliance on commodity exports. Instead of serving as an 'engine of growth', it became apparent that many primary producer prices were unstable, and prone to decline *vis-à-vis* industrialised goods.

International business was only one factor among several in causing the international pattern of specialisation in the world economy. It is not very productive to speculate whether developing host economies would have been 'better off' if their mineral or agricultural resources had not been developed, or had been developed by local enterprise. However, certain aspects of the strategies of international firms reduced the advantages derived by host economies from their exports. In particular, the fact that most minerals and agricultural commodities were exported with only the minimum of processing meant that most value was added to the product in the developed economies, which was usually the MNE home economy. A further set of potential problems arose from the complex patterns of vertical and horizontal integration, which had the result that transfer pricing between the various stages of mining or growing and processing did not take place at arm's length.

The literature on the strategies of manufacturing affiliates over the last thirty years generally shows that they have a high propensity to export, and tend to tilt the industrial structures of host economies towards internationalisation (Dunning 1992: 385–413). The historical development of this pattern is still in the process of being established. In so far as a considerable amount of manufacturing FDI before the Second World War took place as a response to protectionism, it is reasonable to assume that the bulk of the output of subsidiaries was for host country consumption. However, the exporting activities of some affiliates were considerable even in the interwar years. US-owned plants in Canada sometimes exported to the British Empire, where after 1915 they enjoyed tariff preferences. US subsidiaries in Europe sometimes exported to nearby nations or countries within the host nation's empire. The United Kingdom was used as a base to supply empire and sterling area markets in the interwar years. By the 1930s at least one-third of foreign-owned manufacturing subsidiaries in that country were engaged in exporting. From the late 1950s, as European economic integration gathered pace, foreign affiliates were used to export elsewhere in Western Europe (Wilkins 1974a: 140–2; Bostock and Jones 1994: 116–18).

The dynamic role of manufacturing MNEs in the promotion of exports has become very apparent over the more recent period. By the 1980s foreign-owned firms were estimated to be responsible for 23 per cent of US exports, 30 per cent of UK exports, and 32 per cent of French exports (Julius 1990: 45). In some cases, MNE investments enabled these developed hosts to re-emerge as major exporters of products which their indigenously-owned companies had ceased to manufacture. This was the case of colour television production in the United Kingdom, which became a major exporting industry thanks to Japanese-owned affiliates in that country (Eltis and Fraser 1992).

The role of foreign MNEs in the trade expansion of certain of the fast-growing East Asian economies has also been considerable. Singapore provided an extreme case where over 80 per cent of total manufacturing exports in the 1980s were accounted for by foreign affiliates, but the percentages have also been high for a number of other countries. In the same period foreign affiliates accounted for 37 per cent of Thailand's manufactured exports and 41 per cent of Malaysia's (United Nations 1992: 334). While the potential of MNEs to make an important contribution to export promotion in developing countries is clear, certain limitations need to be noted. The foreign exchange benefits are often limited because of the low value added locally in products such as electronic components. Foreign firms often limit export opportunities for subsidiaries. Moreover, in two of the most important newly industrial countries (NICs) – South Korea and Hong Kong – local firms accounted for the bulk of export promotion, although trading companies – especially *sogo shosha* – were sometimes very important. This was the case in Taiwan, where the *sogo shosha* handled over 50 per cent of that country's total exports in the early 1980s (Cho 1987: 62). The *sogo shosha* performed a strategic role in finding markets for products of Taiwan's numerous small and medium-size firms.

An additional consideration in assessing the trade effects of manufacturing MNEs in both developed and developing economies is their propensity to import. In general, MNE affiliates are more import-intensive than domestic firms. During the initial establishment of foreign affiliates, MNEs can have high import propensities because of limited knowledge of market conditions in host countries and locally available inputs. Over time, foreign affiliates may switch to a greater use of domestic goods and services. However, MNEs might also favour foreign sources of supply in order to maintain greater control over quality and reliability of supply, or take advantage of bulk purchases for the firm as a whole. A high import propensity will limit the net balance of payments effect of MNEs on a host economy even if they are very active in exporting, though the importing activities of MNEs can serve as an engine of growth. For example, by importing capital and intermediate goods MNEs can relieve supply constraints in developing countries.

The growth of intra-firm trade in manufacturing over the last twenty years resulted in a deep and profound interlinking of international trade and FDI. During the 1980s around one-third of US exports and over two-fifths of US imports were intra-firm transactions. This meant that trade flows were heavily influenced by the distribution of FDI. The significance of this can be seen in the cases of Japan and the United States. Japanese FDI in the United States far exceeded the amount of US FDI in Japan and, moreover, US affiliates in Japan were organised in a different fashion than in the reverse relationship. Intra-firm trade generally flows between MNE parents and majority-owned subsidiaries. The fact that most US subsidiaries in Japan were minority-owned meant that they made relatively few purchases from the US parent. Japanese companies, on the other hand, largely operated in the United States through majority subsidiaries. This is an important influence behind the persistent US trade deficit with Japan (Encarnation 1992). Into the 1990s 'trade disputes' between the United States, Japan and Europe continued to be conducted as if the world consisted of national firms exporting from their home bases, but in reality this world no longer existed. It had been replaced by one in which world trade flows could only be understood in the context of the operations of the MNEs.

## MARKET STRUCTURE AND LINKAGES

MNEs influence the structure of markets in host economies and impact the competitive environment in host economies through their linkages with local enterprises. The impact on the structure of markets and the performance of firms within these markets might considerably affect the efficiency of resource allocation within the host economy. Unfortunately, as with the other topics, almost all of the empirical research on this subject has been concerned with the manufacturing sector over the last thirty years. This causes obvious distortions in the literature: for example, there can be little dispute about the association between FDI and high concentration levels in most of the natural resource industries.

There are conflicting possibilities about the effects on market structure. MNE activities are particularly pronounced in manufacturing sectors characterised by market imperfections, such as oligopolistic competition, extensive product differentiation and entry barriers. This might suggest that the effect of MNEs will be to increase concentration levels. The alternative possibility is that MNEs might increase competition and reduce industrial concentration by their entry into existing markets. The empirical testing of either hypothesis is difficult, partly because concentration ratios are affected by many other factors than FDI, and partly because it is difficult to arrive at a dynamic model of cause and effect. The overall conclusion of the research which has been undertaken is that (once again) the nature of the impact on market structure will depend on industry – and host country – specific factors.

For the most part, studies of inward FDI in manufacturing in developed economies since the 1950s suggest no correlation with increased concentration (Steuer 1973). In broad terms, MNEs have often increased competition, and may have reduced concentration levels. Nevertheless, it has been quite common for foreign MNEs to hold dominant market positions at certain times in developed host economies. Before the First World War the US cotton thread industry was controlled by a group of interlinked British companies, of which J & P Coats was the most influential (Wilkins 1989: 361–8). Ford – whose first British assembly plant opened in 1911 – accounted for almost a quarter of British automobile production a decade later (Church 1994: 37). The dominant market positions held by these MNEs was fully explicable by their possession of technological, managerial and other ownership advantages but these positions were almost never a stable long-term phenomenon. Dominant positions were eroded by new competitors or the loss of competitive vigour, as in the case of Ford in interwar Europe. US antitrust proceedings awaited foreign firms with dominant market shares in the United States – this was the fate of the cotton thread companies in 1914 (Wilkins 1989: 386).

The entry of MNEs into the small markets of developing countries may have a more significant impact on concentration levels. The growth of MNEs in Malaysia, Mexico and a number of other developing countries in the 1960s and 1970s appeared to raise concentration levels by introducing new capital-intensive processes and differentiated products (Lall 1979; Blumström 1986).

The impact of MNEs on the performance of domestic firms is important. This impact occurs in several ways. Direct linkages occur through the impact of foreign affiliates on their local suppliers and customers. The effect of such linkages varies greatly from case to case, however, as firms and industries differ in the amount of inputs purchased locally. There are also differences in the qualitative impact made on local suppliers. In manufacturing, foreign affiliates are often more demanding in their specifications and delivery targets, while more willing to provide assistance and advice to local firms. The role of Japanese affiliates in raising the standards and productivity of domestic suppliers has been widely observed since the 1970s, but in fact this is part of a much longer trend. In the interwar years and later, US affiliates in Europe and elsewhere had the same effect (Dunning 1958, 1986).

Assessments of the impact of MNEs on suppliers become more complicated if foreign investors are accompanied by suppliers from their own country, as has been the norm in the multinational automobile industry. When US automobile companies invested in Europe in the interwar years, they were accompanied by US car body builders, tyre companies and manufacturers of wheels, batteries, spark plugs and window glass (Wilkins 1974a: 75-6). In some cases, their factories were physically located in host countries next to the main automobile assembly plant (Bostock and Jones 1994: 102). The same phenomenon occurred when the Japanese automobile firms invested in the United States in the 1980s (see p. 268).

If foreign-owned suppliers completely replaced local suppliers, the linkage effect might be regarded as weak. Wilkins distinguishes between technology transfer and technology absorption: 'only when nationals on their own (or virtually on their own) are able to produce the product does true diffusion – in contrast with mere geographical transfer – of the technology occur' (Wilkins 1974b). From this perspective, if all local suppliers are foreign-owned, there is an argument that no significant technological 'absorption' has occurred in the host economy. In practice there is usually a mixture of outcomes. Both in interwar Britain and the United States in the 1980s, some locally-owned suppliers improved their performance to meet the standards of the foreign entrants.

The presence of MNEs can exercise a powerful 'demonstration effect' on locally-owned firms. Workers and managers trained by foreign companies may change jobs and transfer to local companies the skills and attitudes learned with foreign employers. Greater competition can force them to adopt more efficient production methods. This effect can be seen in the British pharmaceuticals industry. After the Second World War foreign, mainly US, companies invested heavily in pharmaceutical manufacture in that country, and also established extensive R & D facilities. The result was a competitive stimulus on local competitors which at that time were small and generally dependent on foreign technology obtained under licence. It provided the background for the emergence of a cluster of world-class UK pharmaceutical companies, headed by Glaxo (Brech and Sharp 1984: 41–62).

The alternative scenario is that the activities of MNEs can displace domestic firms not able to resist the competitive pressures of foreign rivals. A study of the Latin American tobacco industry showed how the dominant local firms were replaced by US affiliates in the 1960s. Contraband was an important means of market penetration into the protected national markets. Contraband cigarettes weakened the national firms – enabling the MNEs to buy them – and changed tastes in favour of US brands (Shepherd 1989). The result was the 'denationalisation' of most of the Latin American cigarette industry.

Spillover effects can be very limited in the case of the enclavist-type investments which were common in the natural resource sector. The linkage effects of banana production are slight. There are very few inputs of local origin, and much of the value added occurs after the product has left the exporting country. However there are wide variations between minerals and crops in their local forward and backward linkages. Tin, rubber and tea production in Asian economies has been shown to have stimulated transport facilities and engineering capacity, which can be easily turned to other uses (Thoburn 1977). Some recent forms of MNE investment in developing country agriculture have produced significant welfare gains. In some developing countries MNE contracts with smallholders have resulted in the cultivation of new crops, the spread of more advanced farming practices, and income increases due to access to foreign markets. However, the outcome has varied greatly with the exact type of contractual and institutional arrangement. When MNEs do not deal with direct producers but with local plantation owners, the wages and working conditions of workers have been poorer than on company plantations (Glover 1986).

The enclave problem arose in a new guise through the location of much manufacturing FDI in export processing zones in developing countries. Taiwan and South Korea experimented with such zones in the mid-1960s and the early 1970s. They offered tax holidays and other incentives for foreign firms to locate factories in them, which appeared to be attractive strategy to develop export industries without some of the political and other costs that a general liberalisation of trade policy would entail. These zones were subsequently adopted on a large scale in some other Asian and Latin American economies. The case of Malaysia is discussed below (see pp. 264–6). In countries where export-oriented FDI has been concentrated within such zones, linkages with local firms have often been weak. In such situations, MNEs had to cross the 'border' in order to source locally, and they often preferred to source in neighbouring countries (United Nations 1992: 122).

Among the negative linkages which have arisen from MNE practices have been the distortion of traditional consumption patterns by powerful marketing which can induce the adoption of socially undesirable practices. In the late 1970s and early 1980s a boycott of Nestlé products was initiated by activists in the United States who claimed that the Swiss firm's aggressive baby food promotions made mothers in developing countries so eager to use Nestlé's formula that they used it any way they could. This often resulted in mixing the formula with polluted water or trying to make the expensive supplies last longer by using an insufficient amount of formula, thereby starving their infants. Nestlé eventually stopped promoting the product through advertising and free samples. Nestlé was one of a group of MNEs whose marketing of baby foods in developing countries seems to have contributed to sharp declines in breast-feeding by mothers. This posed serious health risks given the environmental and economic conditions of many countries (Bader 1980).

The promotion of cigarette consumption by the major MNEs, already noted in the case of Latin America, can also be regarded as having extremely negative consequences. As consumption faltered in the developed world through health concerns, the major tobacco MNEs increasingly marketed their products in developing countries and, from the late 1980s, in Eastern Europe and China.

While the promotion of powdered milk and cigarettes in poor countries represent clear-cut cases, much of the criticism of MNEs for spreading 'socially undesirable' practices is subjective. The expansion of Coca-Cola in France in the late 1940s provoked widespread attacks from competing wine and mineral water interests, and from critics of 'Coca-Colonisation' who regarded the company as a symbol of US economic imperialism. There were legislative moves to ban the importation, manufacture and sale of Coca-Cola, though eventually the US company was able to overcome its problems in that country (Giebelhaus 1994: 207–8). While it is theoretically conceivable that the habit of drinking Coca-Cola had some adverse impact on French lifestyles, it does seem unlikely, and would certainly be impossible to quantify.

## SOVEREIGNTY AND CULTURE

MNEs have an impact on the sovereignty of their host economies. Because ultimate decision-making in an MNE resides with the parent rather than the subsidiary, host governments have less control over foreign-owned firms than over local firms. MNEs may also use the international nature of their organisation to circumvent host government policies or – in extreme cases – attempt to subvert governments. This section will focus on three specific issues: the dependency critique of MNEs; the exercise of political influence; and their cultural impact.

A number of radical theories have treated MNEs as 'agents' of imperialism, which assumed an important role after the end of the colonial era, and whose behaviour forms part of a political and economic system which exploits developing countries and retards their development. The *dependencia* school, originating in Latin America, initially regarded MNEs as major obstacles to development through their roles in transferring technologies which caused mass unemployment and displaced local businesses. This critique was later modified to take account of Latin America's rapid industrialisation from the 1960s. MNEs came to be seen as engines of growth, but of a lop-sided development, the costs of which included too great an emphasis on luxury consumer durables and widening income disparities (Cardoso and Faleto 1979).

The role of MNEs in the growth of Brazil, Mexico and similar countries was regarded as 'dependent development'. Dependence on MNEs imposed strict limits on national policies, for it was necessary to maintain 'good investment climates'. The result was that such countries were 'simply not free to explore a welfare-oriented version of capitalist development' (Gereffi and Evans 1981: 32, 54). These dependency relations were solidified by a 'triple alliance' between MNEs, host country governments and externally oriented segments of the local business community. Local firms provided the skills in political manoeuvring, MNEs provided the technology, while governments provided the institutional framework and established a common set of goals (Evans 1979).

The *dependencia* analysis provides a corrective to simplistic views that MNEs are an automatic cure-all for developing countries, but it rests on an excessive level of generalisation. Discussion of 'local capital' as a single entity overlooks the many differences within the private sector of developing countries, while the supply and marketing linkages which developed between MNEs and local firms pointed to a more symbiotic than dependent relationship (Haggard 1989: 186–90). Domestic firms have not always played a subordinate role to MNEs in developing countries over the last three decades. Powerful domestic enterprises have been evident in both Asia and Latin America, a number of which have themselves become MNEs.

The exercise of political influence on host governments has usually been discussed in terms of developing economies. A number of *cause célèbres* – such as ITT's intervention in Chilean politics in the early 1970s – stand out as worst-case examples of the abuse of national sovereignty. However such spectacular cases have been very rare. More typically, foreign MNEs have been able to influence political decisions in their favour, especially when their role in a particular host economy has been very powerful.

The question of political influence has also arisen in the case of developed hosts. The growth in importance of inward FDI into the United States from the 1970s caused concern about the ability of foreign firms to influence the political process through lobbying. Japanese firms in particular were identified as using resources to influence voting and legislation, and using their bargaining power to extract special treatment (Choate 1990: xvi). A further issue was the expensive competition among states and localities to attract foreign firms. The Japanese automobile assemblers which invested in the United States were able to secure favourable conditions such as waiver of property taxes, provision of free land, and government funded new roads and training programmes. However it is not evident that such political lobbying by foreign firms should be treated as reducing the sovereignty of the United States. As a prominent feature of the political system of the United States is the extensive lobbying by business, unions and other interest groups designed to influence policy, foreign MNEs have adapted to the host country environment rather than introducing a new phenomenon (Graham and Krugman 1989: 68–9).

The extent to which cultural sovereignty is undermined by international business raises complex problems. There have been periodic waves of hostility to foreign ownership in many host economies. In the 1880s and 1890s there was a wave of criticism in the United States against foreign investments, with particular resentment of foreign – especially British – ownership of land. The criticism of foreign ownership extended into dislike for the alien culture of the owners. The British were disliked for their aristocratic and superior behaviour – unwelcome reminders of America's colonial past (Wilkins 1989: 566–78).

From the late nineteenth century US FDI in Europe stimulated waves of anti-American feelings. Between 1897 and 1902 there was a flurry of discussion about the American invasion of Europe, with a number of books being published with titles such as *The Americanization of the World* (Wilkins 1970: 70–71). In the late 1920s there was another public debate in Britain and elsewhere in Europe about US takeovers of national firms and the spread of US influence (Wilkins 1974a: 153–5). The issue surfaced again in the 1960s, and the debates of that period were symbolised in the publication of Servan-Schreiber's *Le Défi Americain* (*The American Challenge*) in 1967. The issue has continued to feature in US-European negotiations in the 1990s about the liberalisation of service industries such as films, where some Europeans have identified a cultural threat posed by Americans.

The cultural tensions between Americans and Europeans have been rarely serious in their consequences, but the difficulties have sometimes been greater when the cultural differences between home and host economies have been more substantial, as in the case with Western FDI in developing countries, or Japanese FDI in the United States and Europe. The underlying point is that MNEs transfer cultural values and ideas along with technology, management and capital (Sauvant and Mennis 1980: 278–9). In so far as the values create jobs and enhance productivity they are welcomed, but they can also be seen as a threat or simply an unwelcome intrusion.

## HOST ECONOMIES OVER TIME

The following case studies examine the impact of international business on host economies at various periods since the late nineteenth century. They are not designed to be 'representative' so much as to indicate the diversity of national and sectoral experience. They draw on extensive pieces of research which were designed to get beyond the generalisations which prevail in much of the literature on the impact of MNEs.

### Mining and development in late nineteenth century Spain

The experience of Spain in the late nineteenth century provides an opportunity to examine the impact on a developing economy of FDI in natural resources. The Spanish economy was backward and undeveloped in this period, though with a number of regional enclaves where modern industrialisation was underway. A large number of foreign, especially British, mining companies entered the country during the second half of the nineteenth century to exploit its rich reserves of raw materials. Spain emerged as one of the world's principal mining nations, accounting for almost a quarter of world lead production and almost a fifth of world copper production. This prominence as a world mining exporter was short-lived, however, and the Spanish mining sector entered absolute and protracted decline after the First World War.

The role of foreign enterprises in the Spanish mining industries was criticised both by contemporaries and later historians. Foreign firms were regarded as earning and transferring out of the country excessive profits, while the enclavist nature of mining provided few linkages for more broadly-based development. The exploitative nature of the process was seen as being facilitated by the alliance between the foreign firms and the corrupt political élite, who provided a permissive regulatory and taxation framework for the mining companies.

Harvey and Taylor (1987) reassessed these issues in a study of 174 British registered mining companies formed to operate in Spain between 1851 and 1913. A disaggregation of the mining companies showed that most of them were short-lived, while a small number of large and successful operating companies accounted for the greater part of investment and production. There were many failures. Only one in five ventures was profitable, a reflection of the high-risk nature of mining in Spain. The period of high profits for the successful ventures between the mid-1880s and 1913 came after earlier periods when investments had exceeded earnings – and consequently have to be seen in the context of a return on capital invested. The major losses were made by the British companies drawn into the industry by the high dividends, as most of the best prospects had been discovered early in the development of the industry.

The impact of the foreign mining companies was heavily influenced by the nature of the host economy. In northern Spain, the business elites from the Basque region took advantage of the opportunities of the mineral export boom. There was a substantial growth in industries related to mining – such as iron and steel and shipbuilding – and banking. The foreign mining companies sometimes participated directly in these activities in collaborative ventures, while local entrepreneurs also copied their technological and managerial systems. In contrast, in southern Spain the entrepreneurial response to foreign mining firms was very muted. There were few joint ventures between them and local companies. This encouraged an enclavist-type of development, in which the mining companies stuck to their core business, and mining operations were centred on company towns. Even in these regions, the foreign mining companies provided well-paid and secure employment.

The foreign mining companies emerge strongly as an 'engine of growth' in late nineteenth century Spain. Foreign capital and enterprise created 'employment and prosperity where none had existed before', and stimulated responsive local entrepreneurs to engage in industrial modernisation. Mining was a risky business in which most firms failed. Profits were not exceptionally high given the time characteristics of investment and profit flows. In so far as Spain did not capture more fully the benefits of foreign mining activities, Harvey and Taylor suggest that the primary responsibility rested with the host government, which pursued inadequate taxation policies and practices (Harvey and Taylor 1987: 204–6).

## Oil and banking in Iran before the 1950s

Before the interwar years Iran was one of the poorest and least developed economies on earth. The great majority of the population were employed in subsistence agriculture and had extremely low incomes, and there was a dearth of modern infrastructure from education to transport. The economy was dominated by foreign enterprises. The two most important of these were the British-owned bank and oil company. The Imperial Bank of Persia, formed in 1889, was a state bank, and held a *de facto* monopoly on modern banking until the late 1920s. The Anglo-Persian Oil Company (later British Petroleum) discovered oil in the south west of the country in 1908. By 1914 it had built a pipeline to the coast and a refinery at Abadan.

The most obvious benefits for Iran arose from the success of the two British companies in achieving their aims. Iran emerged as a major world oil exporter, and oil was by far the country's largest export in the interwar years. The Imperial Bank created a nationwide modern banking system and provided administrative and financial support for a government which lacked resources or power. Yet costs are also transparent. Both the

Imperial Bank and the Anglo-Persian Oil Company operated on the basis of monopoly concessions which gave them enormous privileges. The Imperial Bank's concession, which lasted for sixty years, made it the state bank of Iran with the exclusive right of note issue, and exempted it from all taxes (Jones 1986c: 23). The Anglo-Persian Oil Company operated on the basis of a concession which awarded a monopoly on petroleum exploitation and development over virtually all of Iran. Exports and imports were free of all taxes, though the government possessed an ill-defined right to receive a proportion of the annual profit of companies formed to work the concession (Ferrier 1982: 42–3).

The British investments, especially Anglo-Persian, were highly enclavist in nature. Because of the geographical isolation of the oilfields, as well as the decentralisation of government before the mid-1920s, the oil company had to provide its own economic and social infrastructure. In southern Iran it constructed and operated a vast network of services including roads, electricity and water supplies, telephone lines, transportation, education and security. It responded to the lack of local industry and the absence of skilled labour by becoming entirely self-sufficient. Abadan, where the refinery was located, became a self-sufficient industrial complex with few local contractors or other contacts with the local economy. Even by the end of the 1930s only about 5 per cent of Anglo-Iranian's total production was consumed in Iran. The Imperial Bank was also widely criticised for 'enclavism'. The bank was perceived as concentrating on the finance of foreign trade and as discriminating against Iranians in lending policies (Jones 1986c: 45–8, 94–9).

The calculation of the costs and benefits of this inward investment in Iran is complex. There was no possibility that Iran could have developed an oil industry or a modern banking system without the transfer of enterprise and technology from the foreign companies. The exemptions from taxation and other concession terms appear exploitative, but were indicative of the high risks involved in the proposed investments. There was no other way that any investor would have risked funds searching for oil in a country lacking infrastructure and political stability. The concession policy can be regarded as an embryonic development strategy which recognised that foreign interests were essential if modernisation was to begin: in this sense, they were the forerunners of the export processing zones of today.

The linkage effects were not ideal, but nor were they completely absent. The royalties paid by the British oil company to the government, together with its sales of foreign exchange to secure the local currency needed for its operations, provided the largest single source of foreign exchange for the economy in the interwar years. The foreign companies had a large impact on employment. The oil company employed 27,000 Iranians in 1930, and was the largest employer in the modern industrial sector.

A growing number of Iranians were given technical training. A special training school at Abadan took school-leavers and put them through an apprenticeship course. Though most workers stayed with the company, a minority left, and Iranian industrial occupations became full of persons who had been trained by the oil company. The Imperial Bank's staff numbers were smaller – never exceeding 400 – and it was slower to promote Iranians to management positions and provide formal training. Yet the on-the-job training it did provide was not available elsewhere in Iran before the 1930s, and former staff from the bank provided a valuable source of labour for the economy (Jones 1987b; Bostock and Jones 1989: 63–6; Bamberg 1994: 80–103).

For many Iranians, however, the most serious cost of the British oil and banking investments was the effect on the country's sovereignty. Iran reacted with extreme hostility to foreign business and other influence. Both the country's Islamic culture and its political history help explain the high level of sensitivity. In 1907 Iran was divided into 'spheres of influence' which recognised Russia's 'interest' in the north and Britain's 'interest' in the south. During the First World War it became a battleground for competing armies, and the British and the Soviets occupied it again in the Second World War. Iran's focal position as a centre of diplomatic rivalries forced home governments and their business interests into a close, if not always harmonious, relationship. Both the Imperial Bank and the Anglo-Persian Oil Company had close contacts with the British government. The relationship became closer still when the British government acquired its shareholding in the oil company in 1914. To most Iranians, Anglo-Persian became the symbol of British imperialism.

The unwelcome symbolic role of British business provoked a violent reaction from modernising Iranian governments from the 1920s. The government became determined to maximise both its control over, and its revenue from, the Anglo-Persian Oil Company, as part of a strategy to develop the Iranian economy and to reverse foreign political and economic domination. Oil, as the major source of foreign exchange, became regarded as a vital resource for national progress. When the onset of the Great Depression reduced demand in the world oil industry, and cut state oil revenues, company–government relations deteriorated. In 1932 the company's concession was unilaterally cancelled. A new concession was finally agreed in the following year, which reduced the concession area and improved the financial terms for the Iranian government, but in fact the episode proved a curtain-raiser for a more dramatic attack against the British company twenty years later (Ferrier 1982: 588–622; Bamberg 1994: 33–50). The Imperial Bank was replaced as a state bank by a government-owned bank in 1928. It was subsequently subjected to discriminatory legislation which sharply reduced its market share by the end of the 1930s. After a brief wartime respite, the bank withdrew from Iran in 1952 (Jones 1986c).

A positive interpretation of the impact of inward FDI into Iran would highlight the creation of new industries, especially petroleum which was to result in a permanent and long-term improvement in Iran's income; the linkage effects in employment and government revenues; and the transfer of social technologies. A negative interpretation would stress the exploitative concession terms which remained in force long after the level of risk had changed out of recognition; the enclavist nature of the development which was achieved; and the abuse of sovereignty caused by having strategic natural resources controlled by a foreign company, especially a company partly owned by the government of a hostile imperialist country.

## MNEs and the German machinery industry before 1918

In the late nineteenth century US machinery firms acquired large market shares in Germany in machinery products, which were reinforced by the establishment of factories in that country. The companies included some of the most dynamic US MNEs of the period, such as Singer, which had sold its sewing machines in Germany since 1861, and which established a factory in 1904, National Cash Register (NCR), United Shoe Machinery, and Otis Elevator. These investments in manufacturing facilities were stimulated by German tariffs and patent legislation, but the competitive advantages of the US enterprises rested on their superior production techniques and the effectiveness of their marketing organisations (Blaich 1984: 1–11; Chandler 1990: 199–201).

German companies produced and sold almost all the products manufactured by the American firms – but their production costs were higher and their marketing methods less efficient. The US companies transferred advanced technological and managerial techniques into Germany through their affiliates. Singer utilised US-style mass production which reduced the production costs of sewing machines in Germany. The firm also applied its distinctive marketing methods, creating a direct sales network and providing credit facilities for purchasers. The United Shoe Machinery Company's production technology enabled it to produce a complete range of quality machines which shoe manufacturers found easy to use. After-sales service was provided by the company as well as a leasing system. The linkage effects for German shoe manufacturers were very positive. The US-owned factories also became significant employers. Singer had 2,000 employees by 1914, all but a handful of whom were German (Blaich 1984).

The impact of the US machinery companies on their German competitors took several forms. In cash registers, NCR adopted an aggressive strategy designed to eliminate its German competitors by price-cutting and patent suits. The Americans were able to eliminate two of the three local competitors in large cash registers, though the third company survived. An unforeseen consequence of the aggressive US strategy was that it attracted the attention of the German authorities to the product. During the First World War they favoured German-owned companies, and Krupp – the large German metals firm – entered production. It had captured over half of the market by the early 1920s (Blaich 1984: 40–9).

In other products German companies responded to the Americans in several ways. They either copied US production methods, or else diversified into the manufacture of other products. German sewing machine companies reacted variously to Singer by specialising in particular types of machines and by diversification into other products such as office machines, automobiles and calculating machines. The new businesses were on occasion such a success that the firms never returned to sewing machines. This was the case for Opel, which became Germany's largest automobile manufacturer. A number of other companies, notably Pfaff, stayed with sewing machines. They reduced their production costs and adopted American manufacturing methods, and developed a distribution system which could compete with the Americans. Pfaff also encouraged a US manufacturer of sewing machine parts to establish a German subsidiary. This venture, which began production in 1912, provided high quality parts for Pfaff (Blaich 1984: 36–40).

There was little concern about the sovereignty impact of the US machinery companies. The German government welcomed US FDI in the machinery sector. State purchasing agencies declined requests from domestic suppliers asking to be favoured, arguing that the foreign competitors offered superior technologies and production capacity. Accusations that US subsidiaries manipulated their balance sheets to avoid taxation and repatriate capital did not produce any action from the German government (Blaich 1984: 96–8).

This case study of the impact of manufacturing FDI in the pre-1914 period shows the positive impact it can exercise on local competitor firms in a developed economy. Although some firms were driven out of business or forced to diversify – in at least one case by predatory practices – the stronger German enterprises were able to absorb the technologies and organisational skills of the Americans. As a result, US MNEs facilitated the creation of a number of competitive firms, such as Pfaff, which were able to survive the disruption of the First World War, and emerge as important international rivals to US firms in the interwar years (Chandler 1990: 524–6).

### MNEs and the Brazilian automobile industry 1956–80

The creation of an automobile industry in Brazil by MNEs illustrates their potential as an 'engine of growth'. In the early 1950s Brazil had only the beginnings of an industrial base. Coffee still accounted for more than 50 per cent of the country's exports. Virtually all the vehicles used in Brazil were imported as knocked-down kits and assembled locally. Between 1956 – when the Brazilian government banned all car imports – and 1968 the situation was transformed. By the latter date eight firms, all foreign-controlled, manufactured 280,000 vehicles in the country. A further surge of growth resulted in annual production of over one million vehicles by 1980, giving Brazil the tenth largest automobile industry in the world.

Recent research emphasises the critical role of the host government in securing this positive outcome (Shapiro 1991, 1993, 1994). In 1956 the government began a comprehensive programme to develop a local industry when it set up the *Grupo Ejectivo de la Industria Automovilistica* (GEIA) responsible for promoting the industry. The Brazilians – and later other Latin American governments – saw automobiles as a vital industry in their import substitution strategies. In the early 1950s, the industry accounted for around 14 per cent of total imports, causing a considerable drain on foreign exchange.

It was the threat of market closure in 1956 when prohibitively high tariffs were imposed which attracted and set the timing of foreign invest-ment. Even more critical was state policy towards the level of local content. GEIA established local content targets for the industry which were to rise from between 35 per cent and 50 per cent of vehicle weight in 1956 to 90–95 per cent by 1961. These high domestic content levels meant that firms were forced to produce the 'technological heart' of their vehicles in Brazil, which was definitely not on their agenda (Shapiro 1994: 128–9). Participating firms were offered fiscal incentives such as exemption from duties and taxes on imports of parts and machinery, and special credit machinery. GEIA enforced domestic content requirements by withholding foreign exchange allocations from those firms that did not comply. These policies proved effective. Within five years, eleven firms had initiated vehicle production. By 1961 Brazilian total vehicle production had reached 145,000 units, with an average domestic content share of 93 per cent by weight (Shapiro 1991: 877).

Clearly there were a number of elements which favoured the birth and growth of the Brazilian automobile industry. The GEIA plan coincided with the internationalisation of motor vehicle production. The emergence of European competitors in the 1950s loosened the power of the US auto-mobile MNEs, and so increased Brazil's bargaining power. Competition for foreign markets was intensifying in the industry, especially in Europe, and firms responded by following each other to these markets. It was very important that the threats of market closure and deadlines were credible. The automobile MNEs did not want to manufacture in Brazil and constantly tested the resolve of the government. The credibility of GEIA's threats rested on its possession of sufficient authority and coherence to make it costly for firms not to follow its programme. It was also undoubtedly assisted by the large size of the Brazilian market, which made a domestic industry viable and offered considerable growth potential (Shapiro 1994).

There were marked differences in the strategies pursued by different automobile companies. The most positive response to the government's plans came from Germany's Volkswagen, which at that time had no foreign manufacturing plants and was anxious to expand abroad. It established production facilities to make its 'Beetle' cars in Brazil, establishing a commanding position in the Brazilian passenger car market. The US MNEs opted out of the passenger car market, and it was only after 1968 that Ford and General Motors entered the passenger car market, becoming the second and third largest automobile producers after Volkswagen. The Italian company Fiat entered Brazil later still, beginning production in 1976, but by virtue of extensive subsidies from a state government, was able to establish a large business.

The relationship between the MNEs and the government was dynamic once the industry was established. Government policies created conditions under which vehicle demand grew and labour costs were kept down. By influencing factor costs, maintaining protection and limiting new entry, the Brazilian government enabled the firms to earn sufficient profits despite the relatively small and still fragmented market.

During the 1970s the government focused on providing export promotion incentives. In 1972 the BEFIEX (Export Fiscal Benefits) programme was established. This allowed for tax exemptions against export performance commitments. Following the first oil shock in 1974, all incentives for local production were removed except those available under BEFIEX. The result was a remarkable growth in Brazilian automobile exports. In 1970 none of the total production of over 300,000 units were exported; by 1980 around 15 per cent of the production in excess of 900,000 units were exported. This outcome was again facilitated by a coincidence of policy aims and wider trends in the world automobile industry, especially the increased resort to offshore sourcing for parts and components, and the growing integration of plants in countries with lower labour costs (Fritsch and Franco 1991: 111–22).

The industry had high linkage effects, stimulating – for example – the development of new sectors to produce its intermediate inputs, particularly in the metallurgical industry (Shapiro 1994: 1–3, 186–90). Linkages were fostered by a high domestic content requirements combined with policies that banned the importation of components and parts for which there were domestically produced equivalents. This resulted in Brazil acquiring a large supplier network – larger than in the case of Mexico, which had lower domestic content requirements. On the other hand, firms were reluctant to change models frequently because of tooling costs, and as a result the country's streets became full of antiquated car models (Shapiro 1993:211).

While the level of government subsidy needed to create the industry should not be exaggerated – especially when the amount of taxes paid is taken into consideration – more complex issues are raised if a strategic counterfactual perspective is taken. A comparison can be made with South Korea, where the government in the 1960s banned the import of built-up vehicles as a strategy to develop a domestic, South Korean-owned automobile industry. South Korean production grew rapidly in the 1980s, and surpassed that of Brazil in the second half of the decade. Two of its three leading firms, Hyundai and Kia, were dominated by Korean interests, while the third – Daewoo – was half owned by GM. As Shapiro argues, the Brazilian and South Korean strategies both had costs and benefits. Hyundai and Kia were active in developing technological capacity and their own distribution networks, while Daewoo – like the foreign affiliates in Brazil – did little to develop domestic technological capacity and relied on GM's sales network, which would not sell its products in North America. However the Korean companies faced accelerating problems of accessing the latest technologies through non-equity or minority joint venture arrangements. This provided a potential restriction on their continuing ability to upgrade (Shapiro 1993: 240–3).

The creation of the Brazilian automobile industry shows both the positive impact that MNEs can make on the manufacturing sector of a developing economy, and the way that host government policy shaped that impact. The case provides little support for the 'dependent development' models discussed earlier. The state emerges as more effective vis-à-vis MNEs, and the economy as less structually constrained, than such models suggest. However, the case of South Korea shows that alternative strategies to build an automobile industry – involving less reliance on MNEs – were possible in certain conditions.

## MNEs and the British diet in the twentieth century

Foreign, especially American, MNEs had a profound impact on the British diet and lifestyle over the last century. The American impact on the British diet began before the First World War. This impact was concentrated on products which lent themselves to mass processing techniques – canning, freezing, drying – rather than the fresh food sector. In these areas US firms benefited from new technologies and from the application of mass marketing techniques. One of the first areas to be affected was breakfast, a meal at which the British had traditionally eaten a large cooked meal of eggs, bacon and other items or else simply bread. The Quaker Oats Company began selling its branded and advertised oatmeal product in Britain in the late 1870s, and founded its own marketing subsidiary in 1899. On the basis of an aggressive advertising campaign and some adaptation of the basic product to suit local tastes, Quaker Oats had established oatmeal porridge as almost a mass consumption food in Britain by the First World War (Horst 1974: 41).

Another change to the eating habits of the British came when H. J. Heinz introduced canned soup. In 1886 the firm secured an order from the elite London department store Fortnum and Mason for some of the '57 Varieties' of canned soup which it made. This was followed by the creation of a British marketing affiliate, and the opening of a factory in London in 1905. There was no British competitor in this product owing to the British failure to adopt the new high-speed canning technology (Chandler 1990: 262). Subsequently, Heinz introduced a range of other products into the United Kingdom – baked beans, strained baby foods, sauces and pickles – in which it was able to retain a high percentage of the market over a very long term.

During the interwar years the British breakfast diet was further and more radically changed by the introduction of cold, ready-to-eat cereals. The interwar years saw the vigorous targeting of the British market by US manufacturers who, encouraged by rising sales of imports of brands already popular in the United States, began manufacturing in Britain. Shredded Wheat opened a British factory in 1926; Quaker Oats opened a small plant in 1920 and a much larger one in 1936; and Kellogg, which began exporting corn flakes to Britain in 1922, opened a factory – the largest of its kind outside the United States – in 1938. Kellogg undertook an extensive marketing campaign in Britain in the 1930s. By 1939 ready-to-eat cereals were purchased by the majority of British households. Like Heinz, Kellogg established a long-term high market share, which was still 50 per cent in the 1980s (Collins 1994: 239–42).

Through their introduction of products such as breakfast cereals, canned soups and baked beans, US MNEs exerted a considerable influence on the content of British diet and on British eating habits within a relatively short period. These were new products the markets for which were created and made possible by the transfer of product differentiation and advertising strategies, as well as processing technologies, from the United States. In other food products, US firms had important but less radical influences. In chocolate and confectionery, Mars achieved considerable market share for its candy bars after the Second World War, but this was in the context of a large pre-existing market which remained distinctly British rather than American in its preference for sweet tasting 'milk' chocolate.

The entry of the US food retailer McDonald's into the United Kingdom started further radical changes to the British diet and eating habits. Britain had traditional low-cost food service outlets in the form of 'fish and chip' shops and pubs, which served snack foods along with alcoholic beverages, but the poor quality of products offered was notorious.

Following the opening of its first store in the United Kingdom in 1974, McDonald's faced considerable difficulties in trying to provide a quality food product combined with fast efficient service. While in some European countries McDonald's was criticised for lowering food standards, in Britain it encountered the problem that its standards and quality were too high for both consumers and suppliers. British consumers initially preferred the traditional large quantities of poor quality food available at pubs and elsewhere to McDonald's more expensive product. The company also had to establish its own bun and other supplier businesses in order to secure reliable quality suppliers (Love 1987: 439–44). Eventually, as in Japan, McDonald's was able to establish a large business. This was the success which led to the entry into Britain of other US fast food restaurants. The change in the lifestyle of many British consumers was considerable.

The British adoption of cereal breakfasts, baked beans and fast food hamburgers was not the result of an automatic transfer of US lifestyles across the Atlantic, but the consequence of the creation of demand through marketing and other corporate strategies transferred from the United States. The British experience was part of a much wider trend whereby US MNEs spread US lifestyles virtually worldwide. While the roles of the US breakfast cereal companies and fast food retailers have been stressed here, US advertising agencies and hotel chains were also important in this process.

## MNEs and the Malaysian electronics industry after 1970

Malaysia became one of the most important developing host countries from the 1970s. It was surpassed in importance in terms of inflows only by Brazil, Mexico, Singapore and (in the 1980s) China. A good infrastructure, political stability, low wages and the widespread use of English were among the country's locational attractions. Much of this investment was in electronics. Prior to 1971 there were only two Japanese companies – Matsushita and Toshiba – manufacturing in Malaysia. They both assembled black-and-white television receivers for the domestic market. But in the early 1970s US electronics companies began to locate their labour-intensive assembly operations in Malaysia, and Japanese firms followed (Kawabe 1991: 239–44). The growth of the electronics industry was spectacular. By the 1980s Malaysia had become the world's largest single exporter of electronic components (Warr 1987: 30).

Malaysia's electronics industry became a major employer. Employment in electronics companies rose from 577 workers in 1970 to over 80,000 in 1984 (Jesudason 1989: 174). It also emerged as Malaysia's largest exporter. Initially most of these exports went to the United States, reflecting the tight links between the US parents and the affiliates in semiconductors. Wafers manufactured in the United States were air-freighted to Malaysia,

where they were assembled into circuits, and then air-freighted back to
the parent firm. The entry of Japanese companies helped create more
diverse trade patterns. By the late 1980s the United States only accounted
for 30 per cent of semiconductor imports, with Singapore, Japan and
Korea as large sources of supply.

Malaysia's electronics industry was overwhelmingly concentrated in
export processing zones – or free trade zones as they were known locally.
These zones became more important than in any other developing
country, accounting (in 1982) for more than half of Malaysia's total exports
of manufactured goods, and virtually all the electronic components. The
initial impetus for the first of these zones, established in Penang in 1971,
came from the state government, faced by rising unemployment following
the slow withdrawal of the island's free port status (Warr 1987: 31–2).
The promotion of manufacturing was also an important feature of the
Malaysian government's New Economic Policy. This policy was heavily
conditioned by the ethnic situation prevailing in the country. After severe
racial riots in 1969 between the majority Malays and minority Chinese,
employment creation became a major goal, but the Malay-dominated
government was also determined to increase the participation of the
Malays in business and to reduce the domination by Chinese, who represented around two-fifths of the population, but who exercised a
pre-eminent role in business. This ethnic dimension resulted in different
policies than suggested in dependency-style 'triple alliance' models, for
the government was suspicious of local Chinese business rather than
interested in forming an alliance with it (Jesudason 1989: 173–6).

These government policies influenced the strategy towards the free
trade zones. In 1971 free trade zones were established in which products
could be shipped in and out without customs duties. Goods purchased by
firms in the free trade zones from within Malaysia were treated as exports
from Malaysia. Companies were exempted from income tax for periods
of up to ten years. In addition, the government, concerned that foreign
MNEs should not strengthen local Chinese business interests, also allowed
foreign companies to have 100 per cent ownership of their subsidiaries
provided they exported their entire output, thus tacitly discouraging joint
ventures (Phongpaichit 1991: 33).

The concentration of Malaysia's electronics industry in these enclaves
and the ownership structure of industry resulted in rather low linkage
effects. Most of the intermediate products were imported from abroad.
This meant that the industry imported almost as much as it exported in
the 1980s, but it also limited the linkages with local firms, which merely
supplied basics such as cardboard boxes. The industry was also heavily
concentrated in the component sub-sector with an absence of forward
linkages from components to the manufacture of consumer and industrial
products. Part of the problem was that the government had little interest

in encouraging the local Chinese business sector to become involved in products such as television receivers and keyboards (Jesudason 1989: 174–6). Low value-added components – where Malaysian factories usually added only about 30 per cent of the value of the product – accounted for around 80 per cent of the country's electronics sector in the 1980s. Little design and R & D was undertaken in Malaysia. A shortage of graduate scientists and skilled technicians – a reflection of the local preference for studying subjects such as accountancy and business – was part of the explanation, but in contrast to Singapore, the government also provided few incentives for MNEs to upgrade their operations.

While the electronics companies provided employment on a substantial scale, the jobs created were overwhelmingly low-skilled. A cost-benefit analysis of Malaysia's export-oriented industrial enclaves concluded that they contributed to the country's economic welfare mainly through their absorption of unskilled and semi-skilled labour (Warr 1987). Around 90 per cent of the employees in Malaysia's electronics industry were female. From the beginning of operations, the electronics firms preferred to hire women between the ages of 16 and 23, who were more manually dextrous than males, and more easily disciplined. Vertical mobility within the firms was low because there were few skilled and higher level jobs available in the offshore manufacturing plants, and supervisory jobs were held by males. Employment in the electronics factories also imposed a welfare cost on the workers. The nature and pace of the work – which involved looking through a highly magnified microscope for eight hours a day – led to numerous health problems. At least in the early growth period of the industry, mass hysteria was a frequent occurrence on the late-night shifts in Malaysia (Lim 1980).

The MNEs which invested in Malaysia's electronics industry after 1970 created high employment and exports, but the linkages with the rest of the economy were weak. The nature of the industry and of the host economy were important influences on this outcome, but even more important was the framework and nature of incentives provided by the host government.

## Japanese MNEs and the US automobile industry in the 1980s

The growth of Japanese multinational manufacturing in the US automobile industry was rapid after the US government introduced a voluntary export restraint (VER) in 1981 whereby the Japanese government 'voluntarily' agreed to prevent Japanese car makers from increasing exports to the United States. Combined with increasing demand for Japanese cars in the United States, this provided a major incentive to invest in production facilities. The pioneering Japanese automobile maker was Honda, which had a relatively small domestic market share in Japan compared to Nissan and Toyota, and insufficient quota allocation under the VER. Honda had built a motorcycle products plant at Marysville, Ohio, and an automobile plant was established adjacent to this, which produced its first car in 1982. A Nissan plant followed at Smyrna, Tennessee in 1983, while Toyota entered the United States more cautiously by establishing a 50/50 joint venture with General Motors to produce cars at an old GM assembly plant at Fremont, California. This NUMMI plant, which was designed to test the feasibility of transferring the Toyota system to the United States, began production in 1984. Within a few years, by introducing new technology and the Toyota production system, it took only half of the previous workforce to assemble the same number of cars. In 1988 Toyota began production at wholly-owned plants in Kentucky and Ontario, Canada. By the early 1990s Japanese automobile companies had nine major assembly plants in the United States and three in Canada (Kenney and Florida 1993: 95–100).

The Japanese transplants virtually created a new automobile industry in the United States within the space of a decade. By 1990 the Japanese-owned factories had an annual production of 1.5 million cars. Together with imports, Japanese companies controlled around one-third of the US car market. The transplants employed 30,000 American workers, and by the early 1990s were starting to export vehicles to Japan, and other parts of Asia and Europe.

The Japanese companies had a considerable effect on their US competitors. The 'big three' US producers were turned into a 'big five', comprising GM, Ford, Chrysler, Honda and Toyota. Between 1979 and 1991 US car manufacturers reduced their workforces by between 250,000 and 300,000 jobs – partly as a result of shifting production to Mexico and offshore subsidiaries. But there was also considerable learning from the Japanese companies. Ford passed through a major crisis at the beginning of the 1980s, and then introduced many quasi-Japanese production methods over the following decade. Chrysler went through the same cycle a decade later.

The US learning process came from both the competitive challenge of the Japanese and co-operation with them. A complex web of relationships grew up between the US automobile companies and their Japanese competitiors. These gave US manufacturers smaller, fuel-efficient cars and introduced them to the Japanese-style manufacturing methods, while allowing Japanese car companies access to the American market. As early as 1969 Chrysler acquired 35 per cent of Mitsubishi Motors – a shareholding relationship that lasted until 1993 – and in 1971 GM acquired 34 per cent of Isuzu (Mason 1992a: 233–9). Subsequently, other links were formed. Ford purchased 24 per cent of the Japanese car maker Mazda in 1979, while GM secured access to Toyota's technology through the NUMMI joint venture. The US companies used these links to import Japanese models – relabelled with American names – to supplement their domestically produced models. From the 1970s Chrysler marketed a car made by Mitsubishi as one of its Dodge models, called the Colt. The links were also used to learn about Japanese production methods, though organisational rigidities sometimes hindered the transfer of ideas and practices back to the US parent (Womack, Jones and Roos 1990: 237–9).

The Japanese automobile producers transferred parts of their production system to their US factories. There was a widespread use of work teams and a very limited number of job classifications. Open plan offices and single cafeterias for all staff were in use in most cases. Quality circles and Japanese-style employee suggestion schemes were also employed, though less widely than in Japan (Kenney and Florida 1993: 102–18). The extent to which Japanese management was fully transferred remains debatable. A study by Abo concluded that only certain parts of the Japanese system had been transferred to the United States, creating a kind of 'hybrid' factory which was neither Japanese or American in its organisation. There was also a heavy reliance on Japanese expatriates in order to make things work. Abo suggested that, bearing in mind the cost of expatriates, training and expenses incurred by local sourcing of parts and resources, 'the real efficiency of auto assembly transplants, with supposedly the same quality level and with cost factors taken into account, does not exceed 60 per cent of that of the parents' (Abo 1994: 241).

Japanese suppliers followed the assemblers into the United States. By 1990 more than 300 Japanese or joint venture automotive parts suppliers had been established to supply parts to transplant automobile assemblers in the United States. This reflected the close relationship between the Japanese automobile assemblers and their tiers of suppliers, and the critical importance of reliable supplies if the just-in-time production system was to work. Many aspects of the Japanese assembler–supplier relationship were reproduced in the United States, such as the continuous exchange of information in both production and design. The reproduction of these relationships was a potential problem for US-owned suppliers, whose long-term viability was in doubt, although some traditional US automotive parts suppliers became integrated into the supplier complexes. In these cases, the assemblers have exercised a positive impact through raising standards and providing support to enable US suppliers to meet just-in-time delivery schedules (Kenney and Florida 1993: 126–54).

A widespread criticism of the Japanese automobile transplants focused on the belief that their strategy was confined to the establishment of 'screwdriver' factories which would assemble cars from kits imported from Japan, while maintaining higher value activities in Japan (Choate 1990: 149). In reality, the Japanese companies moved quickly to produce high value-added components like engines and transmissions in the United States. There were also substantial developments in R & D and design. By 1990 Japanese assembly transplants operated twenty-two R & D product engineering, and/or design facilities in the United States. The great majority were engaged in adaptive research close to production facilities, but in 1987 Honda established an R & D facility in Ohio aimed at developing R & D and engineering expertise in the United States. The goal was to produce new cars from design to production entirely in the United States (Kenney and Florida 1993: 120–3).

## Conclusions

The above case studies show the diverse impact which international business has exercised on host economies since the late nineteenth century. Despite this diversity, MNEs emerge as facilitators of the more efficient use of global resources and as powerful forces for economic development. Their role has been especially important through the transfer of factors between countries, especially intangibles such as proprietary knowledge, technology and organisation, and through facilitating trade flows. This does not mean that all outcomes were 'optimal'. There were sub-optimal outcomes to which MNE strategies, the nature of the host economy, and host government policies contributed. However it remains an open question if any feasible alternative scenario would have delivered superior results.

## SUMMARY

International business activities have never been spread evenly around the world, and there have been considerable discontinuities in its distribution. Up to the middle of the twentieth century the majority of world FDI was located in developing economies, but subsequently there was a redistribution towards developed economies. There have also been considerable continuities among host economies, especially the long-term importance of the United States and Canada. The relative importance of different host economies can be explained by the distribution of resource endowments, market size, geographical location, culture and government policies.

International business has served as an engine of growth for host economies and for the world economy in general. MNEs have been important in transferring across borders knowledge, technologies and organisations, and in facilitating trade flows. However the influence of international business on host economies has not grown in a linear fashion. The net balance of costs and benefits of inward investment has varied widely over time, between industries, and between different firms pursuing different strategies. The nature of the host economy – including the host government policy – has often been a crucial determinant of the outcome of the inward investment.

# Chapter 8

# Governments and multinationals

## POLICY AND INWARD INVESTMENT

Both the distribution of FDI between host economies and its impact upon them has been greatly influenced by the policies pursued by host governments. Policy approaches towards foreign enterprises can be categorised into three broad types – 'open', 'restrictive' and 'mixed' (Behrman and Grosse 1990: 107). Governments pursuing 'open' policies allow inward FDI in most, if not all, economic sectors; only rarely specify ownership structures; and have relatively few or no regulatory controls over foreign companies other than those imposed on national companies. The 'mixed' approach permits inward FDI, but has far more controls over the entry and behaviour of foreign companies. 'Restrictive' governments have sought to severely limit foreign business in their countries, and promote local business in its place.

The actual policies pursued by host governments have varied considerably over time. A broad categorisation into three periods is possible. In the era of the borderless world before 1930, virtually all governments in the world pursued 'open' policies. Between the 1930s and the 1970s governments became more concerned with MNEs and sought to monitor and restrict their operations. Their impact on resource transfers, trade, market structure and sovereignty made them of great interest to policy makers. Restrictions on MNEs grew virtually worldwide in these decades, and large parts of the globe were closed altogether to their operations. By the 1980s a worldwide policy shift signalled a return to a borderless world, although in practice restrictions of various kinds continued to be operated by host governments.

Although the evolution of all host government policies has followed this broad chronological pattern, policies have nonetheless varied considerably between countries. There have been strong long-term continuities in the policies pursued by different countries towards inward FDI, which have often transcended changes in political party or even in political regime. Two policy extremes have been the United Kingdom and Japan.

British governments have a sustained tradition of 'open' policies towards foreign investors, regardless of whether right or left wing parties were in power. In contrast, Japanese governments of completely different political complexions sought to limit wholly-owned FDI in their country for most of the twentieth century. Among developing economies, India in the post-colonial era consistently displayed a far greater concern than Brazil for national ownership of business assets, though the latter was very concerned about foreign ownership in certain sectors.

A number of factors help to account for such long-term differences in host policies between countries. First, there was a correlation between open policies and the extent of a country's outward FDI. The twentieth century's two largest foreign investors – the United States and the United Kingdom – have both been among the least restrictive host governments. A fundamental consideration in such cases is the danger of retaliation against a country's outward FDI if restrictive policies are pursued against other nations' companies. Conversely, countries with low outward FDI have been more often found with restrictive or mixed policy stances. This was evident in the case of Japan before the early 1970s. Japanese policy towards foreign MNEs was progressively liberalised as Japanese outward FDI became substantial.

Second, the industrial policy background provides an important explanation of differing host government policies. Governments which followed liberal, market-oriented economic policies such as the United States have generally not sought to restrict or tightly control foreign business. Governments which have had more active industrial policies such as Japan have been more inclined to seek to restrict or control foreign MNE activity to some extent, as they reduced their control over the economy.

Third, the industrial distribution of inward FDI has been a factor in host government attitudes to foreign investors. Some activities have been regarded as considerably more politically and economically sensitive than others. Foreign control over natural resources, banks and airlines provoked considerable opposition in a large number of countries as the twentieth century progressed. Inward investment in manufacturing indus-tries was, in most but not all cases, less controversial. However certain manufacturing sectors – including defence, computers and automobiles – were often seen as having implications for national security or national prestige. Inward investment in these industries sometimes aroused the concern of even governments whose general policy thrust was towards 'openness'.

Fourth, the geographical origins of inward FDI have been a factor in host government policies. In developing economies, governments were often particularly hostile to MNEs from former imperial powers. In contrast, linguistic and cultural similarities between home and host countries tended to reduce tensions. A survey of British official attitudes in the 1960s showed that senior civil servants and politicians regarded US MNEs as less 'foreign' than continental European ones (Jones 1990a: 208). In the 1970s and 1980s the prospect of substantial acquisitions of local firms by wealthy Middle Eastern oil producer interests was resisted even by open-oriented governments of Britain, the US and West Germany. In the same period United States opinion was far more alarmed by Japanese multinational investment than the much larger amount of FDI from the United Kingdom, Netherlands and other European investors.

A fifth variable influencing host government policies was the size of their economies. There was a tendency for small economies to be prominent among the followers of more 'open' government policies. This was true over the long term for a number of the smaller European economies – such as Switzerland, Belgium and the Netherlands – and, in more recent decades, the Asian city states of Singapore and Hong Kong. These countries had small national markets, a high degree of trade dependency, and little concern for power or national security guaranteed by their own abilities (Behrman and Grosse 1990: 109). In contrast, the list of the most restrictive countries in the twentieth century includes Russia, China and India.

A final influence on host government policies was the cultural and historical inheritance of the country. This was a potent force in the case of Japan. The long era of self-imposed isolation from the rest of the world during the Edo period from the seventeenth to the nineteenth century both reflected a strong resistance to foreign cultural influence, and reinforced such sentiments. Although the historical inheritance of Japan was peculiar, there were other countries whose historical, cultural or religious development resulted in a suspicion of foreign influence, including business activities. A number of Islamic countries developed a particular antipathy to Western enterprises. Conversely, countries with a long tradition of being open trading economies – such as the United Kingdom and the Netherlands – were usually less concerned about foreign participation in their economies.

MNEs were profoundly affected by changing host government policies, but were not passive recipients of them. MNEs were able to influence policy formation and they had different options in responding to policies. The actual outcome was often the result of a 'bargaining' process in which each side had particular sources of leverage. A powerful tradition in the literature has argued that MNEs were able to skew bargaining outcomes in their favour, especially in developing countries. Such a view has emphasised the large size of some MNEs vis-à-vis their host economies, and the advantage such corporations derive both from their multinationality and their access to technology, organisation skills and finance.

In practice, the balance of power between MNEs and host governments has been shown to rest on a considerable number of factors (Fague and Wells 1982; Doner 1991: 6–22). The more valuable and unique the firm-specific assets possessed by the MNE – such as technology and management skills – the more leverage it has to challenge or modify government policies. A host government's leverage is a function of its possession of resources required by the MNE, such as a large domestic market or natural resources; the degree of competition between different MNEs for access to these resources; and the host country's ability to develop resources capable of substituting for those controlled by foreign MNEs. In low technology extractive industries, a foreign MNE's power is often greatest at the beginning of a project, when its capital and technology is badly needed. Over time, the foreign firm's investment is sunk and knowledge about its techniques has spread, providing more leverage to the host government. Vernon termed this the 'obsolescing bargain' process (Vernon 1971). In industries with rapidly changing technologies, host governments may gain little additional leverage over time. In import-substituting manufacturing industries, the host government can use the promise of access to the local market as a bargaining advantage. The foreign investor is, therefore, weakest at the point of entry. Once manufacturing firms are established, networks of suppliers, distributors, joint-venture partners and consumers can provide a tacit political base of support for MNEs (Haggard 1989: 192).

The balance of power between host governments and foreign firms is considerably influenced by the domestic politics of policy formation towards MNEs. Factors to be considered here range from the political significance of specific industries to the ability of governments to pursue coherent policies, which might be undermined by divisions of opinion or by corruption. Few governments have ever had *one* policy towards MNEs: different parts of any single government have different approaches. The role of indigenous business groups in shaping host policies has been extremely significant. These groups may closely co-operate with MNEs and help influence host governments in their favour; or they may strongly resist foreign companies and encourage their government to restrict their activities (Moran 1993: 7–8).

A further major influence on the bargaining strengths of host governments and foreign firms was the role of home governments. Their influence was particularly important in developing economies, whose ability to challenge MNEs owned by powerful Western nations was greatly circumscribed for much of this century by the threat of home country retaliation.

The following sections examine the evolution of host government policies and MNE responses in developed economies; in Japan; in developing economies; and in India, Brazil and Singapore.

# GOVERNMENT AND MNEs IN DEVELOPED ECONOMIES

## The borderless world

In retrospect, the most striking aspect of host government policies in Western Europe, the United States and Canada in the nineteenth century was their lack of controls over foreign-owned concerns. There were few barriers to their entry by either greenfield investment or acquisition; virtually no controls over the behaviour of foreign firms; and only selected cases of official discrimination in favour of locally-owned firms against foreign firms. As Wilkins has observed in the case of the United States, despite considerable anti-foreign rhetoric at times and a variety of regulations, 'the easy flow of capital from abroad into America is what stands out rather than the impediments' (Wilkins 1989: 607). This openness to MNEs reflected the laissez-faire economic policies in operation in the nineteenth century. Governments intervened in their economies in various ways, including trade protectionism, but the scale of intervention was minimal compared to the twentieth century.

The main constraint on open policies came from restrictions over a limited number of activities regarded as key or sensitive for some reason. In the United States, foreign control over the banking system was regarded as highly sensitive. Banks operated under either federal – 'national' – or state regulation, and in both cases there were considerable restrictions on foreign bank activity. At federal level, the National Bank Act of 1864 restricted national banks from branching and specified that bank directors had to be US citizens resident in the area in which the bank did business. Foreign banks were also subject to state regulations, and these became more restrictive over the course of the late nineteenth century. New York state laws prevented foreign banks from receiving deposits or issuing bank notes. In California, foreign banks played a significant role in the development of that state's banking and finance in the second half of the nineteenth century, but subsequently state regulation became more restrictive. By 1914 Illinois was almost unique among states in permitting banks from other countries to operate. From the late nineteenth century US state goverments introduced wide-ranging restrictions on foreign participation in insurance companies and mortgage lenders. There were also federal and state laws attempting to restrict foreign land ownership. Foreign investors were also barred from coastal shipping on national security grounds (Wilkins 1989: 454–69; 578–85).

During the 1920s the United States introduced further restrictions on foreign ownership in a number of sectors, including shipping, banking and petroleum. In 1920 the Mineral Leasing Law was passed, which excluded from leases of public land the citizens of any country whose laws, regulations or customs similarly denied such privileges to US citizens or corporations. This was used to threaten European governments which blocked US entry to oilfields in their colonies, and was used by the Americans to secure access for their companies to the Dutch East Indies (Venn 1986: 67).

Western European policies were more open towards foreign MNEs than those of the United States. In Britain, Germany and elsewhere there were flurries of alarm about the scale of US penetration of domestic industry but no restrictive controls were exercised over foreign ownership in any sector. In contrast to the American preference to restrict foreign entry to certain key activities, the Western European tendency to encourage national champions was already in evidence before 1914. The British government's investment in the Anglo-Persian Oil Company in 1914 – which effectively became the world's first state oil company – was an early example (see p. 67). The European 'national champions' strategy was reinforced by the nationalistic sentiments generated by the First World War. The sequestrated subsidiaries of German MNEs were sold to local firms with the specific intention of strengthening indigenous enterprise in sectors such as chemicals, electricals and petroleum. During the 1920s several European national champions were promoted. The British government's encouragement of the creation of Imperial Chemical Industries in 1926 was motivated by the desire for a major indigenous chemicals company able to compete with the Americans and Germany (Reader 1970: Chapter 19). In the oil industry, France, Italy and Spain were among the countries which established national oil companies.

During the 1920s the question of the national ownership of business assets was far more of an issue than previously in Europe, although actual restrictions remained limited. In Germany in the 1920s there was considerable discussion about foreign influence over German business, though this did not translate into policy, as was evidenced in 1929 by General Motors' acquisition of Opel, Germany's leading automobile manufacturer, and GE's purchase of almost one-third of the equity of AEG (Feldman 1989: 87–107). Similarly in Britain alarm about the growth of US FDI did not lead to a more restrictionist policy, though government had a list of industries which it did not want to see pass under foreign control. These included finance and defence-related industries, as well as certain important overseas investments, including British-controlled Latin American railroads and South African gold-fields. British regulations were opaque and were never translated into law, though the barriers to foreign entry were real (Jones 1990a: 197–8).

## The growth of restrictions

During the 1930s the spread of exchange controls, the creation of regional currency blocks, and the growth of economic nationalism throughout

Europe represented a major deterioration in the policy environment for MNEs, even if the policies were not specifically designed to affect them. In some countries, governments began to openly discriminate against foreign companies. In a study of the automobile industry, Reich has argued that the Nazi regime favoured the growth of Volkswagen while stifling the development of Ford's German subsidiary, Fordwerke (Reich 1990).

Yet the most striking feature of European host government policies in the 1930s was their continued openness. Even the rabidly nationalistic fascist dictatorships of the period were able to co-exist with the foreign-owned businesses in their midst, a process made easier by the willingness of most MNEs to co-exist with the fascist dictators. In anti-semitic Nazi Germany, for example, there was initially government abuse of the 'Jewish' nature of US enterprises, but most of the companies readily signed statements that they were not under 'Jewish', 'foreign' or 'Marxist' control. United States companies often welcomed the absence of labour problems in Nazi Germany, and some US business leaders – such as Thomas J. Watson, president of IBM – developed a close relationship with Nazi leaders (Wilkins 1974a: 186–8).

Even during the Second World War governments allowed foreign-owned companies considerable freedom of manoeuvre. An example was the German subsidiary of the Norton Company, the US manufacturer of bonded abrasives – important elements of machine tool and mass production manufacture. This company generally co-operated with the industrial policy of the Nazi regime, but was able to blunt any hostility to it by appointing German nationals to the senior management. This management used the political processes of the state to protect the Norton company's interests even after the United States entered the war against Germany, and also strove to protect the Norton subsidiary in occupied France. At various times, the Norton subsidiary's policies on location, finance and production ran counter to the Nazi state's interests (Cheape 1988).

After the Second World War Western European policies towards MNEs were located on a spectrum between 'open' and 'mixed'. There were also some important differences between countries in their policies. In France, the United Kingdom and a number of other European countries, the nationalisation of large parts of industry in the late 1940s closed those sectors to foreign MNEs. In these sectors, policies became far more restrictive than in the United States. In postwar Italy two large state-owned holding companies, IRI and ENI (which included the national oil company AGIP) controlled a range of enterprises engaged in public utilities, energy and manufacturing, providing state-subsidised competition for any MNE that wanted to operate in these sectors. Many governments used exchange controls to 'screen' inward FDI, usually to regulate its balance of payments effects. The British and others used such foreign exchange controls to encourage foreign companies to locate factories in regions of high unemployment (Jones 1990a: 199–203; Gillespie 1972). Some inward investments were blocked by such 'screening', though the actual number was not great.

It was also common for particularly sensitive economic activities to be closed to foreign investors. Foreign ownership of natural resources was widely restricted. During the late 1940s and early 1950s the fascist Spanish government put a high priority on the removal of British control over its mining resources. Rio Tinto's long-standing operations in Spain were termed the country's 'economic Gibraltar' (Mendoza 1994).

Despite exchange controls, screening and the nationalisation of parts of their economies, the general European policy stance towards inward FDI for the two decades after the end of the Second World War remained open. During the 1960s a shift to more restrictionist policies in Europe was combined with a renewed emphasis on the promotion of national champions. These trends were strongly evident in France, whose governments pursued active industrial policies and were especially sensitive to becoming too dependent on foreign – especially American – technology. A number of factors triggered a policy change in France which was particularly focused on suspicion of US MNEs. One was the announcement of substantial redundancies by US-owned subsidiaries in France without prior consultation with the government, which was the conventional practice in France at that time. There was also growing alarm at foreign control over France's high technology sectors, which was crystallised by a bid by GE to take over Machines Bull, France's largest computer firm. During 1965 the French government virtually banned all foreign takeovers of French firms, and for a time blocked all applications for approval of new investments (Gillespie 1972: 403–9).

The policies which emerged from this immediate crisis in France involved a careful screening of applications of foreign investors and a more frequent rejection of proposed investments. The method of rejecting proposed investments was generally that of prolonged delay in acting upon the applications. When foreign takeovers of French firms were proposed, delays were used by the authorities to try to find French purchasers instead. At the same time a number of key sectors were explicitly protected from foreign ownership: these included the defence and armament industries, agricultural land, road and maritime transport, aircraft manufacture, insurance and publishing. Although these policies were at least ostensibly designed to restrict US activity in France, through the 1970s France also sought to restrict takeover activity by firms from other EU countries. It was not until 1980 that France agreed to relax the rules on acquisitions from elsewhere in the EU (Safarian 1993: 208–20).

A particular concern of French policy from the mid-1960s was the preservation of French ownership in those industries in which the most rapid technological change was taking place, such as electronics and computers. Together with the other industries with a high strategic signif-icance, such as aerospace and nuclear power, these sectors came to be regarded by the French as too vital to be left in the hands of foreigners. French national champions were promoted as a result.

Even in the 1960s French policies towards foreign MNEs were not uniformly anti-foreign or anti-American. There was a continued recognition of the technological advantages offered by MNEs. Moreover, it was recog-nised that French policy was constrained by membership of the EU: a foreign investor barred from France could build a plant in another member country, and have unrestricted access to the French market. The importance attached to the need to attract foreign technology to France led the government to acquiesce in takeovers of firms which were held to have let themselves be technologically outpaced by their foreign competitors. There was even a preference for US firms as inward investors rather than those from elsewhere in Europe, as they were believed to possess more autonomy in the areas of purchasing and exports (Caron 1984).

The 1960s also saw a shift in policy towards foreign MNEs in the United Kingdom. The impetus came from the ever-rising volume of inward FDI in that country, as well as the existence of a socialist government between 1964 and 1970. British policy remained open in its general orientation, but this period saw stronger emphasis on negotiation with inward investors, with new governments seeking 'assurances' from foreign MNEs about aspects of their performance, especially concerning employment, capital investment and exports. This policy proved ineffective, both because of a failure to monitor whether firms lived up to their performance requirements, and because governments were never prepared to take real coercive measures against companies which reneged on their 'assurances' (Jones 1990a: 206–7).

The British government also actively sought to promote national champions in selected strategic industries. In 1968 it encouraged the merger of two major British-owned vehicle producers to form the British Leyland Motor Corporation (later known as Rover), which on its forma-tion produced a half of all cars made in Britain. The virtual bankruptcy of this company by 1975 was followed by its nationalisation, and the granting of large subsidies in what proved to be the forlorn hope of creating a viable British-owned car manufacturer (Church 1994: 99–103). In 1968 the government also encouraged a merger of British firms to form a national champion in the computer industry, ICL, and acquired just over 10 per cent of the equity of the enterprise (Campbell-Kelly 1989: 245–64). Subsequently ICL was given government support for its R & D, and some preference in purchases of computers for the central government. British national champion policy was generally characterised by an unwillingness to extend discriminatory support against the British subsidiaries of foreign firms, and this may have undermined the viability of the entire strategy (Wilks 1990). By the 1990s all the British national champions of the 1960s had passed under foreign control.

Compared to France and even the United Kingdom, West German government policies towards inward investment remained very open. There was no authorisation or screening of firms on entry, or of foreign takeovers, except in so far as they affected German antitrust policies, which were the most stringent in Europe after 1945. These laws were not aimed at foreign investors but, as in the United States, their operation sometimes impeded foreign acquisitions. A particular area of government intervention was in the petroleum industry, in which Germany possessed a number of medium-sized firms. In the late 1960s the government objected to foreign takeovers of German petroleum companies on two occasions, and on one occasion successfully found a German buyer (Gillespie 1972: 415–16). During the 1970s the German government became concerned that the governments of OPEC countries might use their new oil wealth to buy up some sectors of German industry. Iran's acquisition of 25 per cent of Krupp, and the government of Kuwait's purchase of a 14 per cent interest in Daimler-Benz, led to measures to restrict such investments. Banks and major companies were asked to report to the government any impending sales of companies or large blocks of shares to foreigners, especially OPEC governments, and in a few cases the government encouraged German investors to buy equity being offered for sale (Safarian 1993: 326).

The United States remained the most open of the major developed host economies. In the postwar period there were no limits on percentage ownership by foreign firms, nor on methods of market entry such as acquisition or joint venture. US regulations on foreign firms were virtually identical to the rules facing domestic US firms. There were, however, a significant number of sectors where federal or state laws limited or restricted foreign investment.

The major federal restrictions on inward investment were concentrated in 'strategic' sectors where foreign ownership was barred or limited. These included, by this period, coastal shipping, radio and television broadcasting, and the operation of nuclear power facilities. The Federal Aviation Act of 1958 restricted air transportation within the United States to domestically controlled firms. The most important restriction was on FDI in the defence sector. Foreign-controlled firms were not eligible for the facility security clearance required to bid on US defence contracts, except under special arrangements. The US definition of foreign control went beyond ownership to include a wider definition of 'influence', including licensing agreements. These restrictions were a real deterrent to foreign acquisitions of US firms with defence interests. Given the enormous size of US defence spending during the Cold War, this represented a considerable limitation on international business activity (Safarian 1993: 385–89).

There were also a wide range of restrictions at state level in the United States. There were considerable, but varied, restrictions on foreign companies in banking and insurance, and limitations on land use and ownership. Virtually all states had special arrangements for out-of-state and out-of country corporations or persons, including both other US and foreign ones. There were sometimes preferences to local corporations in public purchasing, and some states discriminated against foreign-owned firms in their public procurement (Safarian 1993: 389–91).

Foreign firms investing in the United States also encountered difficulties because of certain idiosyncratic features of US law, especially antitrust legislation. A particular peculiarity of the United States was the ability of domestic firms threatened by foreign predators to use litigation – or else direct appeals to federal or state agencies – to create lengthy delays and problems for the foreign investors (Safarian 1993: 392).

During the 1970s a more restrictive tone became apparent in US policy, coinciding with the rapid growth of inward FDI into that country. Particular concern about investments from OPEC countries led to the Committee on Foreign Investment in the United States being established in 1975 within the executive branch. This committee had responsibility for monitoring the impact of both portfolio and direct investment in the United States, though it primarily focused on the latter. In 1978 the federal International Banking Act removed some of the advantages allegedly held by foreign banks over local banks in the United States, especially in the area of inter-state banking. Yet despite growing concern about foreign ownership of US business, the number of actual restrictions remained modest. During the late 1970s the Committee on Foreign Investment encouraged the retention of open policies rather than the reverse, opposing the restriction of foreign investment in energy resources and farmland.

### Liberalisation

From the early 1980s policies to restrict or monitor inward FDI were greatly modified or abolished altogether. The new policy emphasis became more to attract MNEs than to restrict them. There were a number of factors behind this policy shift.

One influence was the globalisation of the capital and money markets. The accelerating pace of innovation in financial instruments in the Euromarkets progressively undermined national controls over banking and financial systems, and over the ability of governments to influence the borrowing and other financial strategies of MNEs. The web of controls over the movement of capital which had grown up in the world economy since the 1920s was fatally undermined.

A second influence towards greater policy liberalisation was the relative failure of many of the restrictive measures taken in the 1960s and 1970s. Governments were unable to monitor MNE behaviour effectively. The European national champion strategy resulted in a record of costly failures in subsidising indigenous firms, while successful national champion firms exhibited a tendency to behave like their international competitors, exporting production to low wage countries, for example (Moran 1993: 11).

A third influence towards more liberal policies was the re-emergence of market-oriented economic policies in the developed world. There were several dimensions to this change including the reaction against Keynesian demand management in favour of monetarist economic policies concerned with the control of inflation, and the election of right wing governments in the United States, Britain and elsewhere. In Britain, the election of the Thatcher government in 1979 was followed by the suspension of exchange controls, the progressive privatisation of the state-owned sector, and the effective abandonment of the national champion strategy. These developments marked the opening stages of the new age of global economic liberalism which was to be the driving force of world economic policy in the 1980s and 1990s.

A fourth major influence towards liberalisation was the growth of unemployment in the developed world. The end of the era of fast economic growth in 1973, the oil shocks of 1973–4 and 1979–81 and the policy reactions to them, technological change and global restructuring combined to raise unemployment rates. The rise in average unemployment in OECD countries from 3.3 per cent in 1973 to 8.6 per cent a decade later changed the policy perception of foreign MNEs. Fears of technological – or even cultural – dependence subsided as the role of MNEs as providers of jobs was emphasised.

From the 1980s the numbers of sectors and activities restricted from foreign MNEs declined. The manufacturing sectors of virtually all developed countries became fully open to FDI, and restrictions on many services began to be lifted. Although the types of industry still restricted varied from country to country, they were mostly concerned with natural resources and certain types of service, especially telecommunications, transportation and media activities. In most developed countries, residual restrictions on transfers of profits and dividends were also abolished. An important element in this process was regional integration. In the European Union in particular, the Single Market programme was designed in part to facilitate regional integration by European MNEs by harmonising national legislation and removing regulatory barriers to trade and factor flows.

Paradoxically, it was the traditionally open United States which saw a growth of restrictive legislation. A number of measures gave the President powers to retaliate against the alleged restrictive FDI policies of other countries and to block takeovers of US firms by foreign interests. The Exon-Florio amendment to the Defence Production Act of 1988 gave the President authority to suspend or prohibit an acquisition by foreign investors of a US firm engaged in inter-state commerce if there was a threat to national security (Safarian 1993: 383–5). These policies formed part of wider US government initiatives to remove worldwide barriers to trade in goods, services and investment, but their practical effect remained small, although not insignificant. Foreign companies faced discrimination in participation in federally funded programmes such as Sematech, a semiconductor research consortium. And at state level, foreign companies encountered a range of takeover barriers, preferential procurement policies and employment creation targets.

The attraction of inward investment became a major policy concern. A number of European countries and regions, particularly ones with high unemployment, had a history of such policies. During the 1950s and 1960s the Republic of Ireland developed an extensive range of incentives for new industries and removed almost all restrictions on foreign ownership of industry. From the 1970s the strategies of European governments to attract foreign MNEs became more organised. In West Germany, France and Britain central government and regional agencies became active in offering incentives to inward FDI. These strategies to attract inward FDI intensified in the following decade, and spread to Canada and to many states of the United States. The most prominent incentives included tax concessions and a broad range of financial incentives, particularly in the form of subsidised sites and other infrastructure facilitation.

In the 1990s governments saw MNEs not as a problem to be 'controlled', but as an opportunity to enhance national competitiveness in a global economy. They competed to attract MNEs not only by providing financial incentives, but also by helping to shape an environment to which MNEs would be attracted to perform desirable value-added activities. The competition between countries in offering financial and other incentives carried considerable potential dangers. In some cases, the overall cost of attracting inward investment projects was extremely high, and there was a risk of major distortions to investment flows.

## JAPAN AND THE MNEs

The low level of inward investment into Japan throughout the twentieth century made that country a special case in the history of international business. Japanese host government policies have been generally given as the primary explanation for this phenomenon (Behrman and Grosse 1990: 157). However this oversimplifies the situation, both because there were significant policy changes over time, and also because there were other influences behind the low level of inward FDI into Japan.

There are also complex issues concerning the motivation behind Japanese policy. The general thrust of most of the literature has been to argue that Japanese governments pursued a long-term 'strategic investment policy' designed to minimise foreign business influence in their country. This is also probably an oversimplification. Mason suggests that domestic Japanese business was highly influential in shaping foreign investment policies. When American firms attempted to undertake or maintain investments in industries in which Japanese firms were already powerful, domestic companies were able to influence the government to block or impede the unwanted foreign investors. However in industries in which Japanese interests did not hold powerful positions, they had much less or no influence over government investment policy. It was in these areas that the exceptional cases of foreign companies with substantial successful operations in Japan were to be found (Mason 1992a).

## Policy before 1930

Between the 1850s – when Japan was obliged to end its isolation – and 1899 foreigners were allowed to operate in the country only within designated port areas, known to contemporaries as the 'Treaty Settlements', where westerners held extraterritorial rights. British and other foreign trading companies, shipping agents and banks established branches in these 'Treaty Settlements', and for a time these institutions occupied an important place in the movement and finance of Japan's foreign trade (Allen and Donnithorne 1954). The Japanese government moved rather quickly to promote or support domestic institutions to challenge these foreign enterprises. The government played a supportive role in the foundation and development of Mitsui Bussan. In 1880 it sponsored the creation of the Yokohama Specie Bank, and five years later it sponsored an alliance of shipping concerns under Mitsubishi's control to create Nippon Yusen Kaisha, which was then heavily subsidised. By the end of the nineteenth century, these Japanese-owned businesses were well-advanced in replacing their foreign rivals.

Inward FDI into Japan was permitted in 1899 and between then and 1930 Japanese government policies were comparatively liberal. The public policy priority was the rapid modernisation of the Japanese economy. It was recognised that this required foreign technology and foreign capital, and governments were even prepared to encourage inward FDI in order to achieve these goals. However policy can be best described as mixed rather than open. Governments encouraged foreign companies with desirable technologies to form joint ventures with Japanese enterprises. Except where the transfer of technology made FDI a necessity, there was an official preference for portfolio rather than direct investment. In 1900 the government established the Industrial Bank of Japan principally to channel investment capital from foreign to Japanese entrepreneurs on a portfolio rather than a direct basis. The government effectively prohibited inward FDI in public utilities, shipping, financial services, mining, dyestuffs and some other activities. Potential foreign investment in railroads was discouraged by the nationalisation of major private railroad companies in 1906 (Mason 1992a: 24–5).

Foreign involvement in other sectors was closely monitored and sometimes curbed by the government. In 1899 American Tobacco acquired 60 per cent of the largest Japanese privately owned cigarette company, Murai Brothers. This subsequently came under the control of the newly founded BAT. Subsequently a violent nationalistic campaign against Murai Brothers led to a government decision in 1904 to expropriate every existing private cigarette firm, including Murai. Thereafter a government monopoly directly imported tobacco from the United States, and controlled the industry in Japan (Cochran 1980: 40–1).

During these decades foreign MNEs were important transferors of technological and organisation skills to Japan (see pp. 237–9). The influence of public policy was not to block FDI absolutely, but to influence the organisational form it took and the industry in which it was located. However the main reason for the low level of inward FDI was probably the underdeveloped nature of the economy at that time. The East Asian market, including Japan, was not a major concern in the global strategy of MNEs before the Second World War (Udagawa 1990: 26).

## 1930s – 1970s

A radical shift occurred in Japanese host government policies in the early 1930s. The trigger was the 'Manchurian Incident' in 1931 which was followed by the Japanese army's conquest of Manchuria from China. The subsequent years saw increasing army influence in Japan, and further territorial expansion leading to the full-scale attack on China in 1937. In this highly nationalistic political atmosphere, foreign companies were increasingly unwelcome. Japanese firms were also very active in pressing the authorities to increase their controls over foreign affiliates (Li 1990: 227–36). Following the Manchurian Incident and into the Second World War, Japanese host policies fell into the 'restrictive' category. Outside the special case of the Soviet Union, Japanese policies emerged as the most antagonistic in the world to inward FDI (Udagawa 1990: 27).

Japanese policies against foreign MNEs in the 1930s had a number of dimensions. There were laws designed to limit foreign ownership in strategic industries such as petroleum, automobiles, machine tools and aircraft manufacturing. In petroleum, the government took powers to allocate oil production and sales. The two foreign companies which had controlled more than 50 per cent of the gasoline market, Standard-Vacuum Oil and Shell, were allocated progressively less than their actual market shares. In automobiles, the once dominant subsidiaries of Ford and General Motors were subjected to such discrimination that they had to divest. To these industry-specific controls on foreign companies were added exchange and import controls used systematically to limit the operations of foreign companies. The imports of foreign-owned firms were strictly controlled so it was impossible for them to replace machine parts or even import items such as telephones (Mason 1992a).

During the 1940s Japan became even more closed to foreign companies. As in the United States and elsewhere, corporate assets sequestrated during the war were transferred to their leading Japanese competitors. After Japan's surrender in 1945, the allied occupation authorities sought to temporarily restrict the re-entry of foreign companies which, it was feared, might complicate the economic recovery programme. It was only in 1949 that inward FDI was again permitted. Although Japan was still under allied occupation, the approval of the Japanese authorities was required before new investment proposals were allowed. In this regulatory environment, and given the unstable and unattractive macro-economic conditions prevailing in postwar Japan, only a few foreign firms re-established operations. The major exceptions were the oil companies, which were able to offer guaranteed supplies of petroleum in return for FDI. IBM also re-established a wholly-owned subsidiary in Japan, though it was subjected to various restrictions (Mason 1992a: 101–49).

Japanese government policies towards inward FDI were highly restrictive in the 1950s and 1960s. The key legislation was the Foreign Investment Law of 1950, which regulated the acquisition by foreign investors of corporate stocks and proprietary interests in Japan. The Foreign Investment Deliberation Council determined whether an individual investment proposal was to be permitted. This consulted widely with government departments and with those Japanese enterprises most directly affected by the foreign application. The result was a lengthy procedure in which the potential competitors of the proposed foreign investors had a considerable influence on the final outcome. The frequent outcome was pressure on foreign investors to abandon their FDI strategies, and license their technology to Japanese companies; if the foreign investor refused to license, then a joint venture with a Japanese firm was proposed. Mason describes this regulatory procedure as a 'Screen Door', designed to discourage most FDI inflows, while encouraging inflows of foreign technology (Mason 1992a: 151).

Foreign companies not approved under the Foreign Investment Law were subject to the Foreign Exchange Control Law promulgated in 1949. This made virtually every international transaction subject to official approval. The government could block the transfer of capital, technology, and other assets from an overseas parent to local subsidiaries, as well as the remittance of all payments from subsidiaries to parents (Mason 1992a: 159–61).

These regulations meant that foreign MNEs determined either to undertake FDI in Japan or expand their business usually had to engage in lengthy negotiations with the Japanese government and frequently with their Japanese competitors as well. The classic example was IBM, which applied in 1956 for permission under the Foreign Investment Law to import the technology and other assets necessary to manufacture electronic computers at its existing subsidiary, and to remit earnings from this activity. IBM was advised by the government that it should form a 49 per cent owned joint venture with a Japanese company, and that it should license to local competitors some of its most basic computer patents. It was only in 1960, after IBM had threatened to abandon any plan to manufacture in Japan, that IBM was finally given the permission it required, and given temporary validation under the Foreign Investment law. In return the US company had to license its basic computer patents to Japanese companies, including all seven major domestic computer manufacturers (Mason 1992a: 187–91).

The restrictions on inward FDI were matched by government promotion of local companies, but this took forms other than the national champion strategy favoured in Europe. In computers, the government did not choose a single firm to favour as a competitor to IBM, but rather created the conditions in which Japanese-owned firms in general were favoured. Thus the IBM technology was licensed to many firms. Then, in the 1960s, government ministries and government-owned companies were required to buy domestically produced computers. Low interest loans were given to a leasing company established by the government which purchased machines from manufacturers and placed them in industry. These measures seeded the whole market for computers and encouraged Japanese-owned firms within it, but left individual firms to compete vigorously. The result was the creation of an internationally competitive industry (Usselman 1993: 23–7).

In retrospect, Japan was fortunate that on the several occasions when the government attempted to pursue national champion strategies, these attempts failed either due to the complexities of decision-making within the Japanese bureaucracy, or because of opposition from Japanese firms. There were failed attempts to create a single national automobile company in the 1950s. Similarly, government attempts in the 1960s to create a national oil champion out of Japan's highly fragmented petroleum industry were unsuccessful, despite a widespread view that the dominance of foreign oil companies needed to be reduced (Samuels 1987: 186–220).

Though the extent of Japanese government restrictions over inward FDI in the 1950s and 1960s cannot be contested, the degree to which they were solely responsible for low inward FDI can be debated. It was not until the late 1950s that high economic growth rates began to make Japan's economic prospects look truly attractive. There were a variety of other factors which made direct investment in Japan look more risky than, say, in Europe: these ranged from language and cultural factors through to the role of business groups. As Mason notes, there were US MNEs which preferred to license or avoid the Japanese market (Mason 1992a: 196; Abeggelen and Stalk 1985: 217).

There was a real problem that many Western MNEs were unprepared to adapt to the many peculiarities of the Japanese market, and used bureaucratic obstacles as an excuse to avoid the country. The problems of operating in Japan ranged from minor inconveniences, such as the complex national language which took Western people a long time to master, to major obstacles, such as the costly and inefficient distribution arrangements and the enterprise group system. When Japanese MNEs made major investments in Europe and the United States from the 1970s, they displayed a far greater willingness to adapt to the peculiarities of these foreign markets. This was evidenced in a range of things, from the readiness of Japanese expatriate staff to communicate in the language of the host economy, to the willingness of Japanese firms to engage in the time-honoured practice of lobbying in Washington.

## Liberalisation

Japanese host government policies towards foreign MNEs began a slow process of liberalisation in the late 1960s. The first stage of the capital liberalisation programme took effect in 1967. The initial measures provided for automatic government approval for up to 100 per cent FDI to establish new corporations in a number of industries, and for up to 50 per cent FDI in additional industries. The first industries selected for liberalisation included ones like soy sauce where substantial inward FDI was unlikely. From the early 1970s the range of industries in which automatic approval was given was extended. In 1980 the Foreign Investment Law was abolished (Mason 1992a: 199–209; Encarnation 1992: 66–80). But into the 1980s and later government restrictions on foreign firms were considerable in financial services, and they were excluded altogether from other industries such as mining, leather and leather products and agriculture. Until 1990 hostile takeover bids of Japanese companies were rendered difficult by laws requiring prior notification, which gave the firms time to defend themselves from unwanted attention.

By the 1990s Japan had effectively an 'open' policy regime regarding inward FDI. Yet even as official barriers to inward investment were dismantled, other factors continued to keep the actual level of foreign MNE activity in Japan low. As a result, attention switched from the role of government to other obstacles to foreign MNE entry into Japan, especially the nature of the enterprise group system and the difficulties in acquiring Japanese firms given the system of cross-shareholding (Lawrence 1992). It remains a moot point, however, if the real handicap faced by US and European MNEs in Japan was their unwillingness to adapt to the Japanese business climate.

## MNEs AND GOVERNMENTS IN DEVELOPING ECONOMIES

### The open economies

There were few restrictions on MNEs in the developing world before the interwar years. The colonial governments which controlled much of Asia and Africa generally followed the same open policies towards inward FDI as their home governments. The colonies provided firms from the imperial countries with a low-risk business environment managed by government officials of their own nationality. In some instances colonial governments discriminated against the firms of other nationalities. This was most evident in a number of 'key' sectors, notably oil. In the 1900s Standard Oil found its attempt to obtain oil concessions in both the Dutch East Indies and British-controlled Burma blocked by their colonial governments (Reed 1958; Wilkins 1970: 84; Jones 1979). It became British policy to exclude non-British companies from oil exploration and production throughout the British Empire (Jones 1981: 106–8). As the Empire contained no major oilfields, this policy was of little significance until it was extended after the First World War to regions of the Middle East under British political influence. In general the US oil companies, supported by the State Department, were able to force entry, primarily because the British government put a greater emphasis on overall good relationships with the United States than on maintaining the Middle East as a preserve of British oil companies (Venn 1986: 54–72). There were major tensions at the end of the 1920s when the British sought to block US companies from securing concessions in the British 'protected' Gulf sheikhdoms of Bahrain and Kuwait, both suspected of possessing rich oil resources, but eventually US oil companies were able to gain entry. Standard Oil of California secured a concession in Bahrain by forming a Canadian subsidiary, which was regarded as 'British', while Gulf Oil formed a 50/50 joint venture in Kuwait with the Anglo-Persian Oil Company (Wilkins 1974a: 120, 213–4; Ferrier 1982: 561–70).

The oil industry was an atypical case, and colonial governments in general did not restrict inward FDI from other countries. There were US manufacturing and distribution investments in India and other parts of the British Empire which entered and operated without restriction (Wilkins 1970, 1974a). Swedish Match established a multi-plant business in India which, by 1932, accounted for half of all Indian match production (Modig 1979). The UK's Lever Brothers was able to secure and operate its enormous concession in the Belgian Congo with few restrictions. A Belgian-registered, but wholly-owned, subsidiary was formed to operate the concession, but ultimate decision-making in Huileries du Congo Belge lay in London. In addition, it was specified that half the company's European employees were to be of Belgian nationality and that its ships were to be Belgian-registered (Wilson 1954, I: 165–79; Fieldhouse 1978: 494–507).

Countries which remained outside Western imperial control – notably Latin America, but also China and Thailand in Asia and Iran in the Middle East – retained greater autonomy in dealing with foreign companies. Yet their acceptance of international property law, their perceived need for foreign entrepreneurship and technology, the weaknesses of state structures, and the diplomatic and military importance of Europe and the United States, seldom left their governments much room for manoeuvre.

There were few restrictions on inward FDI in Latin America during the second half of the nineteenth century. There was a widespread belief in liberal economic policies, including free trade, and a strong conviction that economic modernisation would be facilitated by foreign business (Abel and Lewis 1985: 179). In so far as government restrictions against FDI existed, they were largely found in the financial sector. In Argentina between the mid-1880s and the mid-1890s, there was an attempt to develop a state-owned venture as a quasi state or development bank, and to subject the British banks to taxation. This strategy faltered when it and other local banks collapsed during the Baring Crisis of 1890, and from the mid-1890s there were few government attempts to restrict the activities of the British banks. Elsewhere in Latin America, resentment of foreign banks did not lead to regulatory action, although the British bank in Uruguay was obliged to give up its private note issue in 1904 (Jones 1993a: 107).

## Restrictions and confrontation

The interwar years witnessed a trend away from the former open policy regimes in the sovereign developing countries. Restrictions on inward FDI were industry and region-specific: petroleum was the industry most affected, while hostility to foreign investment was greatest in countries of the Middle East and Latin America.

The nationalisation of the Russian oil industry following the Russian Revolution in 1917 was the first significant act of expropriation of FDI in the petroleum industry's history. The next major host government/ oil company conflict came in Iran with the cancellation and subsequent renegotiation of the Anglo-Persian Oil Company's concession in 1932 (see p. 257).

In Latin America there was also a rise in hostility towards foreign oil companies. During the 1930s many governments directly entered the oil business in competition with existing foreign oil companies, and sometimes at their expense. In Argentina, a state oil company – YPF – had co-existed with foreign companies since 1907, but in the mid-1930s the government reserved for YPF the areas most likely to have petroleum deposits. Subsequently the government forbade both oil imports and exports, and placed oil distribution under strict government regulation. In Venezuela, which had been a haven for foreign oil companies until the death of the dictator Gómez in 1935, legislation from the mid-1930s obliged the companies to provide a wide range of social benefits for their workers, and in 1938 a new law authorised the Venezuelan government to enter the oil industry (Wilkins 1974a: 221–4).

In 1937 Latin American policies towards foreign oil companies took a new turn when the Bolivian government expropriated Jersey Standard's properties in that country. The US company had found oil in Bolivia in the 1920s, but relations with the government had deteriorated at the end of the decade, when Jersey had cut production and stopped exporting in response to an increase in tax rates and the lack of a cheap means of oil transportation. The most noted Latin American nationalisation occurred a year later in 1938, in Mexico. There had been continuing tension between the foreign oil companies and the Mexican government since the adoption of the 1917 constitution, which had vested direct ownership of all subsoil rights in the Mexican nation. A serious area of contention was the Mexican insistence that foreign oil companies obey Mexican labour laws. Finally, in 1938 the government expropriated most of the foreign oil industry, which included large stakes held by Shell and Jersey Standard (Wilkins 1974a: 225–9; Venn 1986: 76–8). This assertion of national sovereignty over natural resources was of enormous significance, as was the fact that the Mexicans succeeded in their goals without retaliation from Western governments, thanks in part to the fortuitous outbreak of the Second World War.

These specific measures against oil companies formed part of wider regional propensities to restrict inward FDI. In the Middle East, Turkey and Iran's interwar modernisation programmes involved the use of state-owned or sponsored enterprises which challenged existing foreign firms, and left no room for new entrants. Latin American governments introduced new controls over foreign mining companies, obliging them to hire indigenous personnel and to provide welfare benefits. Much FDI in agricultural properties was nationalised, especially in Mexico in the 1930s. Foreign-owned transport and energy utilities, as highly visible 'natural' monopoly producers of essential services and large employers of labour, proved easy targets for nationalistic politicians. They were subjected to new government controls, which added to the burdens they faced from depreciating local currencies, and rate structures fixed and controlled by host governments.

The environment for international business changed markedly in Latin America in the 1930s as a result of these host government policies. Large utilities such as American & Foreign Power found themselves highly regulated. Foreign firms were excluded from some sectors. In 1937 a new Brazilian constitution forbade any company with foreign stockholders from obtaining new hydroelectrical concessions (Wilkins 1974a: 200–2). Despite such mounting pressures, foreign companies retained some freedom of manoeuvre in Brazil and other Latin American countries. Excepting the limited number of actual expropriations, they more often faced a deteriorating business environment in Latin America than total exclusion. Companies were able to maintain contacts with government officials, and negotiate to mitigate the impact of some legislation to find ways to get round new laws (Eakin 1989: 99). The potential for negotiation, evasion and compromise remained far greater in Latin America than in contemporary Japan.

There was a marked shift to more restrictive policies after the Second World War. The most extreme cases came as a result of the spread of communism. The Communist Revolution in China in 1949 was followed by the withdrawal of all privileges from foreign enterprises and the establishment of total state control over foreign trade. In the following year the government took control of all US property in China (Wilkins 1974a: 313). The spread of communism to other Asian countries (North Korea and North Vietnam) and to Cuba after 1961 closed further areas of the world altogether to international business.

Beyond the communist world, there was a spread of mixed and restrictive policies in most developing countries. In the immediate post-colonial period, governments were anxious to establish their national identities, and this often involved seeking to curtail or limit foreign investment in their economies. The association of foreign companies with former colonial powers, their employment of expatriates in senior positions, their past history (real or imagined) of discrimination against local workers, and their embodiment of alien cultural values all contributed to the suspicion with which foreign MNEs were regarded. Foreign control over national resources and public utilities aroused the greatest sensitivities.

Mining and petroleum often dominated economic activity – and especially exports – in developing economies, and .foreign ownership was regarded as incompatable with national control over such vital resources. In the petroleum and minerals industries, the share of revenues taken in tax became a central area of contention. Reactions against MNEs were particularly strong in countries where a handful of MNEs dominated the key industries.

The Middle East became a particular focus of hostility to Western business in the early 1950s. In 1951 Iran nationalised its oil industry. The subsequent boycott of Iranian oil by Western oil companies and a British and American-inspired coup which overthrew the government in 1953 secured the reversal of this policy, though at a cost. The monopoly of the Anglo-Persian Oil Company (renamed British Petroleum in 1954) was broken and it returned to Iran with only a 40 per cent holding in a new oil consortium, with the residual holding shared between other major oil companies (Bamberg 1994: 383–511).

In Egypt, the overthrow of the former monarchy in 1952 and the advent of the more nationalist government of Colonel Nasser led in 1956 to the nationalisation of the Suez Canal Company, a French concessionary company which operated the Suez Canal. The nationalisation led to a violent reaction by France and Britain, whose armies invaded Egypt in collusion with Israel. Their subsequent withdrawal, under US pressure, was followed by the nationalisation of all British and French FDI in 1957. Subsequently Egyptian-style 'Arab socialism' exercised a strong influence on a number of neighbouring countries, especially Syria and Iraq, which nationalised foreign assets in the early 1960s (Jones 1987a: 214–28).

The growth of more restrictive policies took place in the context of an increase in state intervention in many developing countries. During the 1950s and 1960s many governments in Latin America and South Asia adopted import substitution strategies involving a considerable expansion of the government-owned sector of the economy. This was often combined with extensive controls over the residual private sector, including industrial licensing and import restrictions. They had the result of both closing off some activities to foreign participation and controlling the behaviour of foreign firms in the remaining ones. These policies were not always restrictive towards foreign MNEs, especially in manufacturing, and were sometimes designed to attract them, though under specified conditions. In Latin America, MNEs turned out to be the main beneficiaries of measures framed to foster industrial development.

For governments of developing countries seeking to control their national economies, the ability of MNEs to move resources across borders was perceived as a threat rather than as an opportunity. The importance of intra-firm trade in natural resources and, later, manufacturing, raised questions about the prices – transfer prices – charged to affiliates within the MNEs. The ability to set prices in such a way as to maximise overall profits within the group as a whole suggested that MNEs were well-placed to avoid taxation and distort prices. The limited administrative resources of most developing countries rendered counter strategies hard to sustain. An investigation of the transfer pricing issue by the Colombian government for the period 1967–70 estimated that import prices for pharmaceuticals were 87 per cent greater than the world price. Government action against the MNEs

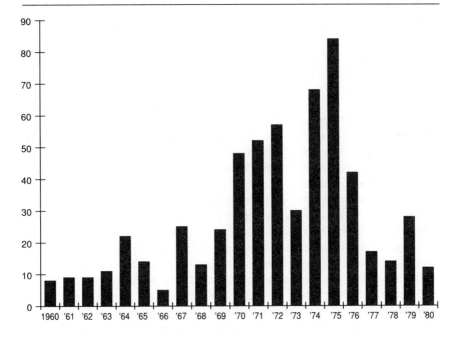

*Figure 8.1* Number of expropriations in developing economies, 1960–80
*Source*: Kennedy 1992: 69

involved resulted in an annual saving of $3.3 million out of an import bill of
$15 million (Lall 1973: 185–8).

During the 1960s the number of expropriations in developing countries
began to increase. Figure 8.1 shows them reaching a peak in the mid-
1970s before falling away.

The very considerable number of expropriations in the 1970s were of
great significance. They demonstrated that the West, and the United States
in particular, was no longer able or willing to use its power to protect foreign
investments. Nonetheless, the issue has to be kept in perspective. Less than
5 per cent of all foreign-owned firms in developing countries were expropriated between 1960 and 1976 (Kobrin 1984: 329). The vast majority of
expropriations were undertaken by only a few political regimes. Less than
thirty countries accounted for over 60 per cent of all expropriation acts. The
great majority of these countries were in Africa or the Middle East.
The other major expropriations occurred in Chile between 1970 and 1973
(thirty acts), Indonesia between 1957 and 1965 (fifteen acts) and Peru
between 1968 and 1975 (twenty-eight acts) (Kennedy 1992). The nationalisations were also heavily concentrated in petroleum, mining, other
natural resources, and public utilities (Williams 1975: 268–9). By 1976 the

nationalisation of large-scale mining and petroleum ventures was virtually complete in the entire developing world (Kobrin 1984: 338).

Expropriation policies were the most extreme manifestation of this era of 'confrontation' between host governments and MNEs in developing economies (Kennedy 1992). Yet the relationships between the parties were always complex, and far from uniformly confrontational. Compensation was given for 40 per cent of nationalised assets between 1956 and 1972, and over two-thirds of assets if the small group of mass expropriators (such as Cuba, Egypt, Iraq and Syria) are excluded (Williams 1975: 272). In many instances, foreign participation continued by means of management and other contracts.

MNEs sometimes used nationalisation as a strategy for strengthening relationships with host governments. The Kenyan government in the late 1960s and early 1970s introduced a range of policy instruments to constrain the operations of foreign companies, and partially nationalised some sectors such as banking, cement manufacturing and bus transport. These nationalisations were often undertaken at the initiative of the MNEs, which desired government partners to ensure access to the machinery of government, or to facilitate repatriation of capital back to head offices. Close symbiotic relationships developed between MNEs and the Kenyan political elite which worked to their mutual benefit. The reality of host government–MNE relations in Kenya was, thus, quite different from that suggested by the public image of expropriation and other control measures (Langdon 1981: 36–43).

During the period of 'confrontation' ownership issues were not confined to expropriations. Many governments which did not seek to exclude foreign companies altogether nonetheless insisted that they should form joint ventures with local partners. Government policies were a major reason why so many MNEs used joint ventures in developing countries. As host government policies liberalised in the 1980s, there was a sharp fall in the formation of joint ventures (Contractor 1990).

In these decades the bargaining power between host developing countries and MNEs appeared to have shifted in the former's favour. However this shift was often more apparent than real. As in previous generations, MNEs often showed considerable resilience and flexibility in response to changed host government policies. They retained access to financial, technological and marketing resources which developing countries needed. Governments discovered that the ownership of resources did not automatically bring real control over their exploitation. As developing country strategies began to shift from import substitution to export promotion, their dependence on MNEs for access to international markets grew. MNEs were, in turn, able to utilise a range of alternatives to wholly-owned FDI, from joint ventures to contractual arrangements, to continue to provide much needed services to developing countries.

## Reconciliation

From the late 1970s governments of developing countries began to enter into a 'reconciliation' phase in their relationships with MNEs. The decline in the number of expropriations was one indicator. The elimination of foreign control over natural resources continued to be pursued, but through other means. Host governments began to switch their attention from ownership towards performance requirements coupled with investment incentives. The new focus of government concern was less sovereignty issues than local value added, domestic research and development, job creation and exports (Guisinger 1985).

A number of factors lay behind this change of emphasis. The nationalisation of the sensitive natural resource industries was virtually complete by the mid-1970s. The passage of time reduced previous sensitivities about colonial dependencies. The symbolism of foreign MNEs declined, enabling governments to view them more objectively 'as a package of benefits and costs whose ratio was subject to manipulation' (Kobrin 1984: 338). Over time the administrative, technical and managerial capabilities of some developing countries increased sufficiently to make regulatory control – rather than simple expropriation – a viable policy option. There was evidence of the growth of host country capabilities over time, though the mass expropriation undertaken by the new Islamic Republic of Iran in 1979–80 occurred in a country which had achieved a high level of regulatory control over MNEs (Kennedy 1992: 80; Kobrin 1984: 340–3).

A further influence on the changed policy emphasis was the relative lack of success of earlier strategies. Many countries – though not all – experienced disappointing results from the nationalisation of their natural resource industries. Productivity fell sharply, new technologies were not introduced, companies were used as employment devices, and managerial inefficiency proliferated. There was sometimes a painful recognition that host government policies were constrained by their ability to implement them. During the 1970s Nigeria pursued an extensive programme of controls over foreign firms, involving indigenisation of equity, local content and personnel, but a great increase in Nigerian 'control' over the economy was not forthcoming. The Nigerian government relied on the indigenous business community to accomplish its objective of greater indigenous control of enterprise. Yet they were more than willing to assist MNE strategies to neutralise government policies through company reorganisations, personnel changes and other arrangements. By developing programmes they could not implement, governments simply created 'channels for corruption, consume[d] valuable resources that could be put to better use, and create[d] unrealistic expectations about [their] capacity' (Biersteker 1987: 297).

From the 1980s many host developing governments followed the developed hosts in liberalising their policies towards inward investment. There was a widespread adoption of policies designed to attract export-oriented manufacturing industries or projects involving advanced technology. Rather more slowly, access to service industries which had been closed to MNEs began to be opened, and certain restrictions in the natural resource sector began to be lifted. In some countries, privatisation reopened access to natural resource industries which had been nationalised in earlier decades. Over the same period there was a widespread abandonment of compulsory joint ventures with government or local private participation, which by the mid-1990s were limited to a small number of 'key' sectors (such as petroleum) in a diminishing number of countries.

The sharpest policy changes of all occurred in the communist or former communist countries which were reopened to FDI. The most dramatic consequences were seen in China, where the gradual opening of the domestic market to FDI in the 1980s and the extension of the liberalisation programme to services in the following decade, facilitated China's sudden emergence as the single largest host economy among the developing countries. Vietnam, which permitted inward FDI in 1988, subsequently also experienced a rapid flow of inward investment. In contrast, although most African countries also underwent a widespread liberalisation of their inward FDI policies in the 1980s, that continent's share of world FDI continued to decline. While a national regulatory framework conducive to FDI was a necessary condition of attracting foreign MNEs, their actual locational decisions rested on other factors. In Africa's case, low growth rates, unstable economic and political conditions, heavy indebtedness, and the lack of a skilled workforce, provided a profoundly unattractive investment climate (United Nations 1994: 91–7).

From the mid-1980s, as in the developed economies, many governments introduced incentives to attract inward FDI. There was a proliferation of export processing zones, and incentives to establish facilities such as science parks. Governments offered protection from import competition and foreign exchange preferences. Fiscal incentives included exemption from import duties and tax holidays, which were typically available for up to five years after an investment, and sometimes for much longer. These incentives were, in some cases, both generous and largely unfocused, although there was a trend towards more specific targeting over time. Competitive bidding for projects posed particular difficulties for poorer countries, which faced even further marginalisation from world FDI flows.

## COMPARATIVE HOST GOVERNMENTS: INDIA, BRAZIL AND SINGAPORE SINCE 1950

This section contrasts the host government policies followed in the three developing economies of India, Brazil and Singapore after 1950. Despite shifts in emphasis over time, these countries can be taken as representative of the restrictive, mixed and open policy options towards inward FDI. Partly as a result of their policies, inward FDI assumed quite different degrees of importance in their economies. As Chapter 7 showed, India's stock of FDI in 1993 was only around 5 per cent of that of Singapore and Brazil, while Singapore's stock of FDI exceeded that of Brazil despite the disparity in their geographical and population sizes.

## India

On independence from Britain in 1947, India possessed a substantial stock of inward FDI. It included both the long-established British trading companies – which controlled diversified operations in services, natural resources and consumer goods manufacturing – and manufacturing MNEs, most of which were initially British firms which had established factories during the interwar years (Tomlinson 1989).

The official policy of the ruling Congress Party was to limit the role of foreign enterprises in India and, ultimately, see the transfer of industries into indigenous hands, but no specific legislation was introduced in the first decade of independence to achieve these goals. Policies towards foreign companies were ambiguous and lacked transparency. There were no restrictions on the 100 per cent ownership of Indian subsidiaries, but the authorities exerted pressure on MNEs to sell part of their equity to local investors (Fieldhouse 1978: 197–204). The overall policy environment was sufficiently unpredictable to discourage new MNE entrants into India, while some companies withdrew rather than permit local capital participation. These included Ford, which was also to be a reluctant participant in Brazil's industrialisation programme at the same time (Wilkins and Hill 1964: 102).

Government policies changed in emphasis following a major foreign exchange crisis in 1957. The crisis threatened to reduce the imports of the foreign technologies which were considered necessary by the government as it pursued a capital-intensive industrialisation policy behind high protective tariffs. The government decided to fund many of the imports of new plant and the licensing of patents through the equity of MNEs. If MNEs brought technology and finance into India, they were allowed to retain full managerial control. The new policy regime encouraged a considerable flow of new FDI in India, while existing MNEs expanded their operations. For a time, foreign-owned companies grew faster in India than the private sector as a whole. While in 1957 MNEs controlled one-tenth of India's corporate assets, ten years later the proportion had risen to one-fifth (Encarnation 1989: 107–9, 180–1).

In the early 1970s, policy changed once more, this time in the direction of becoming highly restrictive to inward FDI. Enterprises with over 40 per cent foreign ownership were classified as FERA (Foreign Exchange Regulation Act) firms. They were offered the choice of diluting their equity or divesting from India. The only exceptions allowed – under which an MNE could retain a 51–74 per cent shareholding – were if they met stiff requirements of employing 'sophisticated' technology, or exported 'significant proportions of output', or operated in 'high-priority industries'. Under the new policy regime, several sectors of industry were closed altogether to foreign firms, while in many others 'official entry conditions were so difficult, cumbersome and restrictive that new capital inflows were effectively excluded' (Lall 1985: 311).

Not surprisingly, the new policies led to India experiencing in the 1970s a net outflow of capital, as some MNEs divested while there were few entrants. IBM and Coca-Cola were among the MNEs which divested completely from India in this period because they refused to abandon full ownership of their subsidiaries. This was a minority reaction, as the Indian operations of most MNEs were profitable given the highly protected domestic market. Under the impact of FERA, most MNEs in India reduced their foreign shareholdings to 40 per cent or less. A number of companies which qualified for government exemptions – including the subsidiaries of Unilever and ICI, which were counted among India's twenty largest business groups – retained larger shareholdings, usually distributing the residual among numerous private investors. The MNEs which remained in India relied on reinvested earnings and local capital markets for their growth while new inward FDI fell to tiny amounts (Lall 1985: 318).

India's policies were effective in 'dislodging' MNEs from many industries which they had previously dominated. In contrast to Brazil and Singapore, local enterprises – both public and private – came to occupy pre-eminent positions in a wide range of industries, including chemicals, machinery and transport equipment and pharmaceuticals (Encarnation 1989: 5–7).

This outcome was the result of complex bargaining processes between the state, Indian business and MNEs. Indian firms were able to increase their bargaining power *vis-à-vis* the MNEs over time, partly because – as in the computer industry – they were able to access foreign technology through licensing agreements by exploiting growing competition among foreign firms (Grieco 1982: 609–32). Local firms were also able to draw on state finance to buy foreign technology, and had preferential access to state permits. After 1973, Indian firms also received state assistance to develop their own technological resources. MNEs were also able to 'bargain' – by, for example, restricting the kind of technology they offered to India – but they were handicapped by the many restrictions on their ownership and operation, and generally by their weak position in the Indian political economy. They lacked access to the political networks that guaranteed preferential access to government licences and state financing.

They had few joint ventures with either the large Indian business groups, or the state-owned enterprises, which again restricted access to state decision-making (Encarnation 1989: 180–93).

India became an unusual developing economy in respect to international business. It had a fairly large industrial sector, which was largely in national hands, and achieved considerable self-reliance in technology. During the 1970s India itself emerged as a significant direct investor, almost entirely in other developing economies. Yet India's escape from 'dependency' on MNEs did not translate into a satisfactory economic performance. Export performance was poor, and India experienced low average growth in per capita income, which between 1960 and 1980 was only 1.4 per cent, compared to 7 per cent for Singapore. The highly restrictive policies towards inward FDI and licensing have been widely accepted as part of the reason for this overall weak performance. Not only did India have too few MNEs entering the country, but existing affiliates were unable or unwilling to bring new techniques, products and methods into the country, nor could they offer a strong competitive spur for indigenous firms (Lall 1985).

During the 1990s Indian policies towards MNEs began to be radically revised. The first liberalisation in 1991 provided automatic approval of FDI project proposals with up to 51 per cent foreign equity ownership in thirty-four priority industries. In 1993 full ownership was allowed for foreign firms on a case by case basis. This liberalisation resulted in the return of prominent MNEs such as IBM and Coca-Cola which had disinvested in the 1970s and 1980s, though India's continuous complex web of regulatory controls, widespread bureaucratic corruption and lack of adequate infrastructure provided major constraints on the attraction of large amounts of FDI (United Nations 1994: 81–4).

## Brazil

Brazilian economic policies after the Second World War initially shared some similarities with those of India. As in most of Latin America, an import substitution strategy was in place in the 1950s. This was accompanied by a large state-owned sector: in 1973 state-owned enterprises accounted for two-fifths of Brazil's corporate asssets (Encarnation, 1989: 194). However, protectionism was combined with few restrictions on entry by foreign firms and strategies to attract them. In contrast to India, FDI flowed into Brazil in considerable quantities. In constant US dollar terms (1986 prices), the stock of inward investment increased fivefold over the period 1947–86 (Fritsch and Franco 1991: 23). Brazil's overall economic performance was also different to that of India. Between 1945 and 1980 Brazilian industrial production grew at over 8 per cent per annum on average (Fritsch and Franco 1991: 23).

As in the case of India, Brazilian policies shifted over time. Through to the mid-1950s the import substitution strategy which had been adopted in the Great Depression remained in place. It focused on the development of local manufacture of light consumer goods. This involved the limitation of foreign control in key strategic sectors, such as steel, as well as pressures on foreign subsidiaries to increase local content. There were high rates of effective protection against imports. However policies fluctuated with political events. In 1950 the re-election of President Vargas – the Brazilian dictator from 1930 to 1945 – was followed by a period of economic nationalism and hostility to some foreign-owned enterprises. In 1953 Brazil established the state-owned Petrobras with a monopoly over most phases of the oil industry. Yet the overall concern of the Brazilians was to attract FDI, especially from the US, because of a desire to reduce a severe shortage of hard currency. As a result, Brazil was able to attract nearly one-fifth of total US FDI in manufacturing between 1946 and 1954 (Fritsch and Franco 1991: 24).

In the mid-1950s, Brazilian policies were re-oriented towards broadening the range of local production to include consumer durables, especially automobiles, and building up local manufacture of capital and intermediate goods (Gereffi and Evans 1981: 39–42). This policy shift assumed an active role for MNEs in achieving industrialisation. High tariffs and quantitative controls on imports of manufactured goods were combined with a variety of incentives such as subsidies on imports of machinery and equipment. Another policy reversal occurred during the left wing presidencies of Quadros and Goulart in the early 1960s, which saw the expropriation of Jersey Standard, Shell and an ITT subsidiary, but in 1964 a coup resulted in a military government which welcomed inward FDI as a means to promote economic development. The era of military dictatorship lasted until 1985.

By the beginning of the 1970s MNEs held about half the assets of the largest manufacturing firms in Brazil. Their role in the creation and growth of the Brazilian automobile industry was discussed in Chapter 7. There were almost no restrictions on entry to foreign firms. By contrast with the position under India's FERA legislation, MNEs could serve the Brazilian market through wholly-owned subsidiaries. Foreign companies could also acquire Brazilian firms. Again, in contrast to the situation in India, MNEs became involved in extensive joint venture and collaborative arrangements with leading Brazilian private sector enterprises, and with the state-owned companies (Encarnation 1989: 193–6).

Brazilian economic policies shifted towards a more outward-oriented stance at the beginning of the 1970s. Export promotion policies were adopted, and again considerable success was achieved. Brazilian exports of manufactured goods grew at 19.5 per cent between 1965 and 1980. Foreign-owned firms were particularly prominent in this process (Fritsch and Franco 1991: 31–5). This was the era of the 'economic miracle', when Brazil experienced some of the fastest growth rates in the world – though it accumulated one of the world's largest debts in the process. During this period Brazilian policies on foreign ownership remained flexible and pragmatic. There were some efforts to increase local ownership but there were great variations between industries and sectors.

This latter point can be seen in the case of electronics, where government policies varied widely between sectors in the 1970s. The telecommunications industry was dominated by foreign firms up to the mid-1970s, when government policy insisted on the transformation of affiliates into minority joint ventures controlled by private nationals in order to improve technology transfer. The MNEs initially resisted, but by the end of the decade followed this route because of the threat of being excluded from government procurement. Ericsson, Siemens and NEC were among the firms forming joint ventures. In contrast, in consumer electronics there were no restrictions on full ownership, although many firms did form joint ventures.

In computers, an industry which had been almost entirely foreign owned, the government introduced a 'market reserve' policy which represented a considerable departure from the previous liberal policy towards inward FDI. In 1979 the industry was divided. Microcomputers were reserved for completely national firms – not even minority joint ventures were admitted – while mainframes were left to existing MNEs. This was combined with a high local content requirement. The consequences of the policy were controversial. It enabled Brazilian firms to enter the computer industry's lower end, a technologically mature segment, but the level of technological development was low, prices of products were high, and productivity lower (Fritsch and Franco 1991: 89–107).

Brazil's 'mixed' policy stance was an important reason why inward FDI was attracted to the country, but it was certainly never the sole reason. Despite persistent policy failures which led to almost continuous inflation, Brazil was an attractive large market which included an affluent middle class. Its 'cheap' labour force became a valuable locational advantage. These assets greatly enforced the 'bargaining' position of the Brazilian government when dealing with foreign automobile and other MNEs. There is no reason to assume Brazilian host policies would have necessarily produced similar outcomes in different environments. During the 1980s the severe economic dislocation following the debt crisis led to a major decline in new FDI inflows into the country.

### Singapore

Singaporean host government policies contrasted with those of both India and Brazil. Virtually from the state's full independence in the mid-1960s,

Singapore had one of the most open policy regimes anywhere in the world. The country's development strategy rested fundamentally on the attraction of foreign MNEs. Foreign MNEs became the driving force behind Singapore's extremely rapid and sustained economic growth rate as one of the four East Asian 'tigers'. By the 1990s Singapore was ranked among the world's ten richest economies.

Singapore's strategy was conditioned by the economic situation it faced in the mid-1960s. During its long history as a British colony, Singapore had served as an entrepôt, but during the 1950s trade patterns changed as the European empires were dismantled and neighbouring countries began to raise tariff barriers. For a short period, Singapore planned a strategy of mild import substitution based on access to the larger market of Malaya, which had become independent from Britain in 1957. Singapore joined the Federation of Malaysia in 1963, but political tensions led to separation only two years later. As a small island lacking in resources, an import substitution strategy was not practical. The result was the adoption of a strategy of growth through labour-intensive industrialisation (Mirza 1986: 33–6; Hughes 1988).

The policy of export-led growth rested on the attraction of foreign MNEs. Tariffs and non-tariff barriers to trade were sharply reduced to encourage export-oriented industries. A wide range of investment incentives were offered in the form of low taxes and minimum control over operations. The government introduced one of the world's most liberal policies towards inward investors. There were almost no controls on foreign exchange and licensing, the extent of foreign ownership, imports of machinery, local content requirements, employment of foreign personnel, ownership of real estate or acquisitions. There were also no laws regulating competition or market dominance (Lecraw 1985: 390).

The Singaporean outward-looking policy coincided with the new strategies of MNEs in electronics and other industries to embark on policies of worldwide sourcing. Singapore's cheap and flexible labour force made it an attractive location for export platform investments. However the government's role in attracting inward FDI was very far from passive and *laissez-faire*. The government, which since independence has remained in the hands of a single party, intervened vigorously in the economy to provide an attractive investment climate. This involved extensive investment in communications, education and other infrastructure facilities, and the creation of state-owned or partly-owned companies operating in the manufacturing, banking and service sectors. These state enterprises, which included Singapore Airlines and the Development Bank of Singapore, played key roles in the government's strategy to create an attractive environment for international business, and to constantly upgrade it. There were also tight controls over wages, working conditions and labour–management relations. In the late 1960s all labour disputes were made subject to compulsory arbitration, and subsequently a National Wages Council was formed which set wage levels annually by decree (Mirza 1986: 40).

The Singaporean policy was to influence the behaviour of foreign MNEs not by direct controls, but by shaping their environment. Policy was characterised by a constant drive to upgrade and diversify the value-added activities undertaken in the country. In the early 1970s policies were introduced to encourage Singapore's development as an international financial centre. Foreign banks were given incentives to locate in Singapore to operate in the global money and capital markets, though not domestic commercial banking. In manufacturing industry, as other 'cheap labour' economies began to compete for inward FDI, the government made extensive investments to upgrade Singapore's technology and services to attract higher, value-added activities.

Given the successful economic performance of the Asian newly industrial countries (NICs), it is worth noting that they pursued quite different policies towards MNEs. Singapore combined an open policy stance with extensive government intervention to upgrade its locational advantages. The British colonial administration in Hong Kong pursued a *laissez-faire* policy with open access to all MNEs. Both South Korea and Taiwan pursued restrictive policies towards foreign MNEs. Their governments operated Japanese-style restrictions on inward FDI, restricting foreign participation in many sectors and encouraging it to take the form of joint ventures or licensing in others. Both governments sought to combine the acquisition of foreign technology with the development of local innovative capabilities. The East Asian economic miracles were not the result of a single policy towards international business.

**Conclusion**

In the post-1950 decades, India, Brazil and Singapore represented three alternative host government policy options towards foreign MNEs. The policy regimes provide important parts of the explanation for the different levels of inward FDI in these countries, although other factors were important also. The experience of these three countries also suggests a correlation between the degree of policy openness and economic performance. The role of MNEs in Singapore's export-led growth and the growth of the large Brazilian automobile industry lend support to such a view. However the lessons are more complex. Neither Singapore nor Brazil were simply 'open', but rather their governments sought to guide foreign investors in certain directions. The problem of Indian policy lay not so much in restricting foreign MNEs *per se* – which South Korea and Taiwan also did – but in failing to secure access to foreign technologies by other modes, and in sheltering its industries from international competition.

## SUMMARY

Government policies towards foreign MNEs have evolved in a circular direction over the last century. Before 1930 host governments had few restrictions on MNEs, except in a number of strategic sectors. Between 1930 and the 1970s there was a worldwide growth in restrictions. Communist states excluded MNEs altogether, while developing governments nationalised their natural resources and introduced many other restrictions on the operation of foreign firms. From the 1980s these trends were again reversed in a worldwide reversion to a borderless world.

There were marked national differences within these general patterns. The United States had a long-term orientation towards an open policy on MNEs, while Japanese governments had a long-term disinclination to encourage wholly-owned MNE affiliates in their country, although from the 1970s these policy stances converged. The same policy differences were seen among developing countries after the Second World War. Singapore's open policy contrasted sharply with that of restrictive India. These long-term national differences may be explained by the extent of outward FDI; the industrial policies pursued by governments; the industrial distribution of inward FDI; the geographical origins of inward FDI; the size of the host economy; and the cultural and historical inheritance.

During the twentieth century the national state secured a degree of power and an ability to control affairs far greater than in previous centuries. This development represented a major challenge to MNEs. Governments which sought to and had the ability to control and influence their national economies did not share an identity of interests with business enterprises which co-ordinated economic activities across national borders. For much of the twentieth century, national governments sought – in varying degrees – to restrict, control or ban MNEs as a solution to this conflict. The difficulty was the lack of alternatives to MNEs to gain access to the latest technologies and organisational skills, and to markets. As the pace of global integration and technological change accelerated, policies shifted from restricting MNEs to seeking to attract them.

# Chapter 9

# Conclusion

## TRENDS OVER TIME

The main trends in the development of international business can be summarised briefly. After it became easier and safer to sustain managerial control over direct investments in the early nineteenth century, there was a growth in multinational activity. For a period between the 1880s and the First World War, and probably extending until the end of the 1920s, international business increased rapidly and came to represent a significant share of world output. Multinationals originated from a small number of developed economies in Western Europe and North America, but they invested widely over the world. They were engaged in manufacturing, services and the exploitation of natural resources.

The enterprises which engaged in international business in this period were very diverse. Large and small firms, managerial and family firms operated across borders. Numerous entrepreneurial firms were formed to exploit resources on the world's frontiers. The European firms which ventured abroad were often joined in networks of various kinds with other firms. They employed a variety of equity and non-equity modes. Large integrated MNEs came to occupy central roles in manufacturing industries with complex technologies and in some natural resources, but they co-existed with enterprises whose boundaries were blurred. This institutional diversity makes the quantification of international business in this period especially hazardous, and great uncertainties remain about the level and composition of FDI flows in these years.

The largest and most dynamic sector for international business was natural resources. From the early nineteenth century there was a growth in FDI in mining, and from the 1870s the international mining industry boomed. Multinational oil companies established distribution facilities worldwide and searched for new sources of supply. Foreign-owned companies became major elements in the world's supply of commodities such as sugar, bananas and rubber. Integration strategies resulted in the growing importance of intra-firm trade in many resources. By the 1920s either the ownership or the control of many of the world's natural resources was in the hands of international business.

An important aspect of international business activities in services was concerned with facilitating these resource investments. During the nineteenth century multinational trading companies, banks and utilities created a global infrastructure which permitted natural resources to be exploited, transported and distributed, and exports of manufacturers from the industrialised world to be sold in exchange. Service MNEs were major facilitators of the accelerating trade flows of the late nineteenth century and important institutional forces behind the incorporation of peripheral regions into the global economy. At the same time trading companies in particular emerged as co-ordinators and controllers of value-adding activities in other sectors. European trading companies diversified into resource exploitation, infrastructure investment and manufacturing, and this route was followed subsequently by Japan's *sogo shosha*.

The growth of multinational manufacturing was evident from the 1830s, expanded in the middle of the nineteenth century, and was an important element of the world economy by 1914. From this early period MNEs were engaged in moving the latest and the newest technological products and processes around the industrialising nations of the world. They were prominent in chemicals, machinery and branded consumer products. Although the amount of FDI in manufacturing was smaller than in resources or services, numerous multinational manufacturing investments were made and large multi-plant operations were in evidence by the First World War. The level of integration and of intra-firm trade was very much lower than in resources at this time, although it was not entirely absent, and in the interwar years certain MNEs experienced a considerable internationalisation of their R & D operations.

From the 1920s the rapid growth of international business in the world economy halted. The Great Depression, the collapse of primary commodity prices and the political uncertainties leading to the outbreak of the Second World War provided an unattractive environment for FDI, and international cartels proliferated as an alternative. When multinational enterprise expanded again from the 1950s, many countries and sectors were closed or restricted. The countries which recovered their sovereignty as the European colonial empires were dismantled sought to confirm their independence by taking control of strategic natural resources and utilities from foreign companies. The borderless world had been replaced by a world of numerous borders.

MNEs remained of considerable importance in these decades. Even in the 1930s multinational manufacturing continued to expand in the world's most advanced industries such as automobiles. International cartels were sometimes used not only to restrict output and maintain prices, but also to transfer technologies across borders. After the decade of disruption caused by the Second World War MNEs resumed their growth in the context of the booming economies of the developed world. However the sources of multinational investment were surprisingly narrow. The United States alone accounted for a high proportion of new FDI. The United States, Britain and the Netherlands were the pre-eminent homes of MNEs. The firms of other developed nations preferred to take advantage of booming world trade by exporting. FDI flows increasingly went to other developed economies in Western Europe and North America.

Multinational manufacturing grew steadily in relative importance in the middle decades of the twentieth century. After the Second World War US MNEs took the lead in diffusing the latest innovations in petrochemicals, computers and semiconductors to other developed countries. The level of integration within large manufacturing firms was rather low. During the 1950s and 1960s intra-firm trade was still very low in manufacturing. Although the 'typical' manufacturing MNE of this period was a large firm with strong organisational boundaries, the operations of national subsidiaries within these enterprises were not integrated.

International business in resources no longer grew dynamically. During the 1930s falling primary product prices encouraged the spread of international cartels, though the ability of companies to control prices varied widely between industries. Entrepreneurial firms gave way to large integrated corporations in both renewable and non-renewable resources. However from the 1950s vertical integration strategies began to fragment. A major reason for this trend was that developing country host governments pursued policies to increase national ownership over natural resources. This trend culminated in the late 1960s and 1970s with the widespread nationalisation of MNE assets. As a result, the significance of intra-firm trade fell significantly in one commodity after another.

Service MNEs were also adversely affected by the policies of governments. Their roles as the facilitators of international business and providers of infrastructure were curbed by governments in many countries. Foreign ownership of energy and communication utilities was challenged and prohibited in developing countries. Multinational investment in airlines was impossible almost everywhere. However from the 1950s there were new waves of international business in advertising agencies, accounting, hotels, fast food restaurants and retailing, usually in developed countries and employing a wide range of equity and non-equity modes. International trading companies found new roles in the world economy. The *sogo shosha* functioned as Japan's leading MNEs, not only handling a high proportion of Japan's foreign trade, but also undertaking diversified investments in manufacturing and resources. Finally, the emergence of the Eurodollar market at the end of the 1950s not only completely revolutionised the nature of multinational banking, but gave banks an entirely new significance as the facilitators of international business.

From the 1970s international business entered a new environment and a new growth phase. It regained the level of importance in the world economy which it had held before the 1920s. Germany, France, a number of other European countries and Japan re-emerged as major outward investors. The Asian newly industrial countries (NICs) emerged as new sources of multinational investment. The borders which had been constructed against MNEs crumbled. They re-entered areas such as China and Eastern Europe, and activities such as air transportation and utilities, from which they had been excluded for decades. Although many more borders – in the shape of regulations and controls – still existed than in the nineteenth century, there were strong parallels with the previous era of dynamic growth.

As in the late nineteenth century, MNEs were powerful forces for economic integration. The growth of intra-firm trade in manufacturing, especially in high technology industries, testified to the growing and deep integration of international production by MNEs. Multinational investment overtook trade as the driving force in international economic relations. By the 1990s one-third of total world trade was intra-firm. In this dynamic context, the boundaries of firms became blurred again. Alliances between large MNEs engaged in the most advanced manufacturing industries proliferated. Hierarchies gave way to networks as the pace of innovation and the need for flexibility intensified.

During these decades the resource MNEs proved able to continue to exercise a considerable influence over the world's resources despite the elimination of vertical integration down to production level in many cases. The formidable organisational and technological capacities of the large oil and mining MNEs ensured them an important role in transportation, processing and marketing, while the use of contracts and joint ventures enabled them to exert a continuing influence over the production of many commodities.

However it was in services that multinational investment strategies re-emerged as the most dynamic over the last two decades. The worldwide spread of deregulation and liberalisation reopened sectors such as telecommunications, public utilities and airlines to MNEs. The need to rebuild and upgrade infrastructure after years of neglect in many developing countries provided boundless opportunities for MNEs. As the creation of, and access to, information became ever more fundamental in business, so service activities became ever more central to international business.

The history of international business is a striking mixture of continuities and discontinuities. International business as a whole has grown in a discontinuous fashion. Periods of fast growth alternated with periods of slow growth or even stagnation. At some times international collaborative agreements between firms were more important than in other periods.

The relative importance of resources, manufacturing and services has varied in different time periods. In important respects, the only constant about international business is change, and the only prediction about its future is that it will continue to change.

The persistent national influence on international business has been one of the most striking features of continuity, though the histories of individual home and host economies have shown different patterns. The firms of the United States and a number of European countries – led by the British and the Dutch, and including Sweden and Switzerland – have had a persistent tendency to engage in FDI. On the other hand, German and probably French firms were very active outward investors before 1914, but engaged in relatively low levels of FDI until the 1970s, before resuming the dynamic strategies evident before the First World War. The Japanese economy also falls into this discontinuous pattern. By the interwar years Japanese companies had created a complex international business system and possessed a high level of outward FDI compared to the overall size of the Japanese economy, but after the Second World War Japanese outward FDI remained at low levels until the 1970s.

The outward investment patterns of countries show strong continuities. Each home country has a distinctive profile despite the inevitable evolution over time. Japanese multinational investment was persistently skewed towards services and, for a long time, textiles. The United States, the United Kingdom and the Netherlands had a long-term strength in petroleum. Given the capital intensity of that industry, this was one reason for their prominence as outward investors. Swedish FDI was concentrated in manufacturing and, within manufacturing, engineering and machines. The same continuities were evident in the geographical direction of multinational investment flows. The distribution of US and Japanese FDI has always been skewed towards the Americas and Asia respectively. The British had a long-term preference for investment in other English-speaking economies, whether in their Empire or in the United States.

Among the host economies, there are striking discontinuities and continuities. Among the former, Russia flourished as a major host economy before 1917, and then disappeared. China was of major significance as a host economy before 1949, then disappeared, and then dramatically reappeared in the 1990s. On the other hand, there were also striking long-term continuities in the distribution (or lack of it) of multinational investment. From the nineteenth century the United States and Canada have always been among the world's largest host economies. Although the growth of inward FDI into the United States since the 1970s and the change in that country's relative investment position has been a subject of great comment, over a long period foreign MNEs have made substantial investments in the United States. A second major continuity has been the persistently low level of inward FDI in Japan. This has not meant that foreign MNEs have been unimportant for the Japanese economy – in the first three decades of the twentieth century they were important conduits of technology transfer into the country – but overall and in aggregate terms the level of foreign ownership of value-added activities in Japan has been and remains very low.

If there is one generalisation which stands out sharply about international business over the long term, it is that its distribution over the world has been remarkably uneven. In each generation particular countries and regions have always attracted disproportionately more investment than others. This trend is as persistent in the 1990s as in previous generations. Although MNEs are said to be engaged in global integration strategies, the process of 'globalisation' continues to leave Africa, and many Latin American, Asian and Eastern European economies, comparatively unaffected.

## CENTRAL ISSUES

### Why

The complex history of international business does not prove any single theory of the multinational enterprise. There was no inherent and single logic behind the growth of MNEs. The expansion of MNEs was not linear. Corporate failures alternated with corporate successes. Chance events – such as the sequestration of German and Japanese overseas assets as a result of world wars – resulted in long-term shifts in corporate strategies.

These 'lessons' of history do not mean that the growth of international business was a random process, but it is evident that systematic factors behind its growth must not be oversimplified. The expansion of international business in resources in the nineteenth century was driven by the need for raw materials and foodstuffs in the industrialised world. The high transaction costs in many markets and the capital intensity of mining operations provided systematic factors behind the growth of large integrated MNEs. The global search for resources stimulated in turn multinational service activities to provide the necessary infrastructure to exploit and distribute them. Multinational manufacturing was driven by the desire of firms to exploit and protect the proprietary technology and brands which became so important in the late nineteenth century. The complexity of writing contracts for intricate technologies made it difficult to exploit them in foreign countries through alternative market-based transactions.

MNEs sought to exploit ownership advantages in foreign countries, but the historical evidence shows some of the problems involved in applying this concept. Nineteenth century MNEs, especially in resources and services, frequently had no local competitor over whom they needed an 'advantage'. Once established, their advantages lay in incumbency and the common governance of geographically dispersed assets. The many failed investments in each generation of multinational investment indicated that the ownership advantages possessed by many firms was insufficient to sustain their business.

The most important ownership advantages for MNEs were found in organisation and innovatory capacity, but there were always a considerable variety of organisational forms employed in international business at any one time. No single model emerges as universally the most successful even in the same period of time. A number of models have related long-term trends in international business to shifting national advantages in organising ability, usually by describing a progression from British-style management, to US-style, to Japanese-style. The weakness of such models is the tendency to focus excessively on advanced manufacturing industries, and the failure to acknowledge that other influences are at work in international business, including inherited investment preferences and cultural orientations. Multinational activity is only a partial – and potentially misleading – proxy of national competitiveness, as the United Kingdom's continuing role after the Second World War as one of the world's leading multinational investors demonstrates.

The influence of governments was a fundamental feature of the history of international business. Governments opened up most of the world for international business in the nineteenth century through the spread of imperialism and international property law. Subsequently they restricted and confined MNEs before, towards the end of the twentieth century, reverting to more open policies. While governments often proved less than successful in regulating or replacing MNEs, their interventions in markets have greatly stimulated multinational business by hindering other means of operating abroad, or else providing a stimulus to escape to foreign countries. Tariffs in the late nineteenth century, and voluntary export restraints (VERs) in the 1970s and 1980s, caused major surges of multinational manufacturing as firms jumped trade barriers. The tight regulation of national financial systems after the Second World War led to the explosive growth of non-regulated global financial markets.

The relationship between MNEs and their environment was a complex one. MNE strategies were conditioned by the policy and economic environment in which they operated – although different enterprises often made different choices in the same environment. But MNEs also shaped that environment by transferring technology and organisation across borders, and by influencing policies. The interaction between MNEs and their environment was a two-way dynamic process.

## How

The co-ordination of business in different countries has posed constant challenges. Firms which operate in their domestic market face a constantly shifting environment, as political and economic circumstances change and technologies evolve. But the firms which operated in several countries had to respond to multiple environments changing in different ways and at different speeds. The political, legal, linguistic, cultural and other differences between countries intensified the problems of responding successfully to the managerial challenge.

In view of the problems of exercising control, it is not surprising that improvements in transport and communications have exercised a considerable impact on the development of international business by reducing the time and cost of traversing space. During the nineteenth century the advent of the railroads, improvements in sea transportation, the cutting of ship canals and invention of the telegraph and, later the telephone, both enabled managers to exercise sustained control over foreign operations, and permitted the co-ordination of movements of goods and services across the globe. In the late twentieth century, developments in information technology have been critical to the complex integration strategies pursued by MNEs. However, international business was never a passive recipient of the developments in transport and communications, for multinational service firms played a considerable role in their worldwide spread.

Despite the improvements of transport and communities, it is surprising – especially in the nineteenth century – that international business could develop at such a speed. One important reason was that MNEs reduced the risks of operating abroad by investing in 'nearby' areas. From the nineteenth century multinational investment was often placed in geographically neighbouring countries or in colonies. This multi-regional and colonial investment still encountered the risks of operating under foreign political and legal systems or (as in the case of the colonies) at a large geographical distance, but the risks were reduced. Although over time the empires disappeared, flows of multinational investment continued to be influenced by geographical or cultural proximity. The MNEs of the Asian newly industrial countries (NICs) were following in a long tradition when in the 1970s they invested first in neighbouring Asian countries, before venturing elsewhere. On a larger scale, a great deal of multinational investment over the last one hundred years has consisted of firms from one English-speaking country investing in another English-speaking country.

The ability to sustain direct investments in the nineteenth century rested on the advent of stronger organisational structures. There were inevitable constraints on the international growth of small firms managed by their owners, even if many such firms invested across borders in the nineteenth century. The separation of ownership from control, and the growth of large managerial enterprises during the second half of the nineteenth century, was a very important development in the growth of multinational investment, especially in the capital-intensive manufacturing industries. These firms had the organisational capabilities to achieve economies of scale and scope. They developed corporate competencies in innovation which were sustained generation after generation.

The long-term nature of these competencies is evident in the list of the world's largest MNEs given in Appendix 1. It is striking how many of the US and European firms in the list were prominent MNEs in their industries one hundred years previously. But the absence of the names of other pioneers – such as Singer – demonstrates that there was nothing automatic about the process of corporate survival. In each generation firms had to reinvent their organisational structures in response to changing circumstances. The optimal form of organisation in one generation frequently became the obstacle to innovation and survival in the next generation. The prominent role of Japanese electronics and vehicle companies among the largest MNEs in 1992 provides ample demonstration that new organisational methods could provide the basis for firms to challenge long-established world leaders in their industries.

There has never been a universal international management structure. The large managerial enterprises which developed in the late nineteenth century evolved managerial hierarchies which were able to exert control over foreign operations. However the extensive European international businesses at the time often employed socialisation strategies to control far-flung operations. These strategies worked particularly well when transport and communication difficulties made formal hierarchical methods of control difficult. But during the twentieth century European MNEs continued to employ less bureaucratic forms of control than their US equivalents.

The boundaries of firms showed a persistent tendency to blur when they crossed borders. There has always been extensive inter-firm collaboration in response to the risks and pressures of international business. In periods of fast globalisation, such as the late nineteenth and late twentieth centuries, networks and alliances of firms showed a particular tendency to proliferate, and were used as components of dynamic strategies. During the 1930s international cartels flourished as a more defensive reaction to adverse circumstances. In all periods, joint ventures and other equity and non-equity modes have been employed. Although such arrangements had a tendency to be more unstable than wholly-owned direct investments, their persistence showed their use as ways of responding to foreign environments and, more widely, as potentially more flexible tools than wholly-owned affiliates.

## Impact

In each generation MNEs have served as engines of growth in the world economy. They have been major facilitators of trade flows. They have transferred technologies and organisational skills across borders. Multinational strategies have been prominent in nearly all of the world's most dynamic manufacturing industries since the late nineteenth century. In each generation they have spread innovations across borders and transformed living standards and lifestyles in the process. Both service and resource MNEs have also been highly significant as transferors of organisational and technological systems across borders.

There are, however, no easy generalisations about the consequences of multinational investment. The historical evidence remains full of uncertainties and under-researched topics, but it points to a diversity of outcomes. The impact of MNEs on individual host economies has depended on the type of investment undertaken, its quality as well as its quantity, the source of the investment, the mode of entry, the institutional and contractual form employed, and the alternatives at any one time. The nature of the host economy – including its stage of development and its culture – and the response to foreign investors have been crucial in determining the impact of multinational investment.

These considerations mean that generalisations about impact between countries and across time are seriously misleading unless they are carefully specified. It has been shown that a striking feature of the history of international business in Japan has been the low level of inward FDI compared to the overall size of the economy, while the United Kingdom has been one of the world's largest host economies throughout the twentieth century. But it would be entirely misleading to draw the policy conclusion that governments should seek to restrict FDI in their economies if they want to emulate the Japanese economic miracle and avoid the mediocre economic performance of the British. It is evident that certain features of the Japanese business system, especially the ability to absorb technologies at a fast rate, permitted the highly successful absorption of foreign innovations through modes such as joint ventures and licensing agreements. The success of this process in Japan reveals little about its viability elsewhere, or indeed about whether Japan in the 1990s would gain from a substantial increase in inward FDI.

The difficulties of assessing the impact of MNEs on host economies arise from the many ways in which they can make an impact. They create employment, but many drive out local competitors. They can expand exports, but also increase imports. The new technologies which they introduce may be accompanied by a package of cultural values which may or may not be unwelcome or unwanted. The employment and promotion of women by foreign MNEs in a socially conservative society may be welcomed by the female half of a host economy but not by the males. An entrepreneurial and risk-taking investment in one generation might appear as a rapacious foreign investor draining profits out of a country in the next.

The available evidence on the long-term impact of international business on home economies is equally ambiguous. Countries gain from the receipt of dividends and income from the foreign operations of their MNEs, but may lose if MNEs transfer resources from their home economies to other economies. MNEs have assisted in the economic restructuring of economies by shifting low value-added activities abroad and permitting the upgrading of the use of domestic resources. But there is also evidence that they may 'hollow out' an economy by transferring out innovatory capabilities and manufacturing capacity without any compensatory upgrading of the remaining resources. The uncertainties about the consequences of outward FDI remain great, and the historical evidence can at best only confirm that the possession of a large stock of outward FDI does not necessarily either reflect or sustain a country's overall competitive situation.

The continuing uncertainties about the impact of international business over time carry important implications for contemporary policy makers. Having been criticised and restrained for half a century, MNEs are again fashionable worldwide. However while it makes no sense to maintain policy regimes which exclude them, liberalisation policies based on assumptions that FDI is a panacea to a country's economic problems also rest on illusions. The package of resources that MNEs can transfer across borders has great potential to increase welfare and incomes, but policy-makers need to be aware that there are costs as well as benefits in multinational investment, and that both the exact nature of the package and – above all – the nature of the host economy will be crucial determinants of the final outcome.

# Appendix 1
## The top fifty MNEs ranked by foreign assets, 1992[1]

| Rank | Corporation | Country | Industry | Foreign assets[2] | Total assets | Foreign sales | Total sales | Foreign employment | Total employment |
|---|---|---|---|---|---|---|---|---|---|
| | | | | (Billions of dollars) | | | | (Thousands of employees) | |
| 1 | Royal Dutch/Shell[3] | United Kingdom/Netherlands | Petroleum refining | 69.4 | 100.8 | 45.5 | 96.6 | 91.0 | 127.0 |
| 2 | Exxon | United States | Petroleum refining | 48.2 | 85.0 | 93.1 | 115.7 | 59.0 | 95.0 |
| 3 | IBM | United States | Computers | 45.7 | 86.7 | 39.9 | 64.5 | 143.9 | 301.5 |
| 4 | General Motors | United States | Motor vehicles and parts | 41.8 | 191.0 | 42.3 | 132.4 | 272.0 | 750.0 |
| 5 | Hitachi | Japan | Electronics | – | 66.6 | 13.9 | 58.4 | – | 324.2 |
| 6 | Matsushita Electric | Japan | Electronics | 28.7 | 74.4 | 29.9 | 60.8 | 94.8 | 252.1 |
| 7 | Nestlé | Switzerland | Food | 28.0 | 31.3 | 37.7 | 38.4 | 211.3 | 218.0 |
| 8 | Ford | United States | Automobiles | 24.2 | 180.5 | 33.2 | 100.1 | 167.0 | 325.3 |
| 9 | Alcatel Alsthom | France | Electronics | 22.9 | 44.4 | 18.0 | 30.7 | 106.3 | 203.0 |
| 10 | General Electric | United States | Electronics | 22.6 | 192.9 | 8.4 | 57.1 | 58.0 | 231.0 |
| 11 | Philips Electronics | Netherlands | Electronics | 22.4 | 28.6 | 31.0 | 33.3 | 225.8 | 257.7 |
| 12 | Mobil | United States | Petroleum refining | – | 40.6 | 49.7 | 64.1 | 28.2 | 63.7 |
| 13 | Asea Brown Boveri | Switzerland | Electronics, electrical equipment | – | 25.9 | 26.3 | 29.6 | 198.8 | 213.4 |
| 14 | Elf Aquitaine | France | Petroleum refining | – | 45.1 | 13.2 | 36.2 | – | 87.9 |
| 15 | Volkswagen | Germany | Motor vehicles and parts | – | 46.6 | 29.4 | 54.7 | 109.0 | 273.0 |
| 16 | Toyota Motor Co | Japan | Motor vehicles and parts | 20.7 | 76.7 | 22.0 | 81.3 | 16.3 | 108.2 |
| 17 | Siemens | Germany | Electronics | – | 44.6 | 27.0 | 50.3 | 160.0 | 413.0 |
| 18 | Daimler-Benz | Germany | Transport and communication | – | 52.5 | 35.8 | 63.1 | 74.0 | 376.5 |
| 19 | British Petroleum | United Kingdom | Petroleum refining | – | 31.5 | 34.0 | 58.6 | 71.7 | 97.7 |
| 20 | Unilever | United Kingdom/Netherlands | Food | 19.4 | 24.2 | 35.0 | 43.7 | 247.9 | 283.2 |
| 21 | Fiat | Italy | Motor vehicles and parts | 19.2 | 58.0 | 20.3 | 40.1 | 82.6 | 285.5 |
| 22 | Sony | Japan | Electronics | 19.0 | 39.1 | 13.4 | 34.4 | 71.1 | 126.0 |
| 23 | Hanson | United Kingdom | Building materials | 17.5 | 36.6 | 8.2 | 15.7 | 54.0 | 75.0 |

| | Company | Country | Industry | | | | | | |
|---|---|---|---|---|---|---|---|---|---|
| 24 | ENI | Italy | Petroleum refining | — | 54.9 | 12.9 | 33.8 | 25.2 | 124.0 |
| 25 | Du Pont | United States | Chemicals | 16.0 | 38.9 | 17.5 | 37.8 | 36.9 | 128.7 |
| 26 | BAT Industries | United Kingdom | Tobacco | 14.2 | 43.6 | 24.1 | 31.2 | 183.0 | 198.0 |
| 27 | Philip Morris | United States | Food | 13.8 | 50.0 | 20.0 | 59.1 | 70.0 | 161.0 |
| 28 | Nissho Iwai | Japan | Trading | — | 40.7 | 35.0 | 91.6 | 2.1 | 7.3 |
| 29 | Grand Metropolitan | United Kingdom | Food | 13.0 | 16.7 | 11.2 | 79.8 | — | 102.4 |
| 30 | Bayer | Germany | Chemicals | 12.8 | 23.7 | 20.7 | 26.4 | 79.0 | 156.4 |
| 31 | Chrysler | United States | Motor vehicles and parts | — | 40.7 | 4.3 | 36.9 | 35.1 | 113.0 |
| 32 | Lyonnaise des Eaux | France | Construction | — | 24.3 | 7.4 | 16.4 | 83.9 | 161.1 |
| 33 | Total | France | Petroleum refining | — | 20.9 | 14.9 | 25.9 | 28.5 | 51.1 |
| 34 | Seagram | Canada | Beverages | 11.3 | 11.8 | 5.9 | 6.1 | 9.3 | 15.8 |
| 35 | Saint Gobain | France | Building materials | — | 17.2 | 9.1 | 14.1 | 66.9 | 100.4 |
| 36 | Dow Chemical | United States | Chemicals | 10.8 | 25.4 | 9.4 | 18.9 | 28.2 | 61.4 |
| 37 | Xerox | United States | Scientific and photo equipment | — | 34.1 | 9.1 | 18.3 | — | 107.5 |
| 38 | Toshiba | Japan | Electronics | — | 45.0 | 11.0 | 37.0 | 29.0 | 173.0 |
| 39 | Ciba-Geigy | Switzerland | Chemicals | 10.4 | 21.0 | 10.5 | 15.9 | 68.4 | 90.6 |
| 40 | Procter & Gamble | United States | Soaps and cosmetics | 10.2 | 24.9 | 15.9 | 30.4 | 59.4 | 103.5 |
| 41 | BASF | Germany | Chemicals | — | 24.7 | 18.2 | 28.1 | 41.9 | 112.0 |
| 42 | Chevron | United States | Petroleum refining | 10.1 | 34.0 | 13.2 | 41.4 | 10.1 | 49.3 |
| 43 | Michelin | France | Rubber and plastics | 9.7 | 14.2 | 10.4 | 12.7 | — | 130.7 |
| 44 | Petrofina | Belgium | Petroleum industry | — | 10.7 | — | 16.7 | 10.5 | 15.5 |
| 45 | Honda | Japan | Motor vehicles and parts | — | 24.1 | 19.5 | 29.3 | — | 90.9 |
| 46 | Sandoz | Switzerland | Pharmaceuticals | 9.3 | 12.7 | 9.8 | 10.2 | 45.8 | 53.4 |
| 47 | Bridgestone | Japan | Rubber and plastics | — | 14.8 | 7.5 | 14.0 | 54.0 | 85.8 |
| 48 | Texaco | United States | Petroleum refining | 9.2 | 26.0 | 17.2 | 36.8 | 13.1 | 38.0 |
| 49 | Hoechst | Germany | Chemicals | — | 22.9 | 22.1 | 29.4 | 90.3 | 177.7 |
| 50 | Electrolux | Sweden | Electronics | — | 21.0 | 5.4 | 22.0 | 82.0 | 372.0 |

*Source:* UN 1994: 6

*Notes:*
(1) This table excludes banking and finance
(2) Data on foreign assets is not available for the companies for which no figure is given. The ranking is according to foreign assets estimated on the basis of the ratio of foreign to total employment, foreign to total fixed assets, and other ratios
(3) Foreign sales figures are outside Europe whereas foreign employment figures are outside the United Kingdom and the Netherlands

# Definition of key terms

*Agency house*   A trading company active in Southeast Asia in the nineteenth and twentieth centuries.

*Antitrust*   Laws against monopolies or restrictive practices in uncompetitive market conditions.

*Brand*   A name which facilitates product differentiation.

*Cartel*   A group of firms which enter into an agreement to set mutually acceptable prices or a restriction on the output of a commodity.

*Commonwealth*   Informal grouping of former constituents of British Empire.

*Culture*   The learned attitudes of a society. It can refer to an organisation or to a nation.

*Economies of scale*   These arise when expansion of the scale of production causes total production costs to increase less than proportionately with output.

*Economies of scope*   These arise when diversification into new product lines permits a reduction of unit costs.

*Exchange controls*   The control by governments of dealings in foreign currencies and gold.

*Eurodollars*   Dollars held by individuals and institutions outside the United States.

*European Union*   Formed as European Economic Community as a result of Treaty of Rome (1957) and consisting of France, West Germany, Italy, Belgium, Netherlands and Luxembourg. Subsequently known as the European Community and (from 1993) the European Union. Enlarged to include the United Kingdom, Denmark and Ireland in 1973, Greece in 1981, Spain and Portugal in 1986, and Sweden, Finland and Austria in 1995.

*First mover advantages*   These are held by the firms which exploit first a new technology, distribution system or organisation system. The resulting strong competitive positions represent barriers to entry by 'follower' firms.

*Foreign direct investment (FDI)*   An investment in a foreign firm which involves managerial control.

*Franchising*   An arrangement whereby one party gives an independent party the use of a trademark that is an essential asset and continued assistance in the operation of the business.

*Free-standing company*   A firm that did not grow out of an existing domestic business but was established specifically to operate in a foreign country. This form of company existed in great numbers before 1914, and is currently regarded as a form of FDI.

*Gold Standard*   The international monetary system prevalent before 1914 (and in the 1920s) whereby the value of national currencies was fixed to gold and central banks were obliged to give gold in exchange for any of their currency presented to them.

*Greenfield investment* When an MNE opens a new facility in a foreign country as opposed to entering a market by acquiring an existing facility.

*Home economy* The country where an MNE is headquartered.

*Host economy* The recipient country of an MNE investment.

*Horizontal integration* The establishment of plants to make the same or similar goods.

*Intangible asset* Knowledge about technology or market owned and possessed by a firm which yields a rent to the firm.

*Inward investment* FDI by foreign enterprises into a host economy.

*Intra-firm trade* Trade flows across borders but between affiliates of the same company.

*Joint ventures* When two or more firms share in the ownership of a direct investment.

*Keiretsu* A vertical grouping of companies in Japan. Usually used to describe vertical production *keiretsu* that consist of a core manufacturing company and its numerous subcontractors and affiliates.

*Kigyo shudan* A horizontal grouping of companies in Japan.

*Lean production* A production system developed by the Toyota Motor Company in which materials and parts are produced and delivered just before they are needed. Also known as the just-in-time system or Toyota production system. Lean production is used more widely to describe many aspects of Japanese management, including quality control and related human resource management (HRM) practices.

*Licensing* An agreement whereby one firm gives to another the use of assets such as trademarks and patents.

*Location-specific factors* Factors which are specific to particular locations and have to be used in those locations, and which are available on the same terms to all firms.

*Managerial capitalism* A term used to describe a system where the ownership of firms has been separated from the control. Managerial firms are controlled by hierarchies of salaried executives. Developed in the United States and Europe in the last quarter of the nineteenth century.

*Mass production* A production system pioneered by Henry Ford before the First World War involving the use of interchangeable parts and assembly line process. Also known as Fordism.

*Multidivisional company (M-form)* A decentralised form of firm organisation under which managerial control over functions such as R & D and sales was located in each corporate division, freeing upper management to make long-term decisions and allocate resources throughout an organisation. First adopted before 1914 by Siemens in Germany and by Du Pont in the United States around 1920.

*Nationalisation* Ownership and control by the state.

*Newly industrializing countries (NICs)* A number of developing economies which have undergone rapid growth since the 1960s. The growth of the four Asian 'tigers' – Singapore, Hong Kong, South Korea and Taiwan – was greatest. The term is applied to a number of other Asian economies which underwent fast growth subsequently – such as Malaysia and Thailand – and a number of Latin American countries, especially Brazil and Mexico.

*Oligopoly* A type of market in which there is a relatively high degree of concentration where a small number of firms account for a large proportion of output.

*Opportunism*   This refers to various forms of dishonest or guileful behaviour.

*Outsourcing*   A situation in which a domestic company uses foreign suppliers for components or finished products.

*Outward investment*   FDI by domestic enterprises from their home economy to a foreign country.

*Personal capitalism*   A term used to describe family-owned and controlled business in contrast to managerial enterprises. Chandler (1990) uses the term more widely – with reference to British management – to include a personal 'style' of management not involving the use of complex layers of professional managers.

*Portfolio investment*   The acquisition of foreign securities by individuals or institutions without any control over the management of the companies concerned.

*Privatisation*   The transfer of assets owned by the state into private ownership.

*Sequestration*   The forced acquisition and sale of business assets, typically during a war.

*Sogo shosha*   A Japanese general trading company.

*Soviet Union*   Socialist and centrally planned economy in existence between 1917 and 1989. Collapsed in 1989 and replaced by a number of independent republics, including Russia and Ukraine.

*Strategic alliance*   A collaborative agreement between firms for various reasons, but often concerned with technology or marketing.

*Tariff*   A government tax usually on imports levied on goods shipped internationally.

*Transaction cost*   The costs of transacting in a market arising from bounded rationality, opportunism and asset-specificity. MNEs arise from internalising across borders markets with high transactions costs.

*Vertical integration*   The undertaking by a single firm of successive stages in the process of production of particular goods.

*Voluntary export restraint (VER)*   A non-tariff barrier and form of import quota whereby a foreign government agrees to 'restrain' exports from its firms to a foreign country.

*Zaibatsu*   The family-owned business conglomerates which were influential elements of the Japanese business system before 1945. Dissolved during the Allied occupation after the Second World War.

# Appendix 3

# Brief historical chronology

| | |
|---|---|
| c.1760–c.1830 | First Industrial Revolution |
| 1792–1815 | French Revolutionary and Napoleonic Wars |
| 1852 | London and Paris joined by telegraph |
| 1859 | World's first oil well in Pennsylvania, United States |
| 1861–65 | American Civil War |
| 1868 | Meiji Restoration in Japan |
| 1869 | Opening of Suez Canal |
| c.1870-c.1900 | Second Industrial Revolution |
| 1890 | McKinlay Act in United States raises tariffs |
| 1908 | Oil discovered in Iran |
| c.1910 | Henry Ford develops mass production |
| 1914–18 | First World War |
| 1915 | Opening of Panama Canal |
| 1917 | Communist Revolution in Russia |
| 1929–30s | Great Depression |
| 1933–45 | Nazi regime in Germany |
| 1939–45 | Second World War |
| 1947 | Indian independence from British Empire |
| 1947 | General Agreement on Tariffs and Trade (GATT) signed |
| 1948 | Fabrication of first successful transistor at Bell Laboratories |
| 1949 | Communist Revolution in China |
| 1950–53 | Korean War |
| 1950s/60s | 'Economic miracles' in Western Europe and Japan |
| 1957 | Treaty of Rome and formation of European Economic Community |
| 1959–60 | Origins of Eurodollar market |
| 1965 | Intelsat 1 satellite launched |
| 1965–73 | Vietnam War |
| 1971 | United States abandons fixed exchange rate |
| 1973 | First World Oil Crisis |
| 1979 | Second World Oil Crisis |
| 1982 | Outbreak of World Debt Crisis |
| 1989 | Collapse of Communism in Eastern Europe |
| 1990 | Federal Republic of Germany merges with German Democratic Republic |
| 1994 | North American Free Trade Agreement |

# Bibliography

This bibliography contains references to all works cited in the text and a number of others. It is not intended to be a fully comprehensive guide to the literature on the history of international business. Jones (1993b) provides a more extensive bibliography on the historical literature, while Dunning (1992) has the best bibliography on all aspects of multinationals.

Abeggelen, James and Stalk, George (1985) *Kaisha: The Japanese Corporation*, New York: Basic Books.

Abel, Christopher and Lewis, Colin (eds) (1985) *Latin America, Economic Imperialism and the State*, London: Athlone.

Abo, Tetsuo (1982) 'ITT's international business activities, 1920–40: the remarkable advance and setback of a "pure international utility company"', *Annals of the Institute of Social Science*, University of Tokyo, No. 24.

—— (ed.) (1994) *Hybrid Factory. The Japanese Production System in the United States*, New York: Oxford University Press.

Abreu, Marcelo de Paiva (1990) 'Brazil as a creditor: sterling balances, 1940–1952', *Economic History Review* 43(3): 450–69.

Aharoni, Yair (ed.) (1993) *Coalitions and Competition: The Globalization of Professional Business Services*, London: Routledge.

Alford, B. W. E. and Harvey, Charles (1980) 'Copperbelt merger: the formation of the Rhokana Corporation 1930–1932', *Business History Review* 54(3): 330–58.

Allen, G. C. and Donnithorne, A. G. (1954) *Western Enterprise in Far Eastern Economic Development*, London: Allen & Unwin.

Alvesson, Mats and Lindkvist, Lars (1993) 'Transaction costs, clans and corporate culture', *Journal of Management Studies* 30(3): 427–52.

Armstrong, Christopher and Nelles, H. V. (1988) *Southern Exposure: Canadian Promoters in Latin America and the Caribbean, 1896–1930*, Toronto: University of Toronto Press.

Bader, Michael B. (1980) 'Breast-feeding: the role of multinational corporations in Latin America', in K. Kumar (ed.) *Transnational Enterprises: Their Impact on Third World Societies and Cultures*, Boulder: Westview.

Bagchi, Amiya Kumar (1972) *Private Investment in India 1900–1939*, Cambridge: Cambridge University Press.

Balasubramanyam, V. N. (1993) 'Entrepreneurship and the growth of the firm: the case of the British food and drink industries in the 1980s', in J. Brown and M. B. Rose (eds) *Entrepreneurship, Networks and Modern Business*, Manchester: Manchester University Press.

Bamberg, J. H. (1994) *The History of the British Petroleum Company*, Vol. 2, Cambridge: Cambridge University Press.

Barbezat, Daniel (1991) 'A price for every product, every place: the international steel export cartel, 1933–39', *Business History* 33(4) 68–86.

Barjot, Dominique (1986) 'An opportunity seized early: French entrepreneurs in the export market for major public works (1857–1914)' in W. Fischer, R. M. McInnis and J. Schneider (eds) *The Emergence of a World Economy 1500–1914*, Part II: 1850–1914, Wiesbaden: Franz Steiner Verlag.

Bartlett, Christopher A. and Ghoshal, S. (1989) *Managing Across Borders*, Boston, Mass: Harvard Business School Press.

Beaud, Claude (1986) 'Investments and profits of the multinational Schneider group: 1894–1943', in A. Teichova, M. Lévy-Leboyer and H. Nussbaum (eds), *Multinational Enterprise in Historical Perspective*, Cambridge: Cambridge University Press.

Behrman, Jack N. and Grosse, Robert E. (1990) *International Business and Governments*, Columbia: University of South Carolina Press.

Belderbos, R. A. (1992) 'Large multinational enterprises based in a small economy: effects on domestic investment', *Weltwirtschaftliches Archiv* 128(3): 543–57.

Biersteker, Thomas J. (1987) *Multinationals, the State, and Control of the Nigerian Economy*, Princeton: Princeton University Press.

Blaich, Fritz (1984) *Amerikanische Firmen in Deutschland 1890–1918*, Wiesbaden: Franz Steiner Verlag.

Blomström, Magnus (1986) 'Multinationals and market structure in Mexico', *World Development* 14: 523–30.

—— (1990) 'The competitiveness of firms and countries', in J. H. Dunning, B. Kogut and M. Blomström, *Globalisation of Firms and the Competitiveness of Nations*, Lund: Lund University Press.

Blomström, Magnus and Kokko, A. (1994) 'Home country effects of foreign direct investment: evidence from Sweden', National Bureau of Economic Research Working Paper No. 4639.

Blomström, Magnus and Lipsey, R. E. (1989) 'The export performance of US and Swedish multinationals', *Review of Income and Wealth* 35(3): 245–64

Blussé, L. and Gaastra, F. (eds) (1981) *Companies and Trade*, Leiden: Leiden University Press.

Boisot, Max H. (1986) 'Markets and hierarchies in a cultural perspective', *Organization Studies* 7(2): 135–58.

Bolle, Jacques (1968) *Solvay*, Brussells: Sodi.

Bosson, Rex and Varon, Bension (1977) *The Mining Industry and the Developing Countries*, Oxford: Oxford University Press.

Bostock, Frances and Jones, Geoffrey (1989) 'British business in Iran, 1860s-1970s', in R. P. T. Davenport-Hines and Geoffrey Jones (eds) *British Business in Asia since 1860*, Cambridge: Cambridge University Press.

—— (1994) 'Foreign multinationals in British Manufacturing, 1850–1962', *Business History* 36(1): 89–126

Boyd-Barrett (1989) 'Multinational news agencies', in P. Enderwick (ed.) *Multinational Service Firms*, London: Routledge.

Brech, M. and Sharp, M. (1984) *Inward Investment: Policy Options for the United Kingdom*, London: Routledge & Kegan Paul.

Broehl, Wayne G. (1992) *Cargill. Trading the World's Grain*, Hanover: University Press of New England.

Brown, Martin and McKern, Bruce (1987) *Aluminium, Copper and Steel in Developing Countries*, Paris: OECD.

Brown, Rajeswary A. (1994) *Capital and Entrepreneurship in Southeast Asia*, London: Macmillan.

Brown, S. R. (1979) 'The transfer of technology to China in the nineteenth century: the role of foreign direct investment', *Journal of Economic History* 39(1): 181–97.

Buckley, Peter J. (1988) 'Organisational forms and multinational companies', in S. Thompson and M. Wright (eds) *Internal Organisation, Efficiency and Profit*, Oxford: Philip Allen.

Buckley, Peter J. and Casson, M. (1976) *The Future of the Multinational Enterprise*, London: Macmillan.

—— (1985) *The Economic Theory of the Multinational Enterprise*, London: Macmillan.

—— (1989) 'Multinational enterprises in less-developed countries: cultural and economic interactions', University of Reading Discussion Papers in International Investment and Business Studies, Series B, No. 126.

Bussière, Eric (1983) 'The interests of the Banque de l'Union Parisienne in Czechoslovakia, Hungary and the Balkans 1919–30', in A. Teichova and P. L. Cottrell (eds) *International Business and Central Europe, 1918–1939*, Leicester: Leicester University Press.

Cain, P. J. and Hopkins, A. G. (1993) *British Imperialism: Crisis and Deconstruction 1914–1990*, London: Longman.

Calder, Kent E. (1993) *Strategic Capitalism*, Princeton: Princeton University Press.

Cameron, Rondo and Bovykin, V. I. (eds) (1991) *International Banking 1870–1914*, New York: Oxford University Press.

Campbell-Kelly, Martin (1989) *ICL. A Business and Technical History*, Oxford: Clarendon Press.

Cantwell, J. A. (1989) *Technological Innovation and Multinational Corporations*, Oxford: Basil Blackwell.

—— (1991) 'A survey of theories of international production', in Christos N. Pitelis and Roger Sugden (eds) *The Nature of the Transnational Firm*, London: Routledge.

—— (1992) 'Innovation and technological competitiveness', in Peter J. Buckley and Mark Casson (eds) *Multinational Enterprises in the World Economy*, Aldershot: Edward Elgar.

—— (1995) 'The globalisation of technology: what remains of the product cycle model?' *Cambridge Journal of Economics* 19: 155–74

Cantwell, J. A. and Bellak, Christian (1994) 'Measuring the importance of international production: the re-estimation of foreign direct investment at current values', University of Reading Discussion Papers in International Investment and Business Studies, Series B, VII, No. 192.

Cardoso, Fernando Henrique and Faletto, Enzo (1979) *Dependency and Development in Latin America*, Berkeley: University of California Press.

Carlos, Ann and Nicholas, Stephen (1988) 'Giants of an earlier capitalism: the chartered trading companies as modern multinationals', *Business History Review* 62(3): 398–419.

Caron, F. (1984) 'Foreign investments and technology transfers', in A. Okochi and T. Inoue (eds), *Overseas Business Activities*, Tokyo: University of Tokyo Press.

Carosso, Vincent P. and Sylla, R. (1991) 'US banks in international finance', in Rondo Cameron and V. I. Bovykin (eds) *International Banking 1870–1914*, New York: Oxford University Press.

Carstensen, Fred V. (1984) *American Enterprise in Foreign Markets. Singer and*

*International Harvester in Imperial Russia,* Chapel Hill: University of North Carolina Press.

Casson, M. (1982) *The Entrepreneur. An Economic Theory,* Oxford: Martin Robertson.

—— (1983) (ed.) *The Growth of International Business,* London: Allen & Unwin.

—— (1985) 'Entrepreneurship and the dynamics of foreign direct investment', in Peter J. Buckley and Mark Casson *The Economic Theory of the Multinational Enterprise,* London: Macmillan.

—— (1986) 'Contractual arrangements for technology transfer: new evidence from business history', *Business History* 28(4): 5–35.

—— (1987) *The Firm and the Market,* Oxford: Basil Blackwell.

—— (1990a) 'Evolution of multinational banks: a theoretical perspective', in Geoffrey Jones (ed.) *Banks as Multinationals,* London: Routledge.

—— (1990b) *Enterprise and Competitiveness: A Systems View of International Business,* Oxford: Clarendon Press.

—— (1991a) *Economics of Business Culture: Game Theory, Transactions Costs and Economic Performance,* Oxford: Clarendon Press.

—— (ed.) (1991b) *Global Research Strategy and International Competitiveness,* Oxford: Basil Blackwell.

—— (1994a) 'Institutional diversity in overseas enterprise: explaining the free-standing company', *Business History* 36(4): 95–108.

—— (1994b) 'Why are firms hierarchical?', *Journal of the Economics of Business* 1(1): 47–76.

—— (1995) 'Information costs and the organizational structure of the multinational enterprise', University of Reading Discussion Papers in International Investment and Business Studies, Series B, VII, No. 193.

Casson, M., Barry D. and Horner, D. (1986) 'The shipping industry', in Mark Casson (ed.) *Multinationals and World Trade,* London: Allen & Unwin.

Caves, Richard E. (1982) *Multinational Enterprise and Economic Analysis,* Cambridge: Cambridge University Press.

Chalmin, Philippe (1985) *Negociants et Chargeurs,* Paris: Economica.

—— (1986) 'The strategy of a multinational in the world sugar economy: the case of Tate and Lyle: 1870–1980', in A. Teichova, M. Lévy-Leboyer and H. Nussbaum (eds) *Multinational Enterprise in Historical Perspective,* Cambridge: Cambridge University Press.

—— (1987) 'The rise of international commodity trading companies in Europe in the nineteenth century', in S. Yonekawa and H. Yoshihara (eds) *Business History of General Trading Companies,* Tokyo: University of Tokyo Press.

—— (1990) *The Making of a Sugar Giant. Tate and Lyle 1859–1989,* Char: Harwood.

Chandler, A. D. (1962) *Strategy and Structure,* Cambridge, Mass: Harvard University Press.

—— (1977) *The Visible Hand,* Cambridge, Mass: Harvard University Press.

—— (1980) 'The growth of the transnational industrial firm in the United States and the United Kingdom: a comparative analysis', *Economic History Review* 33(3): 396 - 410.

—— (1986) 'The evolution of modern global competition', in Michael E. Porter (ed.) *Competition in Global Industries,* Boston, Mass: Harvard Business School Press.

—— (1990) *Scale and Scope,* Cambridge, Mass: Harvard University Press.

—— (1994) 'The competitive performance of US industrial enterprises since the Second World War', *Business History Review* 68(1): 1–72.

Channon, Derek F. (1973) *The Strategy and Structure of British Enterprise*, London: Macmillan.

Chapman, K. (1991) *The International Petrochemical Industry*, Oxford: Blackwell.

Chapman, S. D. (1985) 'British-based investment groups before 1914', *Economic History Review* 38(2): 230–51.

—— (1987) 'Investment groups in India and South Africa', *Economic History Review* 40(2): 275–80.

—— (1992) *Merchant Enterprise in Britain*, Cambridge: Cambridge University Press.

Cheape, Charles (1988) 'Not politicians but sound businessmen: Norton Company and the Third Reich', *Business History Review* 62(3): 444–66.

Chen, Edward K. Y. (ed.) (1994) *Technology Transfer to Developing Countries*, London: Routledge.

Child, J. and Kieser, A. (1979) 'Organizational and managerial roles in British and West German companies', in C. J. Lammers and D. J. Hickson (eds) *Organisations Alike and Unlike*, London: Routledge & Kegan Paul.

Cho, Dong-Sung (1984) 'The Anatomy of the Korean General Trading Company', *Journal of Business Research* 12: 241–55.

—— (1987) *The General Trading Company*, Lexington, Mass: Lexington Books.

Choate, Pat (1990) *Agents of Influence*, New York: Alfred A. Knopf.

Church, Roy (1986) 'The effects of American multinationals in the British motor industry, 1911–83', in A. Teichova, M. Lévy-Leboyer and H. Nussbaum (eds) *Multinational Enterprises in Historical Perspective*, Cambridge: Cambridge University Press.

—— (1994) *The Rise and Decline of the British Motor Industry*, London: Macmillan.

Clayton, Lawrence A. (1985) *Grace. W.R. Grace & Co. The Formative Years 1850–1930*, Ottawa, Illinois: Jameson Books.

Clegg, J. (1987) *Multinational Enterprises and World Competition*, London: Macmillan.

Cleveland, Harold van B. and Huertas, Thomas F. (1985) *Citibank 1812–1970*, Cambridge, Mass: Harvard University Press.

Coase, R. H. (1937) 'The nature of the firm', *Economica* 4: 386–405.

Cobbe, James H. (1979) *Governments and Mining Companies in Developing Countries*, Boulder, Colorado: Westview.

Cochran, Sherman (1980) *Big Business in China*, Cambridge, Mass: Harvard University Press.

Coleman, D. C. (1969) *Courtaulds*, 2 vols, Oxford: Clarendon Press.

Collins, E. J. T. (1994) 'Brands and breakfast cereals in Britain', in Geoffrey Jones and Nicholas J. Morgan (eds) *Adding Value. Brands and Marketing in Food and Drink*, London: Routledge.

Contractor, Farok J. (1990) 'Ownership patterns of US joint ventures abroad and the liberalization of foreign government regulations in the 1980s: evidence from the benchmark surveys', *Journal of International Business Studies* 21(1): 55–73

Coquery-Vidrovitch, Catherine (1975) 'L'impact des intérêts coloniaux: S.C.O.A. et C.F.A.O. dans l'Ouest Africain, 1910–1965', *Journal of African History* 16(4): 595–621.

Corley, T. A. B. (1983) *A History of the Burmah Oil Company 1886–1924*, London: Heinemann.

—— (1986) *A History of the Burmah Oil Company 1924–1966*, London: Heinemann.

—— (1989) 'The nature of multinationals, 1870–1939', in A. Teichova, M. Lévy-

Leboyer and H. Nussbaum (eds), *Historical Studies in International Corporate Business*, Cambridge: Cambridge University Press.

—— (1993) 'Foreign direct investment and British economic decline 1870–1914', University of Reading Discussion Papers in International Investment and Business Studies, Series B, VI, No. 176.

—— (1994) 'Britain's overseas investments in 1914 revisited', *Business History* 36(1): 71–88.

Cortada, James W. (1993) *Before the Computer*, Princeton: Princeton University Press.

Cox, Howard (1989) 'Growth and ownership in the international tobacco industry: BAT 1902–1927', *Business History* 31(1): 44–67.

Crisp, Olga (1976) *Studies in the Russian Economy before 1914*, London: Macmillan.

Daniels, P. W. (1986) 'Foreign banks and metropolitan development: a comparison of London and New York', *Tidjschrift voor Economische en Sociale Geografie* 77(4): 269–87.

Daniels, P. W., Thrift, N.J. and Leyshon, A. (1989) 'Internationalisation of professional producer services: accountancy conglomerates', in Peter Enderwick (ed.) *Multinational Service Firms*, London: Routledge.

Darby, Michael R. (1986) 'The internationalization of American banking and finance: structure, risk, and world interest rates', *Journal of International Money and Finance* 5: 403–28.

Dassbach, Carl H. A. C. (1989) *Global Enterprises and the World Economy*, New York: Garland.

Davenport-Hines, R. P. T. (1986) 'Vickers as a multinational before 1945', in Geoffrey Jones (ed.) *British Multinationals: Origins, Management and Performance*, Aldershot: Gower.

Davenport-Hines, R. P. T. and Jones, Geoffrey (eds) (1989a) *British Business in Asia since 1860*, Cambridge: Cambridge University Press.

—— (1989b) 'British business in Japan since 1868', in R. P. T. Davenport-Hines and Geoffrey Jones (eds) *British Business in Asia since 1860*, Cambridge: Cambridge University Press.

Davenport-Hines, R. P. T. and Slinn, Judy (1992) *Glaxo: A History to 1962*, Cambridge: Cambridge University Press.

Davies, Howard (1977) 'Technology transfer through commercial transactions', *Journal of Industrial Economics* 26(2): 161–75.

Davies, Peter N. (1973) *The Trade Makers: Elder Dempster in West Africa 1852–1972*, London: Allen & Unwin.

—— (1977) 'The impact of the expatriate shipping lines on the economic development of British West Africa', *Business History* 19(1): 3–17.

—— (1990) *Fyffes and the Banana: Musa Sapientum*, London: Athlone.

Davies, Robert Bruce (1976) *Peacefully Working to Conquer the World. Singer Sewing Machines in Foreign Markets, 1854–1920*, New York: Arno Press.

Daviet, Jean-Pierre (1989) *Une multinationale à la Française*, Paris: Fayard.

Deloitte, Plender, Griffiths & Co. (1958) *Deloitte & Co. 1845–1956*, London: Deloitte, Plender, Griffiths & Co.

Demsetz, H. (1978) 'The theory of the firm revisited', *Journal of Law, Economics and Organisation* 4: 141–61.

Devos, Greta (1993) 'Agfa-Gevaert and Belgian multinational enterprise', in Geoffrey Jones and Harm G. Schröter (eds) *The Rise of Multinationals in Continental Europe*, Aldershot: Edward Elgar.

Dicken, Peter (1992) *Global Shift*, London: Paul Chapman.

Dierikx, Marc L. J. (1991) 'Struggle for prominence: clashing Dutch and British interests on the colonial air routes, 1918–42', *Journal of Contemporary History* 26: 335–51.

Donaldson, Robert A. (1984) 'Canadianization', in J. M. Spence and W. P. Rosenfeld (eds) *Foreign Investment Review Law in Canada*, Toronto: Butterworths.

Doner, Richard F. (1991) *Driving a Bargain. Automobile Industrialization and Japanese Firms in Southeast Asia*, Berkeley: University of California Press.

Dosi, Giovanni (1988) 'Sources, procedures, and microeconomic effects of innovation', *Journal of Economic Literature* 26 (September): 1120–71.

Drabble, J. H. (1991) *Malayan Rubber: The Interwar Years*, London: Macmillan.

Drabble, J. H. and Drake, P. J. (1981) 'The British agency houses in Malaysia: survival in a changing world', *Journal of Southeast Asian Studies* 12(2): 297–328.

Dumett, Raymond E. (1988) 'Sources for mining company history in Africa: the history and records of the Ashanti Goldfields Corporation (Ghana) Ltd', *Business History Review* 62(3): 502–15.

Dumoulin, Michel (1990) *Les Relations Économiques Italo-Belges (1861–1914)*, Brussels: Palais des Académies.

Dunning, J. H. (1958) *American Investment in British Manufacturing Industry*, London: Allen & Unwin.

—— (1970) *Studies in International Investment*, London: Allen & Unwin.

—— (1978) 'Ownership and country specific characteristics of Britain's international competitive position', University of Reading Discussion Papers in International Investment and Business Studies, No. 40.

—— (1981) 'Explaining the international direct investment position of countries: towards a dynamic or developmental approach', *Weltwirtschaftliches Archiv* 117: 30–64.

—— (1983) 'Changes in the level and structure of international production: the last one hundred years', in Mark Casson (ed.) *The Growth of International Business*, London: Allen & Unwin.

—— (ed.) (1985) *Multinational Enterprises, Economic Structure and International Competitiveness*, Chichester: John Wiley & Sons.

—— (1986) *Japanese Participation in British Industry*, London: Croom Helm.

—— (1988a) *Explaining International Production*, London: Unwin Hyman.

—— (1988b) *Multinationals, Technology and Competitiveness*, London: Unwin Hyman.

—— (1989) 'Multinational enterprise and the growth of services: some conceptual and theoretical issues', *The Service Industries Journal* 9(1): 5–39.

—— (1992) *Multinational Enterprises and the Global Economy*, Wokingham: Addison-Wesley.

—— (1993) *The Globalization of Business*, London: Routledge.

—— (1994) 'The strategy of Japanese and US manufacturing investment in Europe', in M. Mason and D. Encarnation (eds) *Does Ownership Matter?*, Clarendon Press: Oxford.

Dunning, J. H. and Archer, Howard (1987) 'The eclectic paradigm and the growth of UK multinational enterprise 1870–1983', *Business and Economic History* 16: 3–49.

Dunning, J. H., Cantwell, John and Corley, T. A. B. (1986) 'The theory of international production: some historical antecedents', in P. Hertner and G. Jones (eds) *Multinationals: Theory and History*, Aldershot: Gower.

Dunning, J. H. and Pearce, R. (1985) *The World's Largest Industrial Enterprises, 1962–1983*, Farnborough: Gower.

Dupuy, C., Milelli, C. and Savary, J. (1991) *Stratégies des Multinationales*, Montpellier-Paris: Reclus.

Dyer, Davis and Silicia, David B. (1990) *Labors of a Modern Hercules*, Boston, Mass: Harvard Business School Press.

Eakin, Marshall C. (1989) *British Enterprise in Brazil*, Durham: Duke University Press.

Egelhoff, W. G. (1984) 'Patterns of control in US, UK and European multinational corporations', *Journal of International Business Studies* 15(1): 73–83.

Eltis, W. and Fraser, Douglas (1992) 'The Contribution of Japanese industrial success to Britain and to Europe', *National Westminster Bank Quarterly Review* November: 2–19.

Encarnation, Dennis J. (1989) *Dislodging Multinationals. India's Strategy in Comparative Perspective*, Ithaca: Cornell University Press.

—— (1992) *Rivals beyond Trade*, Ithaca: Cornell University Press.

Enderwick, Peter (1989) 'Some economics of service-sector multinational enterprises', in Peter Enderwick (ed.), *Multinational Service Firms*, London: Routledge.

Ericsson, Magnus and Tegen, Andreas (1993) 'The corporate structure in the international mining industry: the present situation and the outlook for the mid-1990s', *Raw Material Report* 8(4): 4–11.

Evans, Peter B. (1979) *Dependent Development: The Alliance of Multinational, State and Local Capital in Brazil*, Princeton: Princeton University Press.

Fague, N. and Wells, L. T. (1982) 'Bargaining power of multinationals and host governments', *Journal of International Business Studies* 13(1): 9–23.

Falkus, Malcolm (1989) 'Early British business in Thailand', in R. P. T. Davenport-Hines and Geoffrey Jones (eds), *British Business in Asia since 1860*, Cambridge: Cambridge University Press.

Feinstein, Charles (1990) 'Britain's overseas investments in 1913', *Economic History Review* 43(2): 280–95.

Feldenkirchen, Wilfried (1992) *Werner von Siemens*, Berlin: Siemens Aktiengesellschaft.

Feldman, G. (1989) 'Foreign penetration of German enterprises after the First World War: the problem of Überfremdung', in A. Teichova, M. Lévy-Leboyer and H. Nussbaum (eds) *Historical Studies in International Corporate Business*, Cambridge: Cambridge University Press.

Ferrier, R. W. (1982) *The History of the British Petroleum Company*,Vol. 1, Cambridge: Cambridge University Press.

Fieldhouse, D. K. (1978) *Unilever Overseas*, London: Croom Helm.

—— (1986) 'The multinational: a critique of a concept', in A. Teichova, M. Lévy-Leboyer and H. Nussbaum (eds) *Multinational Enterprise in Historical Perspective*, Cambridge: Cambridge University Press.

—— (1994) *Merchant Capital and Economic Decolonization*, Oxford: Clarendon Press.

Finch, M. H. J. (1985) 'British imperialism in Uruguay: the public utility companies and the Batista State, 1900–1930', in Christopher Abel and Colin M. Lewis (eds) *Latin America, Economic Imperialism and the State*, London: Athlone.

Franko, L. (1974) 'The origins of multinational manufacturing by continental European firms', *Business History Review* 48(3): 272–302.

—— (1976) *The European Multinationals*, London: Harper & Row.

—— (1978) 'Organizational structures and multinational strategies of continental European enterprises', in M. Ghertman and J. Leontiades (eds) *European Research in International Business*, Amsterdam: North Holland.

—— (1989) 'Global corporate competition: who's winning, who's losing, and the R & D Factor as one reason why', *Strategic Management Journal* 10: 451–3.

—— (1991) 'Global corporate competition II: is the large American firm an Endangered Species?', *Business Horizons* November–December: 14–22.

French, M. J. (1987) 'The emergence of a US multinational enterprise: the Goodyear Tire and Rubber Company, 1910–1939', *Economic History Review* 40(1): 64–79.

—— (1991) *The US Tire Industry. A History*, Boston: Twayne.

Fridenson, P. (1986) 'The growth of multinational activities in the French motor industry, 1890–1979', in Peter Hertner and Geoffrey Jones (eds) *Multinationals: Theory and History*, Aldershot: Gower.

Fritsch, W. and Franco, G. (1991) *Foreign Direct Investment in Brazil: Its Impact on Industrial Restructuring*, Paris: OECD.

Fruin, W. Mark (1992) *The Japanese Enterprise System*, Oxford: Clarendon Press.

Fuji Xerox (1994) *Three Decades of Fuji Xerox 1962–1992*, Tokyo: Fuji Xerox.

Fursenko, A. A. (1991) 'The oil industry', in Rondo Cameron and V. I. Bovykin (eds) *International Banking 1870–1914*, New York: Oxford University Press.

Gales, Ben P. A. and Sluyterman, Keetie E. (1993) 'Outward bound. The rise of Dutch multinationals', in Geoffrey Jones and Harm Schröter (eds) *The Rise of Multinationals in Continental Europe*, Aldershot: Edward Elgar.

Gereffi, G. and Evans, P. (1981) 'Transnational corporations, dependent development, and state policy in the semiperiphery: a comparison of Brazil and Mexico', *Latin American Research Review* 16: 31–64.

Gerlach, Michael L. (1992) *Alliance Capitalism: The Social Transformation of Japanese Business*, Berkeley: University of California Press.

Giebelhaus, August W. (1994) 'The pause that refreshed the world: the evolution of Coca Cola's global marketing strategy', in Geoffrey Jones and Nicholas J. Morgan (eds) *Adding Value: Brands and Marketing in Food and Drink*, London: Routledge.

Gillespie, R. W. (1972) 'The policies of England, France and Germany as recipients of foreign direct investment', in F. Machlup, W. S. Salant and L. Tarshis (eds) *International Mobility and Movement of Capital*, New York: Columbia University Press.

Girault, R. (1973) *Emprunts Russes et Investissements Français en Russie, 1887–1914*, Paris: Libraire Armond Colin.

Glover, Daniel J. (1986) 'Multinational corporations and Third World agriculture', in H. Moran (ed.) *Investing in Development: New Roles for Private Capital*, Washington, D. C.: Overseas Development Council.

Goldberg, Lawrence G. and Johnson, Denise (1990) 'The determinants of US banking activity abroad', *Journal of International Money and Finance* 9: 123–37.

Gomes-Casseres, Benjamin (1990) 'Firm ownership preferences and host government restrictions: an integrated approach', *Journal of International Business Studies* 21(1): 1–22.

Gonjo, Yasuo (1993) *Banque Coloniale ou Banque d'Affaires. La Banque de l'Indochine sous la IIIe Republique*, Paris: Comité pour l'histoire économique et financière de la France.

Goodman, John B. (1993) 'Insurance: domestic regulation and international service competition', in David B. Yoffie (ed.) *Beyond Free Trade. Firms, Governments, and Global Competition*, Boston, Mass: Harvard Business School Press.

Graham, Edgar and Floering, Ingrid (1984) *The Modern Plantation in the Third World*, London: Croom Helm.

Graham, E. M. (1978) 'Transatlantic investment by multinational firms: a rivalistic phenomenon', *Journal of Post-Keynesian Economics* 1: 82–99.

Graham, E. M. and Krugman, Paul R. (1989) *Foreign Direct Investment in the United States*, Washington, D. C.: Institute for International Economics.

—— (1993) 'The surge in foreign direct investment in the 1980s', in Kenneth A. Froot (ed.) *Foreign Direct Investment*, Chicago: University of Chicago Press.

Graham, Richard (1968) *Britain and the Onset of Modernization in Brazil 1850–1914*, Cambridge: Cambridge University Press.

Gray, Jean M. and Gray, H. Peter (1981) 'The multinational bank: a financial MNC?', *Journal of Banking and Finance* 5: 33–63.

Greenhill, Robert G. (1995) 'Investment groups, free-standing company or multinational? Brazilian Warrant, 1909–52', *Business History* 37(1): 86–111.

Grieco, J. M. (1982) 'Between dependency and autonomy: India's experience with the international computer industry', *International Organization* 36: 609–32.

Grubel, H. G. (1977) 'A theory of multinational banking', *Banca Nazionale del Lavoro Quarterly Review* December: 342–63.

Guisinger, Stephen E. (1985) *Investment Incentives and Performance Requirements*, New York: Praeger.

Haggard, Stephan (1989) 'The political economy of foreign direct investment in Latin America', *Latin American Research Review* 24: 184–208.

Hakanson, Lars (1990) 'International decentralisation of R & D - the organizational challenges', in C. A. Bartlett, Y. Doz and G. Hedland (eds) *Managing the Global Firm*, London: Routledge.

Hamill, J. (1988) 'British acquisitions in the United States', *National Westminster Bank Quarterly Review* August: 2–17.

—— (1991) 'Strategic restructuring through international acquisitions and divestments', *Journal of General Management* 17(1): 27–44.

Hara, Terashi and Kudo, Akira (1992) 'International cartels in business history', in Akira Kudo and Terashi Hara (eds) *International Cartels in Business History*, Tokyo: University of Tokyo Press.

Harvey, Charles (1981) *The Rio Tinto Company. An Economic History of a Leading International Mining Concern 1873–1954*, Penzance: Alison Hodge.

Harvey, Charles and Press, Jon (1990a) 'The city and international mining, 1870–1914', *Business History* 32(3): 98–119.

—— (1990b) 'Issues in the history of mining and metallurgy', *Business History* 32(3): 1–11.

Harvey, Charles and Taylor, P. (1987) 'Mineral wealth and economic development: foreign direct investment in Spain, 1851–1913', *Economic History Review* 40(2): 185–208.

Heer, Jean (1966) *World Events 1866–1966. The First Hundred Years of Nestlé*, Rivaz: Nestlé.

Hennart, J. F. (1982) *A Theory of Multinational Enterprise*, Ann Arbor, Mich: University of Michigan Press.

—— (1986a) 'Internalisation in practice: early foreign direct investments in Malaysian tin mining', *Journal of International Business Studies* 17(2): 131–43.

—— (1986b) 'The tin industry', in Mark Casson (ed.) *Multinationals and World Trade*, London: Allen & Unwin.

—— (1987) 'Transactions costs and the multinational enterprise: the case of tin', *Business and Economic History* 16: 147–59.

—— (1991a) 'The transaction cost theory of the multinational enterprise', in Christos N. Pitelis and Roger Sugden (eds), *The Nature of the Transnational Firm*, London: Routledge.

—— (1991b) 'The transaction costs theory of joint ventures: an empirical study of Japanese subsidiaries in the United States', *Management Science* 37(4): 483–97.

—— (1993) 'Explaining the swollen middle: why most transactions are a mix of "market" and "hierarchies"', *Organization Science* 4(4): 529–47.

—— (1994a) 'International financial capital transfers: a transaction cost framework', *Business History* 36(1): 51–70.

—— (1994b) 'Free-standing firms and the internalization of markets for financial capital: a response to Casson', *Business History* 36(4): 118–31.

Hennart, J. F. and Larimo, J. (1995) 'The impact of culture on the strategy of multinational enterprises: does national origin affect ownership decisions?' (mimeo).

Heras, Raul Garcia (1987) 'Hostage private companies under restraint: British railways and transport co-ordination in Argentina during the 1930s', *Journal of Latin American Studies* 19: 41–67.

Hertner, Peter (1979) 'Fallstudien zu deutschen multinationalen Unternehmen vor dem ersten Weltkrieg', in N. Horn and J. Kocka (eds) *Law and the Formation of the Big Enterprises in the 19th and early 20th Centuries*, Gottingen: Vanderschoek & Ruprecht.

—— (1984) *Il capitale tedesco in Italia dall Unità alla Prima Guerra Mondiale Banche miste e sviluppo economico italiano*, Bologna: Il Mulino.

—— (1986) 'German multinational enterprise before 1914: some case studies', in Peter Hertner and Geoffrey Jones (eds) *Multinationals: Theory and History*, Aldershot: Gower.

—— (ed.) (1987a) *Per La Storia dell'Imprese Multinazionale in Europa*, Milan: Franco Angeli.

—— (1987b) 'Les sociétés financières suisses et le développement de l'industrie électrique jusqu'à la Première Guerre Mondiale', in F. Cardot (ed.) *1880–1980. Un Siécle d'Électricité dans le Monde*, Paris: PUF.

—— (1990) 'German banks abroad before 1914' in Geoffrey Jones (ed.) *Banks as Multinationals*, London: Routledge.

—— (1993) 'The German electrotechnical industry in the Italian market before the Second World War', in Geoffrey Jones and Harm G. Schröter (eds), *The Rise of Multinationals in Continental Europe*, Aldershot: Edward Elgar.

Hertner, Peter and Geoffrey Jones (eds) (1986) *Multinationals: Theory and History*, Aldershot: Gower.

Hildebrand, Karl-Gustaf (1985) *Expansion. Crisis. Reconstruction. Swedish Match 1917–1939*, Stockholm: Liber Förlag.

Hill, N. K. (1950) 'The history of the Imperial Continental Gas Association 1824–1900', unpublished PhD thesis, University of London.

Hirtle, Beverly (1991) 'Factors affecting the competitiveness of internationally active financial institutions', *Federal Reserve Bank of New York Quarterly Review* 16(1): 38–51.

Hofstede, G. (1980) *Cultures Consequences*, Beverly Hills, CA: Sage.

—— (1991) *Cultures and Organizations*, London: McGraw Hill.

Hollander, Stanley C. (1970) *Multinational Retailing*, East Lansing: Michigan State University Press.

Hood, Neil and Young, Stephen (1979) *The Economics of Multinational Enterprise*, London: Longman.

Hopkins, A. G. (1976a) 'Imperial business in Africa. Part 1: sources', *Journal of African History* 17(1): 29–48.

—— (1976b) 'Imperial business in Africa. Part 2: interpretations', *Journal of African History* 17(2) 267–90.

Horst, Thomas (1974) *At Home Abroad*, Cambridge, Mass: Ballinger.

Houston, Tom and Dunning, John H. (1976) *UK Industry Abroad*, London: Financial Times.

Huertas, Thomas F. (1990) 'US multinational banking: history and prospects', in Geoffrey Jones (ed.) *Banks as Multinationals*, London: Routledge.

Hughes, Helen (1988) *Achieving Industrialization in East Asia*, Cambridge: Cambridge University Press.

Humes, Samuel (1993) *Managing the Multinational*, Hemel Hempstead: Prentice Hall.

Innes, Duncan (1984) *Anglo American and the Rise of Modern South Africa*, London: Heinemann.

Jacob-Wendler, von, Gerhart (1982) *Deutsche Elektroindustrie in Lateinamerika. Siemens und AEG (1890–1914)*, Stuggart: Klett-Cotta.

Jemain, Alain (1982) *Michelin. Un Siècle de Secrets*, Paris: Calmann-Lévy.

Jesudason, James V. (1989) *Ethnicity and the Economy*, Singapore: Oxford University Press.

Jones, Charles A. (1987) *International Business in the Nineteenth Century*, Brighton: Wheatsheaf.

Jones, Geoffrey (1979) 'The state and economic development in India 1890–1947: the case of oil', *Modern Asian Studies* 13(3): 353–75.

—— (1981) *The State and the Emergence of the British Oil Industry*, London: Macmillan.

—— (1982) 'Lombard Street on the Riviera: the British clearing banks and Europe, 1900–1960', *Business History* 24(2): 186–210.

—— (1984a) 'The expansion of British multinational manufacturing, 1890–1939', in A. Okochi and T. Inoue (eds), *Overseas Business Activities*, Tokyo: University of Tokyo Press.

—— (1984b) 'The growth and performance of British multinational firms before 1939: the case of Dunlop', *Economic History Review* 36(1): 35–53;

—— (1984c) 'Multinational chocolate: Cadbury overseas 1918–1939', *Business History* 26(1): 59–76.

—— (1985) 'The Gramophone Company: an Anglo-American multinational, 1898–1931', *Business History Review* 59(1): 76–100.

—— (ed.) (1986a) *British Multinationals: Origins, Management and Performance*, Aldershot: Gower.

—— (1986b) 'Courtaulds in continental Europe, 1920–1945', in Geoffrey Jones (ed.) *British Multinationals: Origins, Management and Performance*, Aldershot: Gower.

—— (1986c) *Banking and Empire in Iran*, Cambridge: Cambridge University Press.

—— (1986d) 'The performance of British multinational enterprise, 1890–1945', in Peter Hertner and Geoffrey Jones (eds), *Multinationals: Theory and History* Aldershot: Gower.

—— (1987a) *Banking and Oil*, Cambridge: Cambridge University Press.

—— (1987b) 'The Imperial Bank of Iran and Iranian economic development 1890–1952', *Business and Economic History* 16: 69–80.

—— (1988) 'Foreign multinationals and British industry before 1945', *Economic History Review* 41(3): 429–53.

—— ( 1990a) 'The British government and foreign multinationals before 1970', in M. Chick (ed.), *Governments, Industries and Markets*, Aldershot: Edward Elgar.

—— (ed.) (1990b) *Banks as Multinationals*, London: Routledge.

—— (1992a) 'British business in Germany since the nineteenth century', in H. Pohl (ed.) *Der Einfluss ausländischer Unternehmen auf die deutsche Wirtschaft vom*

*Spättmittelalter bis zur Gegenwart*, Stuttgart: Franz Steiner.
—— (1992b) 'International financial centres in Asia, the Middle East and Australia: a historical perspective' in Y. Cassis (ed.) *Finance and Financiers in European History, 1880–1960*, Cambridge: Cambridge University Press.
—— (1993a) *British Multinational Banking 1830–1990*, Oxford: Clarendon Press.
—— (ed.) (1993b) *Transnational Corporations: A Historical Perspective*, London: Routledge.
—— (1994) 'British multinationals and British business since 1850', in M. W. Kirby and M. B. Rose (eds) *Business Enterprise in Modern Britain from the Eighteenth to the Twentieth Centuries*, London: Routledge.
Jones, Geoffrey and Schröter, Harm (eds) (1993a) *The Rise of Multinationals in Continental Europe*, Aldershot: Edward Elgar.
—— (1993b) 'Continental European multinationals, 1850–1992', in Geoffrey Jones and Harm Schröter (eds), *The Rise of Multinationals in Continental Europe*, Aldershot: Edward Elgar.
Jones, Geoffrey and Trebilcock, C. (1982) 'Russian industry and British business 1910–1930: oil and armaments', *Journal of European Economic History* 11(1): 61–103.
Jones, Stephanie (1986) *Two Centuries of Overseas Trading*, London: Macmillan.
—— (1987) 'The overseas trading company in Britain: the case of the Inchcape Group', in S. Yonekawa and H. Yoshihara (eds) *Business History of General Trading Companies*, Tokyo: University of Tokyo Press.
Julius, DeAnne (1990) *Global Companies and Public Policy*, London: Pinter.
Kaplan, David E. (1983) 'The internationalisation of South African capital', *African Affairs* 82(329): 465–94.
Kawabe, N. (1987) 'Development of overseas operations by general trading companies 1868–1945' in S. Yonekawa and H. Yoshihara (eds) *Business History of General Trading Companies*, Tokyo: University of Tokyo Press.
—— (1989) 'Japanese business in the United States before the Second World War: the case of Mitsui and Mitsubishi', in A. Teichova, M. Lévy-Leboyer and H. Nussbaum (eds), *Historical Studies in International Corporate Business*, Cambridge: Cambridge University Press.
—— (1990) 'Overseas activities and their organisation', in S. Yonekawa (ed.) *General Trading Companies*, Tokyo: United Nations University Press.
—— (1991) 'Problems of and perspectives on Japanese management in Malaysia', in S. Yamashita (ed.) *Transfer of Japanese Technology and Management to the ASEAN Countries*, Tokyo: University of Tokyo Press.
Keeble, S. (1992) *The Ability to Manage*, Manchester: Manchester University Press.
Kelly, Janet (1977) *Bankers and Borders*, Cambridge, Mass: Ballinger.
Kennedy, Charles R. (1992) 'Relations between transnational corporations and governments in host countries: a look to the future', *Transnational Corporations*, I.
Kenney, Martin and Florida, Richard (1993) *Beyond Mass Production*, New York: Oxford University Press.
Kenwood, A. G. and Lougheed, A. L. (1992) *The Growth of the International Economy, 1820–1990*, London: Allen & Unwin.
Keswick, M. (1982) *The Thistle and the Jade*, London: Octopus.
Kim, J. and Daniels, J. (1991) ' Marketing channel decisions of foreign manufacturing subsidiaries', *Management International Review* 31: 123–38.
Kindleberger, Charles P. (1985) 'Multinational ownership of shipping activities', *World Economy* 8: 249–65.

King, F. H. H. (1991) *The Hongkong Bank in the Period of Development and Nationalism, 1941–1984*, Cambridge: Cambridge University Press.

Kirzner, I. M. (1973) *Competition and Entrepreneurship*, Chicago: University of Chicago Press.

—— (1979) *Perception, Opportunity and Profit*, Chicago: University of Chicago Press.

Klein, Herbert S. (1965) 'The Creation of the Patiño Tin Empire', *Inter-American Economic Affairs* 19: 3–23.

Knickerbocker, F. T. (1973) *Oligopolistic Reaction and the Multinational Enterprise*, Cambridge, Mass: Harvard University Press.

Knight, F. H. (1921) *Risk, Uncertainty and Profit*, Boston, Mass: Houghton Mifflin.

Kobrin, Stephen J. (1984) 'Expropriation as an attempt to control foreign firms in LDCs: trends from 1969 to 1979', *International Studies Quarterly* 18: 329–48.

—— (1985) 'Diffusion as an explanation of oil nationalization', *Journal of Conflict Resolution* 29(1): 3–32.

Kogut, Bruce (1991) 'Country capabilities and the permeability of borders', *Strategic Management Journal* 12: 33–47.

Kogut, Bruce and Parkinson, David (1993) 'The diffusion of American organizing principles to Europe', in Bruce Kogut (ed.) *Country Competitiveness. Technology and the Organizing of Work*, New York: Oxford University Press.

Kogut, Bruce and Singh, H. (1988) 'The effect of national culture on the choice of entry mode', *Journal of International Business Studies* 19: 411–32.

Krugman, Paul (1994) 'Competitiveness: A dangerous obsession', *Foreign Affairs* 73(2): 28–44.

Kudo, Akira (1994) 'IG Farben in Japan: the transfer of technology and management skills', *Business History* 36(1): 159–83.

Kurgen van Hentenryk, G. and Laureyssens, J. (1986) *Un Siècle d'Investissements Belges au Canada*, Brussels: Editions de l'Université de Bruxelles.

Kuwahara, T. (1989) 'The Japanese cotton spinners' direct investments into China before the Second World War', in A. Teichova, M. Lévy-Leboyer and H. Nussbaum (eds) *Historical Studies in International Corporate Business*, Cambridge: Cambridge University Press.

—— (1990) 'Trends in research on overseas expansion by Japanese enterprises prior to World War II', *Japanese Yearbook on Business History* 7: 61–81.

Lall, Sanjaya (1973) 'Transfer pricing by multinational manufacturing firms', *Oxford Bulletin of Economics and Statistics* 35(3): 173–95.

—— (1979) 'Multinationals and market structure in an open developing economy: the case of Malaysia', *Weltwirtschaftliches Archiv* 115: 325–48.

—— (1983) *The New Multinationals: The Spread of Third World Enterprises*, Chichester: John Wiley.

—— (1985) 'India' in J. H. Dunning (ed.), *Multinational Enterprises, Economic Structure and International Competitiveness*, Chichester: John Wiley.

—— (ed.) (1993) *Transnational Corporations and Economic Development*, London: Routledge.

Lall, Sanjaya and Streeten, P. (1977) *Foreign Investment, Transnationals and Developing Countries*, London: Macmillan.

Lane, Christel (1989) *Management and Labour in Europe*, Aldershot: Edward Elgar.

Langdon, Steven W. (1981) *Multinational Corporations in the Political Economy of Kenya*, London: Macmillan.

Langlois, Richard N., Pugel, Thomas A., Haklish, Carmela S., Nelson, Richard

R., and Egelhoff, William G. (1988) *Micro-electronics: An Industry in Transition*, Boston: Unwin Hyman.

Lanthier, Pierre (1989) 'Multinationals and the French electrical industry, 1889–1940', in A. Teichova, M. Lévy-Leboyer and H. Nussbaum (eds) *Historical Studies in International Corporate Business*, Cambridge: Cambridge University Press.

Laster, David S. and McCauley, Robert N. (1994) 'Making sense of the profits of foreign firms in the United States', *Federal Reserve Bank of New York Quarterly Bulletin* 19(2): 44–75.

Laurent, André (1983) 'The cultural diversity of western conceptions of management', *International Studies of Management and Organisation* 13: 75–96.

Laux, James M. (1992) *The European Automobile Industry*, New York: Twayne Publishers.

Lawrence, Robert Z. (1992) 'Japan's low levels of inward investment: the role of inhibitions on acquisitions', *Transnational Corporations* 1(3): 47–75.

Lazonick, William (1990) *Competitive Advantage on the Shop Floor*, Cambridge, Mass: Harvard University Press.

—— (1991) *Business Organisation and the Myth of the Market Economy*, Cambridge: Cambridge University Press.

Lecraw, Donald (1985) 'Singapore' in J. H. Dunning (ed.) *Multinational Enterprises, Economic Structure and International Competitiveness*, Chichester: John Wiley & Sons.

Lewis, Cleona (1938) *America's Stake in International Investments*, Washington D. C.: The Brookings Institution.

Lewis, Colin M. (1983a) *British Railways in Argentina 1857–1914*, London: Athlone.

—— (1983b) 'The financing of railway development in Latin America, 1850–1914', *Ibero-Amerikanisches Archiv* 9: 255–78.

—— (1985) 'Railways and industrialization: Argentina and Brazil, 1870–1929', in Christopher Abel and Colin M. Lewis (eds) *Latin America, Economic Imperialism and the State*, London: Athlone.

Li, Jin-Mieung (1990) 'L'Air Liquide, pioneer of French industrial presence in Japan between 1910 and 1945', in T. Yuzawa and M. Udagawa (eds) *Foreign Business in Japan before World War II*, Tokyo: University of Tokyo Press.

Lim, Linda Y. C. (1980) 'Women workers in multinational corporations: the case of the electronics industry in Malaysia and Singapore', in Krisha Kumar (ed.) *Transnational Enterprises: Their Impact on Third World Societies and Cultures*, Boulder, Colorado: Westview Press.

Lindgren, Hakan (1979) *Corporate Growth. The Swedish Match Industry in its Global Setting*, Stockholm: Liber.

Lipsey, Robert E. (1988) 'Changing patterns of international investment in and by the United States', in Martin Feldstein (ed.) *The United States in the World Economy*, Chicago: University of Chicago Press.

—— (1993) 'Foreign direct investment in the United States: changes over three decades', in Kenneth A. Froot (ed.) *Foreign Direct Investment*, Chicago: University of Chicago Press.

—— (1994) 'Outward direct investment and the US economy', National Bureau of Economic Research Working Paper No. 469.

Lipsey, Robert E. and Kravis, Irving B. (1987) 'The competitiveness and comparative advantage of US multinationals 1957–1984', *Banca Nationale Del Lavoro Quarterly Review*: 147–65.

Lipson, Charles (1985) *Standing Guard: Protecting Foreign Capital in the Nineteenth and Twentieth Centuries*, Berkeley: University of California Press.

Little, Douglas J. (1979) 'Twenty years of turmoil: ITT, the State Department, and Spain, 1924–1944', *Business History Review* 53(4): 449–72.

Locke, Robert R. (1984) *The End of the Practical Man*, Greenwich, Conn: JAI Press Inc.

Lorange, Peter and Roos, Johan (1992) *Strategic Alliances*, Oxford: Basil Blackwell.

Love, John F. (1987) *McDonalds, Behind the Arches*, New York: Bantam.

Lundström, Ragnhild (1986a) 'Swedish multinational growth before 1930', in P. Hertner and G. Jones (eds) *Multinationals: Theory and History*, Aldershot: Gower.

—— (1986b) 'Banks and early Swedish multinationals', in A. Teichova, M. Lévy-Leboyer and H. Nussbaum (eds) *Multinational Enterprise in Historical Perspective*, Cambridge: Cambridge University Press.

—— (1992) 'The Scandinavian influence on German business and enterprises', in H. Pohl (ed.) *Der Einfluss ausländischer Unternehmen auf die deutsche Wirtschaft vom Spätmittelalter bis zur Gegenwart*, Stuttgart: Franz Steiner Verlag.

McCauley, Robert N. and Eldridge, Don P. (1990) 'The British invasion: explaining the strength of UK acquisitions of US firms in the late 1980s', in *International Private Capital Flows*, Basle: Bank for International Settlements.

McDowall, Duncan (1988) *The Light: Brazilian Traction, Light and Power Company Limited, 1899–1945*, Toronto: University of Toronto Press.

McKay, J. P. (1970) *Pioneers for Profit. Foreign Entrepreneurship and Russian Industrialization 1885–1913*, Chicago: University of Chicago Press.

—— (1982) 'Entrepreneurship and the emergence of the Russian petroleum industry, 1813–1883', in Paul Uselding (ed.) *Research in Economic History*, Vol. 8.

McKern, R. B. (1976) *Multinational Enterprise and Natural Resources*, Sydney: McGraw-Hill.

—— (ed.) (1993) *Transnational Corporations and the Exploitation of Natural Resources*, London: Routledge.

McKinlay, Alan and Starkey, Ken (1994) 'After Henry: continuity and change in Ford Motor Company', *Business History* 36(1): 184–205.

McManus, J. C. (1972) 'The theory of the multinational firm', in G. Paquet (ed.) *The Multinational Firm and the National State*, Don Mills, Ont.: Collier-Macmillan.

Maeda, Kazutoshi (1990) 'General trading companies in pre-War Japan; a sketch' in Shin'ichi Yonekawa (ed.) *General Trading Companies: A Comparative and Historical Study*, Tokyo: United Nations University Press.

Mariti, P. and Smiley, R. H. (1983) 'Co-operative agreements and the organization of industry', *Journal of Industrial Economics* 31(4): 437–51.

Mason, M. (1987) 'Foreign direct investment and Japanese economic development, 1899–1931', *Business and Economic History* 16: 3–17.

—— (1990) 'With reservations: pre-war Japan as host to Western Electric and ITT', in T. Yuzawa and M. Udgawa (eds) *Foreign Business in Japan before World War II*, Tokyo: University of Tokyo Press.

—— (1992a) *American Multinationals and Japan*, Cambridge, Mass: Harvard University Press.

—— (1992b) 'The origins and evolution of Japanese direct investment in Europe', *Business History Review*, 66(3): 435–74.

Mataloni, Raymond J. and Goldberg, Lee (1994) 'Gross product of US multinational companies, 1977–91', *Survey of Current Business* February: 42–63.

Maxcy, George (1981) *The Multinational Motor Industry*, London: Croom Helm.

Mejcher, Helmut (1989) 'Banking and the German oil industry, 1890–1939', in R. W. Ferrier and A. Fursenko (ed.) *Oil in the World Economy*, London: Routledge.

Melby, Eric D. K. (1981) *Oil and the International System: The Case of France, 1918–1969*, New York: Arno.

Mendoza, Antonio Gómez (1994) *El 'Gibraltar Economico': Franco y Rio Tinto, 1936–1954*, Madrid: Editorial Civitas.

Merret, David (1985) *ANZ Bank*, Sydney: Allen & Unwin.

Meuleau, Marc (1990) *Des Pionniers en Extrême-Orient*, Paris: Fayard.

Michalet, Charles-Albert and Chevallier, Thérèse (1985) 'France' in J. H. Dunning (ed.) *Multinational Enterprises, Economic Structure and International Competitiveness*, Chichester: John Wiley & Sons.

Michie, Ranald C. (1992) *The City of London*, London: Macmillan.

Mikesell, Raymond F. and Whitney, John W. (1987), *The World Mining Industry*, Boston: Allen & Unwin.

Miller, Rory (1982) 'Small business in the Peruvian oil industry: Lobitos Oilfields Limited before 1934', *Business History Review* 56(3): 400–23.

—— (1993) *Britain and Latin America in the Nineteenth and Twentieth Centuries*, London: Longman.

Mirza, Hafiz (1986) *Multinationals and the Growth of the Singapore Economy*, Beckenham: Croom Helm.

Modig, Hans (1979) *Swedish Match Interests in British India during the Interwar Years*, Stockholm: Liber.

Montenegro, Angelo (1993) 'The development of Pirelli as an Italian multinational, 1872–1992' in Geoffrey Jones and Harm Schröter (eds), *The Rise of Multinationals in Continental Europe*, Aldershot: Edward Elgar.

Moran, Theodore H. (1974) *Multinational Corporations and the Politics of Dependence*, Princeton: Princeton University Press.

—— (ed.) (1993) *Governments and Transnational Corporations*, London: Routledge.

Morris, Deigan and Hergert, Michael (1987) 'Trends in international collaborative agreements', *Columbia Journal of World Business* 22(2): 15–21.

Munro, J. Forbes (1981) 'Monopolists and speculators: British investment in West African rubber, 1905–1914', *Journal of African History* 22(2): 263–78.

—— (1987) 'Shipping subsidies and railway guarantees: William Mackinnon, Eastern Africa and the Indian Ocean, 1860–93', *Journal of African History* 28(2): 209–30.

—— (1988) 'Scottish overseas enterprise and the lure of London: the Mackinnon Shipping Group, 1847–1893', *Scottish Economic and Social History* 8: 73–87.

Navin, Thomas R. (1978) *Copper Mining and Management*, Tucson: University of Arizona Press.

Neebe, Reinhard (1991) *Überseemärkte und Exportstrategien in der westdeutschen Wirtschaft 1945 bis 1966*, Stuttgart: Franz Steiner Verlag.

Nelson, Richard R. and Winter, S. (1982) *An Evolutionary Theory of Economic Change*, Cambridge, Mass: Harvard University Press.

—— (1991) 'Why do firms differ, and how does it matter?', *Strategic Management Journal* 12: 61–74.

Nicholas, S. (1982) 'British multinational investment before 1939', *Journal of European Economic History* 11(3): 605–30.

—— (1983) 'Agency contracts, institutional modes, and the transition to foreign direct investment by British manufacturing multinationals before 1939', *Journal of Economic History*  43: 675–86.

—— (1989) 'Locational choice, performance and the growth of British multinational firms', *Business History*  31(3): 122–41.

Nowell, Gregory P. (1994) *Mercantile States and the World Oil Cartel, 1900–1939*, Ithaca: Cornell University Press.

O'Brien, Thomas F. (1989) 'Rich beyond the dreams of avarice: the Guggenheims in Chile', *Business History Review* 63(1): 122–59.

Ohmae, K. (1990) *The Borderless World*, London: Collins.

Okochi, A. and Inoue, T. (eds) (1984) *Overseas Business Activities*, Tokyo: University of Tokyo Press.

Olsson, Ulf (1993) 'Securing the markets. Swedish multinationals in a historical perspective', in Geoffrey Jones and Harm Schröter (eds) *The Rise of Multinationals in Continental Europe*, Aldershot: Edward Elgar.

Ouchi, W. G. (1980) 'Markets, bureaucracies, and clans', *Administrative Science Quarterly* 25: 129–41.

Ozawa, Terutomo (1992) 'Foreign direct investment and economic development', *Transnational Corporations* 1(1): 27–54.

Panic, M. (1982) 'International direct investment in conditions of structural disequilibrium: UK experience since the 1960s', in J. Black and J. H. Dunning (eds) *International Capital Movements*, London: Macmillan.

Paterson, D. G. (1976) *British Direct Investment in Canada, 1890–1914*, Toronto: University of Toronto Press.

Pavitt, Keith and Soete, Luc (1982) 'International dynamics of innovation' in H. Giersch (ed.) *Emerging Technologies*, Tubingen: J. C. B. Mohr.

Pearce, Robert and Singh, Satwinder (1992) *The Globalisation of Research and Development*, London: Macmillan.

Pearson, Scott R. (1971) 'The economic imperialism of the Royal Niger Company', *Food Research Institute Studies* 10(1): 69–88.

Penrose, Edith T. (1968) *The Large International Firm in Developing Countries. The International Petroleum Industry*, London: George Allen & Unwin.

Perrow, C. (1986) *Complex Organizations: A Critical Essay*, New York: Random House.

Phongpaichit, Pasuk (1991) 'Japan's investment and local capital in ASEAN since 1985', in S. Yamashita (ed.) *Transfer of Japanese Technology and Management to the ASEAN Countries*, Tokyo: University of Tokyo Press.

Platt, D. C. M. (1980) 'British portfolio investment before 1870: some doubts', *Economic History Review*  33(1): 1–16.

—— (1986) *Britain's Investment Overseas on the eve of the First World War*, London: Macmillan.

Plumpe, Gottfried (1990) *Die IG Farbenindustrie AG*, Berlin: Duncker & Humblot.

Pohl, Hans (1989) 'The Steaua Romana and the Deutsche Bank (1903–1920)' *Studies on Economic and Monetary Problems and on Banking History*, No. 24, Mainz: v. Hase & Koehler Verlag.

Pohl, Manfred (1987) *Deutsche Bank Buenos Aires 1887–1987*, Mainz: Hase & Koehler Verlag.

Pointon, A. C. (1964) *The Bombay Burmah Trading Corporation Limited 1863–1963*, Southampton: Millbrook Press.

Pollard, Sidney (1985) 'Capital exports, 1870–1914: harmful or beneficial?',

*Economic History Review* 38(4): 489–514.

Porter, Michael (1990) *The Competitive Advantage of Nations*, London: Macmillan.

Powell, Walter W. (1990) 'Neither market nor hierarchy: network forms of organization', *Research in Organizational Behaviour* 12: 295–336.

Purcell, W. R. (1966) 'The development of Japan's trading company network in Australia 1890–1941', *Australian Economic History Review* XXI(2): 114–32.

Quigley, Neil (1989) 'The Bank of Nova Scotia in the Caribbean, 1889–1940', *Business History Review* 63(4): 797–838.

Radetzki, Marian (1989) 'The role of state-owned enterprises in the international metal mining industry', *Resources Policy* 15: 45–57.

Ramanchandran, N. (1963) *Foreign Plantation Investment in Ceylon 1889–1958*, Colombo: Central Bank of Ceylon.

Read, Robert (1983) 'The growth and structure of multinationals in the banana export trade', in Mark Casson (ed.) *The Growth of International Business*, London: Allen & Unwin.

—— (1986a) 'The banana industry: oligopoly and barriers to entry', in Mark Casson (ed.) *Multinationals and World Trade*, London: Allen & Unwin.

—— (1986b) 'The copper industry', in Mark Casson (ed.) *Multinationals and World Trade*, London: Allen & Unwin.

Reader, W. J. (1970) *Imperial Chemical Industries: A History*, Vol. 1, London: Oxford University Press.

—— (1975) *Imperial Chemical Industries: A History*, Vol. 2, London: Oxford University Press.

—— (1976) *Metal Box: A History*, London: Heinemann.

Reddaway, W. B. (1968) *Effects of UK Direct Investment Overseas*, Cambridge: Cambridge University Press.

Reed, Howard Curtis (1981) *The Pre-eminence of International Financial Centres*, New York: Praeger.

Reed, P. M. (1958) 'Standard Oil in Indonesia 1898–1928', *Business History Review* 32(3): 311–37.

Regalsky, Andrés M. (1989) 'Foreign capital, local interests and railway development in Argentina: French investments in railways, 1900–1914', *Journal of Latin American Studies* 21: 425–52.

Reich, Leonard S. (1992) 'General Electric and the world cartelisation of electric lamps', in Akira Kudo and Terashi Hara (eds), *International Cartels in Business History*, Tokyo: University of Tokyo Press.

Reich, Robert B. (1990) 'Who is us?' *Harvard Business Review* 68(1): 53–64.

—— (1992) *The Work of Nations*, New York: Vintage Books.

Reich, Robert B. and Mankin, Eric D. (1986) 'Joint ventures with Japan give away our future', *Harvard Business Review* 64(2): 78–86.

Reich, S. (1990) *Fruits of Fascism: Post-War Prosperity in Historical Perspective*, Ithaca: Cornell.

Remer, C. F. (1933) *Foreign Investments in China*, New York: Macmillan

Richardson, Peter (1987) 'The origins and development of the Collins House Group, 1915–1951', *Australian Economic History Review* 27: 3–29.

Rippy, J. Fred (1959) *British Investments in Latin America, 1822–1949*, Hamden, Conn: Archon Books.

Roberts, Richard (1992) *Schroders. Merchants & Bankers*, London: Macmillan.

Rodman, Kenneth A. (1988) *Sanctity vs Sovereignty: The United States and the Nationalization of Natural Resource Investments*, New York: Colombia University Press.

Rodrik, Dani (1982) 'Changing patterns of ownership and integration in the international bauxite-aluminium industry' in Leroy P. Jones (ed.) *Public Enterprise in Less-Developed Countries*, Cambridge: Cambridge University Press.

Roehl, T. (1983) 'A transactions cost approach to international trading structures: the case of the Japanese general trading companies', *Hitotsubashi Journal of Economics* 24: 119–35.

Safarian, A. E. (1993) *Multinational Enterprise and Public Policy*, Aldershot: Edward Elgar.

Sakamoto, M. (1990) 'Diversification: the case of Mitsui Bussan', in S. Yonekawa (ed.) *General Trading Companies*, Tokyo: United Nations University Press.

Samuels, Richard J. (1987) *The Business of the Japanese State*, Ithaca: Cornell University Press.

Sauvant, Karl P. and Mallampally, Padma (eds) (1993) *Transnational Corporations in Services*, London: Routledge.

Sauvant, Karl P. and Mennis, B. (1980) 'Sociocultural investments and the international political economy of North-South relations: the role of transnational enterprises', in K. Kumar (ed.) *Transnational Enterprises: Their Impact on Third World Societies and Cultures*, Boulder: Westview.

Savary, Julien (1984) *French Multinationals*, London: Frances Pinter.

Schell, William (1990) 'American investment in tropical Mexico: rubber plantations, fraud and dollar diplomacy, 1897–1913', *Business History Review* 64(2): 217–54.

Schmitz, C. (1979) *World Non-Ferrous Metal Production and Prices, 1700–1976*, London: Frank Cass.

—— (1986) 'The rise of big business in the world copper industry, 1870–1930', *Economic History Review* 39(3): 392–410.

—— (1993) *The Growth of Big Business in the United States and Western Europe, 1850–1939*, London: Macmillan.

—— (ed.) (1995) *Big Business in Mining and Petroleum*, Aldershot: Edward Elgar.

Schröter, Harm G. (1988a) 'Risk and control in multinational enterprise: German businesses in Scandinavia, 1918–1939', *Business History Review* 62(3): 420–43.

—— (1990a) 'Die Auslandsinvestitionen der deutschen chemischen Industrie 1870 bis 1930', *Zeitschrift für Unternehmensgeschichte* 35(1): 1–22.

—— (1990b) 'Etablierungs- und Verteilungsmuster der schweizerischen Auslandsproduktion von 1870 bis 1914', in Paul Bairoch and Martin Körner (eds), *Die Schweiz in der Weltwirtschaft*, Zürich: Chronos Verlag.

—— (1990c) 'Cartels as a form of concentration in industry: the example of the international dyestuffs cartel from 1927 to 1939', *German Yearbook on Business History 1988*, Berlin: Springer-Verlag.

—— (1991) *Multinationale Unternehmen aus Kleinen Staaten 1870 bis 1930*, Berlin: Free University of Berlin.

—— (1993a) 'Continuity and change: German multinationals since 1850', in Geoffrey Jones and Harm G. Schröter (eds), *The Rise of Multinationals in Continental Europe*, Aldershot: Edward Elgar.

—— (1993b) 'Swiss multinational enterprise in historical perspective', in Geoffrey Jones and Harm G. Schröter (eds), *The Rise of Multinationals in Continental Europe*, Aldershot: Edward Elgar.

—— (1993c) *Aufstieg der Kleinen: multinationale Unternehmen aus fünf Kleinen Staaten vor 1914*, Berlin: Duncker und Humbolt.

—— (forthcoming) 'Die Auslandsinvestitionen der deutschen chemischen Industrie 1930 bis 1965'.

Schröter, Verena (1984) *Die Deutsche Industrie auf dem Weltmarkt 1929 bis 1933*, Frankfurt: Peter Lang.

Schumpeter, J. A. (1943) *Capitalism, Socialism and Democracy*, London: Unwin University Books.

Scott-Quinn, Brian (1990) 'US investment banks as multinationals', in Geoffrey Jones (ed.) *Banks as Multinationals*, London: Routledge.

Segreto, Luciano (1987) 'Le Nuove Strategie Delle Società Finanziarie Svizzere Per L'Industria Elettrica (1919–1939)', *Studi Storici* 4: 861–907.

—— (1992) 'Du "Made in Germany" au "Made in Switzerland"', in M. Trédé-Boulmer (ed.) *Electricité et Électrification dans le Monde 1880–1980*, Paris: PUF.

—— (1994) 'Le rôle des investissements suisses dans l'industrie électrique française jusqu'à la Deuxième Guerre mondiale', in M. Trédé-Boulmer (ed.) *Le Financement de l'Industrie Électrique 1880–1980*, Paris: PUF.

Seth, Rama and Quijano, Alicia (1991) 'Japanese banks' customers in the United States', *Federal Reserve Bank of New York Quarterly Review* 16(1): 79–82.

Shafer, Michael (1983) 'Capturing the mineral multinationals: advantage or disadvantage?', *International Organization* 37(1): 93–120.

Shapiro, Helen (1991) 'Determinants of firm entry into the Brazilian automobile manufacturing industry, 1956–1968', *Business History Review* 65(4): 876–947.

—— (1993) 'Automobiles: from import substitution to export promotion in Brazil and Mexico', in David B. Yoffie (ed.) *Beyond Free Trade. Firms, Governments and Global Competition*, Boston, Mass: Harvard Business School Press.

—— (1994) *Engines of Growth. The State and Transnational Auto Companies in Brazil*, Cambridge: Cambridge University Press.

Shelp, R. K. (ed.) (1984) *Service Industries and Economic Development*, New York: Praeger.

Shepherd, David, Silbertson, Aubrey and Strange, Roger (1985) *British Manufacturing Investment Overseas*, London: Metheun.

Shepherd, Phil (1989) 'Transnational corporations and the denationalization of the Latin American cigarette industry', in A. Teichova, M. Lévy-Leboyer and H. Nussbaum (eds) *Historical Studies in International Corporate Business*, Cambridge: Cambridge University Press.

Sklar, Richard L. (1975) *Corporate Power in an African State*, Berkeley: University of California Press.

Sluyterman, Keetie E. (1992) 'From licensor to multinational enterprise: the small Dutch firm Océ-van der Grinten in the international world, 1920–66', *Business History* 34(2): 28–49.

—— (1994) 'Dutch free-standing companies between 1870 and 1940: a typical colonial phenomenon' (mimeo).

Smith, David N. and Wells, Louis T. (1975) *Negotiating Third World Mineral Agreements*, Cambridge, Mass: Ballinger.

Smith, George David (1988) *From Monopoly to Competition. The Transformation of Alcoa 1886–1986*, Cambridge: Cambridge University Press.

Smith, John Kenley (1992) 'National goals, industry structure, and corporate strategies: chemical cartels between the Wars', in Akira Kudo and Terashi Hara (eds) *International Cartels in Business History*, Tokyo: University of Tokyo Press.

Southard, F.A. (1931) *American Industry in Europe*, Boston: Houghton-Mifflin.

Spar, Debora L. (1994) *The Co-operative Edge: The Internal Politics of International Cartels*, Ithaca: Cornell University Press.

Spender, J. A. (1930) *Weetman Pearson. First Viscount Cowdray 1856–1927*, London: Cassel and Co.

Stanton, J. (1984) 'Protection, market structure and firm behaviour: inefficiency in the early Australian tyre industry,' *Australian Economic History Review* 24(2): 91–113.

Stephenson, John C. (1984) 'Technology transfer by the Bechtel Organisation', in Ronald K. Shelp (ed.) *Service Industries and Economic Development*, New York: Praeger.

Steuer, M. D., Abell, P., Gennard, J., Perlman, M., Rees, R., Scott, B. and Wallis, K. (1973) *The Impact of Foreign Direct Investment in the United Kingdom*, London: HMSO.

Stevens, Gary V. G. and Lipsey, Robert E. (1992) 'Interactions between domestic and foreign investment', *Journal of International Money and Finance* 11: 40–62.

Stocking, George W. and Watkins, Myron W. (1946) *Cartels in Action*, New York: The Twentieth Century Fund.

Stone, I. (1977) 'British direct and portfolio investment in Latin America before 1914', *Journal of Economic History* 37(3): 690–722.

Stopford, John M. and Dunning John, H. (1983) *Multinationals. Company Performance and Global Trends*, London: Macmillan.

Stopford, John M. and Strange, S. (1991) *Rival States, Rival Firms*, Cambridge: Cambridge University Press.

Stopford, John M. and Wells, Louis T. (1972) *Managing the Multinational Enterprise*, London: Longman.

—— (1974) 'The origins of British-based multinational manufacturing enterprises', *Business History Review* 48(3): 303–45.

Strange, Roger (1993) *Japanese Manufacturing Investment in Europe*, London: Routledge.

Sugiyama, Shinja (1987) 'A British trading firm in the Far East: John Swire & Sons, 1867–1914', in S. Yonekawa and H. Yoshihara (eds) *Business History of General Trading Companies*, Tokyo: University of Tokyo Press.

Sunkel, O. (1972) 'Big business and "dependencia": a Latin American view', *Foreign Affairs* 50(3): 517–31.

Suzuki, Tsuneo (1990) 'Post-war development of general trading companies', in S. Yonekawa (ed.) *General Trading Companies*, Tokyo: United Nations University Press.

Svedberg, P. (1978) 'The portfolio – direct composition of private foreign investment in 1914 revisited', *Economic Journal* 80: 763–77.

Swenson, D. L. (1993) 'Foreign mergers and acquisitions in the United States', in Kenneth A. Froot (ed.) *Foreign Direct Investment*, Chicago: University of Chicago Press.

Tamaki, Norio (1990) 'The Yokohama Specie Bank: a multinational in the Japanese interest 1879–1931', in Geoffrey Jones (ed.) *Banks as Multinationals*, London: Routledge.

Taylor, Graham D. (1981) 'Management relations in a multinational enterprise: the case of Canadian Industries Ltd, 1928–1948', *Business History Review*, 55(3): 337–58.

—— (1994) 'Negotiating technology transfer within multinational enterprises: perspectives from Canadian history', *Business History* 36(1): 127–58.

Taylor, Graham D. and Sudnik, Patricia E. (1984) *Du Pont and the International Chemical Industry*, Boston, Mass: Twayne.

Teichova, Alice and Cottrell, P. L. (eds) (1983) *International Business and Central Europe 1918–1939*, Leicester: Leicester University Press.

Teichova, Alice, Lévy-Leboyer, M. and Nussbaum, H. (eds) (1986) *Multinational Enterprise in Historical Perspective*, Cambridge: Cambridge University Press.

—— (eds) (1989) *Historical Studies in International Corporate Business*, Cambridge: Cambridge University Press.

Terpstra, Vern and Yu, Chwo-Ming (1988) 'Determinants of foreign investment by US advertising agencies', *Journal of International Business Studies* 19(1): 34–46.

Terrell, Henry S., Dohner, Robert S. and Lowrey, Barbara R. (1989) 'The US and UK activities of Japanese banks: 1980–1988', International Finance Discussion Papers, Federal Reserve System, No. 361.

Thoburn, John (1977) *Primary Commodity Exports and Economic Development*, London: John Wiley.

—— (1981) *Multinationals, Mining and Development. A Study of the Tin Industry*, Aldershot: Gower.

Tilly, Richard (1993) 'The internationalization of West German banks, 1945–87', in Geoffrey Jones and Harm G. Schröter (eds), *The Rise of Multinationals in Continental Europe*, Aldershot: Edward Elgar.

Tolentino, Paz E. E. (1993) *Technological Innovation and Third World Multinationals*, London: Routledge.

Tomlinson, B. R. (1981) 'Colonial firms and the decline of colonialism in Eastern India 1914–47', *Modern Asian Studies* 15(3): 455–86.

—— (1989) 'British business in India, 1860–1970', in R. P. T. Davenport-Hines and Geoffrey Jones (eds) *British Business in Asia since 1860*, Cambridge: Cambridge University Press.

Triandis, Harry C. (1993) 'Collectivism and individualism as cultural syndromes', *Cross-Cultural Research* 27(3): 155–80.

Truitt, Nancy Sherwood (1984) 'Mass merchandising and economic development: Sears, Roebuck and Co. in Mexico and Peru', in Ronald K. Shelp (ed.) *Service Industries and Economic Development*, New York: Praeger.

Turrell, Rob and van Helten, Jean-Jacques (1986) 'The Rothschilds, the Exploration Company and Mining Finance', *Business History* 28(2): 181.

—— (1987) 'The investment group: the missing link in British overseas expansion before 1914', *Economic History Review*, 40(2): 267–74.

Tweedale, Geoffrey (1986) 'Transatlantic speciality steels: Sheffield high-trade steel firms and the USA, 1860–1940', in Geoffrey Jones (ed.) *British Multinationals, Origins, Management and Performance*, Aldershot: Gower.

Udagawa, M. (1990) 'Business management and foreign-affiliated companies in Japan before World War II', in T. Yuzawa and M. Udagawa (eds) *Foreign Business in Japan before World War II*, Tokyo: University of Tokyo Press.

United Nations Centre on Transnational Corporations (1980) *Transnational Corporations in the Copper Industry*, New York: UNCTC.

—— (1987) *Transnational Corporations and Non-fuel Primary Commodities in Developing Countries*, New York: UNCTC.

—— (1991) *World Investment Report: The Triad in Foreign Direct Investment*, New York: UNCTC.

—— (1992) *World Investment Report: Transnational Corporations as Engines of Growth*, New York: UNCTC.

—— (1993) *World Investment Report: Transnational Corporations and Integrated International Production*, New York: UNCTC.

—— (1994) *World Investment Report: Transnational Corporations, Employment and the Workplace*, New York: UNCTC

—— (1995) *World Investment Report: Transnational Corporations and Competitiveness*, New York: UNCTC.

Usselman, Steven W. (1993) 'IBM and its imitators: organizational capabilities and the emergence of the international computer industry', *Business and Economic History* 22(2): 1–35.

Van der Laan, H. Laurens (1981) 'Modern inland transport and the European trading firms in Colonial West Africa', *Cahiers d'Études Africaines* 84: 547–75.

Van der Wee, Herman and Goossens, Martine (1991) 'Belgium' in Rondo Cameron and V. I. Bovykin (eds) *International Banking 1870–1914*, New York: Oxford University Press.

Van Helten, Jean-Jacques and Jones, Geoffrey (1989) 'British business in Malaysia and Singapore since the 1870s', in R. P. T. Davenport-Hines and Geoffrey Jones (eds) *British Business in Asia since 1860*, Cambridge: Cambridge University Press.

Vaupel, J. W. and Curhan, J. P. (1969) *The Making of Multinational Enterprise*, Cambridge, Mass: Harvard University Press.

Venn, Fiona (1986) *Oil Diplomacy in the Twentieth Century*, London: Macmillan.

Vernon, Raymond (1966) 'International investment and international trade in the product cycle', *Quarterly Journal of Economics* May: 190–207.

—— (1971) *Sovereignty at Bay: The Multinational Spread of US Enterprises*, New York: Basic Books.

—— (1979) 'The Product Cycle Hypothesis in a New International Environment', *Oxford Bulletin of Economics and Statistics* 41(4): 255–67.

—— (1983) *Two Hungry Giants. The United States and Japan in the Quest for Oil and Ores*, Cambridge, Mass: Harvard University Press.

Vernon, Raymond and Levy, Brian (1982) 'State-owned enterprises in the world economy: the case of iron ore', in Leroy P. Jones (ed.) *Public Enterprise in Less-Developed Countries*, Cambridge: Cambridge University Press.

Wainwright, David (nd) *Brooke Bond. A Hundred Years*, np: Newman Neame.

Warr, Peter G. (1987) 'Malaysia's industrial enclaves: benefits and costs', *The Developing Economies* 25(1): 30–55.

Wavre, Pierre-Alain (1988) 'Swiss investments in Italy from the XVIIIth to the XXth century', *Journal of European Economic History* 17(1): 85–102.

Weiher, von, Sigfrid and Goetzeler, Herbert (1977) *The Siemens Company - Its Historical Role in the Progress of Electrical Engineering 1847–1980*, Berlin: Siemens.

Wells, Louis T. (1993) 'Minerals: eroding oligopolies', in David B. Yoffie (ed.) *Beyond Free Trade. Firms, Governments, and Global Competition*, Boston, Mass: Harvard Business School Press.

Wengenroth, Ulrich (1991) 'Iron and steel', in Rondo Cameron and V. I. Bovykin (eds), *International Banking 1870–1914*, New York: Oxford University Press.

West, Douglas C. (1987) 'From T-square to T-plan: the London office of the J. Walter Thompson Advertising Agency, 1919–70', *Business History* 29(2): 199–217.

—— (1988) 'Multinational competition in the British advertising agency business, 1936–1987', *Business History Review* 62(3): 467–501.

Westall, Oliver M. (1992) *The Provincial Insurance Company 1903–38*, Manchester: Manchester University Press.

White, Christine (1986) 'Ford in Russia: in pursuit of the chimeral market', *Business History* 28(4): 77–97.

Wilkins, M. (1970) *The Emergence of Multinational Enterprise*, Cambridge, Mass: Harvard University Press.

—— (1974a) *The Maturing of Multinational Enterprise*, Cambridge, Mass: Harvard University Press.

—— (1974b) 'The role of private business in the international diffusion of technology', *Journal of Economic History* 34(1): 166–88.

—— (1977) 'Modern European economic history and the multinationals', *The Journal of European Economic History*, 6(3): 575–95.

—— (1982) 'American-Japanese direct foreign investment relationships, 1930–1952', *Business History Review* 56(4): 497–518.

—— (1986a) 'Defining a firm: history and theory', in P. Hertner and Geoffrey Jones (eds), *Multinationals: Theory and History*, Aldershot: Gower.

—— (1986b) 'Japanese multinational enterprise before 1914', *Business History Review* 60(2): 199–231.

—— (1986c) 'The history of European multinationals: a new look', *The Journal of European Economic History*, 15(3): 483–510.

—— (1988a) 'The free-standing company, 1870–1914: an important type of British foreign direct investment', *Economic History Review* 41(2): 259–85.

—— (1988b) 'European and North American multinationals, 1870–1914: comparisons and contrasts', *Business History* 30(1): 8–45.

—— (1989) *The History of Foreign Investment in the United States before 1914*, Cambridge, Mass: Harvard University Press.

—— (1990a) 'The contributions of foreign enterprises to Japanese economic development', in T. Yuzawa and M. Ugadawa (eds) *Foreign Business in Japan Before World War II*, Tokyo: University of Tokyo Press.

—— (1990b) 'Japanese multinationals in the United States: continuity and change, 1879–1990', *Business History Review* 64(4): 585–629.

—— (1993a) 'Cosmopolitan finance in the 1920s' (Paper prepared for Congrès International de Paris, 23–5 September 1993).

—— (1993b) 'French multinationals in the United States. An historical perspective', *Enterprises et Histoire* 3: 14–29.

—— (1994a) 'Comparative Hosts', *Business History* 36(1): 18–50.

—— (1994b) 'When and why brand names in food and drink', in Geoffrey Jones and Nicholas J. Morgan (eds), *Adding Value. Brands and Marketing in Food and Drink*, London: Routledge.

—— (forthcoming) *The History of Foreign Investment in the United States since 1914*.

Wilkins, M. and Hill, F. E. (1964) *American Business Abroad: Ford on Six Continents*, Detroit, Mich: Wayne State University Press.

Wilks, Stephen (1990) 'Institutional insularity: government and the British motor industry since 1945' in M. Chick (ed.) *Governments, Industries and Markets*, Aldershot: Edward Elgar.

Williams, M. L. (1975) 'The extent and significance of the nationalization of foreign-owned assets in developing countries, 1956–1972', *Oxford Economic Papers* 27(2): 260–72.

Williamson, O. E. (1975) *Markets and Hierarchies*, New York: Free Press.

—— (1981) 'The modern corporation: origins, evolution, attributes', *Journal of Economic Literature* 19(4): 1537–68.

—— (1985) *The Economic Institutions of Capitalism*, New York: Free Press.

Wilson, Charles (1954) *The History of Unilever*, Vols 1–2, London: Cassell.

—— (1968) *The History of Unilever*, Vol. 3, London: Cassell.

Womack, James P., Jones, Daniel T. and Roos, Daniel (1990) *The Machine that Changed the World*, New York: Rawson Associates.

Wray, William D. (1984) *Mitsubishi and the NYK 1870–1914*, Cambridge, Mass: Harvard University Press.

Wright, Winthrop R. (1974) *British-Owned Railways in Argentina*, Austin:

University of Texas Press.

Wurm, Clemens (1993) *Business, Politics and International Relations*, Cambridge: Cambridge University Press.

Yamazaki, H. (1987) 'The logic of the formation of general trading companies in Japan', in S. Yonekawa and H. Yoshihara (eds) *Business History of General Trading Companies*, Tokyo: University of Tokyo Press.

Yamazawa, Ippei and Hohama, Kirohisa (1985) 'Trading companies and the expansion of foreign trade: Japan, Korea, and Thailand', in K. Ohkawa and G. Ranis (eds) *Japan and the Developing Countries*, London: Basil Blackwell.

Yasumuro, Ken'ichi (1984) 'The contribution of sogo shosha to the multinationalization of Japanese industrial enterprises in historical perspective' in A. Okochi and T. Inoue (eds) *Overseas Business Activities*, Tokyo: University of Tokyo Press.

—— (1993a) 'Conceptualizing an adaptable marketing system: The end of mass marketing', in Richard S. Tedlow and Geoffrey Jones (eds) *The Rise and Fall of Mass Marketing*, London: Routledge.

—— (1993b) 'Cultural diversity and tacit management theory', in S. Yano (ed.) *Global Management and Innovation Strategies*, Tokyo: Chikura-Shobo.

Yoffie, David B. (1993) 'Foreign direct investment in semiconductors', in Kenneth A. Froot (ed.) *Foreign Direct Investment*, Chicago: University of Chicago Press.

Yonekawa, Shin'ichi (1985) 'The formation of general trading companies: a comparative study', *Japanese Yearbook on Business History*: 1–31.

—— (1990) *General Trading Companies: A Comparative and Historical Study*, Tokyo: United Nations University Press.

Yonekawa, Shin'ichi and H. Yoshihara (eds) (1987) *Business History of General Trading Companies*, Tokyo: University of Tokyo Press.

Yoshihara, H. (1984) 'Multinational growth of Japanese manufacturing enterprises in the postwar period', in A. Okochi and T. Inoue (eds) *Overseas Business Activities*, Tokyo: University of Tokyo Press.

—— (1987) 'Some questions on Japan's sogo shosha', in S. Yonekawa and H. Yoshihara (eds) *Business History of General Trading Companies*, Tokyo: University of Tokyo Press.

Yuzawa, T. and Ugadawa, M. (eds) (1990) *Foreign Business in Japan Before World War II*, Tokyo: University of Tokyo Press.

# Index